ALL GLORY TO ŚRĪ GURU AND GAURĀṄGA

ŚRĪMAD BHĀGAVATAM

of

KṚṢṆA-DVAIPĀYANA VYĀSA

यस्य राष्ट्रे प्रजाः सर्वास्त्रस्यन्ते साध्व्यसाधुभिः ।
तस्य मत्तस्य नश्यन्ति कीर्तिरायुर्भगो गतिः ॥
एष राज्ञां परो धर्मो ह्यार्तानामार्तिनिग्रहः ।
अत एनं वधिष्यामि भूतद्रुहमसत्तमम् ॥

yasya rāṣṭre prajāḥ sarvās
trasyante sādhvy asādhubhiḥ
tasya mattasya naśyanti
kīrtir āyur bhago gatiḥ

eṣa rājñāṁ paro dharmo
hy ārtānām ārti-nigrahaḥ
ata enaṁ vadhiṣyāmi
bhūta-druham asattamam (p. 246)

BOOKS by
His Divine Grace A. C. Bhaktivedanta Swami Prabhupāda

Bhagavad-gītā As It Is
Śrīmad-Bhāgavatam, Cantos 1–8 (24 Vols.)
Śrī Caitanya-caritāmṛta (17 Vols.)
Teachings of Lord Caitanya
The Nectar of Devotion
The Nectar of Instruction
Śrī Īśopaniṣad
Easy Journey to Other Planets
Kṛṣṇa Consciousness: The Topmost Yoga System
Kṛṣṇa, the Supreme Personality of Godhead (3 Vols.)
Perfect Questions, Perfect Answers
Dialectic Spiritualism—A Vedic View of Western Philosophy
Transcendental Teachings of Prahlād Mahārāja
Kṛṣṇa, the Reservoir of Pleasure
Life Comes from Life
The Perfection of Yoga
Beyond Birth and Death
On the Way to Kṛṣṇa
Rāja-vidyā: The King of Knowledge
Elevation to Kṛṣṇa Consciousness
Kṛṣṇa Consciousness: The Matchless Gift
Back to Godhead Magazine (Founder)

A complete catalogue is available upon request

The Bhaktivedanta Book Trust
3764 Watseka Avenue
Los Angeles, California 90034

Puranas. Bhagavatapurana.

ŚRĪMAD BHĀGAVATAM

First Canto
"Creation"

(Part Three—Chapters 13-19)

With the Original Sanskrit Text, Its Roman Transliteration, Synonyms, Translation and Elaborate Purports

by

His Divine Grace
A.C. Bhaktivedanta Swami Prabhupāda
Founder-*Ācārya* of the International Society for Krishna Consciousness

THE BHAKTIVEDANTA BOOK TRUST
New York · Los Angeles · London · Bombay

Readers interested in the subject matter of this book
are invited by the International Society for Krishna Consciousness
to correspond with its Secretary.

International Society for Krishna Consciousness
3764 Watseka Avenue
Los Angeles, California 90034

Library of Congress Catalogue Card Number: 73-169353
International Standard Book Number: 0-912776-34-X

First printing, 1972: 10,000
Second printing, 1973: 10,000
Third printing, 1976: 50,000

Printed in the United States of America

Table of Contents

CHAPTER NINETEEN
The Appearance of Śukadeva Gosvāmī

Appendixes

Preface

We must know the present need of human society. And what is that need? Human society is no longer bounded by geographical limits to particular countries or communities. Human society is broader than in the Middle Ages, and the world tendency is toward one state or one human society. The ideals of spiritual communism, according to *Śrīmad-Bhāgavatam*, are based more or less on the oneness of the entire human society, nay, on the entire energy of living beings. The need is felt by great thinkers to make this a successful ideology. *Śrīmad-Bhāgavatam* will fill this need in human society. It begins, therefore, with the aphorism of Vedānta philosophy (*janmādy asya yataḥ*) to establish the ideal of a common cause.

Human society, at the present moment, is not in the darkness of oblivion. It has made rapid progress in the field of material comforts, education and economic development throughout the entire world. But there is a pinprick somewhere in the social body at large, and therefore there are large-scale quarrels, even over less important issues. There is need of a clue as to how humanity can become one in peace, friendship and prosperity with a common cause. *Śrīmad-Bhāgavatam* will fill this need, for it is a cultural presentation for the re-spiritualization of the entire human society.

Śrīmad-Bhāgavatam should be introduced also in the schools and colleges, for it is recommended by the great student devotee Prahlāda Mahārāja in order to change the demonic face of society.

kaumāra ācaret prājño
dharmān bhāgavatān iha
durlabhaṁ mānuṣaṁ janma
tad apy adhruvam arthadam
(*Bhāg.* 7.6.1)

Disparity in human society is due to lack of principles in a godless civilization. There is God, or the Almighty One, from whom everything emanates, by whom everything is maintained and in whom everything is merged to rest. Material science has tried to find the ultimate source of creation very insufficiently, but it is a fact that there is one ultimate source of everything that be. This ultimate source is explained rationally and authoritatively in the beautiful *Bhāgavatam* or *Śrīmad-Bhāgavatam.*

Śrīmad-Bhāgavatam is the transcendental science not only for knowing the ultimate source of everything but also for knowing our relation with Him and our duty towards perfection of the human society on the basis of this perfect knowledge. It is powerful reading matter in the Sanskrit language, and it is now rendered into English elaborately so that simply by a careful reading one will know God perfectly well, so much so that the reader will be sufficiently educated to defend himself from the onslaught of atheists. Over and above this, the reader will be able to convert others to accept God as a concrete principle.

Śrīmad-Bhāgavatam begins with the definition of the ultimate source. It is a bona fide commentary on the *Vedānta-sūtra* by the same author, Śrīla Vyāsadeva, and gradually it develops into nine cantos up to the highest state of God realization. The only qualification one needs to study this great book of transcendental knowledge is to proceed step by step cautiously and not jump forward haphazardly as with an ordinary book. It should be gone through chapter by chapter, one after another. The reading matter is so arranged with its original Sanskrit text, its English transliteration, synonyms, translation and purports so that one is sure to become a God realized soul at the end of finishing the first nine cantos.

The Tenth Canto is distinct from the first nine cantos, because it deals directly with the transcendental activities of the Personality of Godhead Śrī Kṛṣṇa. One will be unable to capture the effects of the Tenth Canto without going through the first nine cantos. The book is complete in twelve cantos, each independent, but it is good for all to read them in small installments one after another.

I must admit my frailties in presenting *Śrīmad-Bhāgavatam,* but still I am hopeful of its good reception by the thinkers and leaders of society on the strength of the following statement of *Śrīmad-Bhāgavatam.*

tad-vāg-visargo janatāgha-viplavo
yasmin pratiślokam abaddhavaty api

nāmāny anantasya yaśo 'ṅkitāni yac
chṛṇvanti gāyanti gṛṇanti sādhavaḥ
(*Bhāg.* 1.5.11)

"On the other hand, that literature which is full with descriptions of the transcendental glories of the name, fame, form and pastimes of the unlimited Supreme Lord is a transcendental creation meant to bring about a revolution in the impious life of a misdirected civilization. Such transcendental literatures, even though irregularly composed, are heard, sung and accepted by purified men who are thoroughly honest."

Oṁ tat sat

A. C. Bhaktivedanta Swami

Introduction

"This *Bhāgavata Purāṇa* is as brilliant as the sun, and it has arisen just after the departure of Lord Kṛṣṇa to His own abode, accompanied by religion, knowledge, etc. Persons who have lost their vision due to the dense darkness of ignorance in the age of Kali shall get light from this *Purāṇa.*" (*Śrīmad-Bhāgavatam* 1.3.43)

The timeless wisdom of India is expressed in the *Vedas*, ancient Sanskrit texts that touch upon all fields of human knowledge. Originally preserved through oral tradition, the *Vedas* were first put into writing five thousand years ago by Śrīla Vyāsadeva, the "literary incarnation of God." After compiling the *Vedas*, Vyāsadeva set forth their essence in the aphorisms known as *Vedānta-sūtras*. *Śrīmad-Bhāgavatam* is Vyāsadeva's commentary on his own *Vedānta-sūtras*. It was written in the maturity of his spiritual life under the direction of Nārada Muni, his spiritual master. Referred to as "the ripened fruit of the tree of Vedic literature," *Śrīmad-Bhāgavatam* is the most complete and authoritative exposition of Vedic knowledge.

After compiling the *Bhāgavatam*, Vyāsa impressed the synopsis of it upon his son, the sage Śukadeva Gosvāmī. Śukadeva Gosvāmī subsequently recited the entire *Bhāgavatam* to Mahārāja Parīkṣit in an assembly of learned saints on the bank of the Ganges at Hastināpura (now Delhi). Mahārāja Parīkṣit was the emperor of the world and was a great *rājarṣi* (saintly king). Having received a warning that he would die within a week, he renounced his entire kingdom and retired to the bank of the Ganges to fast until death and receive spiritual enlightenment. The *Bhāgavatam* begins with Emperor Parīkṣit's sober inquiry to Śukadeva Gosvāmī:

> "You are the spiritual master of great saints and devotees. I am therefore begging you to show the way of perfection for all persons, and especially for one who is about to die. Please let me know what a man should hear, chant, remember and worship, and also what he should not do. Please explain all this to me."

Śukadeva Gosvāmī's answer to this question, and numerous other questions posed by Mahārāja Parīkṣit, concerning everything from the nature of the self to the origin of the universe, held the assembled sages in rapt attention continuously for the seven days leading to the King's death. The sage Sūta Gosvāmī, who was present on the bank of the Ganges when Śukadeva Gosvāmī first recited *Śrīmad-Bhāgavatam*, later repeated the *Bhāgavatam* before a gathering of sages in the forest of Naimiṣāraṇya. Those sages, concerned about the spiritual welfare of the people in general, had gathered to perform a long, continuous chain of sacrifices to counteract the degrading influence of the incipient age of Kali. In response to the sages' request that he speak the essence of Vedic wisdom, Sūta Gosvāmī repeated from memory the entire eighteen thousand verses of *Śrīmad-Bhāgavatam*, as spoken by Śukadeva Gosvāmī to Mahārāja Parīkṣit.

The reader of *Śrīmad-Bhāgavatam* hears Sūta Gosvāmī relate the questions of Mahārāja Parīkṣit and the answers of Śukadeva Gosvāmī. Also, Sūta Gosvāmī sometimes responds directly to questions put by Śaunaka Ṛṣi, the spokesman for the sages gathered at Naimiṣāraṇya. One therefore simultaneously hears two dialogues: one between Mahārāja Parīkṣit and Śukadeva Gosvāmī on the bank of the Ganges, and another at Naimiṣāraṇya between Sūta Gosvāmī and the sages at Naimiṣāraṇya Forest, headed by Śaunaka Ṛṣi. Furthermore, while instructing King Parīkṣit, Śukadeva Gosvāmī often relates historical episodes and gives accounts of lengthy philosophical discussions between such great souls as the saint Maitreya and his disciple Vidura. With this understanding of the history of the *Bhāgavatam*, the reader will easily be able to follow its intermingling of dialogues and events from various sources. Since philosophical wisdom, not chronological order, is most important in the text, one need only be attentive to the subject matter of *Śrīmad-Bhāgavatam* to appreciate fully its profound message.

The translator of this edition compares the *Bhāgavatam* to sugar candy—wherever you taste it, you will find it equally sweet and relishable. Therefore, to taste the sweetness of the *Bhāgavatam*, one may begin by reading any of its volumes. After such an introductory taste, however, the serious reader is best advised to go back to Volume One of the First Canto and then proceed through the *Bhāgavatam*, volume after volume, in its natural order.

This edition of the *Bhāgavatam* is the first complete English translation of this important text with an elaborate commentary, and it is the first widely available to the English-speaking public. It is the product of the scholarly and devotional effort of His Divine Grace A. C. Bhaktivedanta Swami Prabhupāda, the world's most distinguished teacher of Indian religious and philosophical thought. His consummate Sanskrit scholarship and intimate familiarity with Vedic culture and thought as well as the modern way of life combine to reveal to the West a magnificent exposition of this important classic.

Readers will find this work of value for many reasons. For those interested in the classical roots of Indian civilization, it serves as a vast reservoir of detailed information on virtually every one of its aspects. For students of comparative philosophy and religion, the *Bhāgavatam* offers a penetrating view into the meaning of India's profound spiritual heritage. To sociologists and anthropologists, the *Bhāgavatam* reveals the practical workings of a peaceful and scientifically organized Vedic culture, whose institutions were integrated on the basis of a highly developed spiritual world view. Students of literature will discover the *Bhāgavatam* to be a masterpiece of majestic poetry. For students of psychology, the text provides important perspectives on the nature of consciousness, human behavior and the philosophical study of identity. Finally, to those seeking spiritual insight, the *Bhāgavatam* offers simple and practical guidance for attainment of the highest self-knowledge and realization of the Absolute Truth. The entire multivolume text, presented by the Bhaktivedanta Book Trust, promises to occupy a significant place in the intellectual, cultural and spiritual life of modern man for a long time to come.

—The Publishers

His Divine Grace
A. C. Bhaktivedanta Swami Prabhupāda
Founder-Ācārya of the International Society for Krishna Consciousness

PLATE ONE

When Vidura returned to Hastināpura from his long pilgrimage, he first ate sumptuously and then took sufficient rest. Afterward, when he had arisen, bathed, and was comfortably seated, King Yudhiṣṭhira began to speak to him, and all who were present listened: "O Uncle Vidura, do you remember how you always protected us, along with our mother, from all sorts of calamities? Your partiality, like the wings of a bird, saved us from poisoning and arson. While traveling on the surface of the earth, how did you maintain your livelihood? At which holy places of pilgrimage did you render service? My lord, devotees like your good self are verily holy places personified. Because you carry the Personality of Godhead within your heart, you turn all places into places of pilgrimage." Thus questioned by King Yudhiṣṭhira, Mahātmā Vidura gradually described everything that he had personally experienced, except the unbearable news of the annihilation of the Yadu dynasty. *(pp. 10–17)*

PLATE TWO

In a thatched hut on the bank of the Ganges, King Dhṛtarāṣṭra first controlled the yogic sitting postures and the breathing process, and then he turned his senses toward the Absolute Personality of Godhead. He suspended all the actions of the senses, even from the outside, and became impervious to the interactions of the senses and mind. At that time he became immovably established, beyond all sources of hindrances on the path. Then Dhṛtarāṣṭra amalgamated his pure identity with his intelligence and merged into the Supreme Being with knowledge of his qualitative oneness with Him. Being freed from the blocked sky, he rose to the spiritual sky. Finally, he burned his own body to ashes by self-made mystic fire. After observing her husband burn in the fire along with his thatched cottage, his chaste wife, Gāndhārī, entered the fire with rapt attention. *(pp. 71–75)*

PLATE THREE

When a few months had passed, and Arjuna had not returned from Dvārakā, Mahārāja Yudhiṣṭhira began to observe some inauspicious omens. The King then spoke to his younger brother Bhīmasena: "Just see, O man with a tiger's strength, how the she-jackal cries at the rising sun, vomiting fire, and how the dog barks at me fearlessly! O Bhīmasena, my horses appear to weep upon seeing me. Just see the bolts from the blue and the smoke encircling the sky, and just hear the cloudless thunder! It appears that the earth and mountains are throbbing. The wind blows violently, blasting dust and creating darkness everywhere. And everywhere, clouds are raining bloody disasters. The rays of the sun are declining, and the stars seem to be fighting among themselves. The calves do not suck the teats of the cows, nor do the cows give milk. They are standing with tears in their eyes, and the bulls take no pleasure in the pasturing grounds. The Deities in the temple look like they are crying and perspiring. They seem about to leave. And all the cities, villages, towns, gardens, mines and hermitages are now devoid of beauty and bereft of all happiness. I think that all these earthly disturbances prelude some greater loss to the good fortune of the world. The world was fortunate indeed to have been marked with the footprints of Lord Kṛṣṇa's lotus feet, but these signs indicate that this will no longer be." *(pp. 80–96)*

PLATE FOUR

Arjuna, the celebrated friend of Lord Kṛṣṇa, was griefstricken when the Lord closed His earthly pastimes. Remembering Lord Kṛṣṇa and His well wishes, benefactions, intimate familial relations and His chariot driving, Arjuna, overwhelmed and breathing heavily, began to speak: "O King! The Supreme Personality of Godhead, Hari, who treated me exactly like an intimate friend, has left me alone. Thus my astounding power, which astonished even the demigods, is no longer with me. I have just lost Him whose separation for a moment renders all the universes unfavorable and void, like bodies without life. Because He was near me, it was possible for me to conquer with great dexterity the powerful King of heaven, Indradeva, along with his demigod associates, and thus enable the fire-god to devastate the Khāṇḍava forest. By making them widows, Lord Kṛṣṇa loosened the hair of all the wives of the miscreants who dared open the cluster of your Queen's hair, which had been nicely dressed and sanctified for the great Rājasūya sacrifice. And it was by His influence only that in a fight I was able to astonish the personality of god Lord Śiva, who thus became pleased with me and awarded me his own weapon. O Emperor, now I am separated from my friend and dearmost well-wisher, the Supreme Personality of Godhead, and therefore my heart appears to be void of everything." *(pp. 119–146)*

PLATE FIVE

Draupadī was the most beautiful daughter of King Drupada, and when she was a young girl almost all the princes desired her hand. But King Drupada decided to hand over his daughter to Arjuna only and therefore contrived a peculiar way. A fish protected by a wheel was hung from the inner roof of the house. The condition was that out of the princely order, one must be able to pierce the fish's eyes through the wheel of protection, and no one would be allowed to look up at the target. On the ground there was a waterpot in which the target and wheel were reflected, and one had to fix his aim towards the target by looking at the trembling water in the pot. Only Arjuna and Karṇa were capable of successfully piercing the target, but Draupadī tactfully avoided Karṇa by making it known that she was unable to accept as her husband anyone who was less than a *kṣatriya*. Karṇa, being the son of a carpenter, was a *śūdra*, so Draupadī avoided Karṇa by her plea. Thereafter, Arjuna, in the dress of a poor *brāhmaṇa*, pierced the difficult target and thus gained the valuable hand of Draupadī. *(p. 125)*

PLATE SIX

Jarāsandha was a very powerful king of Magadha, but he possessed one weakness due to the peculiar circumstances of his birth: he was born in two parts and later joined together by a she-demon named Jarā. Because he was a relative of Kaṁsa, King Jarāsandha became a great enemy of Kṛṣṇa after He had killed Kaṁsa, and there were many fights between Jarāsandha and Kṛṣṇa. Lord Kṛṣṇa wanted to kill him, but He also wanted that those who served as military men for Jarāsandha might not be killed. Therefore a plan was adopted whereby Kṛṣṇa, Bhīma and Arjuna together went to Jarāsandha in the dress of poor *brāhmaṇas* and begged charity from him. Jarāsandha never refused charity to any *brāhmaṇa*, and thus he readily agreed to fight with Bhīma alone. After Bhīma and Jarāsandha had fought to a draw every day for several days, Bhīma became disappointed. Then Kṛṣṇa gave Bhīma hints about Jarāsandha's being joined together as an infant, and thus Bhīma dissected him and so killed him. *(pp. 128–129)*

PLATE SEVEN

The military strength of the Kauravas was like an ocean in which there dwelled many invincible existences, and thus it was insurmountable. But because of Kṛṣṇa's friendship, Arjuna, seated on the chariot, was able to cross over it. The great military phalanx made by the Kauravas was expert and more than adequate, but Lord Śrī Kṛṣṇa, while going forward on the battlefield, withdrew the Kauravas' duration of life, speculative power and strength of enthusiasm. Thus, although great generals like Bhīṣma, Droṇa, Karṇa, Bhūriśravā, Suśarmā, Śalya, Jayadratha and Bāhlika all directed their invincible weapons against Arjuna, by Lord Kṛṣṇa's grace they could not touch even a hair of his head. *(pp. 137-144)*

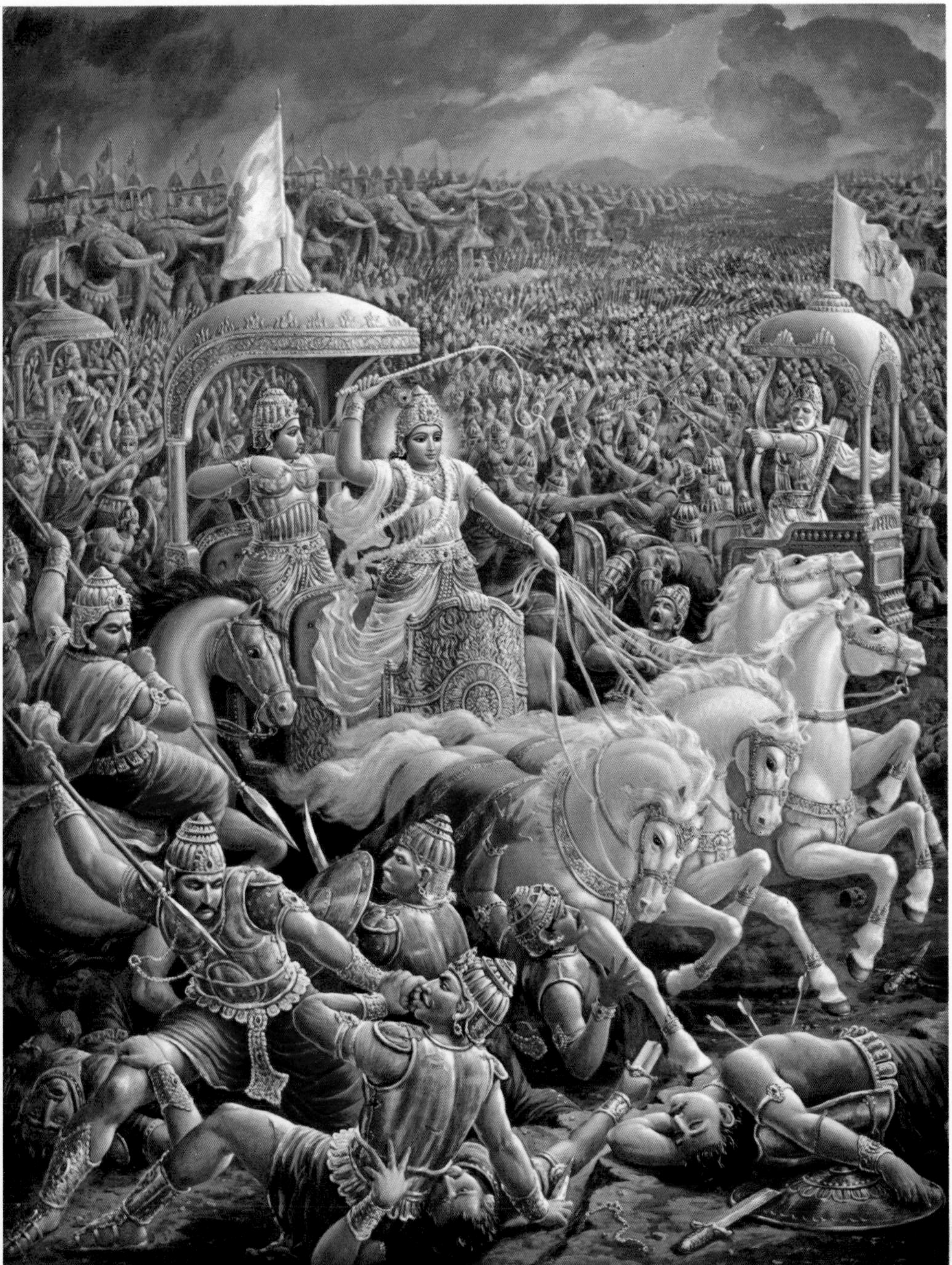

PLATE EIGHT

Generally, Kṛṣṇa and Arjuna used to live together, sleep, sit and enjoy leisure hours together. Arjuna would address the Lord, "O Kṛṣṇa," "O Yādava," "O my friend," without knowing of Kṛṣṇa's glories, and Kṛṣṇa would heartily address Arjuna, "O son of Pṛthā," "O friend," "O beloved son of the Kuru dynasty." At such times, Kṛṣṇa's joking and frank talks were pleasing and beautifully decorated with smiles. Sometimes, if there were any irregularity at the time of advertising for acts of chivalry, Arjuna would reproach Kṛṣṇa by saying, "My friend, You are being too truthful." And even in those hours, when Kṛṣṇa's value was being minimized, He used to tolerate all those utterings of Arjuna's, excusing him exactly as a true friend excuses his true friend, or a father excuses his son. *(pp. 146–148)*

PLATE NINE

The original spiritual planet, Goloka Vṛndāvana, resembles the whorl of a huge lotus flower. It is the abode of Lord Kṛṣṇa, the Supreme Personality of Godhead. Goloka Vṛndāvana emanates an unlimited spiritual effulgence (*brahmajyoti*) within which there are innumerable spiritual planets called Vaikuṇṭhas. Each Vaikuṇṭha planet is ruled by a different four-handed plenary expansion of Lord Kṛṣṇa, such as Lord Keśava, Lord Trivikrama, Lord Upendra, and so forth. The inhabitants of these planets are ever-liberated living beings. Sometimes a spiritual cloud called the *mahat-tattva* covers a corner of the *brahmajyoti.* At that time the Lord's plenary portion known as Mahā-Viṣṇu lies down on the vast Causal Ocean within the *mahat-tattva*, and as He sleeps there He generates innumerable floating universes by His breathing. These universes scatter throughout the Causal Ocean, where they remain during each exhalation of Mahā-Viṣṇu (a period of about three hundred trillion years). In each universal globe, an expansion of Mahā-Viṣṇu called Garbhodakaśāyī Viṣṇu enters and lies down on the Garbha Ocean, supported by the serpentine Śeṣa incarnation. From the navel of Garbhodakaśāyī Viṣṇu sprouts a lotus, upon which Brahmā, the engineer of the universe, is born. Then Brahmā creates the sun, the planets and living entities of every variety.

Nārāyaṇa
Acyuta
Keśava
Janārdana
Mādhava
Śrīdhara
Hari
Vāsudeva
Govinda
Pradyumna
Saṅkarṣaṇa
Trivikrama
Viṣṇumūrti
Aniruddha
Padmanābha
Hṛṣīkeśa
Kṛṣṇa
Dāmodara
Puruṣottama
Vāmana
Madhusūdana
Adhokṣaja
Nṛsiṁha
Upendra

PLATE TEN

From the very day that Lord Kṛṣṇa left this earthly planet in His selfsame form, the age of Kali became fully manifest to create inauspicious conditions for those who are endowed with a poor fund of knowledge. Mahārāja Yudhiṣṭhira was intelligent enough to understand the influence of the age of Kali (characterized by increasing avarice, falsehood, cheating and violence throughout the land), so he wisely prepared himself to leave home. First he enthroned his grandson, Mahārāja Parīkṣit, at Hastināpura to rule as the emperor of all land bordered by the seas. Then he posted Vajra (the grandson of Lord Kṛṣṇa) at Mathurā as the King of Śūrasena. Afterwards, Mahārāja Yudhiṣṭhira performed a Prājāpatya sacrifice and placed in himself the fire for quitting household life. At once relinquishing all his royal garments, he became completely disinterested in everything mundane. He then freed himself entirely from the material conception of life and became absorbed in Brahman. After that, Mahārāja Yudhiṣṭhira dressed himself in torn clothing, gave up eating all solid foods, voluntarily became dumb and let his hair hang loose. All this combined to make him look like an urchin or a madman with no occupation. He did not depend on his brothers for anything. And, just like a deaf man, he heard nothing. He then started towards the North, treading the path which was accepted by his forefathers and great men, to devote himself completely to the thought of the Supreme Personality of Godhead. And he lived in that way wherever he went. *(pp. 170–181)*

PLATE ELEVEN

Once, when Mahārāja Parīkṣit was on a tour of the world, he saw the master of Kali-yuga, who was lower than a *śūdra*, disguised as a king and beating the legs of a cow and a bull. The bull personified the religious principles of austerity, cleanliness, mercy and truthfulness. But he was now standing on only one leg, representing truthfulness, for his other three legs had been destroyed by Kali. The cow was the earth personified and she was lamenting because Lord Śrī Kṛṣṇa had closed His transcendental pastimes on the face of the earth, and in His absence the age of Kali had spread its influence everywhere. After dismounting from his chariot, Mahārāja Parīkṣit spoke to the *śūdra* with a deep voice, sounding like thunder: "Who are you? You appear to be a godly man, and yet you dare kill, within my protection, those who are helpless? By your dress you pose yourself as a king, but by your deeds you are opposing the principles of brahminical rule. You rogue! Do you dare beat an innocent cow because Lord Kṛṣṇa and Arjuna are out of sight? Since you are beating the innocent in a secluded place, you are considered a culprit and deserve to be killed." Saying this, Mahārāja Parīkṣit took up his sharp sword to kill Kali, who is the cause of all irreligion. When Kali understood that the King was willing to kill him, he at once abandoned the dress of a king and bowed his head in surrender. Mahārāja Parīkṣit did not kill the surrendered and fallen Kali, but smiled compassionately, for he was kind to the poor. "O King," said Kali, "please fix some place where I can live permanently under the protection of your government." Thus petitioned by Kali, King Parīkṣit gave him permission to reside in places where gambling, drinking, prostitution, and animal slaughter are performed, and where large quantities of gold are kept. *(pp. 194–282)*

PLATE TWELVE

Once every 8,640,000,000 years, the Supreme Personality of Godhead appears on earth in His original form so that His devotees can experience the highest ecstasy of loving exchanges with Him. The unique loveliness of this form is said to charm even Cupid. His beautiful figure is tinged with the hue of blue clouds, His eyes are like the petals of a blooming lotus flower, and His head is bedecked with a peacock feather. Around His neck He wears a garland of flowers; His ankles, arms and hands are bedecked with jeweled ornaments; and He wears a charming necklace of brilliant pearls, pearl earrings and a pearl headress beautified by an *indranīla* gem. His special ornament is His flute, which He is very adept at playing. This flute is decorated with *indranīla* gems, and at its two ends rubies glitter beautifully. The body of the flute is plated with gold, set ablaze by diamonds. The sweet sound of this flute, combined with the unsurpassed beauty of the Lord in His Vṛndāvana feature, attracts all living entities to become His loving servants. Thus He is known as Kṛṣṇa, the all-attractive Supreme Personality of Godhead. Those who are desirous of achieving complete perfection in life should submissively hear all topics connected with the transcendental activities and qualities of Kṛṣṇa, for this will open the path to a life of eternal bliss and knowledge. *(p. 301)*

PLATE THIRTEEN

Once, Mahārāja Parīkṣit, while engaged in hunting stags in the forest with bow and arrows, became extremely fatigued, hungry and thirsty. While searching for a reservoir of water, he entered the hermitage of the well-known Śamīka Ṛṣi, and saw the sage sitting silently with closed eyes. He was meditating. His sense organs, breath, mind and intelligence were all restrained from material activities, and he was situated in a trance apart from the three normal states of consciousness, namely wakefulness, dream and unconsciousness. The King, not receiving the amenities of a formal welcome (such as a sitting place, some water and sweet addresses), considered himself neglected, and so thinking, he became angry. Thus, while leaving the hermitage, the King picked up a lifeless snake with his bow and angrily placed it on the shoulder of the sage. Then he returned to his palace. *(pp. 322–328)*

PLATE FOURTEEN

The sage Śamīka had a son named Śṛṅgi, who was very powerful, being a *brāhmaṇa's* son. While playing with his friends, he heard how his father had been garlanded with a snake by King Parīkṣit. Then Śṛṅgi spoke as follows: "Oh, just look at the sins of the rulers, who perpetrate sins against their *brāhmaṇa* masters, contrary to the principles governing servants. The descendants of the kingly orders are definitely designated as watchdogs, and they must keep themselves at the door. On what grounds can dogs enter the house and claim to dine with the master on the same plate? After the departure of Lord Śrī Kṛṣṇa, these upstarts have flourished, our protector being gone. Therefore I myself shall take up this matter and punish them. Just witness my power." Śṛṅgi then touched the water of the River Kauśika and discharged the following thunderbolt of words: "On the seventh day from today a snake-bird will bite the most wretched King Parīkṣit because of his having broken the laws of etiquette by insulting my father." Thereafter, when the boy returned to the hermitage, he saw the snake on his father's shoulder, and out of grief he cried very loudly. When Śamīka Ṛṣi asked his son why he was crying, Śṛṅgi explained to him what had happened. Upon hearing the story, the sage began to lament, "Alas! What a great sinful act has been performed by my son. He has awarded heavy punishment for an insignificant offense." *(pp. 330–339)*

PLATE FIFTEEN

After all the sages and other great personages had seated themselves comfortably on the bank of the Ganges, King Parīkṣit told them of his decision to fast until death: "O sages, the Supreme Personality of Godhead has graciously overtaken me in the form of a *brāhmaṇa's* curse. Due to my being too much attached to family life, the Lord, in order to save me, has appeared before me in such a way that out of fear only I will detach myself from the world. O *brāhmaṇas,* just accept me as a completely surrendered soul, for I have already taken the lotus feet of the Lord into my heart. Let the snake-bird—or whatever magical thing the *brāhmaṇa* has created—bite me at once. I only desire that you all continue singing the deeds of Lord Viṣṇu. Again offering obeisances unto all of you, I pray that if I should again take my birth in the material world, I will have complete attachment to the unlimited Lord Kṛṣṇa, association with His devotees and friendly relations with all living beings." Then, in perfect self-control, Mahārāja Parīkṣit sat down on a seat of straw placed on the southern bank of the Ganges, and he himself faced north. Just previously, he had given over the charge of his kingdom to his sons. Thus King Parīkṣit sat to fast until death, receiving praise from all the great sages assembled there as well as from all the demigods of the higher planets, who in great pleasure continually scattered flowers over the earth and beat celestial drums. *(pp. 368–376)*

Kurukṣetra, the place of pilgrimage where Kṛṣṇa and Arjuna defeated the insurmountable strength of the Kauravas. *(pp. 137–139)*

CHAPTER THIRTEEN

Dhṛtarāṣṭra Quits Home

TEXT 1

सूत उवाच

विदुरस्तीर्थयात्रायां मैत्रेयादात्मनो गतिम् ।
ज्ञात्वागाद्धास्तिनपुरं तयावाप्तविवित्सितः ॥ १ ॥

sūta uvāca
viduras tīrtha-yātrāyāṁ
maitreyād ātmano gatim
jñātvāgād dhāstinapuraṁ
tayāvāpta-vivitsitaḥ

sūtaḥ uvāca—Śrī Sūta Gosvāmī said; *viduraḥ*—Vidura; *tīrtha-yātrāyām*—while traveling to different places of pilgrimage; *maitreyāt*—from the great sage Maitreya; *ātmanaḥ*—of the self; *gatim*—destination; *jñātvā*—by knowing it; *āgāt*—went back; *hāstina-puram*—the city of Hastināpura; *tayā*—by that knowledge; *avāpta*—sufficiently a gainer; *vivitsitaḥ*—being well versed in everything knowable.

TRANSLATION

Śrī Sūta Gosvāmī said: While traveling on a pilgrimage, Vidura received knowledge of the destination of the self from the great sage Maitreya and then returned to Hastināpura. He became as well versed in the subject as he desired.

PURPORT

Vidura: One of the prominent figures in the history of the *Mahābhārata.* He was conceived by Vyāsadeva in the womb of the maidservant of Ambikā, mother of Mahārāja Pāṇḍu. He is the incarnation of Yamarāja. Being cursed by Maṇḍuka Muni, he was to become a *śūdra.* The story is narrated as follows. Once upon a time the state police caught some thieves who had concealed themselves in the hermitage of Maṇḍuka Muni. The police constables, as usual, arrested all the thieves and Maṇḍuka Muni along with them. The Magistrate specifically punished the *muni* to death by being pierced with a lance. When he was just to be pierced, the news reached the king, and he at once stopped the act on consideration of his being a great *muni.* The king personally begged the *muni's* pardon for the mistake of his men, and the saint at once went to Yamarāja, who prescribes the destiny of the living beings. Yamarāja, being questioned by the *muni,* replied that the *muni* in his childhood pierced an ant with a sharpened straw, and for that reason he was put into difficulty. The *muni* thought it unwise on the part of Yamarāja that he was punished for his childish innocence, and thus the *muni* cursed Yamarāja to become a *śūdra,* and this *śūdra* incarnation of Yamarāja was known as Vidura, the *śūdra* brother of Dhṛtarāṣṭra and Mahārāja Pāṇḍu. But this *śūdra* son of the Kuru dynasty was equally treated by Bhīṣmadeva, along with his other nephews, and in due course Vidura was married with a girl who was also born in the womb of a *śūdrāṇī* by a *brāhmaṇa.* Although Vidura did not inherit the property of his father (the brother of Bhīṣmadeva), still he was given sufficient state property by Dhṛtarāṣṭra, the elder brother of Vidura. Vidura was very much attached to his elder brother, and all along he tried to guide him on the right path. During the fratricidal war of Kurukṣetra, Vidura repeatedly implored his elder brother to do justice to the sons of Pāṇḍu, but Duryodhana did not like such interference by his uncle, and thus he practically insulted Vidura. This resulted in Vidura's leaving home for pilgrimage and taking instructions from Maitreya.

TEXT 2

यावतः कृतवान् प्रश्नान् क्षत्ता कौषारवाग्रतः ।
जातैकभक्तिर्गोविन्दे तेभ्यश्चोपरराम ह ॥ २ ॥

yāvataḥ kṛtavān praśnān
kṣattā kauṣāravāgrataḥ

jātaika-bhaktir govinde
tebhyaś copararāma ha

yāvataḥ—all that; *kṛtavān*—did he put; *praśnān*—questions; *kṣattā*—a name of Vidura; *kauṣārava*—a name of Maitreya; *agrataḥ*—in the presence of; *jāta*—having grown up; *eka*—one; *bhaktiḥ*—transcendental loving service; *govinde*—unto Lord Kṛṣṇa; *tebhyaḥ*—regarding further questions; *ca*—and; *upararāma*—retired from; *ha*—in the past.

TRANSLATION

After asking various questions and becoming established in the transcendental loving service of Lord Kṛṣṇa, Vidura retired from putting questions to Maitreya Muni.

PURPORT

Vidura retired from putting questions before Maitreya Muni when he was convinced by Maitreya Ṛṣi that the *summum bonum* of life is to be finally situated in the transcendental loving service of Lord Śrī Kṛṣṇa, who is Govinda, or one who satisfies His devotees in all respects. The conditioned soul, the living being in material existence, seeks happiness by employing his senses in the modes of materialism, but that cannot give him satisfaction. He then searches after the Supreme Truth by the empiric philosophic speculative method and intellectual feats. But if he does not find the ultimate goal, he again goes down to material activities and engages himself in various philanthropic and altruistic works, which all fail to give him satisfaction. So neither fruitive activities nor dry philosophical speculation can give one satisfaction because by nature a living being is the eternal servitor of the Supreme Lord Śrī Kṛṣṇa, and all the Vedic literatures give him direction towards that ultimate end. The *Bhagavad-gītā* (15.15) confirms this statement.

Like Vidura, an inquisitive conditioned soul must approach a bona fide spiritual master like Maitreya and by intelligent inquiries must try to know everything about *karma* (fruitive activities), *jñāna* (philosophical research for the Supreme Truth) and *yoga* (the linking process of spiritual realization). One who is not seriously inclined to put questions before a spiritual master need not accommodate a show-bottle spiritual master, nor should a person who may be a spiritual master for others pose to be so if he is unable to engage his disciple ultimately in the transcendental loving service of Lord Śrī Kṛṣṇa. Vidura was successful in approaching such a spiritual master like Maitreya, and he got the ultimate goal of life: *bhakti* unto Govinda. Thus there was nothing to be known further about spiritual progress.

TEXTS 3–4

तं बन्धुमागतं दृष्ट्वा धर्मपुत्रः सहानुजः ।
धृतराष्ट्रो युयुत्सुश्च सूतः शारद्वतः पृथा ॥ ३ ॥
गान्धारी द्रौपदी ब्रह्मन् सुभद्रा चोत्तरा कृपी ।
अन्याश्च जामयः पाण्डोर्ज्ञातयः ससुताः स्त्रियः॥४॥

taṁ bandhum āgataṁ dṛṣṭvā
dharma-putraḥ sahānujaḥ
dhṛtarāṣṭro yuyutsuś ca
sūtaḥ śāradvataḥ pṛthā

gāndhārī draupadī brahman
subhadrā cottarā kṛpī
anyāś ca jāmayaḥ pāṇḍor
jñātayaḥ sasutāḥ striyaḥ

tam—him; *bandhum*—relative; *āgatam*—having arrived there; *dṛṣṭvā*—by seeing it; *dharma-putraḥ*—Yudhiṣṭhira; *saha-anujaḥ*—along with his younger brothers; *dhṛtarāṣṭraḥ*—Dhṛtarāṣṭra; *yuyutsuḥ*—Sātyaki; *ca*—and; *sūtaḥ*—Sañjaya; *śāradvataḥ*—Kṛpācārya; *pṛthā*—Kuntī; *gāndhārī*—Gāndhārī; *draupadī*—Draupadī; *brahman*—O *brāhmaṇas; subhadrā*—Subhadrā; *ca*—and; *uttarā*—Uttarā; *kṛpī*—Kṛpī; *anyāḥ*—others; *ca*—and; *jāmayaḥ*—wives of other family members; *pāṇḍoḥ*—of the Pāṇḍavas; *jñātayaḥ*—family members; *sa-sutāḥ*—along with their sons; *striyaḥ*—the ladies.

TRANSLATION

When they saw Vidura return to the palace, all the inhabitants—Mahārāja Yudhiṣṭhira, his younger brothers, Dhṛtarāṣṭra, Sātyaki,

Sañjaya, Kṛpācārya, Kuntī, Gāndhārī, Draupadī, Subhadrā, Uttarā, Kṛpī, many other wives of the Kauravas, and other ladies with children—all hurried to him in great delight. It so appeared that they had regained their consciousness after a long period.

PURPORT

Gāndhārī: The ideal chaste lady in the history of the world. She was the daughter of Mahārāja Subala, the King of Gāndhāra (now Kandahar in Kabul), and in her maiden state she worshiped Lord Śiva. Lord Śiva is generally worshiped by Hindu maidens to get a good husband. Gāndhārī satisfied Lord Śiva, and by his benediction to obtain one hundred sons, she was betrothed to Dhṛtarāṣṭra, despite his being blind forever. When Gāndhārī came to know that her would-be husband was a blind man, to follow her life companion she decided to become voluntarily blind. So she wrapped up her eyes with many silk linens, and she was married to Dhṛtarāṣṭra under the guidance of her elder brother Śakuni. She was the most beautiful girl of her time, and she was equally qualified by her womanly qualities, which endeared every member of the Kaurava court. But despite all her good qualities, she had the natural frailties of a woman, and she was envious of Kuntī when the latter gave birth to a male child. Both the queens were pregnant, but Kuntī first gave birth to a male child. Thus Gāndhārī became angry and gave a blow to her own abdomen. As a result, she gave birth to a lump of flesh only, but since she was a devotee of Vyāsadeva, by the instruction of Vyāsadeva the lump was divided into one hundred parts, and each part gradually developed to become a male child. Thus her ambition to become the mother of one hundred sons was fulfilled, and she began to nourish all the children according to her exalted position. When the intrigue of the Battle of Kurukṣetra was going on, she was not in favor of fighting with the Pāṇḍavas; rather, she blamed Dhṛtarāṣṭra, her husband, for such a fratricidal war. She desired that the state be divided into two parts, for the sons of Pāṇḍu and her own. She was very affected when all her sons died in the Battle of Kurukṣetra, and she wanted to curse Bhīmasena and Yudhiṣṭhira, but she was checked by Vyāsadeva. Her mourning over the death of Duryodhana and Duḥśāsana before Lord Kṛṣṇa was very pitiful, and Lord Kṛṣṇa pacified her by transcendental messages. She was equally aggrieved on the death of Karṇa, and she described to Lord Kṛṣṇa the lamentation of Karṇa's wife. She was pacified by Śrīla Vyāsadeva when he showed her dead sons, then promoted to the heavenly kingdoms. She died along with her husband in the jungles of the Himalayas near the mouth of the Ganges; she burned in a forest fire. Mahārāja Yudhiṣṭhira performed the death ceremony of his uncle and aunt.

Pṛthā: Daughter of Mahārāja Śūrasena and sister of Vasudeva, Lord Kṛṣṇa's father. Later she was adopted by Mahārāja Kuntibhoja, and hence she is known as Kuntī. She is the incarnation of the success potency of the Personality of Godhead. The heavenly denizens from the upper planets used to visit the palace of King Kuntibhoja, and Kuntī was engaged for their reception. She also served the great mystic sage Durvāsā, and being satisfied by her faithful service, Durvāsā Muni gave her a *mantra* by which it was possible for her to call for any demigod she pleased. As a matter of inquisitiveness, she at once called for the sun-god, who desired couplement with her, but she declined. But the sun-god assured her immunity from virgin adulteration, and so she agreed to his proposal. As a result of this couplement, she became pregnant, and Karṇa was born by her. By the grace of the sun, she again turned into a virgin girl, but being afraid of her parents, she quitted the newly born child, Karṇa. After that, when she actually selected her own husband, she preferred Pāṇḍu to be her husband. Mahārāja Pāṇḍu later wanted to retire from family life and adopt the renounced order of life. Kuntī refused to allow her husband to adopt such life, but at last Mahārāja Pāṇḍu gave her permission to become a mother of sons by calling some other suitable personalities. Kuntī did not accept this proposal at first, but when vivid examples were set by Pāṇḍu she agreed. Thus by dint of the *mantra* awarded by Durvāsā Muni she called for Dharmarāja, and thus Yudhiṣṭhira was born. She called for the demigod Vāyu (air), and thus Bhīma was born. She called for Indra, the King of heaven, and thus Arjuna was born. The other two sons, namely Nakula and Sahadeva, were begotten by Pāṇḍu himself in the womb of Mādrī. Later on, Mahārāja Pāṇḍu died at an early age, for which Kuntī was so aggrieved that she fainted. Two co-wives, namely Kuntī and Mādrī, decided that Kuntī should live for the maintenance of the five minor children, the Pāṇḍavas, and Mādrī should accept the *satī* rituals by meeting voluntary death along with her husband. This agreement was endorsed by great sages like Śatasṛṅga and others present on the occasion.

Later on, when the Pāṇḍavas were banished from the kingdom by the intrigues of Duryodhana, Kuntī followed her sons, and she equally faced all sorts of difficulties during those days. During the forest life one demon girl, Hiḍimbā, wanted Bhīma as her husband. Bhīma refused, but when the girl approached Kuntī and Yudhiṣṭhira, they ordered Bhīma to accept her proposal and give her a son. As a result of this combination, Ghaṭotkaca was born, and he fought very valiantly with his father against the Kauravas. In their forest life they lived with a *brāhmaṇa* family that was in trouble because of one Bakāsura demon, and Kuntī ordered Bhīma to kill the Bakāsura to protect the *brāhmaṇa* family against troubles created by the demon. She advised Yudhiṣṭhira to start for the Pāñcāladeśa. Draupadī was gained in this Pāñcāladeśa by Arjuna, but by order of Kuntī all five of the Pāṇḍava brothers became equally the husbands of Pāñcālī, or Draupadī. She was married with five Pāṇḍavas in the presence of Vyāsadeva. Kuntīdevī never forgot her first child, Karṇa, and after Karṇa's death in the Battle of Kurukṣetra she lamented and admitted before her other sons that Karṇa was her eldest son prior to her marriage with Mahārāja Pāṇḍu. Her prayers for the Lord after the Battle of Kurukṣetra, when Lord Kṛṣṇa was going back home, are excellently explained. Later she went to the forest with Gāndhārī for severe penance. She used to take meals after each thirty days. She finally sat down in profound meditation and later burned to ashes in a forest fire.

Draupadī: The most chaste daughter of Mahārāja Drupada and partly an incarnation of goddess Śacī, the wife of Indra. Mahārāja Drupada performed a great sacrifice under the superintendence of the sage Yaja. By his first offering, Dhṛṣṭadyumna was born, and by the second offering, Draupadī was born. She is therefore the sister of Dhṛṣṭadyumna, and she is also named Pāñcālī. The five Pāṇḍavas married her as a common wife, and each of them begot a son in her. Mahārāja Yudhiṣṭhira begot a son named Pratibhit, Bhīmasena begot a son named Sutasoma, Arjuna begot Śrutakīrti, Nakula begot Śatānīka, and Sahadeva begot Śrutakarmā. She is described as a most beautiful lady, equal to her mother-in-law, Kuntī. During her birth there was an aero-message that she should be called Kṛṣṇā. The same message also declared that she was born to kill many a *kṣatriya.* By dint of her blessings from Śaṅkara, she was awarded five husbands, equally qualified. When she preferred to select her own husband, princes and kings were invited from all the countries of the world. She was married with the Pāṇḍavas during their exile in the forest, but when they went back home Mahārāja Drupada gave them immense wealth as a dowry. She was well received by all the daughters-in-law of Dhṛtarāṣṭra. When she was lost in a gambling game, she was forcibly dragged into the assembly hall, and an attempt was made by Duḥśāsana to see her naked beauty, even though there were elderly persons like Bhīṣma and Droṇa present. She was a great devotee of Lord Kṛṣṇa, and by her praying, the Lord Himself became an unlimited garment to save her from the insult. A demon of the name Jatāsura kidnapped her, but her second husband, Bhīmasena, killed the demon and saved her. She saved the Pāṇḍavas from the curse of Maharṣi Durvāsā by the grace of Lord Kṛṣṇa. When the Pāṇḍavas lived incognito in the palace of Virāṭa, Kīcaka was attracted by her exquisite beauty, and by arrangement with Bhīma the devil was killed and she was saved. She was very much aggrieved when her five sons were killed by Aśvatthāmā. At the last stage, she accompanied her husband Yudhiṣṭhira and others and fell on the way. The cause of her falling was explained by Yudhiṣṭhira, but when Yudhiṣṭhira entered the heavenly planet he saw Draupadī gloriously present there as the goddess of fortune in the heavenly planet.

Subhadrā: Daughter of Vasudeva and sister of Lord Śrī Kṛṣṇa. She was not only a very dear daughter of Vasudeva, but also a very dear sister to both Kṛṣṇa and Baladeva. The two brothers and sister are represented in the famous Jagannātha temple of Purī, and the temple is still visited by thousands of pilgrims daily. This temple is in remembrance of the Lord's visit at Kurukṣetra during an occasion of solar eclipse and His subsequent meeting with the residents of Vṛndāvana. The meeting of Rādhā and Kṛṣṇa during this occasion is a very pathetic story, and Lord Śrī Caitanya, in the ecstasy of Rādhārāṇī, always pined for Lord Śrī Kṛṣṇa at Jagannātha Purī. While Arjuna was at Dvārakā, he wanted to have Subhadrā as his queen, and he expressed his desire to Lord Kṛṣṇa. Śrī Kṛṣṇa knew that His elder brother, Lord Baladeva, was arranging her marriage elsewhere, and since He did not dare to go against the arrangement of Baladeva, He advised Arjuna to kidnap Subhadrā. So when all of them were on a pleasure trip on the Raivata Hill, Arjuna managed to kidnap Subhadrā according to the plan of Śrī Kṛṣṇa. Śrī Baladeva was very angry at Arjuna, and He wanted to kill him, but Lord Kṛṣṇa implored

His brother to excuse Arjuna. Then Subhadrā was duly married with Arjuna, and Abhimanyu was born of Subhadrā. At the premature death of Abhimanyu, Subhadrā was very mortified, but on the birth of Parīkṣit she was happy and solaced.

TEXT 5

प्रत्युज्जग्मुः प्रहर्षेण प्राणं तन्व इवागतम् ।
अभिसंगम्य विधिवत् परिष्वङ्गाभिवादनैः ॥ ५ ॥

pratyujjagmuḥ praharṣeṇa
prāṇaṁ tanva ivāgatam
abhisaṅgamya vidhivat
pariṣvaṅgābhivādanaiḥ

prati—towards; *ujjagmuḥ*—went; *praharṣeṇa*—with great delight; *prāṇam*—life; *tanvaḥ*—of the body; *iva*—like; *āgatam*—returned *abhisaṅgamya*—approaching; *vidhi-vat*—in due form; *pariṣvaṅga*—embracing; *abhivādanaiḥ*—by obeisances.

TRANSLATION

With great delight they all approached him, as if life had returned to their bodies. They exchanged obeisances and welcomed each other with embraces.

PURPORT

In the absence of consciousness, the limbs of the body remain inactive. But when consciousness returns, the limbs and senses become active, and existence itself becomes delightful. Vidura was so dear to the members of the Kaurava family that his long absence from the palace was comparable to inactivity. All of them were feeling acute separation from Vidura, and therefore his return to the palace was joyful for all.

TEXT 6

मुमुचुः प्रेमबाष्पौघं विरहौत्कण्ठ्यकातराः ।
राजा तमर्हयाञ्चक्रे कृतासनपरिग्रहम् ॥ ६ ॥

mumucuḥ prema-bāṣpaughaṁ
virahautkaṇṭhya-kātarāḥ
rājā tam arhayāṁ cakre
kṛtāsana-parigraham

mumucuḥ—emanated; *prema*—affectionate; *bāṣpa-ogham*—emotional tears; *viraha*—separation; *autkaṇṭhya*—anxiousness; *kātarāḥ*—being aggrieved; *rājā*—King Yudhiṣṭhira; *tam*—unto him (Vidura); *arhayām cakre*—offered; *kṛta*—performance of; *āsana*—sitting accommodations; *parigraham*—arrangement of.

TRANSLATION

Due to anxieties and long separation, they all cried out of affection. King Yudhiṣṭhira then arranged to offer sitting accommodations and a reception.

TEXT 7

तं भुक्तवन्तं विश्रान्तमासीनं सुखमासने ।
प्रश्रयावनतो राजा प्राह तेषां च शृण्वताम् ॥ ७ ॥

taṁ bhuktavantaṁ viśrāntam
āsīnaṁ sukham āsane
praśrayāvanato rājā
prāha teṣāṁ ca śṛṇvatām

tam—him (Vidura); *bhuktavantam*—after feeding him sumptuously; *viśrāntam*—and having taken rest; *āsīnam*—being seated; *sukham āsane*—on a comfortable seat; *praśraya-avanataḥ*—naturally very gentle and meek; *rājā*—King Yudhiṣṭhira; *prāha*—began to speak; *teṣām ca*—and by them; *śṛṇvatām*—being heard.

TRANSLATION

After Vidura ate sumptuously and took sufficient rest, he was comfortably seated. Then the King began to speak to him, and all who were present there listened.

PURPORT

King Yudhiṣṭhira was expert in reception also, even in the case of his family members. Vidura was well received by all the family members by exchange of embraces and obeisances. After that, bathing and arrangements for a sumptuous dinner were made, and then he was given sufficient rest. After finishing his rest, he was offered a comfortable place to sit, and then the King began to talk about all happenings, both family and otherwise. That is the proper way to receive a beloved friend, or even an enemy. According to Indian moral codes, even an enemy received at home should be so well received that he will not feel any fearful situation. An enemy is always afraid of his enemy, but this should not be so when he is received at home by his enemy. This means that a person, when received at home, should be treated as a relative, so what to speak of a family member like Vidura, who was a well-wisher for all the members of the family. Thus Yudhiṣṭhira Mahārāja began to speak in the presence of all the other members.

TEXT 8

युधिष्ठिर उवाच
अपि स्मरथ नो युष्मत्पक्षच्छायासमेधितान् ।
विपद्गणाद्विषाग्न्यादेर्मोचिता यत्समातृकाः ॥ ८ ॥

yudhiṣṭhira uvāca
api smaratha no yuṣmat-
pakṣac-chāyā-samedhitān
vipad-gaṇād viṣāgnyāder
mocitā yat samātṛkāḥ

yudhiṣṭhiraḥ uvāca—Mahārāja Yudhiṣṭhira said; *api*—whether; *smaratha*—you remember; *naḥ*—us; *yuṣmat*—from you; *pakṣat*—partiality towards us like the wings of a bird; *chāyā*—protection; *samedhitān*—we who were brought up by you; *vipat-gaṇāt*—from various types of calamities; *viṣa*—by administration of poison; *agni-ādeḥ*—by setting on fire; *mocitāḥ*—released from; *yat*—what you have done; *sa*—along with; *mātṛkāḥ*—our mother.

TRANSLATION

Mahārāja Yudhiṣṭhira said: My uncle, do you remember how you always protected us, along with our mother, from all sorts of calamities? Your partiality, like the wings of a bird, saved us from poisoning and arson.

PURPORT

Due to Pāṇḍu's death at an early age, his minor children and widow were the object of special care by all the elderly members of the family, especially Bhīṣmadeva and Mahātmā Vidura. Vidura was more or less partial to the Pāṇḍavas due to their political position. Although Dhṛtarāṣṭra was equally careful for the minor children of Mahārāja Pāṇḍu, he was one of the intriguing parties who wanted to wash away the descendants of Pāṇḍu and replace them by raising his own sons to become the rulers of the kingdom. Mahātmā Vidura could follow this intrigue of Dhṛtarāṣṭra and company, and therefore, even though he was a faithful servitor of his eldest brother, Dhṛtarāṣṭra, he did not like his political ambition for the sake of his own sons. He was therefore very careful about the protection of the Pāṇḍavas and their widow mother. Thus he was, so to speak, partial to the Pāṇḍavas, preferring them to the sons of Dhṛtarāṣṭra, although both of them were equally affectionate in his ordinary eyes. He was equally affectionate to both the camps of nephews in the sense that he always chastised Duryodhana for his intriguing policy against his cousins. He always criticized his elder brother for his policy of encouragement to his sons, and at the same time he was always alert in giving special protection to the Pāṇḍavas. All these different activities of Vidura within the palace politics made him well-known as partial to the Pāṇḍavas. Mahārāja Yudhiṣṭhira has referred to the past history of Vidura before his going away from home for a prolonged pilgrim's journey. Mahārāja Yudhiṣṭhira reminded him that he was equally kind and partial to his grown-up nephews, even after the Battle of Kurukṣetra, a great family disaster.

Before the Battle of Kurukṣetra, Dhṛtarāṣṭra's policy was peaceful annihilation of his nephews, and therefore he ordered Purocana to build a house at Vāraṇāvata, and when the building was finished Dhṛtarāṣṭra desired that his brother's family live there for some time. When the Pāṇḍavas were going there in the presence of all the members of the royal family, Vidura tactfully gave instructions to the Pāṇḍavas about the future plan of Dhṛtarāṣṭra. This is specifically described in the *Mahābhārata* (*Ādi-parva* 114). He indirectly hinted, "A weapon not made of steel or any other material element can be more than sharp to kill an enemy, and he who knows this is never killed." That is to say, he hinted that the party of the Pāṇḍavas was being sent to Vāraṇāvata to be killed, and thus he warned Yudhiṣṭhira to be very careful in their new residential palace. He also gave indications of fire and said that fire cannot extinguish the soul but can annihilate the material body. But one who protects the soul can live. Kuntī could not follow such indirect conversations between Mahārāja Yudhiṣṭhira and Vidura, and thus when she inquired from her son about the purport of the conversation, Yudhiṣṭhira replied that from the talks of Vidura it was understood that there was a hint of fire in the house where they were proceeding. Later on, Vidura came in disguise to the Pāṇḍavas and informed them that the housekeeper was going to set fire to the house on the fourteenth night of the waning moon. It was an intrigue of Dhṛtarāṣṭra that the Pāṇḍavas might die all together with their mother. And by his warning the Pāṇḍavas escaped through a tunnel underneath the earth so that their escape was also unknown to Dhṛtarāṣṭra, so much so that after setting the fire, the Kauravas were so certain of the death of the Pāṇḍavas that Dhṛtarāṣṭra performed the last rites of death with great cheerfulness. And during the mourning period all the members of the palace became overwhelmed with lamentation, but Vidura did not become so, because of his knowledge that the Pāṇḍavas were alive somewhere. There are many such instances of calamities, and in each of them Vidura gave protection to the Pāṇḍavas on one hand, and on the other he tried to restrain his brother Dhṛtarāṣṭra from such intriguing policies. Therefore, he was always partial to the Pāṇḍavas, just as a bird protects its eggs by its wing.

TEXT 9

कया वृत्त्या वर्तितं वश्चरद्भिः क्षितिमण्डलम् ।
तीर्थानि क्षेत्रमुख्यानि सेवितानीह भूतले ॥ ९ ॥

kayā vṛttyā vartitaṁ vaś
caradbhiḥ kṣiti-maṇḍalam

tīrthāni kṣetra-mukhyāni
sevitānīha bhūtale

kayā—by which; *vṛttyā*—means; *vartitam*—maintained your livelihood; *vaḥ*—your good self; *caradbhiḥ*—while traveling; *kṣiti-maṇḍalam*—on the surface of the earth; *tīrthāni*—places of pilgrimage; *kṣetra-mukhyāni*—the principal holy places; *sevitāni*—served by you; *iha*—in this world; *bhūtale*—on this planet.

TRANSLATION

While traveling on the surface of the earth, how did you maintain your livelihood? At which holy places and pilgrimage sites did you render service?

PURPORT

Vidura went out from the palace to detach himself from household affairs, especially political intrigues. As referred to hereinbefore, he was practically insulted by Duryodhana's calling him a son of a *śūdrāṇī*, although it was not out of place to talk loosely in the case of one's grandmother. Vidura's mother, although a *śūdrāṇī*, was the grandmother of Duryodhana, and funny talks are sometimes allowed between grandmother and grandchildren. But because the remark was an actual fact, it was unpalatable talk to Vidura, and it was accepted as a direct insult. He therefore decided to quit his paternal house and prepare for the renounced order of life. This preparatory stage is called *vānaprastha-āśrama*, or retired life for traveling and visiting the holy places on the surface of the earth. In the holy places of India, like Vṛndāvana, Hardwar, Jagannātha Purī, and Prayāga, there are many great devotees, and there are still free kitchen houses for persons who desire to advance spiritually. Mahārāja Yudhiṣṭhira was inquisitive to learn whether Vidura maintained himself by the mercy of the free kitchen houses (*chatras*).

TEXT 10

भवद्विधा भागवतास्तीर्थभूताः स्वयं विभो ।
तीर्थीकुर्वन्ति तीर्थानि स्वान्तःस्थेन गदाभृता ॥१०॥

bhavad-vidhā bhāgavatās
tīrtha-bhūtāḥ svayaṁ vibho
tīrthī-kurvanti tīrthāni
svāntaḥ-sthena gadābhṛtā

bhavat—your good self; *vidhāḥ*—like; *bhāgavatāḥ*—devotees; *tīrtha*—the holy places of pilgrimage; *bhūtāḥ*—converted into; *svayam*—personally; *vibho*—O powerful one; *tīrthī-kurvanti*—make into a holy place of pilgrimage; *tīrthāni*—the holy places; *sva-antaḥ-sthena*—having been situated in the heart; *gadā-bhṛtā*—the Personality of Godhead.

TRANSLATION

My Lord, devotees like your good self are verily holy places personified. Because you carry the Personality of Godhead within your heart, you turn all places into places of pilgrimage.

PURPORT

The Personality of Godhead is omnipresent by His diverse potencies everywhere, just as the power of electricity is distributed everywhere within space. Similarly, the Lord's omnipresence is perceived and manifested by His unalloyed devotees like Vidura, just as electricity is manifested in an electric bulb. A pure devotee like Vidura always feels the presence of the Lord everywhere. He sees everything in the potency of the Lord and the Lord in everything. The holy places all over the earth are meant for purifying the polluted consciousness of the human being by an atmosphere surcharged with the presence of the Lord's unalloyed devotees. If anyone visits a holy place, he must search out the pure devotees residing in such holy places, take lessons from them, try to apply such instructions in practical life and thus gradually prepare oneself for the ultimate salvation, going back to Godhead. To go to some holy place of pilgrimage does not mean only to take a bath in the Ganges or Yamunā or to visit the temples situated in those places. One should also find representatives of Vidura who have no desire in life save and except to serve the Personality of Godhead. The Personality of Godhead is always with such pure devotees because of their unalloyed service, which is without any tinge of fruitive action or utopian speculation. They are in the actual service of the Lord, specifically by the process of hearing and chanting. The pure devotees hear from the authorities and chant, sing and write of the glories of the Lord. Mahāmuni Vyāsadeva heard from Nārada, and then he chanted in writing; Śukadeva Gosvāmī studied from his father, and he described it to Parīkṣit; that is the way of *Śrīmad-Bhāgavatam.* So by their actions the pure devotees of the Lord can render any place into a place of pilgrimage, and the holy places are worth the name only on their account. Such pure devotees are able to rectify the polluted atmosphere of any place, and what to speak of a holy place rendered unholy by the questionable actions of interested persons who try to adopt a professional life at the cost of the reputation of a holy place.

TEXT 11

अपि नः सुहृदस्तात बान्धवाः कृष्णदेवताः ।
दृष्टाः श्रुता वा यदवः स्वपुर्यां सुखमासते ॥११॥

api naḥ suhṛdas tāta
bāndhavāḥ kṛṣṇa-devatāḥ
dṛṣṭāḥ śrutā vā yadavaḥ
sva-puryāṁ sukham āsate

api—whether; *naḥ*—our; *suhṛdaḥ*—well-wishers; *tāta*—O my uncle; *bāndhavāḥ*—friends; *kṛṣṇa-devatāḥ*—those who are always rapt in the service of Lord Śrī Kṛṣṇa; *dṛṣṭāḥ*—by seeing them; *śrutāḥ*—or by hearing about them; *vā*—either; *yadavaḥ*—the descendants of Yadu; *sva-puryām*—along with their residential place; *sukham āsate*—if they are all happy.

TRANSLATION

My uncle, you must have visited Dvārakā. In that holy place are our friends and well-wishers, the descendants of Yadu, who are always rapt in the service of the Lord Śrī Kṛṣṇa. You might have seen them or heard about them. Are they all living happily in their abodes?

PURPORT

The particular word *kṛṣṇa-devatāḥ,* i.e., those who are always rapt in the service of Lord Kṛṣṇa, is significant. The Yādavas and the Pāṇḍavas, who were always rapt in the thought of the Lord Kṛṣṇa and His different transcendental activities, were all pure devotees of the Lord like Vidura. Vidura left home in order to devote himself completely to the service of the Lord, but the Pāṇḍavas and the Yādavas were always rapt in the thought of Lord Kṛṣṇa. Thus there is no difference in their pure devotional qualities. Either remaining at home or leaving home, the real qualification of a pure devotee is to become rapt in the thought of Kṛṣṇa favorably, i.e., knowing well that Lord Kṛṣṇa is the Absolute Personality of Godhead. Kaṁsa, Jarāsandha, Śiśupāla and other demons like them were also always rapt in the thought of Lord Kṛṣṇa, but they were absorbed in a different way, namely unfavorably, or thinking Him to be a powerful man only. Therefore, Kaṁsa and Śiśupāla are not on the same level as pure devotees like Vidura, the Pāṇḍavas and the Yādavas.

Mahārāja Yudhiṣṭhira was also always rapt in the thought of Lord Kṛṣṇa and His associates at Dvārakā. Otherwise he could not have asked all about them from Vidura. Mahārāja Yudhiṣṭhira was therefore on the same level of devotion as Vidura, although engaged in the state affairs of the kingdom of the world.

TEXT 12

इत्युक्तो धर्मराजेन सर्वं तत् समवर्णयत् ।
यथानुभूतं क्रमशो विना यदुकुलक्षयम् ॥१२॥

ity ukto dharma-rājena
sarvaṁ tat samavarṇayat
yathānubhūtaṁ kramaśo
vinā yadu-kula-kṣayam

iti—thus; *uktaḥ*—being asked; *dharma-rājena*—by King Yudhiṣṭhira; *sarvam*—all; *tat*—that; *samavarṇayat*—properly described; *yathā-anubhūtam*—as he experienced; *kramaśaḥ*—one after another; *vinā*—without; *yadu-kula-kṣayam*—annihilation of the Yadu dynasty.

TRANSLATION

Thus being questioned by Mahārāja Yudhiṣṭhira, Mahātmā Vidura gradually described everything he had personally experienced, except news of the annihilation of the Yadu dynasty.

TEXT 13

नन्वप्रियं दुर्विषहं नृणां स्वयमुपस्थितम् ।
नावेदयत् सकरुणो दुःखितान् द्रष्टुमक्षमः ॥१३॥

nanv apriyaṁ durviṣahaṁ
nṛṇāṁ svayam upasthitam
nāvedayat sakaruṇo
duḥkhitān draṣṭum akṣamaḥ

nanu—as a matter of fact; *apriyam*—unpalatable; *durviṣaham*—unbearable; *nṛṇām*—of humankind; *svayam*—in its own way; *upasthitam*—appearance; *na*—did not; *āvedayat*—expressed; *sakaruṇaḥ*—compassionate; *duḥkhitān*—distressed; *draṣṭum*—to see; *akṣamaḥ*—unable.

TRANSLATION

Compassionate Mahātmā Vidura could not stand to see the Pāṇḍavas distressed at any time. Therefore he did not disclose this unpalatable and unbearable incident because calamities come of their own accord.

PURPORT

According to *Nīti-śāstra* (civic laws) one should not speak an unpalatable truth to cause distress to others. Distress comes upon us in its own way by the laws of nature, so one should not aggravate it by propaganda. For a compassionate soul like Vidura, especially in his dealings with the beloved Pāṇḍavas, it was almost impossible to disclose an unpalatable piece of news like the annihilation of the Yadu dynasty. Therefore he purposely refrained from it.

TEXT 14

कञ्चित्कालमथावात्सीत्सत्कृतो देववत्सुखम् ।
भ्रातुर्ज्येष्ठस्य श्रेयस्कृत्सर्वेषां सुखमावहन् ॥१४॥

kañcit kālam athāvātsīt
sat-kṛto devavat sukham

bhrātur jyeṣṭhasya śreyas-kṛt
sarveṣāṁ sukham āvahan

kañcit—for a few days; *kālam*—time; *atha*—thus; *avātsīt*—resided; *sat-kṛtaḥ*—being well treated; *deva-vat*—just like a godly personality; *sukham*—amenities; *bhrātuḥ*—of the brother; *jyeṣṭhasya*—of the elder; *śreyaḥ-kṛt*—for doing good to him; *sarveṣām*—all others; *sukham*—happiness; *āvahan*—made it possible.

TRANSLATION

Thus Mahātmā Vidura, being treated just like a godly person by his kinsmen, remained there for a certain period just to rectify the mentality of his eldest brother and in this way bring happiness to all the others.

PURPORT

Saintly persons like Vidura must be treated as well as a denizen from heaven. In those days denizens of heavenly planets used to visit homes like that of Mahārāja Yudhiṣṭhira, and sometimes persons like Arjuna and others used to visit higher planets. Nārada is a spaceman who can travel unrestrictedly, not only within the material universes but also in the spiritual universes. Even Nārada used to visit the palace of Mahārāja Yudhiṣṭhira and what to speak of other celestial demigods. It is only the spiritual culture of the people concerned that makes interplanetary travel possible, even in the present body. Mahārāja Yudhiṣṭhira therefore received Vidura in the manner of reception offered to the demigods.

Mahātmā Vidura had already adopted the renounced order of life, and therefore he did not return to his paternal palace to enjoy some material comforts. He accepted out of his own mercy what was offered to him by Mahārāja Yudhiṣṭhira, but the purpose of living in the palace was to deliver his elder brother, Dhṛtarāṣṭra, who was too much materially attached. Dhṛtarāṣṭra lost all his state and descendants in the fight with Mahārāja Yudhiṣṭhira, and still, due to his sense of helplessness, he did not feel ashamed to accept the charity and hospitality of Mahārāja Yudhiṣṭhira. On the part of Mahārāja Yudhiṣṭhira, it was quite in order to maintain his uncle in a befitting manner, but acceptance of such magnanimous hospitality by Dhṛtarāṣṭra was not at all desirable. He accepted it because he thought that there was no alternative. Vidura particularly came to enlighten Dhṛtarāṣṭra and to give him a lift to the higher status of spiritual cognition. It is the duty of enlightened souls to deliver the fallen ones, and Vidura came for that reason. But talks of spiritual enlightenment are so refreshing that while instructing Dhṛtarāṣṭra, Vidura attracted the attention of all the members of the family, and all of them took pleasure in hearing him patiently. This is the way of spiritual realization. The message should be heard attentively, and if spoken by a realized soul, it will act on the dormant heart of the conditioned soul. And by continuously hearing, one can attain the perfect stage of self-realization.

TEXT 15

अबिभ्रदर्यमा दण्डं यथावदघकारिषु ।
यावद्दधार शूद्रत्वं शापाद्वर्षशतं यमः ॥१५॥

abibhrad aryamā daṇḍaṁ
yathāvad agha-kāriṣu
yāvad dadhāra śūdratvaṁ
śāpād varṣa-śataṁ yamaḥ

abibhrat—administered; *aryamā*—Aryamā; *daṇḍam*—punishment; *yathāvat*—as it was suitable; *agha-kāriṣu*—unto persons who had committed sins; *yāvat*—as long as; *dadhāra*—accepted; *śūdratvam*—the tabernacle of a *śūdra; śāpāt*—as the result of a curse; *varṣa-śatam*—for one hundred years; *yamaḥ*—Yamarāja.

TRANSLATION

As long as Vidura played the part of a śūdra, being cursed by Maṇḍuka Muni, Aryamā officiated at the post of Yamarāja to punish those who committed sinful acts.

PURPORT

Vidura, born in the womb of a *śūdra* woman, was forbidden even to be a party of royal heritage along with his brothers Dhṛtarāṣṭra and Pāṇḍu. Then how could he occupy the post of a preacher to instruct such learned kings and *kṣatriyas* as Dhṛtarāṣṭra and Mahārāja Yudhiṣṭhira? The first answer is that even though it is accepted that he was a *śūdra* by birth, because he renounced the world for spiritual enlightenment by the authority of Ṛṣi Maitreya and was thoroughly educated by him in transcendental knowledge, he was quite competent to occupy the post of an *ācārya*, or spiritual preceptor. According to Śrī Caitanya Mahāprabhu, anyone who is conversant in the transcendental knowledge, or the science of Godhead, be he a *brāhmaṇa* or a *śūdra*, a householder or a *sannyāsī*, is eligible to become a spiritual master. Even in the ordinary moral codes (maintained by Cāṇakya Paṇḍita, the great politician and moralist) there is no harm in taking lessons from a person who may be by birth less than a *śūdra*. This is one part of the answer. The other is that Vidura was not actually a *śūdra*. He was to play the part of a so-called *śūdra* for one hundred years, being cursed by Maṇḍuka Muni. He was the incarnation of Yamarāja, one of the twelve *mahājanas*, on the level with such exalted personalities as Brahmā, Nārada, Śiva, Kapila, Bhīṣma, Prahlāda, etc. Being a *mahājana*, it is the duty of Yamarāja to preach the cult of devotion to the people of the world, as Nārada, Brahmā, and other *mahājanas* do. But Yamarāja is always busy in his plutonic kingdom punishing the doers of sinful acts. Yamarāja is deputed by the Lord to a particular planet, some hundreds of thousands of miles away from the planet of earth, to take away the corrupt souls after death and convict them in accordance with their respective sinful activities. Thus Yamarāja has very little time to take leave from his responsible office of punishing the wrongdoers. There are more wrongdoers than righteous men. Therefore Yamarāja has to do more work than other demigods who are also authorized agents of the Supreme Lord. But he wanted to preach the glories of the Lord, and therefore by the will of the Lord he was cursed by Maṇḍuka Muni to come into the world in the incarnation of Vidura and work very hard as a great devotee. Such a devotee is neither a *śūdra* nor a *brāhmaṇa*. He is transcendental to such divisions of mundane society, just as the Personality of Godhead assumes His incarnation as a hog, but He is neither a hog nor a Brahmā. He is above all mundane creatures. The Lord and His different authorized devotees sometimes have to play the role of many lower creatures to claim the conditioned souls, but both the Lord and His pure devotees are always in the transcendental position. When Yamarāja thus incarnated himself as Vidura, his post was officiated by Aryamā, one of the many sons of Kaśyapa and Aditi. The Ādityas are sons of Aditi, and there are twelve Ādityas. Aryamā is one of the twelve Ādityas, and therefore it was quite possible for him to take charge of the office of Yamarāja during his one hundred years' absence in the form of Vidura. The conclusion is that Vidura was never a *śūdra*, but was greater than the purest type of *brāhmaṇa.*

TEXT 16

युधिष्ठिरो लब्धराज्यो दृष्ट्वा पौत्रं कुलंधरम् ।
भ्रातृभिर्लोकपालाभैर्मुमुदे परया श्रिया ॥१६॥

yudhiṣṭhiro labdha-rājyo
dṛṣṭvā pautraṁ kulan-dharam
bhrātṛbhir loka-pālābhair
mumude parayā śriyā

yudhiṣṭhiraḥ—Yudhiṣṭhira; *labdha-rājyaḥ*—possessing his paternal kingdom; *dṛṣṭvā*—by seeing; *pautram*—the grandson; *kulam-dharam*—just suitable for the dynasty; *bhrātṛbhiḥ*—by the brothers; *loka-pālābhaiḥ*—who were all expert administrators; *mumude*—enjoyed life; *parayā*—uncommon; *śriyā*—opulence.

TRANSLATION

Having won his kingdom and observed the birth of one grandson competent to continue the noble tradition of his family, Mahārāja Yudhiṣṭhira reigned peacefully and enjoyed uncommon opulence in cooperation with his younger brothers, who were all expert administrators to the common people.

PURPORT

Both Mahārāja Yudhiṣṭhira and Arjuna were unhappy from the beginning of the Battle of Kurukṣetra, but even though they were unwilling to kill their own men in the fight, it had to be done as a matter of duty, for it was planned by the supreme will of Lord Śrī Kṛṣṇa. After the battle, Mahārāja Yudhiṣṭhira was unhappy over such mass killings. Practically there was none to continue the Kuru dynasty after them, the Pāṇḍavas. The only remaining hope was the child in the womb of his daughter-in-law, Uttarā, and he was also attacked by Aśvatthāmā, but by the grace of the Lord the child was saved. So after the settlement of all disturbing conditions and reestablishment of the peaceful order of the state, and after seeing the surviving child, Parīkṣit, well satisfied, Mahārāja Yudhiṣṭhira felt some relief as a human being, although he had very little attraction for material happiness, which is always illusory and temporary.

TEXT 17

एवं गृहेषु सक्तानां प्रमत्तानां तदीहया ।
अत्यक्रामदविज्ञातः कालः परमदुस्तरः ॥१७॥

evaṁ gṛheṣu saktānāṁ
pramattānāṁ tad-īhayā
atyakrāmad avijñātaḥ
kālaḥ parama-dustaraḥ

evam—thus; *gṛheṣu*—in the family affairs; *saktānām*—of persons who are too attached; *pramattānām*—insanely attached; *tat-īhayā*—engrossed in such thoughts; *atyakrāmat*—surpassed; *avijñātaḥ*—imperceptibly; *kālaḥ*—eternal time; *parama*—supremely; *dustaraḥ*—insurmountable.

TRANSLATION

Insurmountable, eternal time imperceptibly overcomes those who are too much attached to family affairs and are always engrossed in their thought.

PURPORT

"I am now happy; I have everything in order; my bank balance is quite enough; I can now give my children enough estate; I am now successful; the poor beggar *sannyāsīs* depend on God, but they come to beg from me; therefore I am more than the Supreme God." These are some of the thoughts which engross the insanely attached householder who is blind to the passing of eternal time. Our duration of life is measured, and no one is able to enhance it even by a second against the scheduled time ordained by the supreme will. Such valuable time, especially for the human being, should be cautiously spent because even a second passed away imperceptibly cannot be replaced, even in exchange for thousands of golden coins amassed by hard labor. Every second of human life is meant for making an ultimate solution to the problems of life, i.e. repetition of birth and death and revolving in the cycle of 8,400,000 different species of life. The material body, which is subject to birth and death, diseases and old age, is the cause of all sufferings of the living being, otherwise the living being is eternal; he is never born, nor does he ever die. Foolish persons forget this problem. They do not know at all how to solve the problems of life, but become engrossed in temporary family affairs not knowing that eternal time is passing away imperceptibly and that their measured duration of life is diminishing every second, without any solution to the big problem, namely repetition of birth and death, disease and old age. This is called illusion.

But such illusion cannot work on one who is awake in the devotional service of the Lord. Yudhiṣṭhira Mahārāja and his brothers the Pāṇḍavas were all engaged in the service of the Lord Śrī Kṛṣṇa, and they had very little attraction for the illusory happiness of this material world. As we have discussed previously, Mahārāja Yudhiṣṭhira was fixed in the service of the Lord Mukunda (the Lord, who can award salvation), and therefore he had no attraction even for such comforts of life as are available in the kingdom of heaven, because even the happiness obtained on the planet Brahmaloka is also temporary and illusory. Because the living being is eternal, he can be happy only in the eternal abode of the kingdom of God (*paravyoma*), from which no one returns to this region of repeated birth and death, disease and old age. Therefore, any comfort of life or any material happiness which does not warrant an eternal life is but illusion for the eternal living being. One who understands this factually is learned, and such a learned person can sacrifice any amount of material happiness to achieve the desired goal known as *brahma-sukham*, or absolute happiness. Real transcendentalists are hungry for this happiness, and as a hungry man cannot be made happy by all comforts of life minus foodstuff, so the man hungry for eternal absolute happiness cannot be satisfied by any amount of material happiness. Therefore, the instruction described in this verse cannot be applied to Mahārāja Yudhiṣṭhira or his brothers and mother. It was meant for persons like Dhṛtarāṣṭra, for whom Vidura came especially to impart lessons.

TEXT 18

विदुरस्तदभिप्रेत्य धृतराष्ट्रमभाषत ।
राजन्निर्गम्यतां शीघ्रं पश्येदं भयमागतम् ॥१८॥

viduras tad abhipretya
dhṛtarāṣṭram abhāṣata
rājan nirgamyatāṁ śīghraṁ
paśyedaṁ bhayam āgatam

viduraḥ—Mahātmā Vidura; *tat*—that; *abhipretya*—knowing it well; *dhṛtarāṣṭram*—unto Dhṛtarāṣṭra; *abhāṣata*—said; *rājan*—O King; *nirgamyatām*—please get out immediately; *śīghram*—without the least delay; *paśya*—just see; *idam*—this; *bhayam*—fear; *āgatam*—already arrived.

TRANSLATION

Mahātmā Vidura knew all this, and therefore he addressed Dhṛtarāṣṭra, saying: My dear King, please get out of here immediately. Do not delay. Just see how fear has overtaken you.

PURPORT

Cruel death cares for none, be he Dhṛtarāṣṭra or even Mahārāja Yudhiṣṭhira; therefore spiritual instruction, as was given to old Dhṛtarāṣṭra, was equally applicable to younger Mahārāja Yudhiṣṭhira. As a matter of fact, everyone in the royal palace, including the King and his brothers and mother, was raptly attending the lectures. But it was known to Vidura that his instructions were especially meant for Dhṛtarāṣṭra, who was too materialistic. The word *rājan* is especially addressed to Dhṛtarāṣṭra significantly. Dhṛtarāṣṭra was the eldest son of his father, and therefore according to law he was to be installed on the throne of Hastināpura. But because he was blind from birth, he was disqualified from his rightful claim. But he could not forget the bereavement, and his disappointment was somewhat compensated after the death of Pāṇḍu, his younger brother. His younger brother left behind him some minor children, and Dhṛtarāṣṭra became the natural guardian of them, but at heart he wanted to become the factual King and hand the kingdom over to his own sons, headed by Duryodhana. With all these imperial ambitions, Dhṛtarāṣṭra wanted to become a king, and he contrived all sorts of intrigues in consultation with his brother-in-law Śakuni. But everything failed by the will of the Lord, and at the last stage, even after losing everything, men and money, he wanted to remain as King, being the eldest uncle of Mahārāja Yudhiṣṭhira. Mahārāja Yudhiṣṭhira, as a matter of duty, maintained Dhṛtarāṣṭra in royal honor, and Dhṛtarāṣṭra was happily passing away his numbered days in the illusion of being a king or the royal uncle of King Yudhiṣṭhira. Vidura, as a saint and as the duty-bound affectionate youngest brother of Dhṛtarāṣṭra, wanted to awaken Dhṛtarāṣṭra from his slumber of disease and old age. Vidura therefore sarcastically addressed Dhṛtarāṣṭra as the "King," which he was actually not. Everyone is the servant of eternal time, and therefore no one can be king in this material world. King means the person who can order. The celebrated English king wanted to order time and tide, but the time and tide refused to obey his order. Therefore one is a false king in the material world, and Dhṛtarāṣṭra was particularly reminded of this false position and of the factual fearful happenings which had already approached him at that time. Vidura asked him to get out immediately, if he wanted to be saved from the fearful situation which was approaching him fast. He did not ask Mahārāja Yudhiṣṭhira in that way because he knew that a king like Mahārāja Yudhiṣṭhira is aware of all the fearful situations of this flimsy world and would take care of himself, in due course, even though Vidura might not be present at that time.

TEXT 19

प्रतिक्रिया न यस्येह कुतश्चित्कर्हिचित्प्रभो ।
स एष भगवान् कालः सर्वेषां नः समागतः ॥१९॥

pratikriyā na yasyeha
kutaścit karhicit prabho

sa eṣa bhagavān kālaḥ
sarveṣāṁ naḥ samāgataḥ

pratikriyā—remedial measure; *na*—there is none; *yasya*—of which; *iha*—in this material world; *kutaścit*—by any means; *karhicit*—or by anyone; *prabho*—O my lord; *saḥ*—that; *eṣaḥ*—positively; *bhagavān*—the Personality of Godhead; *kālaḥ*—eternal time; *sarveṣām*—of all; *naḥ*—of us; *samāgataḥ*—arrived.

TRANSLATION

This frightful situation cannot be remedied by any person in this material world. My lord, it is the Supreme Personality of Godhead as eternal time [kāla] that has approached us all.

PURPORT

There is no superior power which can check the cruel hands of death. No one wants to die, however acute the source of bodily sufferings may be. Even in the days of so-called scientific advancement of knowledge, there is no remedial measure either for old age or for death. Old age is the notice of the arrival of death served by cruel time, and no one can refuse to accept either summon calls or the supreme judgment of eternal time. This is explained before Dhṛtarāṣṭra because he might ask Vidura to find out some remedial measure for the imminent fearful situation, as he had ordered many times before. Before ordering, however, Vidura informed Dhṛtarāṣṭra that there was no remedial measure by anyone or from any source in this material world. And because there is no such thing in the material world, death is identical with the Supreme Personality of Godhead, as it is said by the Lord Himself in the *Bhagavad-gītā* (10.34).

Death cannot be checked by anyone or from any source within this material world. Hiraṇyakaśipu wanted to be immortal and underwent a severe type of penance by which the whole universe trembled, and Brahmā himself approached him to dissuade Hiraṇyakaśipu from such a severe type of penance. Hiraṇyakaśipu asked Brahmā to award him the blessings of immortality, but Brahmā said that he himself was subject to death, even in the topmost planet, so how could he award him the benediction of immortality? So there is death even in the topmost planet of this universe, and what to speak of other planets, which are far, far inferior in quality to Brahmaloka, the residing planet of Brahmā. Wherever there is the influence of eternal time, there is this set of tribulations, namely birth, disease, old age and death, and all of them are invincible.

TEXT 20

येन चैवाभिपन्नोऽयं प्राणैः प्रियतमैरपि ।
जनः सद्यो वियुज्येत किमुतान्यैर्धनादिभिः ॥२०॥

yena caivābhipanno 'yaṁ
prāṇaiḥ priyatamair api
janaḥ sadyo viyujyeta
kim utānyair dhanādibhiḥ

yena—pulled by such time; *ca*—and; *eva*—certainly; *abhipannaḥ*—overtaken; *ayam*—this; *prāṇaiḥ*—with life; *priya-tamaiḥ*—which is most dear to everyone; *api*—even though; *janaḥ*—person; *sadyaḥ*—forthwith; *viyujyeta*—do give up; *kim uta anyaiḥ*—what to speak of any other thing; *dhana-ādibhiḥ*—such as wealth, honor, children, land and house.

TRANSLATION

Whoever is under the influence of supreme kāla [eternal time] must surrender his most dear life, and and what to speak of other things, such as wealth, honor, children, land and home.

PURPORT

A great Indian scientist, busy in the planmaking business, was suddenly called by invincible eternal time while going to attend a very important meeting of the planning commission, and he had to surrender his life, wife, children, house, land, wealth, etc. During the political upsurge in India and its division into Pakistan and Hindustan, so many rich and influential Indians had to surrender life, property and honor due to the influence of time, and there are hundreds and thousands of examples like that all over the world, all over the universe, which are all effects of the influence of time. Therefore, the conclusion is that there is no powerful living being within the universe who can overcome the influence of time. Many poets have written verses lamenting the influence of time. Many devastations have taken place over the universes due to the influence of time, and no one could check them by any means. Even in our daily life, so many things come and go in which we have no hand, but we have to suffer or tolerate them without remedial measure. That is the result of time.

TEXT 21

पितृभ्रातृसुहृत्पुत्रा हतास्ते विगतं वयम् ।
आत्मा च जरया ग्रस्तः परगेहमुपाससे ॥२१॥

pitṛ-bhrātṛ-suhṛt-putrā
hatās te vigataṁ vayam
ātmā ca jarayā grastaḥ
para-geham upāsase

pitṛ—father; *bhrātṛ*—brother; *suhṛt*—well-wishers; *putrāḥ*—sons; *hatāḥ*—all dead; *te*—yours; *vigatam*—expended; *vayam*—age; *ātmā*—the body; *ca*—also; *jarayā*—by invalidity; *grastaḥ*—overcome; *para-geham*—another's home; *upāsase*—you do live.

TRANSLATION

Your father, brother, well-wishers and sons are all dead and passed away. You yourself have expended the major portion of your life, your body is now overtaken by invalidity, and you are living in the home of another.

PURPORT

The King is reminded of his precarious condition, influenced by cruel time, and by his past experience he should have been more intelligent to see what was going to happen to his own life. His father, Vicitravīrya, died long ago, when he and his younger brothers were all little children, and it was due to the care and kindness of Bhīṣmadeva that they were properly brought up. Then again his brother Pāṇḍu died also. Then in the Battlefield of Kurukṣetra his one hundred sons and his grandsons all died, along with all other well-wishers like Bhīṣmadeva, Droṇācārya, Karṇa and many other kings and friends. So he had lost all men and money, and now he was living at the mercy of his nephew, whom he had put into troubles of various types. And despite all these reverses, he thought that he would prolong his life more and more. Vidura wanted to point out to Dhṛtarāṣṭra that everyone has to protect himself by his action and the grace of the Lord. One has to execute his duty faithfully, depending for the result on the supreme authority. No friend, no children, no father, no brother, no state and no one else can protect a person who is not protected by the Supreme Lord. One should, therefore, seek the protection of the Supreme Lord, for the human form of life is meant for seeking that protection. He was warned of his precarious conditions more and more by the following words.

TEXT 22

अन्धः पुरैव वधिरो मन्दप्रज्ञाश्च साम्प्रतं ।
विशीर्णदन्तो मन्दाग्निः सरागः कफमुद्वहन् ।।२२।।

andhaḥ puraiva vadhiro
manda-prajñāś ca sāmpratam
viśīrṇa-danto mandāgniḥ
sarāgaḥ kapham udvahan

andhaḥ—blind; *purā*—from the beginning; *eva*—certainly; *vadhiraḥ*—hard of hearing; *manda-prajñāḥ*—memory shortened; *ca*—and; *sāmpratam*—recently; *viśīrṇa*—loosened; *dantaḥ*—teeth; *manda-agniḥ*—liver action decreased; *sa-rāgaḥ*—with sound; *kapham*—coughing much mucus; *udvahan*—coming out.

TRANSLATION

You have been blind from your very birth, and recently you have become hard of hearing. Your memory is shortened, and your intelligence is disturbed. Your teeth are loose, your liver is defective, and you are coughing up mucus.

PURPORT

The symptoms of old age, which had already developed in Dhṛtarāṣṭra, were all one after another pointed out to him as warning that death was nearing very quickly, and still he was foolishly carefree about his future. The signs pointed out by Vidura in the body of Dhṛtarāṣṭra were signs of *apakṣaya,* or dwindling of the material body before the last stroke of death. The body is born, it develops, stays, creates other bodies, dwindles and then vanishes. But foolish men want to make a permanent settlement of the perishable body and think that their estate, children, society, country, etc., will give them protection. With such foolish ideas, they become overtaken by such temporary engagements and forget altogether that they must give up this temporary body and take a new one, again to arrange for another term of society, friendship and love, again to perish ultimately. They forget their permanent identity and become foolishly active for impermanent occupations, forgetting altogether their prime duty. Saints and sages like Vidura approach such foolish men to awaken them to the real situation, but they take such *sādhus* and saints as parasites of society, and almost all of them refuse to hear the words of such *sādhus* and saints, although they welcome show-bottle *sādhus* and so-called saints who can satisfy their senses. Vidura was not a *sādhu* to satisfy the ill-gotten sentiment of Dhṛtarāṣṭra. He was correctly pointing out the real situation of life, and how one can save oneself from such catastrophies.

TEXT 23

अहो महीयसी जन्तोर्जीविताशा यथा भवान् ।
भीमापवर्जितं पिण्डमादत्ते गृहपालवत् ॥२३॥

aho mahīyasī jantor
jīvitāśā yathā bhavān
bhīmāpavarjitaṁ piṇḍam
ādatte gṛha-pālavat

aho—alas; *mahīyasī*—powerful; *jantoḥ*—of the living beings; *jīvita-āśā*—hope for life; *yathā*—as much as; *bhavān*—you are; *bhīma*—of

Bhīmasena (a brother of Yudhiṣṭhira's); *apavarjitam*—remnants; *piṇḍam*—foodstuff; *ādatte*—eaten by; *gṛha-pāla-vat*—like a household dog.

TRANSLATION

Alas, how powerful are the hopes of a living being to continue his life. Verily, you are living just like a household dog and are eating remnants of food given by Bhīma.

PURPORT

A *sādhu* should never flatter kings or rich men to live comfortably at their cost. A *sādhu* is to speak to the householders about the naked truth of life so that they may come to their senses about the precarious life in material existence. Dhṛtarāṣṭra is a typical example of an attached old man in household life. He had become a pauper in the true sense, yet he wanted to live comfortably in the house of the Pāṇḍavas, of whom Bhīma especially is mentioned because personally he killed two prominent sons of Dhṛtarāṣṭra, namely Duryodhana and Duḥśāsana. These two sons were very much dear to him for their notorious and nefarious activities, and Bhīma is particularly pointed out because he killed these two pet sons. Why was Dhṛtarāṣṭra living there at the house of the Pāṇḍavas? Because he wanted to continue his life comfortably, even at the risk of all humiliation. Vidura, therefore, was astonished how powerful is the urge to continue life. This sense of continuing one's life indicates that a living being is eternally a living entity and does not want to change his bodily habitation. The foolish man does not know that a particular term of bodily existence is awarded to him to undergo a term of imprisonment, and the human body is awarded, after many, many births and deaths, as a chance for self-realization to go back home, back to Godhead. But persons like Dhṛtarāṣṭra try to make plans to live there in a comfortable position with profit and interest, for they do not see things as they are. Dhṛtarāṣṭra is blind and continues to hope to live comfortably in the midst of all kinds of reverses of life. A *sādhu* like Vidura is meant to awaken such blind persons and thus help them go back to Godhead, where life is eternal. Once going there, no one wants to come back to this material world of miseries. We can just imagine how responsible a task is entrusted to a *sādhu* like Mahātmā Vidura.

TEXT 24

अग्निर्निसृष्टो दत्तश्च गरो दाराश्च दूषिताः ।
हृतं क्षेत्रं धनं येषां तद्दत्तैरसुभिः कियत् ॥२४॥

agnir nisṛṣṭo dattaś ca
garo dārāś ca dūṣitāḥ
hṛtaṁ kṣetraṁ dhanaṁ yeṣāṁ
tad-dattair asubhiḥ kiyat

agniḥ—fire; *nisṛṣṭaḥ*—set; *dattaḥ*—given; *ca*—and; *garaḥ*—poison; *dārāḥ*—married wife; *ca*—and; *dūṣitāḥ*—insulted; *hṛtam*—usurped; *kṣetram*—kingdom; *dhanam*—wealth; *yeṣām*—of those; *tat*—their; *dattaiḥ*—given by; *asubhiḥ*—subsisting; *kiyat*—is unnecessary.

TRANSLATION

There is no need to live a degraded life and subsist on the charity of those whom you tried to kill by arson and poisoning. You also insulted one of their wives and usurped their kingdom and wealth.

PURPORT

The system of *varṇāśrama* religion sets aside a part of one's life completely for the purpose of self-realization and attainment of salvation in the human form of life. That is a routine division of life, but persons like Dhṛtarāṣṭra, even at their weary ripened age, want to stay home, even in a degraded condition of accepting charity from enemies. Vidura wanted to point this out and impressed upon him that it was better to die like his sons than accept such humiliating charity. Five thousand years ago there was one Dhṛtarāṣṭra, but at the present moment there are Dhṛtarāṣṭras in every home. Politicians especially do not retire from political activities unless they are dragged by the cruel hand of death or killed by some opposing element. To stick to family life to the end of one's human life is the grossest type of degradation and there is an absolute need for the Viduras to educate such Dhṛtarāṣṭras, even at the present moment.

TEXT 25

तस्यापि तव देहोऽयं कृपणस्य जिजीविषोः ।
परैत्यनिच्छतो जीर्णो जरया वाससी इव ॥२५॥

tasyāpi tava deho 'yaṁ
kṛpaṇasya jijīviṣoḥ
paraity anicchato jīrṇo
jarayā vāsasī iva

tasya—of this; *api*—in spite of; *tava*—your; *dehaḥ*—body; *ayam*—this; *kṛpaṇasya*—of one who is miserly; *jijīviṣoḥ*—of you who desire life; *paraiti*—will dwindle; *anicchataḥ*—even unwilling; *jīrṇaḥ*—deteriorated; *jarayā*—old; *vāsasī*—garments; *iva*—like.

TRANSLATION

Despite your unwillingness to die and your desire to live even at the cost of honor and prestige, your miserly body will certainly dwindle and deteriorate like an old garment.

PURPORT

The words *kṛpaṇasya jijīviṣoḥ* are significant. There are two classes of men. One is called the *kṛpaṇa*, and the other is called the *brāhmaṇa*. The *kṛpaṇa*, or the miserly man, has no estimation of his material body, but the *brāhmaṇa* has a true estimation of himself and the material body. The *kṛpaṇa*, having a wrong estimation of his material body, wants to enjoy sense gratification with his utmost strength, and even in old age he wants to become a young man by medical treatment or otherwise. Dhṛtarāṣṭra is addressed herein as a *kṛpaṇa* because without any estimation of his material body he wants to live at any cost. Vidura is trying to open his eyes to see that he cannot live more than his term and that he must prepare for death. Since death is inevitable, why should he accept such a humiliating position for living? It is better to take the right path, even at the risk of death. Human life is meant for finishing all kinds of miseries of material existence, and life should be so regulated that one can achieve the desired goal. Dhṛtarāṣṭra, due to his wrong conception of life, had already spoiled eighty percent of his achieved energy, so it behooved him to utilize the remaining days of his miserly life for the ultimate good. Such a life is called miserly because one cannot properly utilize the assets of the human form of life. Only by good luck does such a miserly man meet a self-realized soul like Vidura and by his instruction gets rid of the nescience of material existence.

TEXT 26

गतस्वार्थमिमं देहं विरक्तो मुक्तबन्धनः ।
अविज्ञातगतिर्जह्यात् स वै धीर उदाहृतः ॥२६॥

gata-svārtham imaṁ dehaṁ
virakto mukta-bandhanaḥ
avijñāta-gatir jahyāt
sa vai dhīra udāhṛtaḥ

gata-sva-artham—without being properly utilized; *imam*—this; *deham*—material body; *viraktaḥ*—indifferently; *mukta*—being freed; *bandhanaḥ*—from all obligations; *avijñāta-gatiḥ*—unknown destination; *jahyāt*—one should give up this body; *saḥ*—such a person; *vai*—certainly; *dhīraḥ*—undisturbed; *udāhṛtaḥ*—is said to be so.

TRANSLATION

He is called undisturbed who goes to an unknown, remote place and, freed from all obligations, quits his material body when it has become useless.

PURPORT

Narottama dāsa Ṭhākura, a great devotee and *ācārya* of the Gauḍīya Vaiṣṇava sect, has sung: "My Lord, I have simply wasted my life. Having obtained the human body, I have neglected to worship Your Lordship, and therefore I have willingly drunk poison." In other words, the human body is especially meant for cultivating knowledge of devotional service to the Lord, without which life becomes full of anxieties and miserable conditions. Therefore, one who has spoiled his life without such cultural activities is advised to leave home without knowledge of friends and relatives and, being thus freed from all obligations of family, society, country, etc., give up the body at some unknown destination so that others may not know where and how he has met his death. *Dhīra* means one who is not disturbed, even when there is sufficient provocation. One cannot give up a comfortable family life due to his affectionate relation with wife and children. Self-realization is obstructed by such undue affection for family, and if anyone is at all able to forget such a relation, he is called undisturbed, or *dhīra.* This is, however, the path of renunciation based on a frustrated life, but stabilization of such renunciation is possible only by association with bona fide saints and self-realized souls by which one can be engaged in the loving devotional service of the Lord. Sincere surrender unto the lotus feet of the Lord is possible by awakening the transcendental sense of service. This is made possible by association with pure devotees of the Lord. Dhṛtarāṣṭra was lucky enough to have a brother whose very association was a source of liberation for this frustrated life.

TEXT 27

यः स्वकात्परतो वेह जातनिर्वेद आत्मवान् ।
हृदि कृत्वा हरिं गेहात्प्रव्रजेत्स नरोत्तमः ॥२७॥

yaḥ svakāt parato veha
jāta-nirveda ātmavān
hṛdi kṛtvā hariṁ gehāt
pravrajet sa narottamaḥ

yaḥ—anyone who; *svakāt*—by his own awakening; *parataḥ vā*—or by hearing from another; *iha*—here in this world; *jāta*—becomes; *nirvedaḥ*—indifferent to material attachment; *ātmavān*—consciousness; *hṛdi*—within the heart; *kṛtvā*—having been taken by; *harim*—the Personality of Godhead; *gehāt*—from home; *pravrajet*—goes away; *saḥ*—he is; *nara-uttamaḥ*—the first-class human being.

TRANSLATION

He is certainly a first-class man who awakens and understands, either by himself or from others, the falsity and misery of this

material world and thus leaves home and depends fully on the Personality of Godhead residing within his heart.

PURPORT

There are three classes of transcendentalists, namely, (1) the *dhīra*, or the one who is not disturbed by being away from family association, (2) one in the renounced order of life, a *sannyāsī* by frustrated sentiment, and (3) a sincere devotee of the Lord, who awakens God consciousness by hearing and chanting and leaves home depending completely on the Personality of Godhead, who resides in his heart. The idea is that the renounced order of life, after a frustrated life of sentiment in the material world, may be the stepping stone on the path of self-realization, *but real perfection of the path of liberation is attained when one is practiced to depend fully on the Supreme Personality of Godhead*, who lives in everyone's heart as Paramātmā. One may live in the darkest jungle alone out of home, but a steadfast devotee knows very well that he is not alone. The Supreme Personality of Godhead is with him, and He can protect His sincere devotee in any awkward circumstance. One should therefore practice devotional service at home, hearing and chanting the holy name, quality, form, pastimes, entourage, etc., in association with pure devotees, and this practice will help one awaken God consciousness in proportion to one's sincerity of purpose. One who desires material benefit by such devotional activities can never depend on the Supreme Personality of Godhead, although He sits in everyone's heart. Nor does the Lord give any direction to persons who worship Him for material gain. Such materialistic devotees may be blessed by the Lord with material benefits, but they cannot reach the stage of the first-class human being, as above mentioned. There are many examples of such sincere devotees in the history of the world, especially in India, and they are our guides on the path of self-realization. Mahātmā Vidura is one such great devotee of the Lord, and we should all try to follow in his lotus footsteps for self-realization.

TEXT 28

अथोदीचीं दिशं यातु स्वैरज्ञातगतिर्भवान् ।
इतोऽर्वाक्प्रायशः कालः पुंसां गुणविकर्षणः ॥२८॥

athodīcīṁ diśaṁ yātu
svair ajñāta-gatir bhavān
ito 'rvāk prāyaśaḥ kālaḥ
puṁsāṁ guṇa-vikarṣaṇaḥ

atha—therefore; *udīcīm*—northern side; *diśam*—direction; *yātu*—please go away; *svaiḥ*—by your relatives; *ajñāta*—without knowledge; *gatiḥ*—movements; *bhavān*—of yourself; *itaḥ*—after this; *arvāk*—will usher in; *prāyaśaḥ*—generally; *kālaḥ*—time; *puṁsām*—of men; *guṇa*—qualities; *vikarṣaṇaḥ*—diminishing.

TRANSLATION

Please, therefore, leave for the North immediately, without letting your relatives know, for soon that time will approach which will diminish the good qualities of men.

PURPORT

One can compensate for a life of frustration by becoming a *dhīra*, or leaving home for good without communicating with relatives, and Vidura advised his eldest brother to adopt this way without delay because very quickly the age of Kali was approaching. A conditioned soul is already degraded by the material association, and still in the Kali-yuga the good qualities of a man will deteriorate to the lowest standard. He was advised to leave home before Kali-yuga approached because the atmosphere which was created by Vidura, his valuable instructions on the facts of life, would fade away due to the influence of the age which was fast approaching. To become *narottama*, or a first-class human being depending completely on the Supreme Lord Śrī Kṛṣṇa, is not possible for any ordinary man. It is stated in *Bhagavad-gītā* (7.28) that a person who is completely relieved of all taints of sinful acts can alone depend on the Supreme Lord Śrī Kṛṣṇa, the Personality of Godhead. Dhṛtarāṣṭra was advised by Vidura at least to become a *dhīra* in the beginning if it were impossible for him to become a *sannyāsī* or a *narottama*. Persistently endeavoring on the line of self-realization helps a person to rise to the conditions of a *narottama* from the stage of a *dhīra*. The *dhīra* stage is attained after prolonged practice of the *yoga* system, but by the grace of Vidura one can attain the stage immediately simply by willing to adopt the means of the *dhīra* stage, which is the preparatory stage for *sannyāsa.* The *sannyāsa* stage is the preparatory stage of *paramahaṁsa,* or the first-grade devotee of the Lord.

TEXT 29

एवं राजा विदुरेणानुजेन
प्रज्ञाचक्षुर्बोधित आजमीढः ।
छित्त्वा स्वेषु स्नेहपाशान्द्रढिम्नो
निश्चक्राम भ्रातृसंदर्शिताध्वा ॥२९॥

evaṁ rājā vidureṇānujena
prajñā-cakṣur bodhita ājamīḍhaḥ
chittvā sveṣu sneha-pāśān draḍhimno
niścakrāma bhrātṛ-sandarśitādhvā

evam—thus; *rājā*—King Dhṛtarāṣṭra; *vidureṇa anujena*—by his younger brother Vidura; *prajñā*—introspective knowledge; *cakṣuḥ*—eyes; *bodhitaḥ*—being understood; *ājamīḍhaḥ*—Dhṛtarāṣṭra, scion of the family of Ājamīḍha; *chittvā*—by breaking; *sveṣu*—regarding kinsmen; *sneha-pāśān*—strong network of affection; *draḍhimnaḥ*—because of steadfastness; *niścakrāma*—got out; *bhrātṛ*—by his brother; *sandarśita*—direction to; *adhvā*—the path of liberation.

TRANSLATION

Thus Mahārāja Dhṛtarāṣṭra, the scion of the family of Ājamīḍha, firmly convinced by introspective knowledge [prajñā], broke at once the strong network of familial affection by his resolute determination. Thus he immediately left home to set out on the path of liberation, as directed by his younger brother Vidura.

PURPORT

Lord Śrī Caitanya Mahāprabhu, the great preacher of the principles of *Śrīmad-Bhāgavatam,* has stressed the importance of association with *sādhus,* pure devotees of the Lord. He said that even by a moment's association with a pure devotee, one can achieve all perfection. We are not ashamed to admit that this fact was experienced in our practical life. Were we not favored by His Divine Grace Śrīmad Bhaktisiddhānta Sarasvatī Gosvāmī Mahārāja, by our first meeting for a few minutes only, it would have been impossible for us to accept this mighty task of describing *Śrīmad-Bhāgavatam* in English. Without seeing him at that opportune moment, we could have become a very great business magnate, but never would we have been able to walk the path of liberation and be engaged in the factual service of the Lord under instructions of His Divine Grace. And here is another practical example by the action of Vidura's association with Dhṛtarāṣṭra. Mahārāja Dhṛtarāṣṭra was tightly bound in a network of material affinities related to politics, economy and family attachment, and he did everything in his power to achieve so-called success in his planned projects, but he was frustrated from the beginning to the end so far as his material activities were concerned. And yet, despite his life of failure, he achieved the greatest of all success in self-realization by the forceful instructions of a pure devotee of the Lord, who is the typical emblem of a *sādhu*. The scriptures enjoin, therefore, that one should associate with *sādhus* only, rejecting all other kinds of association, and by doing so one will have ample opportunity to hear the *sādhus*, who can cut to pieces the bonds of illusory affection in the material world. It is a fact that the material world is a great illusion because everything appears to be a tangible reality but at the next moment evaporates like the dashing foam of the sea or a cloud in the sky. A cloud in the sky undoubtedly appears to be a reality because it rains, and due to rains so many temporary green things appear, but in the ultimate issue, everything disappears, namely the cloud, rain and green vegetation, all in due course. But the sky remains, and the varieties of sky or luminaries also remain forever. Similarly, the Absolute Truth, which is compared to the sky, remains eternally, and the temporary cloudlike illusion comes and goes away. Foolish living beings are attracted by the temporary cloud, but intelligent men are more concerned with the eternal sky with all its variegatedness.

TEXT 30

पतिं प्रयान्तं सुबलस्य पुत्री
पतिव्रता चानुजगाम साध्वी ।

हिमालयं न्यस्तदण्डप्रहर्षं
मनस्विनामिव सत्सम्प्रहारः ॥३०॥

patiṁ prayāntaṁ subalasya putrī
pati-vratā cānujagāma sādhvī
himālayaṁ nyasta-daṇḍa-praharṣaṁ
manasvinām iva sat samprahāraḥ

patim—her husband; *prayāntam*—while leaving home; *subalasya*—of King Subala; *putrī*—the worthy daughter; *pati-vratā*—devoted to her husband; *ca*—also; *anujagāma*—followed; *sādhvī*—the chaste; *himālayam*—towards the Himalaya Mountains; *nyasta-daṇḍa*—one who has accepted the rod of the renounced order; *praharṣam*—object of delight; *manasvinām*—of the great fighters; *iva*—like; *sat*—legitimate; *samprahāraḥ*—good lashing.

TRANSLATION

The gentle and chaste Gāndhārī, who was the daughter of King Subala of Kandahara [or Gāndhāra], followed her husband, seeing that he was going to the Himalaya Mountains, which are the delight of those who have accepted the staff of the renounced order like fighters who have accepted a good lashing from the enemy.

PURPORT

Saubalinī, or Gāndhārī, daughter of King Subala and wife of King Dhṛtarāṣṭra, was ideal as a wife devoted to her husband. The Vedic civilization especially prepares chaste and devoted wives, of whom Gāndhārī is one amongst many mentioned in history. Lakṣmījī Sītādevī was also a daughter of a great king, but she followed her husband, Lord Rāmacandra, into the forest. Similarly, as a woman Gāndhārī could have remained at home or at her father's house, but as a chaste and gentle lady she followed her husband without consideration. Instructions for the renounced order of life were imparted to Dhṛtarāṣṭra by Vidura, and Gāndhārī was by the side of her husband. But he did not ask her to follow him because he was at that time fully determined, like a great warrior who faces all kinds of dangers in the battlefield. He was no longer attracted to so-called wife or relatives, and he decided to start alone, but as a chaste lady Gāndhārī decided to follow her husband till the last moment. Mahārāja Dhṛtarāṣṭra accepted the order of *vānaprastha*, and at this stage the wife is allowed to remain as a voluntary servitor, but in the *sannyāsa* stage no wife can stay with her former husband. A *sannyāsī* is considered to be a dead man civilly, and therefore the wife becomes a civil widow without connection with her former husband. Mahārāja Dhṛtarāṣṭra did not deny his faithful wife, and she followed her husband at her own risk.

The *sannyāsīs* accept a rod as the sign of the renounced order of life. There are two types of *sannyāsīs*. Those who follow the Māyāvādī philosophy, headed by Śrīpāda Śaṅkarācārya, accept only one rod (*eka-daṇḍa*), but those who follow the Vaiṣṇavite philosophy accept three combined rods (*tri-daṇḍa*). The Māyāvādī *sannyāsīs* are *ekadaṇḍi-svāmīs*, whereas the Vaiṣṇava *sannyāsīs* are known as *tridaṇḍi-svāmīs*, or more distinctly, *tridaṇḍi-gosvāmīs*, in order to be distinguished from the Māyāvādī philosophers. The *ekadaṇḍi-svāmīs* are mostly fond of the Himalayas, but the Vaiṣṇava *sannyāsīs* are fond of Vṛndāvana and Purī. The Vaiṣṇava *sannyāsīs* are *narottamas*, whereas the Māyāvādī *sannyāsīs* are *dhīras*. Mahārāja Dhṛtarāṣṭra was advised to follow the *dhīras* because at that stage it was difficult for him to become a *narottama*.

TEXT 31

अजातशत्रुः कृतमैत्रो हुताग्नि-
विप्रान् नत्वा तिलगोभूमिरुक्मैः ।
गृहं प्रविष्टो गुरुवन्दनाय
न चापश्यत्पितरौ सौबलीं च ॥३१॥

ajāta-śatruḥ kṛta-maitro hutāgnir
viprān natvā tila-go-bhūmi-rukmaiḥ
gṛhaṁ praviṣṭo guru-vandanāya
na cāpaśyat pitarau saubalīṁ ca

ajāta—never born; *śatruḥ*—enemy; *kṛta*—having performed; *maitraḥ*—worshiping the demigods; *huta-agniḥ*—and offering fuel in the fire; *viprān*—the *brāhmaṇas; natvā*—offering obeisances; *tila-go-bhūmi-rukmaiḥ*—along with grains, cows, land and gold; *gṛham*—within the palace; *praviṣṭaḥ*—having entered into; *guru-vandanāya*—for offering respect to the elderly members; *na*—did not; *ca*—also; *apaśyat*—see; *pitarau*—his uncles; *saubalīm*—Gāndhārī; *ca*—also.

TRANSLATION

Mahārāja Yudhiṣṭhira, whose enemy was never born, performed his daily morning duties by praying, offering fire sacrifice to the sun-god, and offering obeisances, grains, cows, land and gold to the brāhmaṇas. He then entered the palace to pay respects to the elderly. However, he could not find his uncles or aunt, the daughter of King Subala.

PURPORT

Mahārāja Yudhiṣṭhira was the most pious king because he personally practiced daily the pious duties for the householders. The householders are required to rise early in the morning, and after bathing they should offer respects to the Deities at home by prayers, by offering fuel in the sacred fire, by giving the *brāhmaṇas* in charity land, cows, grains, gold, etc., and at last offering to the elderly members due respects and obeisances. One who is not prepared to practice injunctions prescribed in the *śāstras* cannot be a good man simply by book knowledge. Modern householders are practiced to different modes of life, namely to rise late and then take bed tea without any sort of cleanliness and without any purificatory practices as mentioned above. The household children are taken to practice what the parents practice, and therefore the whole generation glides towards hell. Nothing good can be expected from them unless they associate with *sādhus.* Like Dhṛtarāṣṭra, the materialistic person may take lessons from a *sādhu* like Vidura and thus be cleansed of the effects of modern life.

Mahārāja Yudhiṣṭhira, however, could not find in the palace his two uncles, namely Dhṛtarāṣṭra and Vidura, along with Gāndhārī, the daughter of King Subala. He was anxious to see them and therefore asked Sañjaya, the private secretary of Dhṛtarāṣṭra.

TEXT 32

तत्र सञ्जयमासीनं पप्रच्छोद्विग्नमानसः ।
गावल्गणे क्व नस्तातो वृद्धो हीनश्च नेत्रयोः ॥३२॥

tatra sañjayam āsīnaṁ
papracchodvigna-mānasaḥ
gāvalgaṇe kva nas tāto
vṛddho hīnaś ca netrayoḥ

tatra—there; *sañjayam*—unto Sañjaya; *āsīnam*—seated; *papraccha*—he inquired from; *udvigna-mānasaḥ*—filled with anxiety; *gāvalgaṇe*—the son of Gavalgaṇa, Sañjaya; *kva*—where is; *naḥ*—our; *tātaḥ*—uncle; *vṛddhaḥ*—old; *hīnaḥ ca*—and bereft of; *netrayoḥ*—the eyes.

TRANSLATION

Mahārāja Yudhiṣṭhira, full of anxiety, turned to Sañjaya, who was sitting there, and said: O Sañjaya, where is our uncle, who is old and blind?

TEXT 33

अम्बा च हतपुत्राऽऽर्ता पितृव्यः क्व गतः सुहृत् ।
अपि मय्यकृतप्रज्ञे हतबन्धुः स भार्यया ।
आशंसमानः शमलं गङ्गायां दुःखितोऽपतत् ॥३३॥

ambā ca hata-putrārtā
pitṛvyaḥ kva gataḥ suhṛt
api mayy akṛta-prajñe
hata-bandhuḥ sa bhāryayā
āśaṁsa-mānaḥ śamalaṁ
gaṅgāyāṁ duḥkhito 'patat

ambā—mother aunt; *ca*—and; *hata-putrā*—who had lost all her sons; *ārtā*—in a sorry plight; *pitṛvyaḥ*—uncle Vidura; *kva*—where; *gataḥ*—gone; *suhṛt*—well-wisher; *api*—whether; *mayi*—unto me; *akṛta-prajñe*—ungrateful; *hata-bandhuḥ*—one who has lost all his sons; *saḥ*—Dhṛtarāṣṭra; *bhāryayā*—with his wife; *āśaṁsa-mānaḥ*—in doubtful mind; *śamalam*—offenses; *gaṅgāyām*—in the Ganges water; *duḥkhitaḥ*—in distressed mind; *apatat*—fell down.

TRANSLATION

Where is my well-wisher, uncle Vidura, and mother Gāndhārī, who is very afflicted due to all her sons' demise? My uncle Dhṛtarāṣṭra was also very mortified due to the death of all his sons and grandsons. Undoubtedly I am very ungrateful. Did he, therefore, take my offenses very seriously and, along with his wife, drown himself in the Ganges?

PURPORT

The Pāṇḍavas, especially Mahārāja Yudhiṣṭhira and Arjuna, anticipated the aftereffects of the Battle of Kurukṣetra, and therefore Arjuna declined to execute the fighting. The fight was executed by the will of the Lord, but the effects of family aggrievement, as they had thought of it before, had come to be true. Mahārāja Yudhiṣṭhira was always conscious of the great plight of his uncle Dhṛtarāṣṭra and aunt Gāndhārī, and therefore he took all possible care of them in their old age and aggrieved conditions. When, therefore, he could not find his uncle and aunt in the palace, naturally his doubts arose, and he conjectured that they had gone down to the water of the Ganges. He thought himself ungrateful because when the Pāṇḍavas were fatherless, Mahārāja Dhṛtarāṣṭra had given them all royal facilities to live, and in return he had killed all Dhṛtarāṣṭra's sons in the Battle of Kurukṣetra. As a pious man, Mahārāja Yudhiṣṭhira took into account all his unavoidable misdeeds, and he never thought of the misdeeds of his uncle and company. Dhṛtarāṣṭra had suffered the effects of his own misdeeds by the will of the Lord, but Mahārāja Yudhiṣṭhira was thinking only of his own unavoidable misdeeds. That is the nature of a good man and devotee of the Lord. A devotee never finds fault with others, but tries to find his own and thus rectify them as far as possible.

TEXT 34

पितर्युपरते पाण्डौ सर्वान्नः सुहृदः शिशून् ।
अरक्षतां व्यसनतः पितृव्यौ क्व गतावितः ॥३४॥

pitary uparate pāṇḍau
sarvān naḥ suhṛdaḥ śiśūn
arakṣatāṁ vyasanataḥ
pitṛvyau kva gatāv itaḥ

pitari—upon my father; *uparate*—falling down; *pāṇḍau*—Mahārāja Pāṇḍu; *sarvān*—all; *naḥ*—of us; *suhṛdaḥ*—well-wishers; *śiśūn*—small children; *arakṣatām*—protected; *vyasanataḥ*—from all kinds of dangers; *pitṛvyau*—uncles; *kva*—where; *gatau*—have departed; *itaḥ*—from this place.

TRANSLATION

When my father, Pāṇḍu, fell down and we were all small children, these two uncles gave us protection from all kinds of calamities. They were always our good well-wishers. Alas, where have they gone from here?

TEXT 35

सूत उवाच
कृपया स्नेहवैक्लव्यात्सूतो विरहकर्शितः ।
आत्मेश्वरमचक्षाणो न प्रत्याहातिपीडितः ॥३५॥

sūta uvāca
kṛpayā sneha-vaiklavyāt
sūto viraha-karśitaḥ
ātmeśvaram acakṣāṇo
na pratyāhātipīḍitaḥ

sūtaḥ uvāca—Sūta Gosvāmī said; *kṛpayā*—out of full compassion; *sneha-vaiklavyāt*—mental derangement due to profound affection; *sūtaḥ*—Sañjaya; *viraha-karśitaḥ*—distressed by separation; *ātma-īśvaram*—his master; *acakṣāṇaḥ*—having not seen; *na*—did not; *pratyāha*—replied; *ati-pīḍitaḥ*—being too aggrieved.

TRANSLATION

Sūta Gosvāmī said: Because of compassion and mental agitation, Sañjaya, not having seen his own master, Dhṛtarāṣṭra, was aggrieved and could not properly reply to Mahārāja Yudhiṣṭhira.

PURPORT

Sañjaya was the personal assistant of Mahārāja Dhṛtarāṣṭra for a very long time, and thus he had the opportunity to study the life of Dhṛtarāṣṭra. And when he saw at last that Dhṛtarāṣṭra had left home without his knowledge, his sorrows had no bound. He was fully compassionate toward Dhṛtarāṣṭra because in the game of the Battle of Kurukṣetra, King Dhṛtarāṣṭra had lost everything, men and money, and at last the King and the Queen had to leave home in utter frustration. He studied the situation in his own way because he did not know that the inner vision of Dhṛtarāṣṭra has been awakened by Vidura and that therefore he had left home in enthusiastic cheerfulness for a better life after departure from the dark well of home. Unless one is convinced of a better life after renunciation of the present life, one cannot stick to the renounced order of life simply by artificial dress or staying out of the home.

TEXT 36

विमृज्याश्रूणि पाणिभ्यां विष्टभ्यात्मानमात्मना ।
अजातशत्रुं प्रत्यूचे प्रभोः पादावनुस्मरन् ॥३६॥

vimṛjyāśrūṇi pāṇibhyāṁ
viṣṭabhyātmānam ātmanā
ajāta-śatruṁ pratyūce
prabhoḥ pādāv anusmaran

vimṛjya—smearing; *aśrūṇi*—tears of the eyes; *pāṇibhyām*—with his hands; *viṣṭabhya*—situated; *ātmānam*—the mind; *ātmanā*—by intelligence; *ajāta-śatrum*—unto Mahārāja Yudhiṣṭhira; *pratyūce*—began to reply; *prabhoḥ*—of his master; *pādau*—feet; *anusmaran*—thinking after.

TRANSLATION

First he slowly pacified his mind by intelligence, and wiping away his tears and thinking of the feet of his master, Dhṛtarāṣṭra, he began to reply to Mahārāja Yudhiṣṭhira.

TEXT 37

संजय उवाच
नाहं वेद व्यवसितं पित्रोर्वः कुलनन्दन ।
गान्धार्या वा महाबाहो मुषितोऽस्मि महात्मभिः ॥३७॥

sañjaya uvāca
nāhaṁ veda vyavasitaṁ
pitror vaḥ kula-nandana
gāndhāryā vā mahā-bāho
muṣito 'smi mahātmabhiḥ

sañjayaḥ uvāca—Sañjaya said; *na*—not; *aham*—I; *veda*—know; *vyavasitam*—determination; *pitroḥ*—of your uncles; *vaḥ*—your; *kula-nandana*—O descendant of the Kuru dynasty; *gāndhāryāḥ*—of Gāndhārī; *vā*—or; *mahā-bāho*—O great King; *muṣitaḥ*—cheated; *asmi*—I have been; *mahā-ātmabhiḥ*—by those great souls.

TRANSLATION

Sañjaya said: My dear descendant of the Kuru dynasty, I have no information of the determination of your two uncles and Gāndhārī. O King, I have been cheated by those great souls.

PURPORT

That great souls cheat others may be astonishing to know, but it is a fact that great souls cheat others for a great cause. It is said that Lord Kṛṣṇa also advised Yudhiṣṭhira to tell a lie before Droṇācārya, and it was also for a great cause. The Lord wanted it, and therefore it was a great cause. Satisfaction of the Lord is the criterion of one who is bona fide, and the highest perfection of life is to satisfy the Lord by one's occupational duty. That is the verdict of *Gītā* and *Bhāgavatam.** Dhṛtarāṣṭra and Vidura, followed by Gāndhārī, did not disclose their determination to Sañjaya, although he was constantly with Dhṛtarāṣṭra as his personal assistant. Sañjaya never thought that Dhṛtarāṣṭra could perform any act without consulting him. But Dhṛtarāṣṭra's going away from home was so confidential that it could not be disclosed even to Sañjaya. Sanātana Gosvāmī also cheated the keeper of the prison house while going away to see Śrī Caitanya Mahāprabhu, and similarly Raghunātha dāsa Gosvāmī also cheated his priest and left home for good to satisfy the Lord. To satisfy the Lord, anything is good, for it is in relation with the Absolute Truth. We also had the same opportunity to cheat the family members and leave home to engage in the service of *Śrīmad-Bhāgavatam.* Such cheating was necessary for a great cause, and there is no loss for any party in such transcendental fraud.

TEXT 38

अथाजगाम भगवान् नारदः सहतुम्बुरुः ।
प्रत्युत्थायाभिवाद्याह सानुजोऽभ्यर्चयन्मुनिम् ॥३८॥

athājagāma bhagavān
nāradaḥ saha-tumburuḥ
pratyutthāyābhivādyāha
sānujo 'bhyarcayan munim

atha—thereafter; *ājagāma*—arrived; *bhagavān*—the godly personality; *nāradaḥ*—Nārada; *saha-tumburuḥ*—along with his *tumburu* (musical instrument); *pratyutthāya*—having gotten up from their seats; *abhivādya*—offering their due obeisances; *āha*—said; *sa-anujaḥ*—along with younger brothers; *abhyarcayan*—thus while receiving in a proper mood; *munim*—the sage.

**yataḥ pravṛttir bhūtānāṁ/ yena sarvam idaṁ tatam*
sva-karmaṇā tam abhyarcya/ siddhiṁ vindati mānavaḥ (Bg. 18.46)

ataḥ pumbhir dvija-śreṣṭhā/ varṇāśrama-vibhāgaśaḥ
svanuṣṭhitasya dharmasya/ saṁsiddhir hari-toṣaṇam (*Bhāg.* 1.2.13)

TRANSLATION

While Sañjaya was thus speaking, Śrī Nārada, the powerful devotee of the Lord, appeared on the scene carrying his tumburu. Mahārāja Yudhiṣṭhira and his brothers received him properly by getting up from their seats and offering obeisances.

PURPORT

Devarṣi Nārada is described herein as *bhagavān* due to his being the most confidential devotee of the Lord. The Lord and His very confidential devotees are treated on the same level by those who are actually engaged in the loving service of the Lord. Such confidential devotees of the Lord are very much dear to the Lord because they travel everywhere to preach the glories of the Lord in different capacities and try their utmost to convert the nondevotees of the Lord into devotees in order to bring them to the platform of sanity. Actually a living being cannot be a nondevotee of the Lord because of his constitutional position, but when one becomes a nondevotee or nonbeliever, it is to be understood that the person concerned is not in a sound condition of life. The confidential devotees of the Lord treat such illusioned living beings, and therefore they are most pleasing in the eyes of the Lord. The Lord says in the *Bhagavad-gītā* that no one is dearer to Him than one who actually preaches the glories of the Lord to convert the nonbelievers and nondevotees. Such personalities as Nārada must be offered all due respects, like those offered to the Personality of Godhead Himself, and Mahārāja Yudhiṣṭhira, along with his noble brothers, were examples for others in receiving a pure devotee of the Lord like Nārada, who had no other business save and except singing the glories of the Lord along with his *vīṇā*, a musical stringed instrument.

TEXT 39

युधिष्ठिर उवाच

नाहं वेद गतिं पित्रोर्भगवन् क्व गतावितः ।
अम्बा वा हतपुत्रार्ता क्व गता च तपस्विनी ॥३९॥

yudhiṣṭhira uvāca
nāhaṁ veda gatiṁ pitror
bhagavan kva gatāv itaḥ
ambā vā hata-putrārtā
kva gatā ca tapasvinī

yudhiṣṭhiraḥ uvāca—Mahārāja Yudhiṣṭhira said; *na*—do not; *aham*—myself; *veda*—know it; *gatim*—departure; *pitroḥ*—of the uncles; *bhagavan*—O godly personality; *kva*—where; *gatau*—gone; *itaḥ*—from this place; *ambā*—mother aunt; *vā*—either; *hata-putrā*—bereft of her sons; *ārtā*—aggrieved; *kva*—where; *gatā*—gone; *ca*—also; *tapasvinī*—ascetic.

TRANSLATION

Mahārāja Yudhiṣṭhira said: O godly personality, I do not know where my two uncles have gone. Nor can I find my ascetic aunt who is griefstricken by the loss of all her sons.

PURPORT

Mahārāja Yudhiṣṭhira, as a good soul and devotee of the Lord, was always conscious of the great loss of his aunt and her sufferings as an ascetic. An ascetic is never disturbed by all kinds of sufferings, and that makes him strong and determined on the path of spiritual progress. Queen Gāndhārī is a typical example of an ascetic because of her marvelous character in many trying situations. She was an ideal woman as mother, wife and ascetic, and in the history of the world such character in a woman is rarely found.

TEXT 40

कर्णधार इवापारे भगवान् पारदर्शकः ।
अथाबभाषे भगवान् नारदो मुनिसत्तमः ॥४०॥

karṇadhāra ivāpāre
bhagavān pāra-darśakaḥ

athābabhāṣe bhagavān
nārado muni-sattamaḥ

karṇa-dhāraḥ—captain of the ship; *iva*—like; *apāre*—in the extensive oceans; *bhagavān*—representative of the Lord; *pāra-darśakaḥ*—one who can give directions to the other side; *atha*—thus; *ababhāṣe*—began to say; *bhagavān*—the godly personality; *nāradaḥ*—the great sage Nārada; *muni-sat-tamaḥ*—the greatest among the devotee-philosophers.

TRANSLATION

You are like a captain of a ship in a great ocean and you can direct us to our destination. Thus addressed, the godly personality, Devarṣi Nārada, greatest of the philosopher devotees, began to speak.

PURPORT

There are different types of philosophers, and the greatest of all of them are those who have seen the Personality of Godhead and have surrendered themselves in the transcendental loving service of the Lord. Among all such pure devotees of the Lord, Devarṣi Nārada is the chief, and therefore he has been described herein as the greatest of all philosopher devotees. Unless one has become a sufficiently learned philosopher by hearing the Vedānta philosophy from a bona fide spiritual master, one cannot be a learned philosopher devotee. One must be very faithful, learned and renounced, otherwise one cannot be a pure devotee. A pure devotee of the Lord can give us direction towards the other end of nescience. Devarṣi Nārada used to visit the palace of Mahārāja Yudhiṣṭhira because the Pāṇḍavas were all pure devotees of the Lord, and the Devarṣi was always ready to give them good counsel whenever needed.

TEXT 41

नारद उवाच
मा कंचन शुचो राजन् यदीश्वरवशं जगत् ।
लोकाः सपाला यस्येमे वहन्ति बलिमीशितुः ।
स संयुनक्ति भूतानि स एव वियुनक्ति च ॥४१॥

nārada uvāca
mā kañcana śuco rājan
yad īśvara-vaśaṁ jagat
lokāḥ sapālā yasyeme
vahanti balim īśituḥ
sa saṁyunakti bhūtāni
sa eva viyunakti ca

nāradaḥ uvāca—Nārada said; *mā*—never; *kañcana*—by all means; *śucaḥ*—do you lament; *rājan*—O King; *yat*—because; *īśvara-vaśam*—under the control of the Supreme Lord; *jagat*—world; *lokāḥ*—all living beings; *sa-pālāḥ*—including their leaders; *yasya*—whose; *ime*—all these; *vahanti*—do bear; *balim*—means of worship; *īśituḥ*—for being protected; *saḥ*—He; *saṁyunakti*—gets together; *bhūtāni*—all living beings; *saḥ*—He; *eva*—also; *viyunakti*—disperses; *ca*—and.

TRANSLATION

Śrī Nārada said: O pious King, do not lament for anyone, for everyone is under the control of the Supreme Lord. Therefore all living beings and their leaders carry on worship to be well protected. It is He only who brings them together and disperses them.

PURPORT

Every living being, either in this material world or in the spiritual world, is under the control of the Supreme Lord, the Personality of Godhead. Beginning from Brahmājī, the leader of this universe, down to the insignificant ant, all are abiding by the order of the Supreme Lord. Thus the constitutional position of the living being is subordination under the control of the Lord. The foolish living being, especially man, artificially rebels against the law of the Supreme and thus becomes chastised as an *asura*, or lawbreaker. A living being is placed in a particular position by the order of the Supreme Lord, and he is again shifted from that place by the order of the Supreme Lord or His authorized agents. Brahmā, Śiva, Indra, Candra, Mahārāja Yudhiṣṭhira or, in modern history, Napoleon, Akbar, Alexander, Gandhi, Shubhash and Nehru all are servants of the Lord, and they are placed in and removed from their respective positions by the supreme will of the Lord. None of them is independent. Even though such men or leaders rebel so as not to recognize the supremacy of the Lord, they are put under still more rigorous laws of the material world by different miseries. Only the foolish man, therefore, says that there is no God. Mahārāja Yudhiṣṭhira was being convinced of this naked truth because he was greatly overwhelmed by the sudden departure of his old uncles and aunt. Mahārāja Dhṛtarāṣṭra was placed in that position according to his past deeds; he had already suffered or enjoyed the benefits accrued to him in the past, but due to his good luck, somehow or other he had a good younger brother, Vidura, and by his instruction he left to achieve salvation by closing all acounts in the material world.

Ordinarily one cannot change the course of one's due happiness and distress by plan. Everyone has to accept them as they come under the subtle arrangement of *kāla*, or invincible time. There is no use trying to counteract them. The best thing is, therefore, that one should endeavor to achieve salvation, and this prerogative is given only to man because of his developed condition of mental activities and intelligence. Only for man are there different Vedic instructions for attainment of salvation during the human form of existence. One who misuses this opportunity of advanced intelligence is verily condemned and put into different types of miseries, either in this present life or in the future. That is the way the Supreme controls everyone.

TEXT 42

यथा गावो नसि प्रोतास्तन्त्यां बद्धाश्च दामभिः ।
वाक्तन्त्यां नामभिर्बद्धा वहन्ति बलिमीशितुः ॥ ४२॥

yathā gāvo nasi protās
tantyāṁ baddhāś ca dāmabhiḥ
vāktantyāṁ nāmabhir baddhā
vahanti balim īśituḥ

yathā—as much as; *gāvaḥ*—cow; *nasi*—by the nose; *protāḥ*—strung; *tantyām*—by the thread; *baddhāḥ*—bound by; *ca*—also; *dāmabhiḥ*—by ropes; *vāktantyām*—in the network of Vedic hymns; *nāmabhiḥ*—by nomenclatures; *baddhāḥ*—conditioned; *vahanti*—carry on; *balim*—orders; *īśituḥ*—for being controlled by the Supreme Lord.

TRANSLATION

As a cow, bound through the nose by a long rope, is conditioned, so also human beings are bound by different Vedic injunctions and are conditioned to obey the orders of the Supreme.

PURPORT

Every living being, whether a man or an animal or a bird, thinks that he is free by himself, but actually no one is free from the severe laws of the Lord. The laws of the Lord are severe because they cannot be disobeyed in any circumstance. The manmade laws may be evaded by cunning outlaws, but in the codes of the supreme lawmaker there is not the slightest possibility of neglecting the laws. A slight change in the course of God-made law can bring about a massive danger to be faced by the lawbreaker. Such laws of the Supreme are generally known as the codes of religion, under different conditions, but the principle of religion everywhere is one and the same, namely, obey the orders of the Supreme God, the codes of religion. That is the condition of material existence. All living beings in the material world have taken up the risk of conditioned life by their own selection and are thus entrapped by the laws of material nature. The only way to get out of the entanglement is to agree to obey the Supreme. But instead of becoming free from the clutches of *māyā*, or illusion, foolish human beings become bound up by different nomenclatures, being designated as *brāhmaṇas*, *kṣatriyas*, *vaiśyas*, *śūdras*, Hindus, Mohammedans, Indians, Europeans, Americans, Chinese, and many others, and thus they carry out the orders of the Supreme Lord under the influence of respective scriptural or legislative injunctions. The statutory laws of the state are imperfect imitation replicas of religious codes. The secular state, or the godless state, allows the citizens to break the laws of God, but restricts them from disobeying the laws of the state; the result is that the people in general suffer more by breaking the laws of God than by obeying the imperfect laws made by man. Every man is imperfect by constitution under conditions of material existence, and there is not the least possibility that even the most materially advanced man can enact perfect legislation. On the other hand, there is no such imperfection in the laws of God. If leaders are educated in the laws of God, there is no necessity of a makeshift legislative council of aimless men. There is necessity of change in the makeshift laws of man, but there is no change in the God-made laws because they are made perfect by the all-perfect Personality of Godhead. The codes of religion, scriptural injunctions, are made by liberated representatives of God in consideration of different conditions of living, and by carrying out the orders of the Lord, the conditioned living beings gradually become free from the clutches of material existence. The factual position of the living being is, however, that he is the eternal servitor of the Supreme Lord. In his liberated state he renders service to the Lord in transcendental love and thus enjoys a life of full freedom, even sometimes on an equal level with the Lord or sometimes more than the Lord. But in the conditioned material world, every living being wants to be the Lord of other living beings, and thus by the illusion of *māyā* this mentality of lording it over becomes a cause of further extension of conditional life. So in the material world the living being is still more conditioned, until he surrenders unto the Lord by reviving his original state of eternal servitorship. That is the last instruction of the *Bhagavad-gītā* and all other recognized scriptures of the world.

TEXT 43

यथा क्रीडोपस्कराणां संयोगविगमाविह ।
इच्छया क्रीडितुः स्यातां तथैवेशेच्छया नृणाम् ॥४३॥

yathā krīḍopaskarāṇāṁ
saṁyoga-vigamāv iha
icchayā krīḍituḥ syātāṁ
tathaiveśecchayā nṛṇām

yathā—as much as; *krīḍa-upaskarāṇām*—playthings; *saṁyoga*—union; *vigamau*—disunion; *iha*—in this world; *icchayā*—by the will of; *krīḍituḥ*—just to play a part; *syātām*—takes place; *tathā*—so also;

eva—certainly; *īśa*—the Supreme Lord; *icchayā*—by the will of; *nṛṇām*—of the human beings.

TRANSLATION

As a player sets up and disperses his playthings according to his own sweet will, so the supreme will of the Lord brings men together and separates them.

PURPORT

We must know for certain that the particular position in which we are now set up is an arrangement of the supreme will in terms of our own acts in the past. The Supreme Lord is present as the localized Paramātmā in the heart of every living being, as it is said in the *Bhagavad-gītā* (13.23), and therefore he knows everything of our activities in every stage of our lives. He rewards the reactions of our actions by placing us in some particular place. A rich man gets his son born with a silver spoon in his mouth, but the child who came as the rich man's son deserved such a place, and therefore he is placed there by the will of the Lord. And at a particular moment when the child has to be removed from that place, he is also carried by the will of the Supreme, even if the child or the father does not wish to be separated from the happy relation. The same thing happens in the case of a poor man also. Neither rich man nor poor man has any control over such meetings or separations of living beings. The example of a player and his playthings should not be misunderstood. One may argue that since the Lord is bound to award the reactionary results of our own actions, the example of a player cannot be applied. But it is not so. We must always remember that the Lord is the supreme will, and He is not bound by any law. Generally the law of *karma* is that one is awarded the result of one's own actions, but in special cases, by the will of the Lord, such resultant actions are changed also. But this change can be affected by the will of the Lord only, and no other. Therefore, the example of the player cited in this verse is quite appropriate, for the Supreme Will is absolutely free to do whatever He likes, and because He is all-perfect, there is no mistake in any of His actions or reactions. These changes of resultant actions are especially rendered by the Lord when a pure devotee is involved. It is assured in the

Bhagavad-gītā (9.30–31) that the Lord saves a pure devotee who has surrendered unto Him without reservation from all sorts of reactions of sins, and there is no doubt about this. There are hundreds of examples of reactions changed by the Lord in the history of the world. If the Lord is able to change the reactions of one's past deeds, then certainly He is not Himself bound by any action or reaction of His own deeds. He is perfect and transcendental to all laws.

TEXT 44

यन्मन्यसे ध्रुवं लोकमध्रुवं वा न चोभयम् ।
सर्वथा न हि शोच्यास्ते स्नेहादन्यत्र मोहजात् ॥४४॥

yan manyase dhruvaṁ lokam
adhruvaṁ vā na cobhayam
sarvathā na hi śocyās te
snehād anyatra mohajāt

yat—even though; *manyase*—you think; *dhruvam*—Absolute Truth; *lokam*—persons; *adhruvam*—nonreality; *vā*—either; *na*—or not; *ca*—also; *ubhayam*—or bothwise; *sarvathā*—in all circumstances; *na*—never; *hi*—certainly; *śocyāḥ*—subject for lamentation; *te*—they; *snehāt*—due to affection; *anyatra*—or otherwise; *moha-jāt*—due to bewilderment.

TRANSLATION

O King, in all circumstances, whether you consider the soul to be an eternal principle, or the material body to be perishable, or everything to exist in the impersonal Absolute Truth, or everything to be an inexplicable combination of matter and spirit, feelings of separation are due only to illusory affection and nothing more.

PURPORT

The actual fact is that every living being is an individual part and parcel of the Supreme Being, and his constitutional position is subordinate cooperative service. Either in his conditional material existence or in his liberated position of full knowledge and eternity, the living entity is eternally under the control of the Supreme Lord. But those who are not conversant with factual knowledge put forward many speculative propositions about the real position of the living entity. It is admitted, however, by all schools of philosophy, that the living being is eternal and that the covering body of the five material elements is perishable and temporary. The eternal living entity transmigrates from one material body to another by the law of *karma*, and material bodies are perishable by their fundamental structures. Therefore there is nothing to be lamented in the case of the soul's being transferred into another body, or the material body's perishing at a certain stage. There are others also who believe in the merging of the spirit soul in the Supreme Spirit when it is uncovered by the material encagement, and there are others also who do not believe in the existence of spirit or soul, but believe in tangible matter. In our daily experience we find so many transformations of matter from one form to another, but we do not lament such changing features. In either of the above cases, the force of divine energy is uncheckable; no one has any hand in it, and thus there is no cause of grief.

TEXT 45

तस्माज्जह्यङ्ग वैक्लव्यमज्ञानकृतमात्मनः ।
कथं त्वनाथाः कृपणा वर्तेरंस्ते च मां विना ॥४५॥

tasmāj jahy aṅga vaiklavyam
ajñāna-kṛtam ātmanaḥ
kathaṁ tv anāthāḥ kṛpaṇā
varteraṁs te ca māṁ vinā

tasmāt—therefore; *jahi*—give up; *aṅga*—O King; *vaiklavyam*—mental disparity; *ajñāna*—ignorance; *kṛtam*—due to; *ātmanaḥ*—of yourself; *katham*—how; *tu*—but; *anāthāḥ*—helpless; *kṛpaṇāḥ*—poor creatures; *varteran*—be able to survive; *te*—they; *ca*—also; *mām*—me; *vinā*—without.

TRANSLATION

Therefore give up your anxiety due to ignorance of the self. You are now thinking of how they, who are helpless poor creatures, will exist without you.

PURPORT

When we think of our kith and kin as being helpless and dependent on us, it is all due to ignorance. Every living creature is allowed all protection by the order of the Supreme Lord in terms of each one's acquired position in the world. The Lord is known as *bhūta-bhṛt,* one who gives protection to all living beings. One should discharge his duties only, for no one but the Supreme Lord can give protection to anyone else. This is explained more clearly in the following verse.

TEXT 46

कालकर्मगुणाधीनो देहोऽयं पाञ्चभौतिकः ।
कथमन्यांस्तु गोपायेत्सर्पग्रस्तो यथा परम् ॥४६॥

kāla-karma-guṇādhīno
deho 'yaṁ pāñca-bhautikaḥ
katham anyāṁs tu gopāyet
sarpa-grasto yathā param

kāla—eternal time; *karma*—action; *guṇa*—modes of nature; *adhīnaḥ*—under the control of; *dehaḥ*—material body and mind; *ayam*—this; *pāñca-bhautikaḥ*—made of the five elements; *katham*—how; *anyān*—others; *tu*—but; *gopāyet*—give protection; *sarpa-grastaḥ*—one who is bitten by the snake; *yathā*—as much as; *param*—others.

TRANSLATION

This gross material body made of five elements is already under the control of eternal time [kāla], action [karma] and the modes of material nature [guṇa]. How, then, can it, being already in the jaws of the serpent, protect others?

PURPORT

The world's movements for freedom through political, economic, social, and cultural propaganda can do no benefit to anyone, for they are controlled by superior power. A conditioned living being is under the full control of material nature, represented by eternal time and activities under the dictation of different modes of nature. There are three material modes of nature, namely goodness, passion and ignorance. Unless one is situated in the mode of goodness, one cannot see things as they are. The passionate and the ignorant cannot even see things as they are. Therefore a person who is passionate and ignorant cannot direct his activities on the right path. Only the man in the quality of goodness can help to a certain extent. Most persons are passionate and ignorant, and therefore their plans and projects can hardly do any good to others. Above the modes of nature is eternal time, which is called *kāla* because it changes the shape of everything in the material world. Even if we are able to do something temporarily beneficial, time will see that the good project is frustrated in course of time. The only thing possible to be done is to get rid of eternal time, *kāla*, which is compared to *kāla-sarpa*, or the cobra snake, whose bite is always lethal. No one can be saved from the bite of a cobra. The best remedy for getting out of the clutches of the cobralike *kāla* or its integrity, the modes of nature, is *bhakti-yoga*, as it is recommended in the *Bhagavad-gītā* (14.26). The highest perfectional project of philanthropic activities is to engage everyone in the act of preaching *bhakti-yoga* all over the world because that alone can save the people from the control of *māyā*, or the material nature represented by *kāla*, *karma* and *guṇa*, as described above. The *Bhagavad-gītā* (14.26) confirms this definitely.

TEXT 47

अहस्तानि सहस्तानामपदानि चतुष्पदाम् ।
फल्गूनि तत्र महतां जीवो जीवस्य जीवनम् ॥४७॥

ahastāni sahastānām
apadāni catuṣ-padām
phalgūni tatra mahatāṁ
jīvo jīvasya jīvanam

ahastāni—those who are devoid of hands; *sa-hastānām*—of those who are endowed with hands; *apadāni*—those who are devoid of legs; *catuḥ-padām*—of those who have four legs; *phalgūni*—those who are weak; *tatra*—there; *mahatām*—of the powerful; *jīvaḥ*—the living being; *jīvasya*—of the living being; *jīvanam*—subsistence.

TRANSLATION

Those who are devoid of hands are prey for those who have hands; those devoid of legs are prey for the four-legged. The weak are the subsistence of the strong, and the general rule holds that one living being is food for another.

PURPORT

A systematic law of subsistence in the struggle for existence is there by the supreme will, and there is no escape for anyone by any amount of planning. The living beings who have come to the material world against the will of the Supreme Being are under the control of a supreme power called *māyā-śakti*, the deputed agent of the Lord, and this *daivī māyā* is meant to pinch the conditioned souls by threefold miseries, one of which is explained here in this verse: *the weak is the subsistence of the strong.* No one is strong enough to protect himself from the onslaught of a stronger, and by the will of the Lord there are systematic categories of the weak, the stronger and the strongest. There is nothing to be lamented if a tiger eats a weaker animal, including a man, because that is the law of the Supreme Lord. But although the law states that a human being must subsist on another living being, there is the law of good sense also, for the human being is meant to obey the laws of the scriptures. This is impossible for other animals. The human being is meant for self-realization, and for that purpose he is not to eat anything which is not first offered to the Lord. The Lord accepts from His devotee all kinds of food preparations made of vegetables, fruits, leaves and grains. Fruits, leaves and milk in different varieties can be offered to the Lord, and after the Lord accepts the foodstuff, the devotee can partake of the *prasāda*, by which all suffering in the struggle for existence will be gradually mitigated. This is confirmed in the *Bhagavad-gītā* (9.26). Even those who are accustomed to eat animals can offer foodstuff, not to the Lord directly, but to an agent of the Lord, under certain conditions of religious rites. Injunctions of the scriptures are meant not to encourage the eaters of animals, but to restrict them by regulated principles.

The living being is the source of subsistence for other, stronger living beings. No one should be very anxious for his subsistence in any circumstances because there are living beings everywhere, and no living being starves for want of food at any place. Mahārāja Yudhiṣṭhira is advised by Nārada not to worry about his uncles' suffering for want of food, for they could live on vegetables available in the jungles as *prasāda* of the Supreme Lord and thus realize the path of salvation.

Exploitation of the weaker living being by the stronger is the natural law of existence; there is always an attempt to devour the weak in different kingdoms of living beings. There is no possibility of checking this tendency by any artificial means under material conditions; it can be checked only by awakening the spiritual sense of the human being by practice of spiritual regulations. The spiritual regulative principles, however, do not allow a man to slaughter weaker animals on one side and teach others peaceful coexistence. If man does not allow the animals peaceful coexistence, how can he expect peaceful existence in human society? The blind leaders must therefore understand the Supreme Being and then try to implement the kingdom of God. The kingdom of God, or Rāma-rājya, is impossible without the awakening of God consciousness in the mass mind of the people of the world.

TEXT 48

तदिदं भगवान् राजन्नेक आत्मात्मनां स्वदृक् ।
अन्तरोऽनन्तरो भाति पश्य तं माययोरुधा ॥४८॥

tad idaṁ bhagavān rājann
eka ātmātmanāṁ sva-dṛk
antaro 'nantaro bhāti
paśya taṁ māyayorudhā

tat—therefore; *idam*—this manifestation; *bhagavān*—the Personality of Godhead; *rājan*—O King; *ekaḥ*—one without a second; *ātmā*—the Supersoul; *ātmanām*—by His energies; *sva-dṛk*—qualitatively like Him; *antaraḥ*—without; *anantaraḥ*—within and by Himself; *bhāti*—so manifests; *paśya*—look; *tam*—unto Him only;

māyayā—by manifestations of different energies; *urudhā*—appears to be many.

TRANSLATION

Therefore, O King, you should look to the Supreme Lord only, who is one without a second and who manifests Himself by different energies and is both within and without.

PURPORT

The Supreme Lord Personality of Godhead is one without a second, but He manifests Himself by different energies because He is by nature blissful. The living beings are also manifestations of His marginal energy, qualitatively one with the Lord, and there are innumerable living beings both within and without the external and internal energies of the Lord. Since the spiritual world is a manifestation of the Lord's internal energy, the living beings within that internal potency are qualitatively one with the Lord without contamination from the external potency. Although qualitatively one with the Lord, the living being, due to contamination of the material world, is pervertedly manifested, and therefore he experiences so-called happiness and distress in the material world. Such experiences are all ephemeral and do not affect the spirit soul. The perception of such ephemeral happiness and distress is due only to the forgetfulness of his qualities, which are equal to the Lord's. There is, however, a regular current from the Lord Himself, from within and without, by which to rectify the fallen condition of the living being. From within He corrects the desiring living beings as localized Paramātmā, and from without He corrects by His manifestations, the spiritual master and the revealed scriptures. One should look unto the Lord; one should not be disturbed by the so-called manifestations of happiness or distress, but he should try to cooperate with the Lord in His outward activities for correcting the fallen souls. By His order only, one should become a spiritual master and cooperate with the Lord. One should not become a spiritual master for one's personal benefit, for some material gain or as an avenue of business or occupation for earning livelihood. Bona fide spiritual masters who look unto the Supreme Lord to cooperate with Him are actually qualitatively one with the Lord, and the forgetful ones are perverted reflections only. Yudhiṣṭhira Mahārāja is advised by Nārada, therefore, not to be disturbed by the affairs of so-called happiness and distress, but to look only unto the Lord to execute the mission for which the Lord has descended. That was his prime duty.

TEXT 49

सोऽयमद्य महाराज भगवान् भूतभावनः ।
कालरूपोऽवतीर्णोऽस्यामभावाय सुरद्विषाम् ॥४९॥

so 'yam adya mahārāja
bhagavān bhūta-bhāvanaḥ
kāla-rūpo 'vatīrṇo 'syām
abhāvāya sura-dviṣām

saḥ—that Supreme Lord; *ayam*—the Lord Śrī Kṛṣṇa; *adya*—at present; *mahārāja*—O King; *bhagavān*—the Personality of Godhead; *bhūta-bhāvanaḥ*—the creator or the father of everything created; *kāla-rūpaḥ*—in the disguise of devouring time; *avatīrṇaḥ*—descended; *asyām*—upon the world; *abhāvāya*—for eliminating; *sura-dviṣām*—those who are against the will of the Lord.

TRANSLATION

That Supreme Personality of Godhead, Lord Śrī Kṛṣṇa, in the guise of all devouring time [kāla-rūpa] has now descended on earth to eliminate the envious from the world.

PURPORT

There are two classes of human beings, namely the envious and the obedient. Since the Supreme Lord is one and the father of all living beings, the envious living beings are also His sons, but they are known as the *asuras*. But the living beings who are obedient to the Supreme Father are called *devatās*, or demigods, because they are not contaminated by the material conception of life. Not only are the *asuras* envious of the Lord in even denying the existence of the Lord, but they are also envious of all other living beings. The predominance of *asuras* in the world is occasionally rectified by the Lord when He eliminates them from the world and establishes a rule of *devatās* like the Pāṇḍavas. His designation as *kāla* in disguise is significant. He is not at all dangerous, but He is the transcendental form of eternity, knowledge and bliss. For the devotees His factual form is disclosed, and for the nondevotees He appears like *kāla-rūpa*, which is causal form. This causal form of the Lord is not at all pleasing to the *asuras*, and therefore they think of the Lord as formless in order to feel secure that they will not be vanquished by the Lord.

TEXT 50

निष्पादितं देवकृत्यमवशेषं प्रतीक्षते ।
तावद् यूयमवेक्षध्वं भवेद् यावदिहेश्वरः ॥५०॥

niṣpāditaṁ deva-kṛtyam
avaśeṣaṁ pratīkṣate
tāvad yūyam avekṣadhvaṁ
bhaved yāvad iheśvaraḥ

niṣpāditam—performed; *deva-kṛtyam*—what was to be done on behalf of the demigods; *avaśeṣam*—the rest; *pratīkṣate*—being awaited; *tāvat*—up to that time; *yūyam*—all of you Pāṇḍavas; *avekṣadhvam*—observe and wait; *bhavet*—may; *yāvat*—as long as; *iha*—in this world; *īśvaraḥ*—the Supreme Lord.

TRANSLATION

The Lord has already performed His duties to help the demigods, and He is awaiting the rest. You Pāṇḍavas may wait as long as the Lord is here on earth.

PURPORT

The Lord descends from His abode (Kṛṣṇaloka), the topmost planet in the spiritual sky, in order to help the demigod administrators of this material world when they are greatly vexed by the *asuras*, who are envious not only of the Lord but also of His devotees. As referred to above, the conditioned living beings contact material association by their own choice, dictated by a strong desire to lord it over the resources of the material world and become imitation lords of all they survey. Everyone is trying to become an imitation God; there is keen competition amongst such imitation gods, and such competitors are generally known as *asuras.* When there are too many *asuras* in the world, then it becomes a hell for those who are devotees of the Lord. Due to the growth of the *asuras,* the mass of people who are generally devoted to the Lord by nature and the pure devotees of the Lord, including the demigods in higher planets, pray to the Lord for relief, and the Lord either descends personally from His abode or deputes some of his devotees to remodel the fallen condition of human society, or even animal society. Such disruptions take place not only in human society but also amongst animals, birds or other living beings, including the demigods in the higher planets. Lord Śrī Kṛṣṇa descended personally to vanquish *asuras* like Kaṁsa, Jarāsandha and Śiśupāla, and during the reign of Mahārāja Yudhiṣṭhira almost all these *asuras* were killed by the Lord. Now he was awaiting the annihilation of His own dynasty, called the Yadu-vaṁśa, who appeared by His will in this world. He wanted to take them away before His own departure to His eternal abode. Nārada, like Vidura, did not disclose the imminent annihilation of the Yadu dynasty, but indirectly gave a hint to the King and his brothers to wait till the incident happened and the Lord departed.

TEXT 51

धृतराष्ट्रः सह भ्रात्रा गान्धार्या च स्वभार्यया ।
दक्षिणेन हिमवत ऋषीणामाश्रमं गतः ॥५१॥

dhṛtarāṣṭraḥ saha bhrātrā
gāndhāryā ca sva-bhāryayā
dakṣiṇena himavata
ṛṣīṇām āśramaṁ gataḥ

dhṛtarāṣṭraḥ—Dhṛtarāṣṭra; *saha*—along with; *bhrātrā*—his brother Vidura; *gāndhāryā*—Gāndhārī also; *ca*—and; *sva-bhāryayā*—his own wife; *dakṣiṇena*—by the southern side; *himavataḥ*—of the Himalaya Mountains; *ṛṣīṇām*—of the *ṛṣis; āśramam*—in shelter; *gataḥ*—he has gone.

TRANSLATION

O King, your uncle, Dhṛtarāṣṭra, his brother Vidura and his wife Gāndhārī have gone to the southern side of the Himalaya Mountains, where there are shelters of the great sages.

PURPORT

To pacify the mourning Mahārāja Yudhiṣṭhira, Nārada first of all spoke from the philosophical point of view, and then he began to describe the future movements of his uncle, which he could see by his foreseeing powers, and thus began to describe as follows.

TEXT 52

स्रोतोभिः सप्तभिर्या वै स्वर्धुनी सप्तधा व्यधात् ।
सप्तानां प्रीतये नाना सप्तस्रोतः प्रचक्षते ॥५२॥

srotobhiḥ saptabhir yā vai
svardhunī saptadhā vyadhāt
saptānāṁ prītaye nānā
sapta-srotaḥ pracakṣate

srotobhiḥ—by currents; *saptabhiḥ*—by seven (divisions); *yā*—the river; *vai*—certainly; *svardhunī*—the sacred Ganges; *saptadhā*—seven branches; *vyadhāt*—created; *saptānām*—of the seven; *prītaye*—for the satisfaction of; *nānā*—various; *sapta-srotaḥ*—seven sources; *pracakṣate*—known by name.

TRANSLATION

The place is called Saptasrota [divided by seven] because there the waters of the sacred Ganges were divided into seven branches. This was done for the satisfaction of the seven great ṛṣis.

TEXT 53

स्नात्वानुसवनं तस्मिन्हुत्वा चाग्नीन्यथाविधि ।
अब्भक्ष उपशान्तात्मा स आस्ते विगतैषणः ॥५३॥

snātvānusavanaṁ tasmin
hutvā cāgnīn yathā-vidhi
ab-bhakṣa upaśāntātmā
sa āste vigataiṣaṇaḥ

snātvā—by taking bath; *anusavanam*—regularly three times (morning, noon and evening); *tasmin*—in that Ganges divided into seven; *hutvā*—by performing the Agni-hotra sacrifice; *ca*—also; *agnīn*—in the fire; *yathā-vidhi*—just according to the tenets of the scripture; *ap-bhakṣaḥ*—fasting by drinking only water; *upaśānta*—completely controlled; *ātmā*—the gross senses and the subtle mind; *saḥ*—Dhṛtarāṣṭra; *āste*—would be situated; *vigata*—devoid of; *eṣaṇaḥ*—thoughts in relation with family welfare.

TRANSLATION

On the banks at Saptasrota, Dhṛtarāṣṭra is now engaged in beginning aṣṭāṅga-yoga by bathing three times daily, in the morning, noon and evening, by performing the Agni-hotra sacrifice with fire and by drinking only water. This helps one control the mind and the senses and frees one completely from thoughts of familial affection.

PURPORT

The *yoga* system is a mechanical way to control the senses and the mind and divert them from matter to spirit. The preliminary processes are the sitting posture, meditation, spiritual thoughts, manipulation of air passing within the body, and gradual situation in trance, facing the Absolute Person, Paramātmā. Such mechanical ways of rising to the spiritual platform prescribe some regulative principles of taking bath daily three times, fasting as far as possible, sitting and concentrating the mind on spiritual matters and thus gradually becoming free from *viṣaya*, or material objectives. Material existence means to be absorbed in the material objective, which is simply illusory. House, country, family, society, children, property, and business are some of the material coverings of the spirit, *ātmā*, and the *yoga* system helps one to become free from all these illusory thoughts and gradually turn towards the Absolute Person, Paramātmā. By material association and education, we learn simply to concentrate on flimsy things, but *yoga* is the process of forgetting them altogether. Modern so-called *yogīs* and *yoga* systems manifest some magical feats, and ignorant persons are attracted by such false things, or they accept the *yoga* system as a cheap healing process for diseases of the gross body. But factually the *yoga* system is the process of learning to forget what we have acquired throughout the struggle for existence. Dhṛtarāṣṭra was all along engaged in improving family affairs by raising the standard of living of his sons or by usurping the property of the Pāṇḍavas for the sake of his own sons. These are common affairs for a man grossly materialistic and without knowledge of the spiritual force. He does not see how this can drag one from heaven to hell. By the grace of his younger brother Vidura, Dhṛtarāṣṭra was enlightened and could see his grossly illusory engagements, and by such enlightenment he was able to leave home for spiritual realization. Śrī Nāradadeva was just foretelling the way of his spiritual progress in a place which was sanctified by the flow of the celestial Ganges. Drinking water only, without solid food, is also considered fasting. This is necessary for advancement of spiritual knowledge. A foolish man wants to be a cheap *yogī* without observing the regulative principles. A man who has no control over the tongue at first can hardly become a *yogī*. *Yogī* and *bhogī* are two opposite terms. The *bhogī*, or the merryman who eats and drinks, cannot be a *yogī*, for a *yogī* is never allowed to eat and drink unrestrictedly. We may note with profit how Dhṛtarāṣṭra began his *yoga* system by drinking water only and sitting calmly in a place with a spiritual atmosphere, deeply absorbed in the thoughts of the Lord Hari, the Personality of Godhead.

TEXT 54

जितासनो जितश्वासः प्रत्याहृतषडिन्द्रियः ।
हरिभावनया ध्वस्तरजःसत्त्वतमोमलः ॥५४॥

jitāsano jita-śvāsaḥ
pratyāhṛta-ṣaḍ-indriyaḥ
hari-bhāvanayā dhvasta-
rajaḥ-sattva-tamo-malaḥ

jita-āsanaḥ—one who has controlled the sitting posture; *jita-śvāsaḥ*—one who has controlled the breathing process; *pratyāhṛta*—turning back; *ṣaṭ*—six; *indriyaḥ*—senses; *hari*—the Absolute Personality of Godhead; *bhāvanayā*—absorbed in; *dhvasta*—conquered; *rajaḥ*—passion; *sattva*—goodness; *tamaḥ*—ignorance; *malaḥ*—contaminations.

TRANSLATION

One who has controlled the sitting postures [the yogic āsanas] and the breathing process can turn the senses toward the Absolute Personality of Godhead and thus become immune to the contaminations of the modes of material nature, namely mundane goodness, passion and ignorance.

PURPORT

The preliminary activities of the way of *yoga* are *āsana, prāṇāyāma, pratyāhāra, dhyāna, dhāraṇā,* etc. Mahārāja Dhṛtarāṣṭra was to attain success in those preliminary actions because he was seated in a sanctified place and was concentrating upon one objective, namely the Supreme Personality of Godhead (Hari). Thus all his senses were being engaged in the service of the Lord. This process directly helps the devotee to get freedom from the contaminations of the three material modes of nature. Even the highest mode, the material mode of goodness, is also a cause of material bondage, and what to speak of the other qualities, namely passion and ignorance. Passion and ignorance increase the material propensities of hankering for material enjoyment, and a strong sense of lust provokes the accumulation of wealth and power. One who has conquered these two base mentalities and has raised himself to the platform of goodness, which is full of knowledge and morality, cannot also control the senses, namely the eyes, the tongue, the nose, the ear and touch. But one who has surrendered himself unto the lotus feet of Lord Hari, as above mentioned, can transcend all influences of the modes of material nature and be fixed in the service of the Lord. The *bhakti-yoga* process, therefore, directly applies the senses to the loving service of the Lord. This prohibits the performer from engaging in material activities. This process of turning the senses from material attachment to the loving transcendental service of the Lord is called *pratyāhāra,* and the very process is called *prāṇāyāma,* ultimately ending in *samādhi,* or absorption in pleasing the Supreme Lord Hari by all means.

TEXT 55

विज्ञानात्मनि संयोज्य क्षेत्रज्ञे प्रविलाप्य तम् ।
ब्रह्मण्यात्मानमाधारे घटाम्बरमिवाम्बरे ॥५५॥

vijñānātmani saṁyojya
kṣetrajñe pravilāpya tam
brahmaṇy ātmānam ādhāre
ghaṭāmbaram ivāmbare

vijñāna—purified identity; *ātmani*—in intelligence; *saṁyojya*—perfectly fixing; *kṣetra-jñe*—in the matter of the living being; *pravilāpya*—merging; *tam*—him; *brahmaṇi*—in the Supreme; *ātmānam*—pure living being; *ādhāre*—in the reservoir; *ghaṭa-ambaram*—sky within the block; *iva*—like; *ambare*—in the supreme sky.

TRANSLATION

Dhṛtarāṣṭra will have to amalgamate his pure identity with intelligence and then merge into the Supreme Being with knowledge of his qualitative oneness, as a living entity, with the Supreme Brahman. Being freed from the blocked sky, he will have to rise to the spiritual sky.

PURPORT

The living being, by his desiring to lord it over the material world and declining to cooperate with the Supreme Lord, contacts the sum total of the material world, namely the *mahat-tattva*, and from the *mahat-tattva* his false identity with the material world, intelligence, mind and senses is developed. This covers his pure spiritual identity. By the yogic process, when his pure identity is realized in self-realization, one has to revert to the original position by amalgamating the five gross elements and the subtle elements, mind and intelligence, into the *mahat-tattva* again. Thus getting freed from the clutches of the *mahat-tattva*, he has to merge in the existence of the Supersoul. In other words, he has to realize that qualitatively he is nondifferent from the Supersoul, and thus he transcends the material sky by his pure identical intelligence and thus becomes engaged in the transcendental loving service of the Lord. This is the highest perfectional development of spiritual identity, which was attained by Dhṛtarāṣṭra by the grace of Vidura and the Lord. The Lord's mercy was bestowed upon him by his personal contact with Vidura, and when he was actually practicing the instructions of Vidura, the Lord helped him to attain the highest perfectional stage.

A pure devotee of the Lord does not live on any planet of the material sky, nor does he feel any contact with material elements. His so-called material body does not exist, being surcharged with the spiritual current of the Lord's identical interest, and thus he is permanently freed from all contaminations of the sum total of the *mahat-tattva.* He is always in the spiritual sky, which he attains by being transcendental to the sevenfold material coverings by the effect of his devotional service. The conditioned souls are within the coverings, whereas the liberated soul is far beyond the cover.

TEXT 56

ध्वस्तमायागुणोदर्को निरुद्धकरणाशयः ।
निवर्तिताखिलाहार आस्ते स्थाणुरिवाचलः ।
तस्यान्तरायो मैवाभूः संन्यस्ताखिलकर्मणः ॥५६॥

dhvasta-māyā-guṇodarko
niruddha-karaṇāśayaḥ
nivartitākhilāhāra
āste sthāṇur ivācalaḥ
tasyāntarāyo maivābhūḥ
sannyastākhila-karmaṇaḥ

dhvasta—being destroyed; *māyā-guṇa*—the modes of material nature; *udarkaḥ*—aftereffects; *niruddha*—being suspended; *karaṇa-āśayaḥ*—the senses and the mind; *nivartita*—stopped; *akhila*—all; *āhāraḥ*—food for the senses; *āste*—is sitting; *sthāṇuḥ*—immovable; *iva*—like; *acalaḥ*—fixed; *tasya*—his; *antarāyaḥ*—hindrances; *mā eva*—never like that; *abhūḥ*—be; *sannyasta*—renounced; *akhila*—all sorts; *karmaṇaḥ*—material duties.

TRANSLATION

He will have to suspend all the actions of the senses, even from the outside, and will have to be impervious to interactions of the

senses, which are influenced by the modes of material nature. After renouncing all material duties, he must become immovably established, beyond all sources of hindrances on the path.

PURPORT

Dhṛtarāṣṭra had attained, by the yogic process, the stage of negation of all sorts of material reaction. The effects of the material modes of nature draw the victim to indefatigable desires of enjoying matter, but one can escape such false enjoyment by the yogic process. Every sense is always busy in searching for its food, and thus the conditioned soul is assaulted from all sides and has no chance to become steady in any pursuit. Mahārāja Yudhiṣṭhira was advised by Nārada not to disturb his uncle by attempting to bring him back home. He was now beyond the attraction of anything material. The material modes of nature (the *guṇas*) have their different modes of activities, but above the material modes of nature is a spiritual mode, which is absolute. *Nirguṇa* means without reaction. The spiritual mode and its effect are identical; therefore the spiritual quality is distinguished from its material counterpart by the word *nirguṇa*. After complete suspension of the material modes of nature, one is admitted to the spiritual sphere, and action dictated by the spiritual modes is called devotional service, or *bhakti*. *Bhakti* is therefore *nirguṇa* attained by direct contact with the Absolute.

TEXT 57

स वा अद्यतनाद् राजन् परतः पञ्चमेऽहनि ।
कलेवरं हास्यति स्वं तच्च भस्मीभविष्यति ॥५७॥

sa vā adya tanād rājan
parataḥ pañcame 'hani
kalevaraṁ hāsyati svaṁ
tac ca bhasmī bhaviṣyati

saḥ—he; *vā*—in all probability; *adya*—today; *tanāt*—from; *rājan*—O King; *parataḥ*—ahead; *pañcame*—on the fifth; *ahani*—day;

kalevaram—body; *hāsyati*—shall quit; *svam*—his own; *tat*—that; *ca*—also; *bhasmī*—ashes; *bhaviṣyati*—will turn into.

TRANSLATION

O King, he will quit his body, most probably on the fifth day from today. And his body will turn to ashes.

PURPORT

Nārada Muni's prophecy prohibited Yudhiṣṭhira Mahārāja from going to the place where his uncle was staying because even after quitting the body by his own mystic power, Dhṛtarāṣṭra would not be in need of any funeral ceremony; Nārada Muni indicated that his body by itself would burn to ashes. The perfection of the *yoga* system is attained by such mystic power. The *yogī* is able to quit his body by his own choice of time and can attain any planet he desires by turning the present body into ashes by self-made fire.

TEXT 58

दह्यमानेऽग्निभिर्देहे पत्युः पत्नी सहोटजे ।
बहिः स्थिता पतिं साध्वी तमग्निमनु वेक्ष्यति ॥५८॥

dahyamāne 'gnibhir dehe
patyuḥ patnī sahoṭaje
bahiḥ sthitā patiṁ sādhvī
tam agnim anu vekṣyati

dahyamāne—while it is burning; *agnibhiḥ*—by the fire; *dehe*—the body; *patyuḥ*—of the husband; *patnī*—the wife; *saha-uṭaje*—along with the thatched cottage; *bahiḥ*—outside; *sthitā*—situated; *patim*—unto the husband; *sādhvī*—the chaste lady; *tam*—that; *agnim*—fire; *anu vekṣyati*—looking with great attention will enter the fire.

TRANSLATION

While outside observing her husband, who will burn in the fire of mystic power along with his thatched cottage, his chaste wife will enter the fire with rapt attention.

PURPORT

Gāndhārī was an ideal chaste lady, a life companion of her husband, and therefore when she saw her husband burning in the fire of mystic *yoga* along with his cottage of leaves, she despaired. She left home after losing her one hundred sons, and in the forest she saw that her most beloved husband was also burning. Now she actually felt alone, and therefore she entered the fire of her husband and followed her husband to death. This entering of a chaste lady into the fire of her dead husband is called the *satī* rite, and the action is considered to be most perfect for a woman. In a later age, this *satī* rite became an obnoxious criminal affair because the ceremony was forced upon even an unwilling woman. In this fallen age it is not possible for any lady to follow the *satī* rite as chastely as it was done by Gāndhārī and others in past ages. A chaste wife like Gāndhārī would feel the separation of her husband to be more burning than actual fire. Such a lady can observe the *satī* rite voluntarily, and there is no criminal force by anyone. When the rite became a formality only and force was applied upon a lady to follow the principle, actually it became criminal, and therefore the ceremony was to be stopped by state law. This prophecy of Nārada Muni to Mahārāja Yudhiṣṭhira forbade him to go to his widowed aunt.

TEXT 59

विदुरस्तु तदाश्चर्यं निशाम्य कुरुनन्दन ।
हर्षशोकयुतस्तस्माद् गन्ता तीर्थनिषेवकः ॥५९॥

viduras tu tad āścaryaṁ
niśāmya kuru-nandana
harṣa-śoka-yutas tasmād
gantā tīrtha-niṣevakaḥ

viduraḥ—Vidura also; *tu*—but; *tat*—that incident; *āścaryam*—wonderful; *niśāmya*—seeing; *kuru-nandana*—O son of the Kuru dynasty; *harṣa*—delight; *śoka*—grief; *yutaḥ*—affected by; *tasmāt*—from that place; *gantā*—will go away; *tīrtha*—place of pilgrimage; *niṣevakaḥ*—for being enlivened.

TRANSLATION

Vidura, being affected with delight and grief, will then leave that place of sacred pilgrimage.

PURPORT

Vidura was astonished to see the marvelous departure of his brother Dhṛtarāṣṭra as a liberated *yogī*, for in his past life he was much attached to materialism. Of course it was only due to Vidura that his brother attained the desirable goal of life. Vidura was therefore glad to learn about it. But he was sorry that he could not make his brother turn into a pure devotee. This was not done by Vidura because of Dhṛtarāṣṭra's being inimical to the Pāṇḍavas, who were all devotees of the Lord. An offense at the feet of a Vaiṣṇava is more dangerous than an offense at the lotus feet of the Lord. Vidura was certainly very liberal to bestow mercy upon his brother Dhṛtarāṣṭra, whose past life was very materialistic. But ultimately the result of such mercy certainly depended on the will of the Supreme Lord in the present life; therefore Dhṛtarāṣṭra attained liberation only, and after many such liberated states of life one can attain to the stage of devotional service. Vidura was certainly very mortified by the death of his brother and sister-in-law, and the only remedy to mitigate such lamentation was to go out to pilgrimage. Thus Mahārāja Yudhiṣṭhira had no chance to call back Vidura, his surviving uncle.

TEXT 60

इत्युक्त्वाथारुहत् स्वर्गं नारदः सहतुम्बुरुः ।
युधिष्ठिरो वचस्तस्य हृदि कृत्वाजहाच्छुचः ॥ ६० ॥

ity uktvāthāruhat svargaṁ
nāradaḥ saha-tumburuḥ
yudhiṣṭhiro vacas tasya
hṛdi kṛtvājahāc chucaḥ

iti—thus; *uktvā*—having addressed; *atha*—thereafter; *āruhat*—ascended; *svargam*—into outer space; *nāradaḥ*—the great sage Nārada; *saha*—along with; *tumburuḥ*—his stringed instrument; *yudhiṣṭhiraḥ*—

Mahārāja Yudhiṣṭhira; *vacaḥ*—instructions; *tasya*—of his; *hṛdi kṛtvā*—keeping in the heart; *ajahāt*—gave up; *śucaḥ*—all lamentations.

TRANSLATION

Having spoken thus, the great sage Nārada, along with his vīṇā, ascended into outer space. Yudhiṣṭhira kept his instruction in his heart and so was able to get rid of all lamentations.

PURPORT

Śrī Nāradajī is an eternal spaceman, having been endowed with a spiritual body by the grace of the Lord. He can travel in the outer spaces of both the material and spiritual worlds without restriction and can approach any planet in unlimited space within no time. We have already discussed his previous life as the son of a maidservant. Because of his association with pure devotees, he was elevated to the position of an eternal spaceman and thus had freedom of movement. One should therefore try to follow in the footsteps of Nārada Muni and not make a futile effort to reach other planets by mechanical means. Mahārāja Yudhiṣṭhira was a pious king, and therefore he could see Nārada Muni occasionally; anyone who desires to see Nārada Muni must first be pious and follow in the footsteps of Nārada Muni.

Thus end the Bhaktivedanta purports of the First Canto, Thirteenth Chapter, of Śrīmad-Bhāgavatam, *entitled "Dhṛtarāṣṭra Quits Home."*

CHAPTER FOURTEEN

The Disappearance of Lord Kṛṣṇa

TEXT 1

सूत उवाच
सम्प्रस्थिते द्वारकायां जिष्णौ बन्धुदिदृक्षया ।
ज्ञातुं च पुण्यश्लोकस्य कृष्णस्य च विचेष्टितम्॥ १ ॥

sūta uvāca
samprasthite dvārakāyāṁ
jiṣṇau bandhu-didṛkṣayā
jñātuṁ ca puṇya-ślokasya
kṛṣṇasya ca viceṣṭitam

sūtaḥ uvāca—Śrī Sūta Gosvāmī said; *samprasthite*—having gone to; *dvārakāyām*—the city of Dvārakā; *jiṣṇau*—Arjuna; *bandhu*—friends and relatives; *didṛkṣayā*—for meeting them; *jñātum*—to know; *ca*—also; *puṇya-ślokasya*—of one whose glories are sung by Vedic hymns; *kṛṣṇasya*—of Lord Kṛṣṇa; *ca*—and; *viceṣṭitam*—further programs of work.

TRANSLATION

Śrī Sūta Gosvāmī said: Arjuna went to Dvārakā to see Lord Śrī Kṛṣṇa and other friends and also to learn from the Lord of His next activities.

PURPORT

As stated in *Bhagavad-gītā*, the Lord descended on earth for the protection of the faithful and annihilation of the impious, so after the Battle of Kurukṣetra and establishment of Mahārāja Yudhiṣṭhira, the mission of the Lord was complete. The Pāṇḍavas, especially Śrī Arjuna, were eternal companions of the Lord, and therefore Arjuna went to Dvārakā to hear from the Lord of His next program of work.

TEXT 2

व्यतीताः कतिचिन्मासास्तदा नायात्ततोऽर्जुनः ।
ददर्श घोररूपाणि निमित्तानि कुरूद्वहः ॥ २ ॥

vyatītāḥ katicin māsās
tadā nāyāt tato 'rjunaḥ
dadarśa ghora-rūpāṇi
nimittāni kurūdvahaḥ

vyatītāḥ—after passing; *katicit*—a few; *māsāḥ*—months; *tadā*—at that time; *na āyāt*—did not return; *tataḥ*—from there; *arjunaḥ*—Arjuna; *dadarśa*—observed; *ghora*—fearful; *rūpāṇi*—appearances; *nimittāni*—various causes; *kuru-udvahaḥ*—Mahārāja Yudhiṣṭhira.

TRANSLATION

A few months passed, and Arjuna did not return. Mahārāja Yudhiṣṭhira then began to observe some inauspicious omens, which were fearful in themselves.

PURPORT

Lord Śrī Kṛṣṇa the Supreme Personality of Godhead is *ad infinitum*, more powerful than the most powerful sun of our experience. Millions and billions of suns are created by Him and annihilated by Him within His one breathing period. In the material world the sun is considered to be the source of all productivity and material energy, and only due to the sun can we have the necessities of life. Therefore, during the personal presence of the Lord on the earth, all paraphernalia for our peace and prosperity, especially religion and knowledge, were in full display because of the Lord's presence, just as there is a full flood of light in the presence of the glowing sun. Mahārāja Yudhiṣṭhira observed some discrepancies in his kingdom, and therefore he became very anxious about Arjuna, who was long absent, and there was also no news about

Dvārakā's well-being. He suspected the disappearance of Lord Kṛṣṇa, otherwise there would have been no possibility of fearful omens.

TEXT 3

कालस्य च गतिं रौद्रां विपर्यस्तर्तुधर्मिणः ।
पापीयसीं नृणां वार्तां क्रोधलोभानृतात्मनाम् ॥ ३ ॥

kālasya ca gatiṁ raudrāṁ
viparyastartu-dharmiṇaḥ
pāpīyasīṁ nṛṇāṁ vārtāṁ
krodha-lobhānṛtātmanām

kālasya—of eternal time; *ca*—also; *gatim*—direction; *raudrām*—fearful; *viparyasta*—reversed; *ṛtu*—seasonal; *dharmiṇaḥ*—regularities; *pāpīyasīm*—sinful; *nṛṇām*—of the human being; *vārtām*—means of livelihood; *krodha*—anger; *lobha*—greed; *anṛta*—falsehood; *ātmanām*—of the people.

TRANSLATION

He saw that the direction of eternal time had changed, and this was very fearful. There were disruptions in the seasonal regularities. The people in general had become very greedy, angry and deceitful. And he saw that they were adopting foul means of livelihood.

PURPORT

When civilization is disconnected from the loving relation of the Supreme Personality of Godhead, symptoms like changes of seasonal regulations, foul means of livelihood, greed, anger and fraudulence become rampant. The change of seasonal regulations refers to one season's atmosphere becoming manifest in another season—for example the rainy season's being transferred to autumn, or the fructification of fruits and flowers from one season in another season. A godless man is invariably greedy, angry and fraudulent. Such a man can earn his livelihood by any means, black or white. During the reign of Mahārāja Yudhiṣṭhira, all the above symptoms were conspicuous by their absence.

But Mahārāja Yudhiṣṭhira was astonished to experience even a slight change in the godly atmosphere of his kingdom, and at once he suspected the disappearance of the Lord. Foul means of livelihood implies deviation from one's occupational duty. There are prescribed duties for everyone, such as the *brāhmaṇa, kṣatriya, vaiśya* and *śūdra,* but anyone who deviates from his prescribed duty and declares another's duty to be his own is following a foul and improper duty. A man becomes too greedy for wealth and power when he has no higher objective in life and when he thinks that this earthly life of a few years is all in all. Ignorance is the cause for all these anomalies in human society, and to remove this ignorance, especially in this age of degradation, the powerful sun is there to distribute light in the shape of *Śrīmad-Bhāgavatam.*

TEXT 4

जिह्मप्रायं व्यवहृतं शाठ्यमिश्रं च सौहृदम् ।
पितृमातृसुहृद्भ्रातृदम्पतीनां च कल्कनम् ॥ ४ ॥

jihma-prāyaṁ vyavahṛtaṁ
śāṭhya-miśraṁ ca sauhṛdam
pitṛ-mātṛ-suhṛd-bhrātṛ-
dam-patīnāṁ ca kalkanam

jihma-prāyam—cheating; *vyavahṛtam*—in all ordinary transactions; *śāṭhya*—duplicity; *miśram*—adulterated in; *ca*—and; *sauhṛdam*—regarding friendly well-wishers; *pitṛ*—father; *mātṛ*—regarding the mother; *suhṛt*—well-wishers; *bhrātṛ*—one's own brother; *dam-patīnām*—regarding husband and wife; *ca*—also; *kalkanam*—mutual quarrel.

TRANSLATION

All ordinary transactions and dealings became polluted with cheating, even between friends. And in familial affairs, there was always misunderstanding between fathers, mothers and sons, between well-wishers, and between brothers. Even between husband and wife there was always strain and quarrel.

PURPORT

A conditioned living being is endowed with four principles of malpractice, namely errors, insanity, inability and cheating. These are signs of imperfection, and out of the four the propensity to cheat others is most prominent. And this cheating practice is there in the conditioned souls because the conditioned souls are primarily in the material world imbued with an unnatural desire to lord it over the material world. A living being in his pure state is not conditioned by the laws because in his pure state he is conscious that a living being is eternally subservient to the Supreme Being, and thus it is always good for him to remain subservient, instead of falsely trying to lord it over the property of the Supreme Lord. In the conditioned state the living being is not satisfied even if he actually becomes the lord of all that he surveys, which he never becomes, and therefore he becomes the victim of all kinds of cheating, even with his nearest and most intimate relations. In such an unsatisfactory state of affairs, there is no harmony, even between father and sons or between husband and wife. But all these contending difficulties can be mitigated by one process, and that is the devotional service of the Lord. The world of hypocrisy can be checked only by counteraction through devotional service to the Lord and nothing else. Mahārāja Yudhiṣṭhira, having observed the disparities, conjectured the disappearance of the Lord from the earth.

TEXT 5

निमित्तान्यत्यरिष्टानि काले त्वनुगते नृणाम् ।
लोभाद्यधर्मप्रकृतिं दृष्ट्वोवाचानुजं नृपः ॥५॥

nimittāny atyariṣṭāni
kāle tv anugate nṛṇām
lobhādy-adharma-prakṛtiṁ
dṛṣṭvovācānujaṁ nṛpaḥ

nimittāni—causes; *ati*—very serious; *ariṣṭāni*—bad omens; *kāle*—in course of time; *tu*—but; *anugate*—passing away; *nṛṇām*—of humanity at large; *lobha-ādi*—such as greed; *adharma*—irreligious; *prakṛtim*—habits; *dṛṣṭvā*—having observed; *uvāca*—said; *anujam*—younger brother; *nṛpaḥ*—the King.

TRANSLATION

In course of time it came to pass that people in general became accustomed to greed, anger, pride, etc. Mahārāja Yudhiṣṭhira, observing all these omens, spoke to his younger brother.

PURPORT

Such a pious king as Mahārāja Yudhiṣṭhira at once became perturbed when there were such inhuman symptoms as greed, anger, irreligiosity and hypocrisy rampant in society. It appears from this statement that all these symptoms of degraded society were unknown to the people of the time, and it was astonishing for them to have experienced them with the advent of the Kali-yuga, or the age of quarrel.

TEXT 6

युधिष्ठिर उवाच
सम्प्रेषितो द्वारकायां जिष्णुर्बन्धुदिदृक्षया ।
ज्ञातुं च पुण्यश्लोकस्य कृष्णस्य च विचेष्टितम् ॥ ६ ॥

yudhiṣṭhira uvāca
sampreṣito dvārakāyāṁ
jiṣṇur bandhu-didṛkṣayā
jñātuṁ ca puṇya-ślokasya
kṛṣṇasya ca viceṣṭitam

yudhiṣṭhiraḥ uvāca—Mahārāja Yudhiṣṭhira said; *sampreṣitaḥ*—has gone to; *dvārakāyām*—Dvārakā; *jiṣṇuḥ*—Arjuna; *bandhu*—friends; *didṛkṣayā*—for the sake of meeting; *jñātum*—to know; *ca*—also; *puṇya-ślokasya*—of the Personality of Godhead; *kṛṣṇasya*—of Lord Śrī Kṛṣṇa; *ca*—and; *viceṣṭitam*—program of work.

TRANSLATION

Mahārāja Yudhiṣṭhira said to his younger brother Bhīmasena, I sent Arjuna to Dvārakā to meet his friends and to learn from the Personality of Godhead Kṛṣṇa of His program of work.

TEXT 7

गताः सप्ताधुना मासा भीमसेन तवानुजः ।
नायाति कस्य वा हेतोर्नाहं वेदेदमञ्जसा ॥ ७ ॥

gatāḥ saptādhunā māsā
bhīmasena tavānujaḥ
nāyāti kasya vā hetor
nāhaṁ vededam añjasā

gatāḥ—has gone; *sapta*—seven; *adhunā*—to date; *māsāḥ*—months; *bhīmasena*—O Bhīmasena; *tava*—your; *anujaḥ*—younger brother; *na*—does not; *āyāti*—come back; *kasya*—for what; *vā*—or; *hetoḥ*—reason; *na*—not; *aham*—I; *veda*—know; *idam*—this; *añjasā*—factually.

TRANSLATION

Since he departed, seven months have passed, yet he has not returned. I do not know factually how things are going there.

TEXT 8

अपि देवर्षिणादिष्टः स कालोऽयमुपस्थितः ।
यदात्मनोऽङ्गमाक्रीडं भगवानुत्सिसृक्षति ॥ ८ ॥

api devarṣiṇādiṣṭaḥ
sa kālo 'yam upasthitaḥ
yadātmano 'ṅgam ākrīḍaṁ
bhagavān utsisṛkṣati

api—whether; *deva-ṛṣiṇā*—by the demigod-saint (Nārada); *ādiṣṭaḥ*—instructed; *saḥ*—that; *kālaḥ*—eternal time; *ayam*—this; *upasthitaḥ*—arrived; *yadā*—when; *ātmanaḥ*—of His own self; *aṅgam*—plenary portion; *ākrīḍam*—manifestation; *bhagavān*—the Personality of Godhead; *utsisṛkṣati*—is going to quit.

TRANSLATION

Is He going to quit His earthly pastimes, as Devarṣi Nārada indicated? Has that time already arrived?

PURPORT

As we have discussed many times, the Supreme Personality of Godhead Lord Śrī Kṛṣṇa has many plenary expansions, and each and every one of them, although equally powerful, executes different functions. In *Bhagavad-gītā* there are different statements by the Lord, and each of these statements is meant for different plenary portions or portions of the plenary portions. For example, Śrī Kṛṣṇa, the Lord, says in *Bhagavad-gītā:*

"Whenever and wherever there is a decline in religious practice, O descendant of Bharata, and a predominant rise of irreligion—at that time I descend Myself." (Bg. 4.7)

"To deliver the faithful, to annihilate the miscreants and also to reestablish the principles of occupational duty, I appear in every age." (Bg. 4.8)

"If I should cease to work, then all humanity would be misdirected. I would also be the cause of creating unwanted population, and I would thereby destroy the peace of all sentient beings." (Bg. 3.24)

"Whatever action a great man performs, common men will follow. And whatever standards he sets by exemplary acts, all the world pursues." (Bg. 3.21)

All the above statements by the Lord apply to different plenary portions of the Lord, namely His expansions such as Saṅkarṣaṇa, Vāsudeva, Pradyumna, Aniruddha and Nārāyaṇa. These are all He Himself in different transcendental expansions, and still the Lord as Śrī Kṛṣṇa functions in a different sphere of transcendental exchange with different grades of devotees. And yet Lord Kṛṣṇa as He is appears once every twenty-four hours of Brahmā's time (or after a lapse of 8,640,000,000 solar years) in each and every universe, and all His transcendental pastimes are displayed in each and every universe in a routine spool. But in that routine spool the functions of Lord Kṛṣṇa, Lord Vāsudeva, etc., are complex problems for the layman. There is no difference between the Lord's Self and the Lord's transcendental body. The expansions execute differential activities. When the Lord, however, appears in His person as Lord Śrī Kṛṣṇa, His other plenary portions also join in Him by His inconceivable potency called *yogamāyā,* and thus the Lord Kṛṣṇa of Vṛndāvana is different from the Lord Kṛṣṇa of Mathurā or the Lord Kṛṣṇa of Dvārakā. The *virāṭ-rūpa* of Lord Kṛṣṇa is also different from

Him, by His inconceivable potency. The *virāṭ-rūpa* exhibited on the Battlefield of Kurukṣetra is the material conception of His form. Therefore it should be understood that when Lord Kṛṣṇa was apparently killed by the bow and arrow of the hunter, the Lord left His so-called material body in the material world. The Lord is *kaivalya*, and for Him there is no difference between matter and spirit because everything is created from Him. Therefore His quitting one sort of body or accepting another body does not mean that He is like the ordinary living being. All such activities are simultaneously one and different by His inconceivable potency. When Mahārāja Yudhiṣṭhira was lamenting the possibility of His disappearance, it was just in pursuance of a custom of lamenting the disappearance of a great friend, but factually the Lord never quits His transcendental body, as is misconceived by less intelligent persons. Such less intelligent persons have been condemned by the Lord Himself in *Bhagavad-gītā*, and they are known as the *mūḍhas*. That the Lord left His body means that He left again His plenary portions in the respective *dhāmas* (transcendental abodes), as He left His *virāṭ-rūpa* in the material world.

TEXT 9

यस्मान्नः सम्पदो राज्यं दाराः प्राणाः कुलं प्रजाः ।
आसन् सपत्नविजयो लोकाश्च यदनुग्रहात् ॥ ९ ॥

yasmān naḥ sampado rājyaṁ
dārāḥ prāṇāḥ kulaṁ prajāḥ
āsan sapatna-vijayo
lokāś ca yad-anugrahāt

yasmāt—from whom; *naḥ*—our; *sampadaḥ*—opulence; *rājyam*—kingdom; *dārāḥ*—good wives; *prāṇāḥ*—existence of life; *kulam*—dynasty; *prajāḥ*—subjects; *āsan*—have become possible; *sapatna*—competitors; *vijayaḥ*—conquering; *lokāḥ*—future accommodation in higher planets; *ca*—and; *yat*—by whose; *anugrahāt*—by the mercy of.

TRANSLATION

From Him only, all our kingly opulence, good wives, lives, progeny, control over our subjects, victory over our enemies, and

future accommodations in higher planets have become possible. All this is due to His causeless mercy upon us.

PURPORT

Material prosperity consists of a good wife, good home, sufficient land, good children, aristocratic family relations, victory over competitors and, by pious work, attainment of accommodations in the higher celestial planets for better facilities of material amenities. These facilities are earned not only by one's hard manual labor or by unfair means, but by the mercy of the Supreme Lord. Prosperity earned by one's personal endeavor also depends on the mercy of the Lord. Personal labor must be there in addition to the Lord's benediction, but without the Lord's benediction no one is successful simply by personal labor. The modernized man of Kali-yuga believes in personal endeavor and denies the benediction of the Supreme Lord. Even a great *sannyāsī* of India delivered speeches in Chicago protesting the benedictions of the Supreme Lord. But as far as Vedic *śāstras* are concerned, as we find in the pages of *Śrīmad-Bhāgavatam*, the ultimate sanction for all success rests in the hands of the Supreme Lord. Mahārāja Yudhiṣṭhira admits this truth in his personal success, and it behooves one to follow in the footsteps of a great king and devotee of the Lord to make life a full success. If one could achieve success without the sanction of the Lord then no medical practitioner would fail to cure a patient. Despite the most advanced treatment of a suffering patient by the most up-to-date medical practitioner, there is death, and even in the most hopeless case, without medical treatment, a patient is cured astonishingly. Therefore the conclusion is that God's sanction is the immediate cause for all happenings, good or bad. Any successful man should feel grateful to the Lord for all he has achieved.

TEXT 10

पश्योत्पातान्नरव्याघ्र दिव्यान् भौमान् सदैहिकान् ।
दारुणान् शंसतोऽदूराद्भयं नो बुद्धिमोहनम् ॥१०॥

paśyotpātān nara-vyāghra
divyān bhaumān sadaihikān
dāruṇān śaṁsato 'dūrād
bhayaṁ no buddhi-mohanam

paśya—just see; *utpātān*—disturbances; *nara-vyāghra*—O man of tigerlike strength; *divyān*—happenings in the sky or by planetary influence; *bhaumān*—happenings on the earth; *sa-daihikān*—happenings of the body and the mind; *dāruṇān*—awfully dangerous; *śaṁsataḥ*—indicating; *adūrāt*—in the near future; *bhayam*—danger; *naḥ*—our; *buddhi*—intelligence; *mohanam*—deluding.

TRANSLATION

Just see, O man with a tiger's strength, how many miseries due to celestial influences, earthly reactions and bodily pains—all very dangerous in themselves—are forboding danger in the near future by deluding our intelligence.

PURPORT

Material advancement of civilization means advancement of the reactions of the threefold miseries due to celestial influence, earthly reactions and bodily or mental pains. By the celestial influence of the stars there are many calamities like excessive heat, cold, rains or no rains, and the after-effects are famine, disease and epidemic. The aggregate result is agony of the body and the mind. Man-made material science cannot do anything to counteract these threefold miseries. They are all punishments from the superior energy of *māyā* under the direction of the Supreme Lord. Therefore our constant touch with the Lord by devotional service can give us relief without our being disturbed in the discharge of our human duties. The *asuras*, however, who do not believe in the existence of God, make their own plans to counteract all these threefold miseries, and so they meet with failures every time. The *Bhagavad-gītā* (7.14) clearly states that the reaction of material energy is never to be conquered, because of the binding effects of the three modes. They can simply be overcome by one who surrenders fully in devotion under the lotus feet of the Lord.

TEXT 11

ऊर्वक्षिबाहवो मह्यं स्फुरन्त्यङ्ग पुनः पुनः ।
वेपथुश्चापि हृदये आराद्दास्यन्ति विप्रियम् ॥११॥

ūrv-akṣi-bāhavo mahyaṁ
sphuranty aṅga punaḥ punaḥ
vepathuś cāpi hṛdaye
ārād dāsyanti vipriyam

ūru—thighs; *akṣi*—eyes; *bāhavaḥ*—the arms; *mahyam*—in my; *sphuranti*—quivering; *aṅga*—left side of the body; *punaḥ punaḥ*—again and again; *vepathuḥ*—palpitations; *ca*—also; *api*—certainly; *hṛdaye*—in the heart; *ārāt*—due to fear; *dāsyanti*—indicating; *vipriyam*—undesirables.

TRANSLATION

The left side of my body, my thighs, arms and eyes are all quivering again and again. I am having heart palpitations due to fear. All this indicates undesirable happenings.

PURPORT

Material existence is full of undesirables. Things we do not want are forced upon us by some superior energy, and we do not see that these undesirables are under the grip of the three modes of material nature. When a man's eyes, arms and thighs all quiver constantly, one must know that something is going to happen which is undesirable. These undesirables are compared to fire in a forest. No one goes into the forest to set fires, but fires automatically take place in the forest, creating inconceivable calamities for the living beings of the forest. Such a fire cannot be extinguished by any human efforts. The fire can be extinguished only by the mercy of the Lord, who sends clouds to pour water on the forest. Similarly, undesirable happenings in life cannot be checked by any number of plans. Such miseries can be removed only by the mercy of the Lord, who sends His bona fide representatives to enlighten human beings and thus save them from all calamities.

TEXT 12

शिवैषोद्यन्तमादित्यमभिरौत्यनलानना ।
मामङ्ग सारमेयोऽयमभिरेभत्यभीरुवत् ॥१२॥

śivaiṣodyantam ādityam
abhirauty analānanā
mām aṅga sārameyo 'yam
abhirebhaty abhīruvat

śivā—jackal; *eṣā*—this; *udyantam*—rising; *ādityam*—unto the sun; *abhi*—towards; *rauti*—crying; *anala*—fire; *ānanā*—face; *mām*—unto me; *aṅga*—O Bhīma; *sārameyaḥ*—dog; *ayam*—this; *abhirebhati*—barks towards; *abhīru-vat*—without fear.

TRANSLATION

Just see, O Bhīma, how the she-jackal cries at the rising sun and vomits fire, and how the dog barks at me fearlessly.

PURPORT

These are some bad omens indicating something undesirable in the near future.

TEXT 13

शस्ताः कुर्वन्ति मां सव्यं दक्षिणं पशवोऽपरे ।
वाहांश्च पुरुषव्याघ्र लक्षये रुदतो मम ॥१३॥

śastāḥ kurvanti māṁ savyaṁ
dakṣiṇaṁ paśavo 'pare
vāhāṁś ca puruṣa-vyāghra
lakṣaye rudato mama

śastāḥ—useful animals like the cow; *kurvanti*—are keeping; *mām*—me; *savyam*—on the left; *dakṣiṇam*—circumambulating; *paśavaḥ apare*—other lower animals like asses; *vāhān*—the horses (carriers); *ca*—also; *puruṣa-vyāghra*—O tiger among men; *lakṣaye*—I see; *rudataḥ*—weeping; *mama*—of mine.

TRANSLATION

O Bhīmasena, tiger amongst men, now useful animals like cows are passing me on my left side, and lower animals like the asses are circumambulating me. My horses appear to weep upon seeing me.

TEXT 14

मृत्युदूतः कपोतोऽयमुलूकः कम्पयन् मनः ।
प्रत्युलूकश्च कुह्वानैर्विश्वम् वैशून्यमिच्छतः ॥१४॥

mṛtyu-dūtaḥ kapoto 'yam
ulūkaḥ kampayan manaḥ
pratyulūkaś ca kuhvānair
viśvaṁ vai śūnyam icchataḥ

mṛtyu—death; *dūtaḥ*—messenger of; *kapotaḥ*—pigeon; *ayam*—this; *ulūkaḥ*—owl; *kampayan*—trembling; *manaḥ*—mind; *pratyulūkaḥ*—the rivals of owls (crows); *ca*—and; *kuhvānaiḥ*—shrieking scream; *viśvam*—the cosmos; *vai*—either; *śūnyam*—void; *icchataḥ*—wishing.

TRANSLATION

Just see! This pigeon is like a messenger of death. The shrieks of the owls and their rival crows make my heart tremble. It appears that they want to make a void of the whole universe.

TEXT 15

धूम्रा दिशः परिधयः कम्पते भूः सहाद्रिभिः ।
निर्घातश्च महांस्तात साकं च स्तनयित्नुभिः॥१५॥

dhūmrā diśaḥ paridhayaḥ
kampate bhūḥ sahādribhiḥ
nirghātaś ca mahāṁs tāta
sākaṁ ca stanayitnubhiḥ

dhūmrāḥ—smoky; *diśaḥ*—all directions; *paridhayaḥ*—encirclement; *kampate*—throbbing; *bhūḥ*—the earth; *saha adribhiḥ*—along with the hills and mountains; *nirghātaḥ*—bolt from the blue; *ca*—also; *mahān*—very great; *tāta*—O Bhīma; *sākam*—with; *ca*—also; *stanayitnubhiḥ*—thundering sound without any cloud.

TRANSLATION

Just see how the smoke encircles the sky. It appears that the earth and mountains are throbbing. Just hear the cloudless thunder and see the bolts from the blue.

TEXT 16

वायुर्वाति खरस्पर्शो रजसा विसृजंस्तमः ।
असृग् वर्षन्ति जलदा बीभत्समिव सर्वतः ॥१६॥

vāyur vāti khara-sparśo
rajasā visṛjaṁs tamaḥ
asṛg varṣanti jaladā
bībhatsam iva sarvataḥ

vāyuḥ—wind; *vāti*—blowing; *khara-sparśaḥ*—sharply; *rajasā*—by the dust; *visṛjan*—creating; *tamaḥ*—darkness; *asṛk*—blood; *varṣanti*—are raining; *jaladāḥ*—the clouds; *bībhatsam*—disastrous; *iva*—like; *sarvataḥ*—everywhere.

TRANSLATION

The wind blows violently, blasting dust everywhere and creating darkness. Clouds are raining everywhere with bloody disasters.

TEXT 17

सूर्यं हतप्रभं पश्य ग्रहमर्दं मिथो दिवि ।
ससंकुलैर्भूतगणैर्ज्वलिते इव रोदसी ॥१७॥

sūryaṁ hata-prabhaṁ paśya
graha-mardaṁ mitho divi
sasaṅkulair bhūta-gaṇair
jvalite iva rodasī

sūryam—the sun; *hata-prabham*—its rays declining; *paśya*—just see; *graha-mardam*—clashes of the stars; *mithaḥ*—among one another;

divi—in the sky; *sa-saṅkulaiḥ*—being mixed with; *bhūta-gaṇaiḥ*—by the living entities; *jvalite*—being ignited; *iva*—as if; *rodasī*—crying.

TRANSLATION

The rays of the sun are declining, and the stars appear to be fighting amongst themselves. Confused living entities appear to be ablaze and weeping.

TEXT 18

नद्यो नदाश्च क्षुभिताः सरांसि च मनांसि च ।
न ज्वलत्यग्निराज्येन कालोऽयं किं विधास्यति ॥१८॥

nadyo nadāś ca kṣubhitāḥ
sarāṁsi ca manāṁsi ca
na jvalaty agnir ājyena
kālo 'yaṁ kiṁ vidhāsyati

nadyaḥ—rivers; *nadāḥ ca*—and the tributaries; *kṣubhitāḥ*—all perturbed; *sarāṁsi*—reservoirs of water; *ca*—and; *manāṁsi*—the mind; *ca*—also; *na*—does not; *jvalati*—ignite; *agniḥ*—fire; *ājyena*—with the help of butter; *kālaḥ*—the time; *ayam*—extraordinary it is; *kim*—what; *vidhāsyati*—going to happen.

TRANSLATION

Rivers, tributaries, ponds, reservoirs and the mind are all perturbed. Butter no longer ignites fire. What is this extraordinary time? What is going to happen?

TEXT 19

न पिबन्ति स्तनं वत्सा न दुह्यन्ति च मातरः ।
रुदन्त्यश्रुमुखा गावो न हृष्यन्त्यृषभा व्रजे ॥१९॥

na pibanti stanaṁ vatsā
na duhyanti ca mātaraḥ
rudanty aśru-mukhā gāvo
na hṛṣyanty ṛṣabhā vraje

na—does not; *pibanti*—suck; *stanam*—breast; *vatsāḥ*—the calves; *na*—do not; *duhyanti*—allow milking; *ca*—also; *mātaraḥ*—the cows; *rudanti*—crying; *aśru-mukhāḥ*—with a tearful face; *gāvaḥ*—the cows; *na*—do not; *hṛṣyanti*—take pleasure; *ṛṣabhāḥ*—the bulls; *vraje*—in the pasturing ground.

TRANSLATION

The calves do not suck the teats of the cows, nor do the cows give milk. They are standing, crying, tears in their eyes, and the bulls take no pleasure in the pasturing grounds.

TEXT 20

दैवतानि रुदन्तीव स्विद्यन्ति ह्युच्चलन्ति च ।
इमे जनपदा ग्रामाः पुरोद्यानाकराश्रमाः ।
भ्रष्टश्रियो निरानन्दाः किमघं दर्शयन्ति नः ॥२०॥

daivatāni rudantīva
svidyanti hy uccalanti ca
ime jana-padā grāmāḥ
purodyānākarāśramāḥ
bhraṣṭa-śriyo nirānandāḥ
kim aghaṁ darśayanti naḥ

daivatāni—the Deities in the temples; *rudanti*—seem to be crying; *iva*—like that; *svidyanti*—perspiring; *hi*—certainly; *uccalanti*—as if going out; *ca*—also; *ime*—these; *jana-padāḥ*—cities; *grāmāḥ*—villages; *pura*—towns; *udyāna*—gardens; *ākara*—mines; *āśramāḥ*—hermitages, etc.; *bhraṣṭa*—devoid of; *śriyaḥ*—beauty; *nirānandāḥ*—bereft of all happiness; *kim*—what sort of; *agham*—calamities; *darśayanti*—shall manifest; *naḥ*—to us.

TRANSLATION

The Deities seem to be crying in the temple, lamenting and perspiring. They seem about to leave. All the cities, villages, towns, gardens, mines and hermitages are now devoid of beauty

and bereft of all happiness. I do not know what sort of calamities are now awaiting us.

TEXT 21

मन्य एतैर्महोत्पातैर्नूनं भगवतः पदैः ।
अनन्यपुरुषश्रीभिर्हीना भूर्हतसौभगा ॥२१॥

manya etair mahotpātair
nūnaṁ bhagavataḥ padaiḥ
ananya-puruṣa-śrībhir
hīnā bhūr hata-saubhagā

manye—I take it for granted; *etaiḥ*—by all these; *mahā*—great; *utpātaiḥ*—upsurges; *nūnam*—for want of; *bhagavataḥ*—of the Personality of Godhead; *padaiḥ*—the marks on the sole of the foot; *ananya*—extraordinary; *puruṣa*—of the Supreme Personality; *śrībhiḥ*—by the auspicious signs; *hīnā*—dispossessed; *bhūḥ*—the earth; *hata-saubhagā*—without the fortune.

TRANSLATION

I think that all these earthly disturbances indicate some greater loss to the good fortune of the world. The world was fortunate to have been marked with the footprints of the lotus feet of the Lord. These signs indicate that this will no longer be.

TEXT 22

इति चिन्तयतस्तस्य दृष्टारिष्टेन चेतसा ।
राज्ञः प्रत्यागमद् ब्रह्मन् यदुपुर्याः कपिध्वजः ॥२२॥

iti cintayatas tasya
dṛṣṭāriṣṭena cetasā
rājñaḥ pratyāgamad brahman
yadu-puryāḥ kapi-dhvajaḥ

iti—thus; *cintayataḥ*—while thinking to himself; *tasya*—he; *dṛṣṭā*—by observing; *ariṣṭena*—bad omens; *cetasā*—by the mind; *rājñaḥ*—the

King; *prati*—back; *āgamat*—came; *brahman*—O *brāhmaṇa; yadu-puryāḥ*—from the kingdom of the Yadus; *kapi-dhvajaḥ*—Arjuna.

TRANSLATION

O Brāhmaṇa Śaunaka, while Mahārāja Yudhiṣṭhira, observing the inauspicious signs on the earth at that time, was thus thinking to himself, Arjuna came back from the city of the Yadus [Dvārakā].

TEXT 23

तं पादयोर्निपतितमयथापूर्वमातुरम् ।
अधोवदनमब्बिन्दून् सृजन्तं नयनाब्जयोः ॥२३॥

taṁ pādayor nipatitam
ayathā-pūrvam āturam
adho-vadanam ab-bindūn
sṛjantaṁ nayanābjayoḥ

tam—him (Arjuna); *pādayoḥ*—at the feet; *nipatitam*—bowing down; *ayathā-pūrvam*—unprecedented; *āturam*—dejected; *adhaḥ-vadanam*—downward face; *ap-bindūn*—drops of water; *sṛjantam*—creating; *nayana-abjayoḥ*—from the lotuslike eyes.

TRANSLATION

When he bowed at his feet, the King saw that his dejection was unprecedented. His head was down, and tears glided from his lotus eyes.

TEXT 24

विलोक्योद्विग्नहृदयो विच्छायमनुजं नृपः ।
पृच्छति स्म सुहृन्मध्ये संस्मरन्नारदेरितम् ॥२४॥

vilokyodvigna-hṛdayo
vicchāyam anujaṁ nṛpaḥ

pṛcchati sma suhṛn madhye
saṁsmaran nāraderitam

vilokya—by seeing; *udvigna*—anxious; *hṛdayaḥ*—heart; *vicchāyam*—pale appearance; *anujam*—Arjuna; *nṛpaḥ*—the King; *pṛcchati sma*—asked; *suhṛt*—friends; *madhye*—amongst; *saṁsmaran*—remembering; *nārada*—Sage Nārada; *īritam*—indicated by.

TRANSLATION

Seeing Arjuna pale due to heartfelt anxieties, the King, remembering the indications of the sage Nārada, questioned him in the midst of friends.

TEXT 25

युधिष्ठिर उवाच
कच्चिदानर्तपुर्यां नः स्वजनाः सुखमासते ।
मधुभोजदशार्हार्हसात्वतान्धकवृष्णयः ॥२५॥

yudhiṣṭhira uvāca
kaccid ānarta-puryāṁ naḥ
sva-janāḥ sukham āsate
madhu-bhoja-daśārhārha-
sātvatāndhaka-vṛṣṇayaḥ

yudhiṣṭhiraḥ uvāca—Yudhiṣṭhira said; *kaccit*—whether; *ānarta-puryām*—of Dvārakā; *naḥ*—our; *sva-janāḥ*—relatives; *sukham*—happily; *āsate*—are passing their days; *madhu*—Madhu; *bhoja*—Bhoja; *daśārha*—Daśārha; *ārha*—Ārha; *sātvata*—Sātvata; *andhaka*—Andhaka; *vṛṣṇayaḥ*—of the family of Vṛṣṇi.

TRANSLATION

Mahārāja Yudhiṣṭhira said: My dear brother, please tell me whether our friends and relatives, such as Madhu, Bhoja, Daśārha, Ārha, Sātvata, Andhaka and the members of the Yadu family are all passing their days in happiness.

TEXT 26

शूरो मातामहः कच्चित्स्वस्त्यास्ते वाथ मारिषः ।
मातुलः सानुजः कच्चित्कुशल्यानकदुन्दुभिः ॥२६॥

śūro mātāmahaḥ kaccit
svasty āste vātha māriṣaḥ
mātulaḥ sānujaḥ kaccit
kuśaly ānakadundubhiḥ

śūraḥ—Śūrasena; *mātāmahaḥ*—maternal grandfather; *kaccit*—whether; *svasti*—all good; *āste*—passing his days; *vā*—or; *atha*—therefore; *māriṣaḥ*—respectful; *mātulaḥ*—maternal uncle; *sa-anu-jaḥ*—with his younger brothers; *kaccit*—whether; *kuśalī*—all well; *ānaka-dundubhiḥ*—Vasudeva.

TRANSLATION

Is my respectable grandfather Śūrasena in a happy mood? And are my maternal uncle Vasudeva and his younger brothers all doing well?

TEXT 27

सप्त स्वसारस्तत्पत्न्यो मातुलान्यः सहात्मजाः ।
आसते सस्नुषाः क्षेमं देवकीप्रमुखाः स्वयम् ॥२७॥

sapta sva-sāras tat-patnyo
mātulānyaḥ sahātmajāḥ
āsate sasnuṣāḥ kṣemaṁ
devakī-pramukhāḥ svayam

sapta—seven; *sva-sāraḥ*—own sisters; *tat-patnyaḥ*—his wives; *mātulānyaḥ*—maternal aunts; *saha*—along with; *ātma-jāḥ*—sons and grandsons; *āsate*—are all; *sasnuṣāḥ*—with their daughters-in-law; *kṣemam*—happiness; *devakī*—Devakī; *pramukhāḥ*—headed by; *svayam*—personally.

TRANSLATION

His seven wives, headed by Devakī, are all sisters. Are they and their sons and daughters-in-law all happy?

TEXTS 28–29

कच्चिद्राजाहुको जीवत्यसत्पुत्रोऽस्य चानुजः ।
हृदीकः ससुतोऽक्रूरो जयन्तगदसारणाः ॥२८॥
आसते कुशलं कच्चिद्ये च शत्रुजिदादयः ।
कच्चिदास्ते सुखं रामो भगवान् सात्वतां प्रभुः ॥२९॥

kaccid rājāhuko jīvaty
asat-putro 'sya cānujaḥ
hṛdīkaḥ sasuto 'krūro
jayanta-gada-sāraṇāḥ

āsate kuśalaṁ kaccid
ye ca śatrujid-ādayaḥ
kaccid āste sukhaṁ rāmo
bhagavān sātvatāṁ prabhuḥ

kaccit—whether; *rājā*—the King; *āhukaḥ*—another name of Ugrasena; *jīvati*—still living; *asat*—mischievous; *putraḥ*—son; *asya*—his; *ca*—also; *anujaḥ*—younger brother; *hṛdīkaḥ*—Hṛdīka; *sa-sutaḥ*—along with son, Kṛtavarmā; *akrūraḥ*—Akrūra; *jayanta*—Jayanta; *gada*—Gada; *sāraṇāḥ*—Sāraṇa; *āsate*—are they all; *kuśalam*—in happiness; *kaccit*—whether; *ye*—they; *ca*—also; *śatrujit*—Śatrujit; *ādayaḥ*—headed by; *kaccit*—whether; *āste*—are they; *sukham*—all right; *rāmaḥ*—Balarāma; *bhagavān*—the Personality of Godhead; *sātvatām*—of the devotees; *prabhuḥ*—protector.

TRANSLATION

Are Ugrasena, whose son was the mischievous Kaṁsa, and his younger brother still living? Is Ugrasena happy? Are Hṛdika and his son Kṛtavarmā happy? Are Akrūra, Jayanta, Gada, Sāraṇa

and Śatrujit all happy? How is Balarāma, the Personality of Godhead and the protector of devotees?

PURPORT

Hastināpura, the capital of the Pāṇḍavas, was situated somewhere near present New Delhi, and the kingdom of Ugrasena was situated in Mathurā. While returning to Delhi from Dvārakā, Arjuna must have visited the city of Mathurā, and therefore the inquiry about the King of Mathurā is valid. Amongst various names of the relatives, the name of Rāma or Balarāma, eldest brother of Lord Kṛṣṇa, is added with the words "the Personality of Godhead" because Lord Balarāma is the immediate expansion of *viṣṇu-tattva* as *prakāśa-vigraha* of Lord Kṛṣṇa. The Supreme Lord, although one without a second, expands Himself as many other living beings. The *viṣṇu-tattva* living beings are expansions of the Supreme Lord, and all of them are qualitatively and quantitatively equal with the Lord. But expansions of the *jīva-śakti*, the category of the ordinary living beings, are not at all equal with the Lord. One who considers the *jīva-śakti* and the *viṣṇu-tattva* to be on an equal level is considered a condemned soul of the world. Śrī Rāma, or Balarāma, is the protector of the devotees of the Lord. Baladeva acts as the spiritual master of all devotees, and by His causeless mercy the fallen souls are delivered. Śrī Baladeva appeared as Śrī Nityānanda Prabhu during the advent of Lord Caitanya, and the great Lord Nityānanda Prabhu exhibited His causeless mercy by delivering a pair of extremely fallen souls, namely Jagāi and Mādhāi. Therefore it is particularly mentioned herein that Balarāma is the protector of the devotees of the Lord. By His divine grace only one can approach the Supreme Lord Śrī Kṛṣṇa, and thus Śrī Balarāma is the mercy incarnation of the Lord, manifested as the spiritual master, the savior of the pure devotees.

TEXT 30

प्रद्युम्नः सर्ववृष्णीनां सुखमास्ते महारथः ।
गम्भीररयोऽनिरुद्धो वर्धते भगवानुत ॥३०॥

pradyumnaḥ sarva-vṛṣṇīnāṁ
sukham āste mahā-rathaḥ

gambhīra-rayo 'niruddho
vardhate bhagavān uta

pradyumnaḥ—Pradyumna (a son of Lord Kṛṣṇa); *sarva*—all; *vṛṣṇīnām*—of the members of the Vṛṣṇi family; *sukham*—happiness; *āste*—are in; *mahā-rathaḥ*—the great general; *gambhīra*—deeply; *rayaḥ*—dexterity; *aniruddhaḥ*—Aniruddha (a grandson of Lord Kṛṣṇa); *vardhate*—flourishing; *bhagavān*—the Personality of Godhead; *uta*—must.

TRANSLATION

How is Pradyumna, the great general of the Vṛṣṇi family? Is He happy? And is Aniruddha, the plenary expansion of the Personality of Godhead, faring well?

PURPORT

Pradyumna and Aniruddha are also expansions of the Personality of Godhead, and thus They are also *viṣṇu-tattva*. At Dvārakā Lord Vāsudeva is engaged in His transcendental pastimes along with His plenary expansions, namely Saṅkarṣaṇa, Pradyumna and Aniruddha, and therefore each and every one of Them can be addressed as the Personality of Godhead, as it is mentioned in connection with the name Aniruddha.

TEXT 31

सुषेणश्चारुदेष्णश्च साम्बो जाम्बवतीसुतः ।
अन्ये च कार्ष्णिप्रवराः सपुत्रा ऋषभादयः ॥३१॥

suṣeṇaś cārudeṣṇaś ca
sāmbo jāmbavatī-sutaḥ
anye ca kārṣṇi-pravarāḥ
saputrā ṛṣabhādayaḥ

suṣeṇaḥ—Suṣeṇa; *cārudeṣṇaḥ*—Cārudeṣṇa; *ca*—and; *sāmbaḥ*—Sāmba; *jāmbavatī-sutaḥ*—the son of Jāmbavatī; *anye*—others; *ca*—also; *kārṣṇi*—the sons of Lord Kṛṣṇa; *pravarāḥ*—all chieftains; *saputrāḥ*—along with their sons; *ṛṣabha*—Ṛṣabha; *ādayaḥ*—etc.

TRANSLATION

Are all the chieftain sons of Lord Kṛṣṇa, such as Suṣeṇa, Cārudeṣṇa, Sāmba the son of Jāmbavatī, and Ṛṣabha, along with their sons, all doing well?

PURPORT

As already mentioned, Lord Kṛṣṇa married 16,108 wives, and each of them had ten sons. Therefore 16,108 x 10 = 161,080 sons. They all grew up, and each of them had as many sons as their father, and the whole aggregate was something near 1,610,800 family members of the Lord. The Lord is the father of all living beings, who are countless in number; therefore only a few of them are called to associate with the Lord in His transcendental pastimes as the Lord of Dvārakā on this earth. It is not astonishing that the Lord maintained a visible family consisting of so many members. It is better to refrain from comparing the Lord's position to ours, and it becomes a simple truth as soon as we understand at least a partial calculation of the Lord's transcendental position. King Yudhiṣṭhira, while inquiring about the Lord's sons and grandsons at Dvārakā, mentioned only the chieftains amongst them, for it was impossible for him to remember all the names of the Lord's family members.

TEXTS 32–33

तथैवानुचराः शौरेः श्रुतदेवोद्धवादयः ।
सुनन्दनन्दशीर्षण्या ये चान्ये सात्वतर्षभाः ॥३२॥
अपि स्वस्त्यासते सर्वे रामकृष्णभुजाश्रयाः ।
अपि स्मरन्ति कुशलमस्माकं बद्धसौहृदाः ॥३३॥

tathaivānucarāḥ śaureḥ
śrutadevoddhavādayaḥ
sunanda-nanda-śīrṣaṇyā
ye cānye sātvatarṣabhāḥ

api svasty āsate sarve
rāma-kṛṣṇa-bhujāśrayāḥ

api smaranti kuśalam
asmākaṁ baddha-sauhṛdāḥ

tathā eva—similarly; *anucarāḥ*—constant companions; *śaureḥ*—of Lord Śrī Kṛṣṇa such as; *śrutadeva*—Śrutadeva; *uddhava-ādayaḥ*—Uddhava and others; *sunanda*—Sunanda; *nanda*—Nanda; *śīrṣaṇyāḥ*—other leaders; *ye*—all of them; *ca*—and; *anye*—others; *sātvata*—liberated souls; *ṛṣabhāḥ*—the best men; *api*—if; *svasti*—doing well; *āsate*—are; *sarve*—all of them; *rāma*—Balarāma; *kṛṣṇa*—Lord Kṛṣṇa; *bhuja-āśrayāḥ*—under the protection of; *api*—if also; *smaranti*—do remember; *kuśalam*—welfare; *asmākam*—about ourselves; *baddha-sauhṛdāḥ*—bound by eternal friendship.

TRANSLATION

Also, Śrutadeva, Uddhava and others, Nanda, Sunanda and other leaders of liberated souls who are constant companions of the Lord are protected by Lord Balarāma and Kṛṣṇa. Are they all doing well in their respective functions? Do they, who are all eternally bound in friendship with us, remember our welfare?

PURPORT

The constant companions of Lord Kṛṣṇa, such as Uddhava, are all liberated souls, and they descended along with Lord Kṛṣṇa to this material world to fulfill the mission of the Lord. The Pāṇḍavas are also liberated souls who descended along with Lord Kṛṣṇa to serve Him in His transcendental pastimes on this earth. As stated in the *Bhagavad-gītā* (4.8), the Lord and His eternal associates, who are also liberated souls like the Lord, come down on this earth at certain intervals. The Lord remembers them all, but His associates, although liberated souls, forget due to their being *taṭasthā śakti*, or marginal potency of the Lord. That is the difference between the *viṣṇu-tattva* and *jīva-tattva.* The *jīva-tattvas* are infinitesimal potential particles of the Lord, and therefore they require the protection of the Lord at all times. And to the eternal servitors of the Lord, the Lord is pleased to give all protection at all times. The liberated souls never, therefore, think themselves as free as the Lord or as powerful as the Lord, but they always seek the protection of the Lord in all circumstances, both in the material world and in the spiritual world. This dependence of the liberated soul is constitutional, for the liberated souls are like sparks of a fire that are able to exhibit the glow of fire along with the fire and not independently. Independently the glow of the sparks is extinguished, although the quality of fire or the glowing is there. Thus those who give up the protection of the Lord and become so-called lords themselves, out of spiritual ignorance, come back again to this material world, even after prolonged *tapasya* of the severest type. That is the verdict of all Vedic literature.

TEXT 34

भगवानपि गोविन्दो ब्रह्मण्यो भक्तवत्सलः ।
कच्चित्पुरे सुधर्मायां सुखमास्ते सुहृद्वृतः ॥३४॥

bhagavān api govindo
brahmaṇyo bhakta-vatsalaḥ
kaccit pure sudharmāyāṁ
sukham āste suhṛd-vṛtaḥ

bhagavān—the Personality of Godhead, Kṛṣṇa; *api*—also; *govindaḥ*—one who enlivens the cows and the senses; *brahmaṇyaḥ*—devoted to the devotees or the *brāhmaṇas; bhakta-vatsalaḥ*—affectionate to the devotees; *kaccit*—whether; *pure*—in Dvārakā Purī; *sudharmāyām*—pious assembly; *sukham*—happiness; *āste*—does enjoy; *suhṛt-vṛtaḥ*—surrounded by friends.

TRANSLATION

Is Lord Kṛṣṇa, the Supreme Personality of Godhead, who gives pleasure to the cows, the senses and the brāhmaṇas, who is very affectionate towards His devotees, enjoying the pious assembly at Dvārakā Purī surrounded by friends?

PURPORT

Here in this particular verse the Lord is described as *bhagavān, govinda, brahmaṇya* and *bhakta-vatsala.* He is *bhagavān svayam*, or the original Supreme Personality of Godhead, full with all opulences, all power, all knowledge, all beauty, all fame and all renunciation. No one is equal to or greater than Him. He is Govinda because He is the pleasure of the cows and the senses. Those who have purified their senses by the devotional service of the Lord can render unto Him real service and thereby derive transcendental pleasure out of such purified senses. Only the impure conditioned living being cannot derive any pleasure from the senses, but being illusioned by false pleasures of the senses, he becomes servant of the senses. Therefore, we need His protection for our own interest. The Lord is the protector of cows and the brahminical culture. A society devoid of cow protection and brahminical culture is not under the direct protection of the Lord, just as the prisoners in the jails are not under the protection of the king but under the protection of a severe agent of the king. Without cow protection and cultivation of the brahminical qualities in human society, at least for a section of the members of society, no human civilization can prosper at any length. By brahminical culture, the development of the dormant qualities of goodness, namely truthfulness, equanimity, sense control, forbearance, simplicity, general knowledge, transcendental knowledge, and firm faith in the Vedic wisdom, one can become a *brāhmaṇa* and thus see the Lord as He is. And after surpassing the brahminical perfection, one has to become a devotee of the Lord so that His loving affection in the form of proprietor, master, friend, son and lover can be transcendentally achieved. The stage of a devotee, which attracts the transcendental affection of the Lord, does not develop unless one has developed the qualities of a *brāhmaṇa* as above mentioned. The Lord is inclined to a *brāhmaṇa* of quality and not of false prestige. Those who are less than a *brāhmaṇa* by qualification cannot establish any relation with the Lord, just as fire cannot be kindled from the raw earth unless there is wood, although there is a relation between wood and the earth. Since the Lord is all-perfect in Himself, there could not be any question of His welfare, and Mahārāja Yudhiṣṭhira refrained from asking this question. He simply inquired about His residential place, Dvārakā Purī, where pious men assemble. The Lord stays only where pious men assemble and takes pleasure in their glorifying the Supreme Truth. Mahārāja Yudhiṣṭhira was anxious to know about the pious men and their pious acts in the city of Dvārakā.

TEXTS 35–36

मङ्गलाय च लोकानां क्षेमाय च भवाय च ।
आस्ते यदुकुलाम्भोधावाद्योऽनन्तसखः पुमान् ॥३५॥
यद्बाहुदण्डगुप्तायां स्वपुर्यां यदवोऽर्चिताः ।
क्रीडन्ति परमानन्दं महापौरुषिका इव ॥३६॥

maṅgalāya ca lokānāṁ
kṣemāya ca bhavāya ca
āste yadu-kulāmbhodhāv
ādyo 'nanta-sakhaḥ pumān

yad bāhu-daṇḍa-guptāyāṁ
sva-puryāṁ yadavo 'rcitāḥ
krīḍanti paramānandaṁ
mahā-pauruṣikā iva

maṅgalāya—for all good; *ca*—also; *lokānām*—of all the planets; *kṣemāya*—for protection; *ca*—and; *bhavāya*—for elevation; *ca*—also; *āste*—is there; *yadu-kula-ambhodhau*—in the ocean of the Yadu dynasty; *ādyaḥ*—the original; *ananta-sakhaḥ*—in the company of Ananta (Balarāma); *pumān*—the supreme enjoyer; *yat*—whose; *bāhu-daṇḍa-guptāyām*—being protected by His arms; *sva-puryām*—in His own city; *yadavaḥ*—the members of the Yadu family; *arcitāḥ*—as they deserve; *krīḍanti*—are relishing; *parama-ānandam*—transcendental pleasure; *mahā-pauruṣikāḥ*—the residents of the spiritual sky; *iva*—like.

TRANSLATION

The original Personality of Godhead, the enjoyer, and Balarāma, the primeval Lord Ananta, are staying in the ocean of the Yadu dynasty for the welfare, protection and general progress of the entire universe. And the members of the Yadu dynasty, being protected by the arms of the Lord, are enjoying life like the residents of the spiritual sky.

PURPORT

As we have discussed many times, the Personality of Godhead Viṣṇu resides within each and every universe in two capacities, namely as the Garbhodakaśāyī Viṣṇu and the Kṣīrodakaśāyī Viṣṇu. The Kṣīrodakaśāyī Viṣṇu has His own planet on the northern top of the universe, and there is a great ocean of milk where the Lord resides on the bed of the Ananta incarnation of Baladeva. Thus Mahārāja Yudhiṣṭhira has compared the Yadu dynasty to the ocean of milk and Śrī Balarāma to the Ananta where Lord Kṛṣṇa resides. He has compared the citizens of Dvārakā to the liberated inhabitants of the Vaikuṇṭhalokas. Beyond the material sky, further than we can see with our eyes and beyond the sevenfold coverings of the universe, there is the Causal Ocean in which all the universes are floating like footballs, and beyond the Causal Ocean there is an unlimited span of spiritual sky generally known as the effulgence of Brahman. Within this effulgence there are innumerable spiritual planets, and they are known as the Vaikuṇṭha planets. Each and every Vaikuṇṭha planet is many, many times bigger than the biggest universe within the material world, and in each of them there are innumerable inhabitants who look exactly like Lord Viṣṇu. These inhabitants are known as the Mahā-pauruṣikas, or persons directly engaged in the service of the Lord. They are happy in those planets and are without any kind of misery, and they live perpetually in full youthfulness, enjoying life in full bliss and knowledge without fear of birth, death, old age or disease, and without the influence of *kāla*, eternal time. Mahārāja Yudhiṣṭhira has compared the inhabitants of Dvārakā to the Mahā-pauruṣikas of Vaikuṇṭhaloka because they are so happy with the Lord. In the *Bhagavad-gītā* there are many references to the Vaikuṇṭhalokas, and they are mentioned there as *mad-dhāma*, or the kingdom of the Lord.

TEXT 37

यत्पादशुश्रूषणमुख्यकर्मणा
सत्यादयो द्व्यष्टसहस्रयोषितः ।
निर्जित्य संख्ये त्रिदशांस्तदाशिषो
हरन्ति वज्रायुधवल्लभोचिताः ॥३७॥

yat-pāda-śuśrūṣaṇa-mukhya-karmaṇā
satyādayo dvy-aṣṭa-sahasra-yoṣitaḥ
nirjitya saṅkhye tri-daśāṁs tad-āśiṣo
haranti vajrāyudha-vallabhocitāḥ

yat—whose; *pāda*—feet; *śuśrūṣaṇa*—administration of comforts; *mukhya*—the most important; *karmaṇā*—by the acts of; *satya-ādayaḥ*—queens headed by Satyabhāmā; *dvi-aṣṭa*—twice eight; *sahasra*—thousand; *yoṣitaḥ*—the fair sex; *nirjitya*—by subduing; *saṅkhye*—in the battle; *tri-daśān*—of the denizens of heaven; *tat-āśiṣaḥ*—what is enjoyed by the demigods; *haranti*—do take away; *vajra-āyudha-vallabhā*—the wives of the personality who controls the thunderbolt; *ucitāḥ*—deserving.

TRANSLATION

Simply by administering comforts at the lotus feet of the Lord, which is the most important of all services, the queens at Dvārakā, headed by Satyabhāmā, induced the Lord to conquer the demigods. Thus the queens enjoy things which are prerogatives of the wives of the controller of thunderbolts.

PURPORT

Satyabhāmā: One of the principal queens of Lord Śrī Kṛṣṇa at Dvārakā. After killing Narakāsura, Lord Kṛṣṇa visited the palace of Narakāsura accompanied by Satyabhāmā. He went to Indraloka also with Satyabhāmā, and she was received by Śacīdevī, who introduced her to the mother of the demigods, Aditi. Aditi was very much pleased with Satyabhāmā, and she benedicted her with the blessings of permanent youth as long as Lord Kṛṣṇa remained on the earth. Aditi also took her with her to show her the special prerogatives of the demigods in the heavenly planets. When Satyabhāmā saw the *pārijāta* flower, she desired to have it in her palace at Dvārakā. After that, she came back to Dvārakā along with her husband and expressed her willingness to have the *pārijāta* flower at her palace. Satyabhāmā's palace was especially bedecked with valuable jewels, and even in the hottest season of summer the inside of the palace remained cool, as if air-conditioned. She decorated her palace with various flags, heralding the news of her great husband's presence there. Once, along with her husband, she met Draupadī, and she was anxious to be instructed by Draupadī in the ways and means of pleasing her husband. Draupadī was expert in this affair because she kept five husbands, the Pāṇḍavas, and all were very much pleased with her. On receipt of Draupadī's instructions, she was very much pleased and offered her good wishes and returned to Dvārakā. She was the daughter of Satrājit. After the departure of Lord Kṛṣṇa, when Arjuna visited Dvārakā, all the queens, including Satyabhāmā and Rukmiṇī, lamented for the Lord with great feeling. At the last stage of her life, she left for the forest to undergo severe penance.

Satyabhāmā instigated her husband to get the *pārijāta* flower from the heavenly planets, and the Lord got it even by force from the demigods, as a common husband secures things to please his wife. As already explained, the Lord had very little to do with so many wives to carry out their orders like an ordinary man. But because the queens accepted the high quality of devotional service, namely administering the Lord all comforts, the Lord played the part of a faithful and complete husband. No earthly creature can expect to have things from the heavenly kingdom, especially the *pārijāta* flowers, which are simply to be used by the demigods. But due to their becoming the Lord's faithful wives, all of them enjoyed the special prerogatives of the great wives of the denizens of heaven. In other words, since the Lord is the proprietor of everything within His creation, it is not very astonishing for the queens of Dvārakā to have any rare thing from any part of the universe.

TEXT 38

यद्बाहुदण्डाभ्युदयानुजीविनो
यदुप्रवीरा ह्यकुतोभया मुहुः ।
अधिक्रमन्त्यङ्घ्रिभिराहृतां बलात्
सभां सुधर्मां सुरसत्तमोचिताम् ॥३८॥

yad bāhu-daṇḍābhyudayānujīvino
yadu-pravīrā hy akutobhayā muhuḥ
adhikramanty aṅghribhir āhṛtāṁ balāt
sabhāṁ sudharmāṁ sura-sattamocitām

yat—whose; *bāhu-daṇḍa*—arms; *abhyudaya*—influenced by; *anujīvinaḥ*—always living; *yadu*—the members of the Yadu dynasty; *pravīrāḥ*—great heroes; *hi akutobhayāḥ*—fearless in every respect; *muhuḥ*—constantly; *adhikramanti*—traversing; *aṅghribhiḥ*—by foot; *āhṛtām*—brought about; *balāt*—by force; *sabhām*—assembly house; *sudharmām*—Sudharmā; *sura-sat-tama*—the best among the demigods; *ucitām*—deserving.

TRANSLATION

The great heroes of the Yadu dynasty, being protected by the arms of Lord Śrī Kṛṣṇa, always remain fearless in every respect. And therefore their feet trample over the Sudharmā assembly house, which the best demigods deserved but which was taken away from them.

PURPORT

Those who are directly servitors of the Lord are protected by the Lord from all fearfulness, and they also enjoy the best of things, even if they are forcibly accumulated. The Lord is equal in behavior to all living beings, but He is partial to His pure devotees, being very affectionate toward them. The city of Dvārakā was flourishing, being enriched with the best of things in the material world. The state assembly house is constructed according to the dignity of the particular state. In the heavenly planets, the state assembly house called Sudharmā was deserving of the dignity of the best of the demigods. Such an assembly house is never meant for any state on the globe because the human being on the earth is unable to construct it, however far a particular state may be materially advanced. But during the time of Lord Kṛṣṇa's presence on the earth, the members of the Yadu family forcibly brought the celestial assembly house to earth and placed it at Dvārakā. They were able to use such force because they were certain of the indulgence and protection of the Supreme Lord Kṛṣṇa. In other words, the Lord is provided with the best things in the universe by His pure devotees. Lord Kṛṣṇa was provided with all kinds of comforts and facilities available within the universe by the members of the Yadu dynasty, and in return such servitors of the Lord were protected and fearless.

A forgetful, conditioned soul is fearful. But a liberated soul is never fearful, just as a small child completely dependent on the mercy of his father is never fearful of anyone. Fearfulness is a sort of illusion for the living being when he is in slumber and forgetting his eternal relation with the Lord. Since the living being is never to die by his constitution, as stated in *Bhagavad-gītā* (2.20), then what is the cause of fearfulness? A person may be fearful of a tiger in a dream, but another man who is awake by his side sees no tiger there. The tiger is a myth for both of them, namely the person dreaming and the person awake, because actually there is no tiger; but the man forgetful of his awakened life is fearful, whereas the man who has not forgotten his position is not at all fearful. Thus the members of the Yadu dynasty were fully awake in their service to the Lord, and therefore there was no tiger for them to be afraid of at any time. Even if there were a real tiger, the Lord was there to protect them.

TEXT 39

कच्चित्तेऽनामयं तात भ्रष्टतेजा विभासि मे ।
अलब्धमानोऽवज्ञातः किं वा तात चिरोषितः ॥३९॥

kaccit te 'nāmayaṁ tāta
bhraṣṭa-tejā vibhāsi me
alabdha-māno 'vajñātaḥ
kiṁ vā tāta ciroṣitaḥ

kaccit—whether; *te*—your; *anāmayam*—health is all right; *tāta*—my dear brother; *bhraṣṭa*—bereft; *tejāḥ*—luster; *vibhāsi*—appear; *me*—to me; *alabdha-mānaḥ*—without respect; *avajñātaḥ*—neglected; *kim*—whether; *vā*—or; *tāta*—my dear brother; *ciroṣitaḥ*—because of long residence.

TRANSLATION

My brother Arjuna, please tell me whether your health is all right. You appear to have lost your bodily luster. Is this due to others disrespecting and neglecting you because of your long stay at Dvārakā?

PURPORT

From all angles of vision, the Mahārāja inquired from Arjuna about the welfare of Dvārakā, but he concluded at last that as long as Lord Śrī

Kṛṣṇa Himself was there, nothing inauspicious could happen. But at the same time, Arjuna appeared to be bereft of his bodily luster, and thus the King inquired of his personal welfare and asked so many vital questions.

TEXT 40

कच्चिन्नाभिहतोऽभावैः शब्दादिभिरमङ्गलैः ।
न दत्तमुक्तमर्थिभ्य आशया यत्प्रतिश्रुतम् ॥४०॥

kaccin nābhihato 'bhāvaiḥ
śabdādibhir amaṅgalaiḥ
na dattam uktam arthibhya
āśayā yat pratiśrutam

kaccit—whether; *na*—could not; *abhihataḥ*—addressed by; *abhāvaiḥ*—unfriendly; *śabda-ādibhiḥ*—by sounds; *amaṅgalaiḥ*—inauspicious; *na*—did not; *dattam*—give in charity; *uktam*—is said; *arthibhyaḥ*—unto one who asked; *āśayā*—with hope; *yat*—what; *pratiśrutam*—promised to be paid.

TRANSLATION

Has someone addressed you with unfriendly words or threatened you? Could you not give charity to one who asked, or could you not keep your promise to someone?

PURPORT

A *kṣatriya* or a rich man is sometimes visited by persons who are in need of money. When they are asked for a donation, it is the duty of the possessor of wealth to give in charity in consideration of the person, place and time. If a *kṣatriya* or a rich man fails to comply with this obligation, he must be very sorry for this discrepancy. Similarly, one should not fail to keep his promise to give in charity. These discrepancies are sometimes causes of despondency, and thus failing, a person becomes subjected to criticism, which might also be the cause of Arjuna's plight.

TEXT 41

कच्चित्त्वं ब्राह्मणं बालं गां वृद्धं रोगिणं स्त्रियम् ।
शरणोपसृतं सत्त्वं नात्याक्षीः शरणप्रदः ॥४१॥

kaccit tvaṁ brāhmaṇaṁ bālaṁ
gāṁ vṛddhaṁ rogiṇaṁ striyam
śaraṇopasṛtaṁ sattvaṁ
nātyākṣīḥ śaraṇa-pradaḥ

kaccit—whether; *tvam*—yourself; *brāhmaṇam*—the *brāhmaṇas; bālam*—the child; *gām*—the cow; *vṛddham*—old; *rogiṇam*—the diseased; *striyam*—the woman; *śaraṇa-upasṛtam*—having approached for protection; *sattvam*—any living being; *na*—whether; *atyākṣīḥ*—not given shelter; *śaraṇa-pradaḥ*—deserving protection.

TRANSLATION

You are always the protector of the deserving living beings, such as brāhmaṇas, children, cows, women and the diseased. Could you not give them protection when they approached you for shelter?

PURPORT

The *brāhmaṇas,* who are always engaged in researching knowledge for the society's welfare work, both materially and spiritually, deserve the protection of the king in all respects. Similarly, the children of the state, the cow, the diseased person, the woman and the old man specifically require the protection of the state or a *kṣatriya* king. If such living beings do not get protection by the *kṣatriya,* or the royal order, or by the state, it is certainly shameful for the *kṣatriya* or the state. If such things had actually happened to Arjuna, Mahārāja Yudhiṣṭhira was anxious to know about these discrepancies.

TEXT 42

कच्चित्त्वं नागमोऽगम्यां गम्यां वासत्कृतां स्त्रियम् ।
पराजितो वाथ भवान्नोत्तमैर्नासमैः पथि ॥४२॥

kaccit tvaṁ nāgamo 'gamyāṁ
gamyāṁ vāsat-kṛtāṁ striyam
parājito vātha bhavān
nottamair nāsamaiḥ pathi

kaccit—whether; *tvam*—yourself *na*—not; *agamaḥ*—did contact; *agamyām*—impeachable; *gamyām*—acceptable; *vā*—either; *asat-kṛtām*—improperly treated; *striyam*—a woman; *parājitaḥ*—defeated by; *vā*—either; *atha*—after all; *bhavān*—your good self; *na*—nor; *ut-tamaiḥ*—by superior power; *na*—not; *asamaiḥ*—by equals; *pathi*—on the road.

TRANSLATION

Have you contacted a woman of impeachable character, or have you not properly treated a deserving woman? Or have you been defeated on the way by someone who is inferior or equal to you?

PURPORT

It appears from this verse that during the time of the Pāṇḍavas free contact between man and woman was allowed in certain conditions only. The higher caste men, namely the *brāhmaṇas* and *kṣatriyas,* could accept a woman of the *vaiśya* or the *śūdra* community, but a man from the lower castes could not contact a woman of the higher caste. Even a *kṣatriya* could not contact a woman of the *brāhmaṇa* caste. The wife of a *brāhmaṇa* is considered one of the seven mothers (namely one's own mother, the wife of the spiritual master or teacher, the wife of a *brāhmaṇa,* the wife of a king, the cow, the nurse, and the earth). Such contact between man and woman was known as *uttama* and *adhama.* Contact of a *brāhmaṇa* with a *kṣatriya* woman is *uttama,* but the contact of a *kṣatriya* with a *brāhmaṇa* woman is *adhama* and therefore condemned. A woman approaching a man for contact should never be refused, but at the same time the discretion as above mentioned may also be considered. Bhīma was approached by Hiḍimbī from a community lower than the *śūdras,* and Yayāti refused to marry the daughter of Śukrācārya because of Śukrācārya's being a *brāhmaṇa.* Vyāsadeva, a *brāhmaṇa,* was called to beget Pāṇḍu and Dhṛtarāṣṭra. Satyavatī belonged to a family of fishermen, but Parāśara, a great *brāhmaṇa,* begot in her Vyāsadeva. So there are so many examples of contacts with woman, but in all cases the contacts were not abominable nor were the results of such contacts bad. Contact between man and woman is natural, but that also must be carried out under regulative principles so that social consecration may not be disturbed or unwanted worthless population be increased for the unrest of the world.

It is abominable for a *kṣatriya* to be defeated by one who is inferior in strength or equal in strength. If one is defeated at all, he should be defeated by some superior power. Arjuna was defeated by Bhīṣmadeva, and Lord Kṛṣṇa saved him from the danger. This was not an insult for Arjuna because Bhīṣmadeva was far superior to Arjuna in all ways, namely age, respect and strength. But Karṇa was equal to Arjuna, and therefore Arjuna was in crisis when fighting with Karṇa. It was felt by Arjuna, and therefore Karṇa was killed even by crooked means. Such are the engagements of the *kṣatriyas,* and Mahārāja Yudhiṣṭhira inquired from his brother whether anything undesirable happened on the way home from Dvārakā.

TEXT 43

अपि स्वित्पर्यभुङ्क्थास्त्वं सम्भोज्यान् वृद्धबालकान् ।
जुगुप्सितं कर्म किंचित्कृतवान्न यदक्षमम् ॥४३॥

api svit parya-bhuṅkthās tvaṁ
sambhojyān vṛddha-bālakān
jugupsitaṁ karma kiñcit
kṛtavān na yad akṣamam

api svit—if it were so that; *parya*—by leaving aside; *bhuṅkthāḥ*—have dined; *tvam*—yourself; *sambhojyān*—deserving to dine together; *vṛddha*—the old men; *bālakān*—boys; *jugupsitam*—abominable; *karma*—action; *kiñcit*—something; *kṛtavān*—you must have done; *na*—not; *yat*—that which; *akṣamam*—unpardonable.

TRANSLATION

Have you not taken care of old men and boys who deserve to dine with you? Have you left them and taken your meals alone?

Have you committed some unpardonable mistake which is considered to be abominable?

PURPORT

It is the duty of a householder to feed first of all the children, the old members of the family, the *brāhmaṇas* and the invalids. Besides that, an ideal householder is required to call for any unknown hungry man to come and dine before he himself goes to take his meals. He is required to call for such a hungry man thrice on the road. The neglect of this prescribed duty of a householder, especially in the matter of the old men and children, is unpardonable.

TEXT 44

कच्चित् प्रेष्ठतमेनाथ हृदयेनात्मबन्धुना ।
शून्योऽस्मि रहितो नित्यं मन्यसे तेऽन्यथा न रुक् ॥४४॥

kaccit preṣṭhatamenātha
hṛdayenātma-bandhunā
śūnyo 'smi rahito nityaṁ
manyase te 'nyathā na ruk

kaccit—whether; *preṣṭha-tamena*—unto the most dear one; *atha*—my brother Arjuna; *hṛdayena*—most intimate; *ātma-bandhunā*—own friend Lord Kṛṣṇa; *śūnyaḥ*—void; *asmi*—I am; *rahitaḥ*—having lost; *nityam*—for all time; *manyase*—you think; *te*—your; *anyathā*—otherwise; *na*—never; *ruk*—mental distress.

TRANSLATION

Or is it that you are feeling empty for all time because you might have lost your most intimate friend, Lord Kṛṣṇa? O my brother Arjuna, I can think of no other reason for your becoming so dejected.

PURPORT

All the inquisitiveness of Mahārāja Yudhiṣṭhira about the world situation was already conjectured by Mahārāja Yudhiṣṭhira on the basis of

Lord Kṛṣṇa's disappearance from the vision of the world and this was now disclosed by him because of the acute dejection of Arjuna, which could not have been possible otherwise. So even though he was doubtful about it, he was obliged to inquire frankly from Arjuna on the basis of Śrī Nārada's indication.

Thus end the Bhaktivedanta purports of the First Canto, Fourteenth Chapter, of the Śrīmad-Bhāgavatam, *entitled "The Disappearance of Lord Kṛṣṇa."*

CHAPTER FIFTEEN

The Pāṇḍavas Retire Timely

TEXT 1

सूत उवाच

एवं कृष्णसखः कृष्णो भ्रात्रा राज्ञाविकल्पितः ।
नानाशङ्कास्पदं रूपं कृष्णविश्लेषकर्शितः ॥ १ ॥

sūta uvāca
evaṁ kṛṣṇa-sakhaḥ kṛṣṇo
bhrātrā rājñā vikalpitaḥ
nānā-śaṅkāspadaṁ rūpaṁ
kṛṣṇa-viśleṣa-karśitaḥ

sūtaḥ uvāca—Sūta Gosvāmī said; *evam*—thus; *kṛṣṇa-sakhaḥ*—the celebrated friend of Kṛṣṇa; *kṛṣṇaḥ*—Arjuna; *bhrātrā*—by his elder brother; *rājñā*—King Yudhiṣṭhira; *vikalpitaḥ*—speculated; *nānā*—various; *śaṅka-āspadam*—based on many doubts; *rūpam*—forms; *kṛṣṇa*—Lord Śrī Kṛṣṇa; *viśleṣa*—feelings of separation; *karśitaḥ*—became greatly bereaved.

TRANSLATION

Sūta Gosvāmī said: Arjuna, the celebrated friend of Lord Kṛṣṇa, was griefstricken because of his strong feeling of separation from Kṛṣṇa, over and above all Mahārāja Yudhiṣṭhira's speculative inquiries.

PURPORT

Being too much aggrieved, Arjuna practically became choked up, and therefore it was not possible for him to reply properly to the various speculative inquiries of Mahārāja Yudhiṣṭhira.

TEXT 2

शोकेन शुष्यद्वदनहृत्सरोजो हतप्रभः ।
विभुं तमेवानुस्मरन्नाशक्नोत्प्रतिभाषितुम् ॥ २ ॥

śokena śuṣyad-vadana-
hṛt-sarojo hata-prabhaḥ
vibhuṁ tam evānusmaran
nāśaknot pratibhāṣitum

śokena—due to bereavement; *śuṣyat-vadana*—drying up of the mouth; *hṛt-sarojaḥ*—lotuslike heart; *hata*—lost; *prabhaḥ*—bodily luster; *vibhum*—the Supreme; *tam*—unto Lord Kṛṣṇa; *eva*—certainly; *anusmaran*—thinking within; *na*—could not; *aśaknot*—be able; *pratibhāṣitum*—properly replying.

TRANSLATION

Due to grief, Arjuna's mouth and lotuslike heart had dried up. Therefore his body lost all luster. Now, remembering the Supreme Lord, he could hardly utter a word in reply.

TEXT 3

कृच्छ्रेण संस्तभ्य शुचः पाणिनामृज्य नेत्रयोः ।
परोक्षेण समुन्नद्धप्रणयौत्कण्ठ्यकातरः ॥ ३ ॥

kṛcchreṇa saṁstabhya śucaḥ
pāṇināmṛjya netrayoḥ
parokṣeṇa samunnaddha-
praṇayautkaṇṭhya-kātaraḥ

kṛcchreṇa—with great difficulty; *saṁstabhya*—by checking the force; *śucaḥ*—of bereavement; *pāṇinā*—with his hands; *āmṛjya*—smearing; *netrayoḥ*—the eyes; *parokṣeṇa*—due to being out of sight; *samunnaddha*—increasingly; *praṇaya-autkaṇṭhya*—eagerly thinking of the affection; *kātaraḥ*—distressed.

TRANSLATION

With great difficulty he checked the tears of grief that smeared his eyes. He was very distressed because Lord Kṛṣṇa was out of his sight, and he increasingly felt affection for Him.

TEXT 4

सख्यं मैत्रीं सौहृदं च सारथ्यादिषु संस्मरन् ।
नृपमग्रजमित्याह बाष्पगद्गदया गिरा ॥ ४ ॥

sakhyaṁ maitrīṁ sauhṛdaṁ ca
sārathyādiṣu saṁsmaran
nṛpam agrajam ity āha
bāṣpa-gadgadayā girā

sakhyam—well-wishing; *maitrīm*—benediction; *sauhṛdam*—intimately related; *ca*—also; *sārathya-ādiṣu*—in becoming the chariot driver; *saṁsmaran*—remembering all these; *nṛpam*—unto the King; *agrajam*—the eldest brother; *iti*—thus; *āha*—said; *bāṣpa*—heavily breathing; *gadgadayā*—overwhelmingly; *girā*—by speeches.

TRANSLATION

Remembering Lord Kṛṣṇa and His well wishes, benefactions, intimate familial relations and His chariot driving, Arjuna, overwhelmed and breathing very heavily, began to speak.

PURPORT

The Supreme Living Being is perfect in all relations with His pure devotee. Śrī Arjuna is one of the typical pure devotees of the Lord reciprocating in the fraternal relationship, and the Lord's dealings with Arjuna are displays of friendship of the highest perfect order. He was not only a well-wisher of Arjuna but actually a benefactor, and to make it still more perfect the Lord tied him into a family relationship by arranging Subhadrā's marriage with him. And above all, the Lord agreed to become a chariot driver of Arjuna in order to protect His friend from warfare risks, and the Lord became actually happy when He established the Pāṇḍavas to rule over the world. Arjuna remembered all these one after another, and thus he became overwhelmed with such thoughts.

TEXT 5

अर्जुन उवाच
वञ्चितोऽहं महाराज हरिणा बन्धुरूपिणा ।
येन मेऽपहृतं तेजो देवविस्मापनं महत् ॥ ५ ॥

arjuna uvāca
vañcito 'haṁ mahā-rāja
hariṇā bandhu-rūpiṇā
yena me 'pahṛtaṁ tejo
deva-vismāpanaṁ mahat

arjunaḥ uvāca—Arjuna said; *vañcitaḥ*—left by Him; *aham*—myself; *mahā-rāja*—O King; *hariṇā*—by the Personality of Godhead; *bandhu-rūpiṇā*—as if an intimate friend; *yena*—by whom; *me*—my; *apahṛtam*—I have been bereft; *tejaḥ*—power; *deva*—the demigods; *vismāpanam*—astonishing; *mahat*—astounding.

TRANSLATION

Arjuna said: O King! The Supreme Personality of Godhead Hari, who treated me exactly like an intimate friend, has left me alone. Thus my astounding power, which astonished even the demigods, is no longer with me.

PURPORT

In the *Bhagavad-gītā* (10.41) the Lord says, "Anyone specifically powerful and opulent in wealth, strength, beauty, knowledge and all that is materially desirable is to be considered but a product of an insignificant portion of the complete whole of My energy." No one, therefore, can be independently powerful in any measure without being endowed by the Lord. When the Lord descends on the earth along with His eternal ever-liberated associates, He not only displays the divine energy possessed by Himself, but also empowers His associate devotees with the required energy to execute His mission of incarnation. It is also stated in the *Bhagavad-gītā* (4.5) that the Lord and His eternal associates descend on the earth many times, but the Lord remembers all the different roles of incarnations, whereas the associates, by His supreme will, forget them. Similarly, the Lord takes away with Him all His associates when He disappears from the earth. The power and energy which were bestowed upon Arjuna were required for fulfillment of the mission of the Lord, but when His mission was fulfilled, the emergency powers were withdrawn from Arjuna because the astounding powers of Arjuna, which were astonishing even to the denizens of heaven, were no longer required, and they were not meant for going back home, back to Godhead. If endowment of powers and withdrawal of powers by the Lord are possible even for a great devotee like Arjuna, or even the demigods in heaven, then what to speak of the ordinary living beings who are but figs compared to such great souls. The lesson is, therefore, that no one should be puffed up for his powers borrowed from the Lord. The sane man should rather feel obliged to the Lord for such benefactions and must utilize such power for the service of the Lord. Such power can be withdrawn at any time by the Lord, so the best use of such power and opulence is to engage them in the service of the Lord.

TEXT 6

यस्य क्षणवियोगेन लोको ह्यप्रियदर्शनः ।
उक्थेन रहितो ह्येष मृतकः प्रोच्यते यथा ॥ ६ ॥

yasya kṣaṇa-viyogena
loko hy apriya-darśanaḥ
ukthena rahito hy eṣa
mṛtakaḥ procyate yathā

yasya—whose; *kṣaṇa*—a moment; *viyogena*—by separation; *lokaḥ*—all the universes; *hi*—certainly; *apriya-darśanaḥ*—everything appears unfavorable; *ukthena*—by life; *rahitaḥ*—being devoid of; *hi*—certainly; *eṣaḥ*—all these bodies; *mṛtakaḥ*—dead bodies; *procyate*—are designated; *yathā*—as it were.

TRANSLATION

I have just lost Him whose separation for a moment would render all the universes unfavorable and void, like bodies without life.

PURPORT

Factually for a living being there is no one dearer than the Lord. The Lord expands Himself by innumerable parts and parcels as *svāṁśa* and *vibhinnāṁśa*. Paramātmā is the *svāṁśa* part of the Lord, whereas the *vibhinnāṁśa* parts are the living beings. As the living being is the important factor in the material body, for without the living being the material body has no value, similarly without Paramātmā the living being has no *status quo*. Similarly, Brahman or Paramātmā has no *locus standi* without the Supreme Lord Śrī Kṛṣṇa. This is thoroughly explained in the *Bhagavad-gītā*. They are all interlinked with one another, or interdependent factors; thus in the ultimate issue the Lord is the *summum bonum* and therefore the vital principle of everything.

TEXT 7

यत्संश्रयाद् द्रुपदगेहमुपागतानां
राज्ञां स्वयंवरमुखे स्मरदुर्मदानाम् ।
तेजो हृतं खलु मयाभिहतश्च मत्स्यः
सज्जीकृतेन धनुषाधिगता च कृष्णा ॥ ७॥

yat-saṁśrayād drupada-geham upāgatānāṁ
rājñāṁ svayaṁvara-mukhe smara-durmadānām
tejo hṛtaṁ khalu mayābhihataś ca matsyaḥ
sajjīkṛtena dhanuṣādhigatā ca kṛṣṇā

yat—by whose merciful; *saṁśrayāt*—by strength; *drupada-geham*—in the palace of King Drupada; *upāgatānām*—all those assembled; *rājñām*—of the princes; *svayaṁvara-mukhe*—on the occasion of the selection of the bridegroom; *smara-durmadānām*—all lusty in thought; *tejaḥ*—power; *hṛtam*—vanquished; *khalu*—as it were; *mayā*—by me; *abhihataḥ*—pierced; *ca*—also; *matsyaḥ*—the fish target; *sajjī-kṛtena*—

by equipping the bow; *dhanuṣā*—by that bow also; *adhigatā*—gained; *ca*—also; *kṛṣṇā*—Draupadī.

TRANSLATION

Only by His merciful strength was I able to vanquish all the lusty princes assembled at the palace of King Drupada for the selection of the bridegroom. With my bow and arrow I could pierce the fish target and thereby gain the hand of Draupadī.

PURPORT

Draupadī was the most beautiful daughter of King Drupada, and when she was a young girl almost all the princes desired her hand. But Drupada Mahārāja decided to hand over his daughter to Arjuna only and therefore contrived a peculiar way. There was a fish hanging on the inner roof of the house under the protection of a wheel. The condition was that out of the princely order, one must be able to pierce the fish's eyes through the wheel of protection, and no one would be allowed to look up at the target. On the ground there was a waterpot in which the target and wheel were reflected, and one had to fix his aim towards the target by looking at the trembling water in the pot. Mahārāja Drupada well knew that only Arjuna or alternately Karṇa could successfully carry out the plan. But still he wanted to hand his daughter to Arjuna. And in the assembly of the princely order, when Dhṛṣṭadyumna, the brother of Draupadī, introduced all the princes to his grown-up sister, Karṇa was also present in the game. But Draupadī tactfully avoided Karṇa as the rival of Arjuna, and she expressed her desires through her brother Dhṛṣṭadyumna that she was unable to accept anyone who was less than a *kṣatriya.* The *vaiśyas* and the *śūdras* are less important than the *kṣatriyas.* Karṇa was known as the son of a carpenter, a *śūdra.* So Draupadī avoided Karṇa by this plea. When Arjuna, in the dress of a poor *brāhmaṇa,* pierced the difficult target, everyone was astonished, and all of them, especially Karṇa, offered a stiff fight to Arjuna, but as usual by the grace of Lord Kṛṣṇa he was able to emerge very successful in the princely fight and thus gain the valuable hand of Kṛṣṇā, or Draupadī. Arjuna was lamentingly remembering the incident in the absence of the Lord, by whose strength only he was so powerful.

TEXT 8

यत्संनिधावहमु खाण्डवमग्नयेऽदा-
मिन्द्रं च सामरगणं तरसा विजित्य ।
लब्धा सभा मयकृताद्भुतशिल्पमाया
दिग्भ्योऽहरन्नृपतयो बलिमध्वरे ते ॥ ८ ॥

yat-sannidhāv aham u khāṇḍavam agnaye 'dām
indraṁ ca sāmara-gaṇaṁ tarasā vijitya
labdhā sabhā maya-kṛtādbhuta-śilpa-māyā
digbhyo 'haran nṛpatayo balim adhvare te

yat—whose; *sannidhau*—being nearby; *aham*—myself; *u*—note of astonishment; *khāṇḍavam*—the protected forest of Indra, King of heaven; *agnaye*—unto the fire-god; *adām*—delivered; *indram*—Indra; *ca*—also; *sa*—along with; *amara-gaṇam*—the demigods; *tarasā*—with all dexterity; *vijitya*—having conquered; *labdhā*—having obtained; *sabhā*—assembly house; *maya-kṛtā*—built by Maya; *adbhuta*—very wonderful; *śilpa*—art and workmanship; *māyā*—potency; *digbhyaḥ*—from all directions; *aharan*—collected; *nṛpatayaḥ*—all princes; *balim*—presentations; *adhvare*—brought; *te*—your.

TRANSLATION

Because He was near me, it was possible for me to conquer with great dexterity the powerful King of heaven, Indradeva, along with his demigod associates and thus enable the fire-god to devastate the Khāṇḍava Forest. And only by His grace was the demon named Maya saved from the blazing Khāṇḍava Forest, and thus we could build our assembly house of wonderful architectural workmanship, where all the princes assembled during the performance of Rājasūya-yajña and paid you tributes.

PURPORT

The demon Maya Dānava was an inhabitant of the forest Khāṇḍava, and when the Khāṇḍava forest was set on fire, he asked protection from Arjuna. Arjuna saved his life, and as a result of this the demon felt obliged. He reciprocated by building a wonderful assembly house for the Pāṇḍavas, which attracted the extraordinary attention of all state princes. They felt the supernatural power of the Pāṇḍavas, and thus without grudge all of them submitted and paid tributes to the Emperor. The demons possess wonderful and supernatural powers to create material wonders. But they are always disturbing elements of the society. The modern demons are the harmful material scientists who create some material wonders for disturbance in the society. For example, the creation of nuclear weapons has caused some panic in human society. Maya was also a materialist like that, and he knew the art of creating such wonderful things. And yet Lord Kṛṣṇa wanted to kill him. When he was chased both by the fire and by the wheel of Lord Kṛṣṇa, he took shelter of such a devotee as Arjuna, who saved him from the wrath of the fire of Lord Śrī Kṛṣṇa. Devotees are therefore more merciful than the Lord, and in devotional service the mercy of a devotee is more valuable than the mercy of the Lord. Both the fire and the Lord ceased from chasing the demon as soon as both of them saw that the demon was given shelter by such a devotee as Arjuna. This demon, feeling obliged to Arjuna, wanted to do him some service to show his gratefulness, but Arjuna declined to accept anything from him in exchange. Lord Śrī Kṛṣṇa, however, being pleased with Maya for his taking shelter of a devotee, asked him to render service unto King Yudhiṣṭhira by building a wonderful assembly house. The process is that by the grace of the devotee the mercy of the Lord is obtained, and by the mercy of the Lord a chance to serve the Lord's devotee is obtained. The club of Bhīmasena was also a gift of Maya Dānava.

TEXT 9

यत्तेजसा नृपशिरोऽङ्घ्रिमहन्मखार्थम्
आर्योऽनुजस्तव गजायुतसत्त्ववीर्यः ।
तेनाहृताः प्रमथनाथमखाय भूपा
यन्मोचितास्तदनयन् बलिमध्वरे ते ॥ ९ ॥

yat-tejasā nṛpa-śiro-'ṅghrim ahan makhārtham
āryo 'nujas tava gajāyuta-sattva-vīryaḥ

tenāhṛtāḥ pramatha-nātha-makhāya bhūpā
yan-mocitās tad-anayan balim adhvare te

yat—whose; *tejasā*—by influence; *nṛpa-śiraḥ-aṅghrim*—one whose feet are adored by the heads of kings; *ahan*—killed; *makha-artham*—for the sacrifice; *āryaḥ*—respectable; *anujaḥ*—younger brother; *tava*—your; *gaja-ayuta*—ten thousand elephants; *sattva-vīryaḥ*—powerful existence; *tena*—by him; *āhṛtāḥ*—collected; *pramatha-nātha*—the lord of the ghosts (Mahābhairava); *makhāya*—for sacrifice; *bhūpāḥ*—kings; *yat-mocitāḥ*—by whom they were released; *tat-anayan*—all of them brought; *balim*—taxes; *adhvare*—presented; *te*—your.

TRANSLATION

Your respectable younger brother, who possesses the strength of ten thousand elephants, killed, by His grace, Jarāsandha, whose feet were worshiped by many kings. These kings had been brought for sacrifice in Jarāsandha's Mahābhairava-yajña, but they were thus released. Later they paid tribute to Your Majesty.

PURPORT

Jarāsandha was a very powerful king of Magadha, and the history of his birth and activities is also very interesting. His father, King Bṛhadratha, was also a very prosperous and powerful King of Magadha, but he had no son, although he married two daughters of the King of Kāśī. Being disappointed in not getting a son from either of the two queens, the King, along with his wives, left home to live in the forest for austerities, but in the forest he was benedicted by one great *ṛṣi* to have a son, and he gave him one mango to be eaten by the queens. The queens did so and were very soon pregnant. The King was very happy to see the queens bearing children, but when the ripe time approached, the queens delivered one child in two parts, one from each of the queens' wombs. The two parts were thrown in the forest, where a great she-demon used to live, and she was glad to have some delicate flesh and blood from the newly born child. Out of curiosity she joined the two parts, and the child became complete and regained life. The she-demon was known as Jarā, and being compassionate on the childless King, she went to the King and presented him with the nice child. The King was very pleased with the she-demon and wanted to reward her according to her desire. The she-demon expressed her desire that the child be named after her, and thus the child was surnamed Jarāsandha, or one who was joined by Jarā, the she-demon. In fact, this Jarāsandha was born as one of the parts and parcels of the demon Vipracitti. The saint by whose benedictions the queens bore the child was called Candra Kauśika, who foretold of the child before his father Bṛhadratha.

Since he possessed demoniac qualities from birth, naturally he became a great devotee of Lord Śiva, who is the lord of all ghostly and demoniac men. Rāvaṇa was a great devotee of Lord Śiva, and so also King Jarāsandha. He used to sacrifice all arrested kings before Lord Mahābhairava (Śiva) and by his military power he defeated many small kings and arrested them to butcher before Mahābhairava. There are many devotees of Lord Mahābhairava, or Kālabhairava, in the province of Bihar, formerly called Magadha. Jarāsandha was a relative of Kaṁsa, the maternal uncle of Kṛṣṇa, and therefore after Kaṁsa's death King Jarāsandha became a great enemy of Kṛṣṇa, and there were many fights between Jarāsandha and Kṛṣṇa. Lord Kṛṣṇa wanted to kill him, but He also wanted that those who served as military men for Jarāsandha might not be killed. Therefore a plan was adopted to kill him. Kṛṣṇa, Bhīma and Arjuna together went to Jarāsandha in the dress of poor *brāhmaṇas* and begged charity from King Jarāsandha. Jarāsandha never refused charity to any *brāhmaṇa*, and he performed many sacrifices also, yet he was not on a par with devotional service. Lord Kṛṣṇa, Bhīma and Arjuna asked Jarāsandha for the facility of fighting him, and it was settled that Jarāsandha would fight with Bhīma only. So all of them were both guests and combatants of Jarāsandha, and Bhīma and Jarāsandha fought every day for several days. Bhīma became disappointed, but Kṛṣṇa gave him hints about Jarāsandha's being joined together as an infant, and thus Bhīma dissected him again and so killed him. All the kings who were detained in the concentration camp to be killed before Mahābhairava were thus released by Bhīma. Feeling thus obliged to the Pāṇḍavas, they paid tribute to King Yudhiṣṭhira.

TEXT 10

पत्न्यास्तवाधिमखक्लृप्तमहाभिषेक-
श्लाघिष्ठचारुकबरं कितवैः सभायाम् ।

स्पृष्टं विकीर्य पदयोः पतिताश्रुमुख्या
यस्तत्स्त्रियोऽकृतहतेशविमुक्तकेशाः॥१०॥

patnyās tavādhimakha-kḷpta-mahābhiṣeka-
ślāghiṣṭha-cāru-kabaraṁ kitavaiḥ sabhāyām
spṛṣṭaṁ vikīrya padayoḥ patitāśru-mukhyā
yas tat-striyo 'kṛta-hateśa-vimukta-keśāḥ

patnyāḥ—of the wife; *tava*—your; *adhimakha*—during the great sacrificial ceremony; *kḷpta*—dressed; *mahā-abhiṣeka*—greatly sanctified; *ślāghiṣṭha*—thus glorified; *cāru*—beautiful; *kabaram*—clustered hair; *kitavaiḥ*—by the miscreants; *sabhāyām*—in the great assembly; *spṛṣṭam*—being caught; *vikīrya*—being loosened; *padayoḥ*—on the feet; *patita-aśru-mukhyāḥ*—of the one who fell down with tears in the eyes; *yaḥ*—He; *tat*—their; *striyaḥ*—wives; *akṛta*—became; *hata-īśa*—bereft of husbands; *vimukta-keśāḥ*—loosened hair.

TRANSLATION

It was He only who loosened the hair of all the wives of the miscreants who dared open the cluster of your Queen's hair, which had been nicely dressed and sanctified for the great Rājasūya sacrificial ceremony. At that time she fell down at the feet of Lord Kṛṣṇa with tears in her eyes.

PURPORT

Queen Draupadī had a beautiful bunch of hair which was sanctified in the ceremonial function of Rājasūya-yajña. But when she was lost in a bet, Duḥśāsana touched her glorified hair to insult her. Draupadī then fell down at the lotus feet of Lord Kṛṣṇa, and Lord Kṛṣṇa decided that all the wives of Duḥśāsana and company should have their hair loosened as a result of the Battle of Kurukṣetra. Thus after the Battle of Kurukṣetra, after all the sons and grandsons of Dhṛtarāṣṭra died in battle, all the wives of the family were obliged to loosen their hair as widows. In other words, all the wives of the Kuru family became widows because of Duḥśāsana's insulting a great devotee of the Lord. The Lord can tolerate insults upon Himself by any miscreant because the father tolerates even insults from the son. But He never tolerates insults upon His devotees. By insulting a great soul, one has to forego all the results of pious acts and benedictions also.

TEXT 11

यो नो जुगोप वन एत्य दुरन्तकृच्छ्राद्
दुर्वाससोऽरिरचितादयुताग्रभुग् यः ।
शाकान्नशिष्टमुपयुज्य यतस्त्रिलोकीं
तृप्तामममंस्त सलिले विनिमग्नसङ्घः ॥११॥

yo no jugopa vana etya duranta-kṛcchrād
durvāsaso 'ri-racitād ayutāgra-bhug yaḥ
śākānna-śiṣṭam upayujya yatas tri-lokīṁ
tṛptām amaṁsta salile vinimagna-saṅghaḥ

yaḥ—one who; *naḥ*—us; *jugopa*—gave protection; *vane*—forest; *etya*—getting in; *duranta*—dangerously; *kṛcchrāt*—trouble; *durvāsasaḥ*—of Durvāsā Muni; *ari*—enemy; *racitāt*—fabricated by; *ayuta*—ten thousand; *agra-bhuk*—one who eats before; *yaḥ*—that person; *śāka-anna-śiṣṭam*—remnants of foodstuff; *upayujya*—having accepted; *yataḥ*—because; *tri-lokīm*—all the three worlds; *tṛptām*—satisfied; *amaṁsta*—thought within the mind; *salile*—while in the water; *vinimagna-saṅghaḥ*—all merged into the water.

TRANSLATION

During our exile, Durvāsā Muni, who eats with his ten thousand disciples, intrigued with our enemies to put us in dangerous trouble. At that time He [Lord Kṛṣṇa], simply by accepting the remnants of food, saved us. By His accepting food thus, the assembly of munis, while bathing in the river, felt sumptuously fed. And all the three worlds were also satisfied.

PURPORT

Durvāsā Muni: A powerful mystic *brāhmaṇa* determined to observe the principles of religion with great vows and under strict austerities. His name is associated with many historical events, and it appears that the great mystic could be both easily satisfied and easily annoyed, like Lord Śiva. When he was satisfied, he could do tremendous good to the servitor, but if he was dissatisfied he could bring about the greatest calamity. Kumārī Kuntī, at her father's house, used to minister all kinds of services to all great *brāhmaṇas*, and being satisfied with her good reception Durvāsā Muni benedicted her with a power to call any demigod she desired. It is understood that he was a plenary incarnation of Lord Śiva, and thus he could be either easily satisfied or annoyed. He was a great devotee of Lord Śiva and by Lord Śiva's order he accepted the priesthood of King Śvetaketu because of the King's performance of sacrifice for one hundred years. Sometimes he used to visit the parliamentary assembly of the heavenly kingdom of Indradeva. He could travel in space by his great mystic powers, and it is understood that he traveled a great distance through space, even up to the Vaikuṇṭha planets beyond material space. He traveled all these long distances within one year, during his quarrel with King Ambarīṣa, the great devotee and Emperor of the world.

He had about ten thousand disciples, and wherever he visited and became a guest of the great *kṣatriya* kings, he used to be accompanied by a number of followers. Once he visited the house of Duryodhana, the enemy cousin of Mahārāja Yudhiṣṭhira. Duryodhana was intelligent enough to satisfy the *brāhmaṇa* by all means, and the great *ṛṣi* wanted to give some benediction to Duryodhana. Duryodhana knew his mystic powers, and he knew also that the mystic *brāhmaṇa*, if dissatisfied, could cause some havoc, and thus he designed to engage the *brāhmaṇa* to show his wrath upon his enemy cousins, the Pāṇḍavas. When the *ṛṣi* wanted to award some benediction to Duryodhana, the latter wished that he should visit the house of Mahārāja Yudhiṣṭhira, who was the eldest and chief among all his cousins. But by his request he would go to him after he had finished his meals with his Queen, Draupadī. Duryodhana knew that after Draupadī's dinner it would be impossible for Mahārāja Yudhiṣṭhira to receive such a large number of *brāhmaṇa* guests, and thus the *ṛṣi* would be annoyed and would create some trouble for his cousin Mahārāja Yudhiṣṭhira. That was the plan of Duryodhana. Durvāsā Muni agreed to this proposal, and he approached the King in exile, according to the plan of Duryodhana after the King and Draupadī had finished their meals.

On his arrival at the door of Mahārāja Yudhiṣṭhira, he was at once well received, and the King requested him to finish his noontime religious rites in the river, for by that time the foodstuff would be prepared. Durvāsā Muni, along with his large number of disciples, went to take a bath in the river, and Mahārāja Yudhiṣṭhira was in great anxiety about the guests. As long as Draupadī had not taken her meals, food could be served to any number of guests, but the *ṛṣi*, by the plan of Duryodhana, reached there after Draupadī had finished her meals.

When the devotees are put into difficulty, they have an opportunity to recollect the Lord with rapt attention. So Draupadī was thinking of Lord Kṛṣṇa in that dangerous position, and the all-pervading Lord could at once know the dangerous position of His devotees. He therefore came there on the scene and asked Draupadī to give whatever food she might have in her stock. On her being so requested by the Lord, Draupadī was sorrowful because the Supreme Lord asked her for some food and she was unable to supply it at that time. She said to the Lord that the mysterious dish which she had received from the sun-god could supply any amount of food if she herself had not eaten. But on that day she had already taken her meals, and thus they were in danger. By expressing her difficulties she began to cry before the Lord as only a woman would do in such a position. The Lord, however, asked Draupadī to bring up the cooking pots to see if there was any particle of foodstuff left, and on Draupadī's doing so, the Lord found some particle of vegetable sticking to the pot. The Lord at once picked it up and ate it. After doing so, the Lord asked Draupadī to call for her guests, the company of Durvāsā.

Bhīma was sent to call them from the river. Bhīma said, "Why are you delaying, sirs? Come on, the food is ready for you." But the *brāhmaṇas*, because of Lord Kṛṣṇa's accepting a little particle of food, felt sumptuously fed, even while they were in the water. They thought that since Mahārāja Yudhiṣṭhira must have prepared many valuable dishes for them and since they were not hungry and could not eat, the King would feel very sorry, so it was better not to go there. Thus they decided to go away.

This incident proves that the Lord is the greatest mystic, and therefore He is known as Yogeśvara. Another instruction is that every householder must offer food to the Lord, and the result will be that everyone, even a company of guests numbering ten thousand, will be satisfied because of the Lord's being satisfied. That is the way of devotional service.

TEXT 12

यत्तेजसाथ भगवान् युधि शूलपाणि-
विस्मापितः सगिरिजोऽस्त्रमदान्निजं मे।
अन्येऽपि चाहममुनैव कलेवरेण
प्राप्तो महेन्द्रभवने महदासनार्धम् ॥१२॥

yat-tejasātha bhagavān yudhi śūla-pāṇir
vismāpitaḥ sagirijo 'stram adān nijaṁ me
anye 'pi cāham amunaiva kalevareṇa
prāpto mahendra-bhavane mahad-āsanārdham

yat—by whose; *tejasā*—by influence; *atha*—at one time; *bhagavān*—the personality of god (Lord Śiva); *yudhi*—in the battle; *śūla-pāṇiḥ*—one who has a trident in his hand; *vismāpitaḥ*—astonished; *sa-giri-jaḥ*—along with the daughter of the Himalaya Mountains; *astram*—weapon; *adāt*—awarded; *nijam*—of his own; *me*—unto me; *anye api*—so also others; *ca*—and; *aham*—myself; *amunā*—by this; *eva*—definitely; *kalevareṇa*—by the body; *prāptaḥ*—obtained; *mahā-indra-bhavane*—in the house of Indradeva; *mahat*—great; *āsana-ardham*—half-elevated seat.

TRANSLATION

It was by His influence only that in a fight I was able to astonish the personality of god Lord Śiva and his wife, the daughter of Mount Himalaya. Thus he [Lord Śiva] became pleased with me and awarded me his own weapon. Other demigods also delivered their respective weapons to me, and in addition I was able to reach the heavenly planets in this present body and was allowed a half-elevated seat.

PURPORT

By the grace of the Supreme Personality of Godhead Śrī Kṛṣṇa, all the demigods, including Lord Śiva, were pleased with Arjuna. The idea is that one who is favored by Lord Śiva or any other demigod may not necessarily be favored by the Supreme Lord Śrī Kṛṣṇa. Rāvaṇa was certainly a great devotee of Lord Śiva, but he could not be saved from the wrath of the Supreme Personality of Godhead Lord Rāmacandra. And there are many instances like that in the histories of the *Purāṇas.* But here is an instance where we can see that Lord Śiva became pleased even in the fight with Arjuna. The devotees of the Supreme Lord know how to respect the demigods, but the devotees of the demigods sometimes foolishly think that the Supreme Personality of Godhead is no greater than the demigods. By such a conception, one becomes an offender and ultimately meets with the same end as Rāvaṇa and others. The instances described by Arjuna during his friendly dealings with Lord Śrī Kṛṣṇa are instructive for all who may be convinced by the lessons that one can achieve all favors simply by pleasing the Supreme Lord Śrī Kṛṣṇa, whereas the devotees or worshipers of the demigods may achieve only partial benefits, which are also perishable, just as the demigods themselves are.

Another significance of the present verse is that Arjuna, by the grace of Lord Śrī Kṛṣṇa, was able to reach the heavenly planet even with the selfsame body and was honored by the heavenly demigod Indradeva, being seated with him half-elevated. One can reach the heavenly planets by the pious acts recommended in the *śāstras* in the category of fruitive activities. And as stated in the *Bhagavad-gītā* (9.21), when the reactions of such pious acts are spent, the enjoyer is again degraded to this earthly planet. The moon is also on the level with the heavenly planets, and only persons who have performed virtues only—performing sacrifices, giving charity and undergoing severe austerities—can be allowed to enter into the heavenly planets after the duration of life of the body. Arjuna was allowed to enter into the heavenly planets in the selfsame body simply by the grace of the Lord, otherwise it is not possible to do so. The present attempts to enter into the heavenly planets by the modern scientists will certainly prove futile because such scientists are not on the level of Arjuna. They are ordinary human beings, without any assets of sacrifice, charity or austerities. The material body is influenced by the three modes of material nature, namely goodness, passion and ignorance. The present population is more or less influenced by the modes of passion and ignorance, and the symptoms for such influence are exhibited in their becoming very lusty and greedy. Such degraded fellows can hardly approach the higher planetary systems. Above the heavenly planets there are many other planets also, which only those who are influenced by goodness can reach. In heavenly and other planets within the universe, the inhabitants are all highly intelligent, many more times than the human beings, and they are all pious in the higher and highest mode of goodness. They are all devotees of the Lord, and although their goodness is not unadulterated, still they are known as demigods possessing the maximum amount of good qualities possible within the material world.

TEXT 13

तत्रैव मे विहरतो भुजदण्डयुग्मं
गाण्डीवलक्षणमरातिवधाय देवाः ।
सेन्द्राः श्रिता यदनुभावितमाजमीढ
तेनाहमद्य मुषितः पुरुषेण भूम्ना ॥१३॥

tatraiva me viharato bhuja-daṇḍa-yugmaṁ
gāṇḍīva-lakṣaṇam arāti-vadhāya devāḥ
sendrāḥ śritā yad-anubhāvitam ājamīḍha
tenāham adya muṣitaḥ puruṣeṇa bhūmnā

tatra—in that heavenly planet; *eva*—certainly; *me*—myself; *viharataḥ*—while staying as a guest; *bhuja-daṇḍa-yugmam*—both of my arms; *gāṇḍīva*—the bow named Gāṇḍīva; *lakṣaṇam*—mark; *arāti*—a demon named Nivātakavaca; *vadhāya*—for killing; *devāḥ*—all the demigods; *sa*—along with; *indrāḥ*—the heavenly King, Indra; *śritāḥ*—taken shelter of; *yat*—by whose; *anubhāvitam*—made it possible to be powerful; *ājamīḍha*—O descendant of King Ajamīḍha; *tena*—by Him; *aham*—myself; *adya*—at the present moment; *muṣitaḥ*—bereft of; *puruṣeṇa*—the personality; *bhūmnā*—supreme.

TRANSLATION

When I stayed for some days as a guest in the heavenly planets, all the heavenly demigods, including King Indradeva, took shelter of my arms, which were marked with the Gāṇḍīva bow, to kill the

demon named Nivātakavaca. O King, descendant of Ajamīḍha, at the present moment I am bereft of the Supreme Personality of Godhead, by whose influence I was so powerful.

PURPORT

The heavenly demigods are certainly more intelligent, powerful and beautiful, and yet they had to take help from Arjuna because of his Gāṇḍīva bow, which was empowered by the grace of Lord Śrī Kṛṣṇa. The Lord is all-powerful, and by His grace His pure devotee can be as powerful as He may desire, and there is no limit to it. And when the Lord withdraws His power from anyone, he is powerless by the will of the Lord.

TEXT 14

यद्बान्धवः कुरुबलाब्धिमनन्तपार-
मेको रथेन ततरेऽहमतीर्यसत्त्वम् ।
प्रत्याहृतं बहु धनं च मया परेषां
तेजास्पदं मणिमयं च हृतं शिरोभ्यः ॥१४॥

yad-bāndhavaḥ kuru-balābdhim ananta-pāram
eko rathena tatare 'ham atīrya-sattvam
pratyāhṛtaṁ bahu dhanaṁ ca mayā pareṣāṁ
tejās-padaṁ maṇimayaṁ ca hṛtaṁ śirobhyaḥ

yat-bāndhavaḥ—by whose friendship only; *kuru-bala-abdhim*—the ocean of the military strength of the Kurus; *ananta-pāram*—which was insurmountable; *ekaḥ*—alone; *rathena*—being seated on the chariot; *tatare*—was able to cross over; *aham*—myself; *atīrya*—invincible; *sattvam*—existence; *pratyāhṛtam*—drew back; *bahu*—very large quantity; *dhanam*—wealth; *ca*—also; *mayā*—by my; *pareṣām*—of the enemy; *tejāḥ-padam*—source of brilliance; *maṇi-mayam*—bedecked with jewels; *ca*—also; *hṛtam*—taken by force; *śirobhyaḥ*—from their heads.

TRANSLATION

The military strength of the Kauravas was like an ocean in which there dwelled many invincible existences, and thus it was

insurmountable. But because of His friendship, I, seated on the chariot, was able to cross over it. And only by His grace was I able to regain the cows and also collect by force many helmets of the kings which were bedecked with jewels that were sources of all brilliance.

PURPORT

On the Kaurava side there were many stalwart commanders like Bhīṣma, Droṇa, Kṛpa and Karṇa, and their military strength was as insurmountable as the great ocean. And yet it was due to Lord Kṛṣṇa's grace that Arjuna alone, sitting on the chariot, could manage to vanquish them one after another without difficulty. There were many changes of commanders on the other side, but on the Pāṇḍavas' side Arjuna alone on the chariot driven by Lord Kṛṣṇa could manage the whole responsibility of the great war. Similarly, when the Pāṇḍavas were living at the palace of Virāṭa incognito, the Kauravas picked a quarrel with King Virāṭa and decided to take away his large number of cows. While they were taking away the cows, Arjuna fought with them incognito and was able to regain the cows along with some booty taken by force, the jewels set on the turbans of the royal order. Arjuna remembered that all this was possible by the grace of the Lord.

TEXT 15

यो भीष्मकर्णगुरुशल्यचमूष्वदभ्र-
राजन्यवर्यरथमण्डलमण्डितासु ।
अग्रेचरो मम विभो रथयूथपाना-
मायुर्मनांसि च दृशा सह ओज आर्च्छत् ॥१५॥

yo bhīṣma-karṇa-guru-śalya-camūṣv adabhra-
rājanya-varya-ratha-maṇḍala-maṇḍitāsu
agrecaro mama vibho ratha-yūthapānām
āyur manāṁsi ca dṛśā saha oja ārcchat

yaḥ—it is He only; *bhīṣma*—Bhīṣma; *karṇa*—Karṇa; *guru*—Droṇācārya; *śalya*—Śalya; *camūṣu*—in the midst of the military phalanx; *adabhra*—immense; *rājanya-varya*—great royal princes;

ratha-maṇḍala—chain of chariots; *maṇḍitāsu*—being decorated with; *agrecaraḥ*—going forward; *mama*—of mine; *vibho*—O great King; *ratha-yūtha-pānām*—all the charioteers; *āyuḥ*—duration of life or fruitive activities; *manāṁsi*—mental upsurges; *ca*—also; *dṛśā*—by glance; *sahaḥ*—power; *ojaḥ*—strength; *ārcchat*—withdrew.

TRANSLATION

It was He only who withdrew the duration of life from everyone and who, in the battlefield, withdrew the speculative power and strength of enthusiasm from the great military phalanx made by the Kauravas, headed by Bhīṣma, Karṇa, Droṇa, Śalya, etc. Their arrangement was expert and more than adequate, but He [Lord Śrī Kṛṣṇa], while going forward, did all this.

PURPORT

The Absolute Personality of Godhead, Lord Śrī Kṛṣṇa, expands Himself by His plenary Paramātmā portion in everyone's heart, and thus He directs everyone in the matter of recollection, forgetfulness, knowledge, the absence of intelligence and all psychological activities (Bg. 15.15). As the Supreme Lord, He can increase or decrease the duration of life of a living being. Thus the Lord conducted the Battle of Kurukṣetra according to His own plan. He wanted that battle to establish Yudhiṣṭhira as the Emperor of this planet, and to facilitate this transcendental business He killed all who were on the opposite party by His omnipotent will. The other party was equipped with all military strength supported by big generals like Bhīṣma, Droṇa and Śalya and it would have been physically impossible for Arjuna to win the battle had the Lord not helped him by every kind of tactic. Such tactics are generally followed by every statesman, even in modern warfare, but they are all done materially by powerful espionages, military tactics and diplomatic maneuvers. But because Arjuna was the Lord's affectionate devotee, the Lord did all this Himself without personal anxiety by Arjuna. That is the way of the devotional service to the Lord.

TEXT 16

यद्दोःषु मा प्रणिहितं गुरुभीष्मकर्ण-
नप्तृत्रिगर्तशल्यसैन्धवबाह्लिकाद्यैः ।

अस्त्राण्यमोघमहिमानि निरूपितानि
नोपस्पृशुर्नृहरिदासमिवासुराणि ॥१६॥

yad-doḥṣu mā praṇihitaṁ guru-bhīṣma-karṇa-
naptṛ-trigarta-śalya-saindhava-bāhlikādyaiḥ
astrāṇy amogha-mahimāni nirūpitāni
nopaspṛśur nṛhari-dāsam ivāsurāṇi

yat—under whose; *doḥṣu*—protection of arms; *mā praṇihitam*—myself being situated; *guru*—Droṇācārya; *bhīṣma*—Bhīṣma; *karṇa*—Karṇa; *naptṛ*—Bhūriśravā; *trigarta*—King Suśarmā; *śalya*—Śalya; *saindhava*—King Jayadratha; *bāhlika*—brother of Mahārāja Śāntanu (Bhīṣma's father); *ādyaiḥ*—etc.; *astrāṇi*—weapons; *amogha*—invincible; *mahimāni*—very powerful; *nirūpitāni*—applied; *na*—not; *upaspṛśuḥ*—touched; *nṛhari-dāsam*—servitor of Nṛsiṁhadeva (Prahlāda); *iva*—like; *asurāṇi*—weapons employed by the demons.

TRANSLATION

Great generals like Bhīṣma, Droṇa, Karṇa, Bhūriśravā, Suśarmā, Śalya, Jayadratha, and Bāhlika all directed their invincible weapons against me. But by His [Lord Kṛṣṇa's] grace they could not even touch a hair on my head. Similarly, Prahlāda Mahārāja, the supreme devotee of Lord Nṛsiṁhadeva, was unaffected by the weapons the demons used against him.

PURPORT

The history of Prahlāda Mahārāja, the great devotee of Nṛsiṁhadeva, is narrated in the Seventh Canto of *Śrīmad-Bhāgavatam.* Prahlāda Mahārāja, a small child of only five years, became the object of envy for his great father, Hiraṇyakaśipu, only because of his becoming a pure devotee of the Lord. The demon father employed all his weapons to kill the devotee son, Prahlāda, but by the grace of the Lord he was saved from all sorts of dangerous actions by his father. He was thrown in a fire, in boiling oil, from the top of a hill, underneath the legs of an elephant, and he was administered poison. At last the father himself took up a chopper to kill his son, and thus Nṛsiṁhadeva appeared and killed the heinous father in the presence of the son. Thus no one can kill the devotee of the Lord. Similarly, Arjuna was also saved by the Lord, although all dangerous weapons were employed by his great opponents like Bhīṣma.

Karṇa: Born of Kuntī by the sun-god prior to her marriage with Mahārāja Pāṇḍu, Karṇa took his birth with bangles and earrings, extraordinary signs for an undaunted hero. In the beginning his name was Vasusena, but when he grew up he presented his natural bangles and earrings to Indradeva, and thenceforward he became known as Vaikartana. After his birth from the maiden Kuntī, he was thrown in the Ganges. Later he was picked up by Adhiratha, and he and his wife Rādhā brought him up as their own offspring. Karṇa was very charitable, especially toward the *brāhmaṇas.* There was nothing he could not spare for a *brāhmaṇa.* In the same charitable spirit he gave in charity his natural bangles and earrings to Indradeva, who, being very much satisfied with him, gave him in return a great weapon called Śakti. He was admitted as one of the students of Droṇācārya, and from the very beginning there was some rivalry between him and Arjuna. Seeing his constant rivalry with Arjuna, Duryodhana picked him up as his companion, and this gradually grew into greater intimacy. He was also present in the great assembly of Draupadī's *svayaṁvara* function, and when he attempted to exhibit his talent in that meeting, Draupadī's brother declared that Karṇa could not take part in the competition because of his being the son of a *śūdra* carpenter. Although he was refused in the competition, still when Arjuna was successful in piercing the fish target on the ceiling and Draupadī bestowed her garland upon Arjuna, Karṇa and the other disappointed princes offered an unusual stumbling block to Arjuna while he was leaving with Draupadī. Specifically, Karṇa fought with him very valiantly, but all of them were defeated by Arjuna. Duryodhana was very much pleased with Karṇa because of his constant rivalry with Arjuna, and when he was in power he enthroned Karṇa in the state of Aṅga. Being baffled in his attempt to win Draupadī, Karna advised Duryodhana to attack King Drupada, for after defeating him both Arjuna and Draupadī could be arrested. But Droṇācārya rebuked them for this conspiracy, and they refrained from the action. Karṇa was defeated many times, not only by Arjuna but also by Bhīmasena. He was the king of the kingdom of Bengal, Orissa and Madras combined. Later on he took an active part in the Rājasūya sacrifice of Mahārāja

Yudhiṣṭhira, and when there was gambling between the rival brothers, designed by Śakuni, Karṇa took part in the game, and he was very pleased when Draupadī was offered as a bet in the gambling. This fed his old grudge. When Draupadī was in the game he was very enthusiastic to declare the news, and it is he who ordered Duḥśāsana to take away the garments of both the Pāṇḍavas and Draupadī. He asked Draupadī to select another husband because, being lost by the Pāṇḍavas, she was rendered a slave of the Kurus. He was always an enemy of the Pāṇḍavas, and whenever there was an opportunity, he tried to curb them by all means. During the Battle of Kurukṣetra, he foresaw the conclusive result, and he expressed his opinion that due to Lord Kṛṣṇa's being the chariot driver of Arjuna, the battle should be won by Arjuna. He always differed with Bhīṣma, and sometimes he was proud enough to say that within five days he could finish up the Pāṇḍavas, if Bhīṣma would not interfere with his plan of action. But he was much mortified when Bhīṣma died. He killed Ghaṭotkaca with the Śakti weapon obtained from Indradeva. His son, Brisasena, was killed by Arjuna. He killed the largest number of Pāṇḍava soldiers. At last there was a severe fight with Arjuna, and it was he only who was able to knock off the helmet of Arjuna. But it so happened that the wheel of his chariot stuck in the battlefield mud, and when he got down to set the wheel right, Arjuna took the opportunity and killed him, although he requested Arjuna not to do so.

Naptā, or *Bhūriśravā:* Bhūriśravā was the son of Somadatta, a member of the Kuru family. His other brother was Śalya. Both the brothers and the father attended the *svayaṁvara* ceremony of Draupadī. All of them appreciated the wonderful strength of Arjuna due to his being the devotee friend of the Lord, and thus Bhūriśravā advised the sons of Dhṛtarāṣṭra not to pick any quarrel or fight with them. All of them also attended the Rājasūya *yajña* of Mahārāja Yudhiṣṭhira. He possessed one *akṣauhiṇī* regiment of army, cavalry, elephants and chariots, and all these were employed in the Battle of Kurukṣetra on behalf of Duryodhana's party. He was counted by Bhīma as one of the *yūtha-patis.* In the Battle of Kurukṣetra he was especially engaged in a fight with Sātyaki, and he killed ten sons of Sātyaki. Later on, Arjuna cut off his hands, and he was ultimately killed by Sātyaki. After his death he merged into the existence of Viśvadeva.

Trigarta, or *Suśarmā:* Son of Mahārāja Vṛddhakṣetra, he was the king of Trigartadeśa, and he was also present in the *svayaṁvara* ceremony of Draupadī. He was one of the allies of Duryodhana, and he advised Duryodhana to attack the Matsyadeśa (Darbhaṅga). During the time of cow-stealing in Virāṭa-nagara, he was able to arrest Mahārāja Virāṭa, but later Mahārāja Virāṭa was released by Bhīma. In the Battle of Kurukṣetra he also fought very valiantly, but at the end he was killed by Arjuna.

Jayadratha: Another son of Mahārāja Vṛddhakṣetra. He was the king of Sindhudeśa (modern Sind Pakistan). His wife's name was Duḥśalā. He was also present in the *svayaṁvara* ceremony of Draupadī, and he desired very strongly to have her hand, but he failed in the competition. But since then he always sought the opportunity to get in touch with Draupadī. When he was going to marry in the Śalyadeśa, on the way to Kāmyavana he happened to see Draupadī again and was too much attracted to her. The Pāṇḍavas and Draupadī were then in exile, after losing their empire in gambling, and Jayadratha thought it wise to send news to Draupadī in an illicit manner through Koṭiśaṣya, one of his associates. Draupadī at once refused vehemently the proposal of Jayadratha, but being so much attracted by the beauty of Draupadī, he tried again and again. Every time he was refused by Draupadī. He tried to take her away forcibly on his chariot, and at first Draupadī gave him a good dashing, and he fell like a cut-root tree. But he was not discouraged, and he was able to force Draupadī to sit on the chariot. This incident was seen by Dhaumya Muni, and he strongly protested the action of Jayadratha. He also followed the chariot, and through Dhātreyikā the matter was brought to the notice of Mahārāja Yudhiṣṭhira. The Pāṇḍavas then attacked the soldiers of Jayadratha and killed them all, and at last Bhīma caught hold of Jayadratha and beat him very severely, almost dead. Then all but five hairs were cut off his head and he was taken to all the kings and introduced as the slave of Mahārāja Yudhiṣṭhira. He was forced to admit himself to be the slave of Mahārāja Yudhiṣṭhira before all the princely order, and in the same condition he was brought before Mahārāja Yudhiṣṭhira. Mahārāja Yudhiṣṭhira was kind enough to order him released, and when he admitted to being a tributary prince under Mahārāja Yudhiṣṭhira, Queen Draupadī also desired his release. After this incident, he was allowed to return to his country. Being so insulted, he went to Gaṅgātri in the Himalayas and undertook a severe type of penance to please Lord Śiva. He asked his benediction to defeat all the

Pāṇḍavas, at least one at a time. Then the Battle of Kurukṣetra began, and he took sides with Duryodhana. In the first day's fight he was engaged with Mahārāja Drupada, then with Virāṭa and then with Abhimanyu. While Abhimanyu was being killed, mercilessly surrounded by seven great generals, the Pāṇḍavas came to his help, but Jayadratha, by the mercy of Lord Śiva, repulsed them with great ability. At this, Arjuna took a vow to kill him, and on hearing this, Jayadratha wanted to leave the warfield and asked permission from the Kauravas for this cowardly action. But he was not allowed to do so. On the contrary, he was obliged to fight with Arjuna, and while the fight was going on Lord Kṛṣṇa reminded Arjuna that the benediction of Śiva upon Jayadratha was that whoever would cause his head to fall on the ground would die at once. He therefore advised Arjuna to throw the head of Jayadratha directly onto the lap of his father, who was engaged in penances at the Samanta-pañcaka pilgrimage. This was actually done by Arjuna. Jayadratha's father was suprised to see a severed head on his lap, and he at once threw it to the ground. The father immediately died, his forehead being cracked in seven pieces.

TEXT 17

सौत्ये वृतः कुमतिनात्मद ईश्वरो मे
यत्पादपद्ममभवाय भजन्ति भव्याः ।
मां श्रान्तवाहमरयो रथिनो भुविष्ठं
न प्राहरन् यदनुभावनिरस्तचित्ताः ॥१७॥

sautye vṛtaḥ kumatinātmada īśvaro me
yat-pāda-padmam abhavāya bhajanti bhavyāḥ
māṁ śrānta-vāham arayo rathino bhuviṣṭhaṁ
na prāharan yad-anubhāva-nirasta-cittāḥ

sautye—regarding a chariot driver; *vṛtaḥ*—engaged; *kumatinā*—by bad consciousness; *ātma-daḥ*—one who delivers; *īśvaraḥ*—the Supreme Lord; *me*—my; *yat*—whose; *pāda-padmam*—lotus feet; *abhavāya*—in the matter of salvation; *bhajanti*—do render service; *bhavyāḥ*—the intelligent class of men; *mām*—unto me; *śrānta*—thirsty; *vāham*—my horses; *arayaḥ*—the enemies; *rathinaḥ*—a great general; *bhuviṣṭham*—while standing on the ground; *na*—did not; *prāharan*—attack; *yat*—whose; *anubhāva*—mercy; *nirasta*—being absent; *cittāḥ*—mind.

TRANSLATION

It was by His mercy only that my enemies neglected to kill me when I descended from my chariot to get water for my thirsty horses. And it was due to my lack of esteem for my Lord that I dared engage Him as my chariot driver, for He is worshiped and offered services by the best men to attain salvation.

PURPORT

The Supreme Lord, the Personality of Godhead Śrī Kṛṣṇa, is the object of worship both by impersonalists and by the devotees of the Lord. The impersonalists worship His glowing effulgence, emanating from His transcendental body of eternal form, bliss and knowledge, and the devotees worship Him as the Supreme Personality of Godhead. Those who are below even the impersonalists consider Him to be one of the great historical personalities. The Lord, however, descends to attract all by His specific transcendental pastimes, and thus He plays the part of the most perfect master, friend, son and lover. His transcendental relation with Arjuna was in friendship, and the Lord therefore played the part perfectly, as He did with His parents, lovers and wives. While playing in such a perfect transcendental relation, the devotee forgets, by the internal potency of the Lord, that his friend or son is the Supreme Personality of Godhead, although sometimes the devotee is bewildered by the acts of the Lord. After the departure of the Lord, Arjuna was conscious of his great friend, but there was no mistake on the part of Arjuna, nor any ill estimation of the Lord. Intelligent men are attracted by the transcendental acting of the Lord with a pure, unalloyed devotee like Arjuna.

In the warfield, scarcity of water is a well-known fact. Water is very rare there, and both the animals and men, working strenuously on the warfield, constantly require water to quench their thirst. Especially wounded soldiers and generals feel very thirsty at the time of death, and it sometimes so happens that simply for want of water one has to die unavoidably. But such scarcity of water was solved in the Battle of Kurukṣetra by means of boring the ground. By God's grace, water can be easily obtained from any place if there is facility for boring the ground. The modern system works on the same principle of boring the ground, but modern engineers are still unable to dig immediately wherever necessary. It appears, however, from the history as far back as the days of the Pāṇḍavas, that big generals like Arjuna could at once supply water even to the horses, and what to speak of men, by drawing water from underneath the hard ground simply by penetrating the stratum with a sharp arrow, a method still unknown to the modern scientists.

TEXT 18

नर्माण्युदाररुचिरस्मितशोभितानि
हे पार्थ हेऽर्जुन सखे कुरुनन्दनेति ।
संजल्पितानि नरदेव हृदिस्पृशानि
स्मर्तुर्लुठन्ति हृदयं मम माधवस्य ॥१८॥

narmāṇy udāra-rucira-smita-śobhitāni
he pārtha he 'rjuna sakhe kuru-nandaneti
sañjalpitāni nara-deva hṛdi-spṛśāni
smartur luṭhanti hṛdayaṁ mama mādhavasya

narmāṇi—conversation in jokes; *udāra*—talked very frankly; *rucira*—pleasing; *smita-śobhitāni*—decorated with a smiling face; *he*—note of address; *pārtha*—O son of Pṛthā; *he*—note of address; *arjuna*—Arjuna; *sakhe*—friend; *kuru-nandana*—son of the Kuru dynasty; *iti*—and so on; *sañjalpitāni*—such conversation; *nara-deva*—O King; *hṛdi*—heart; *spṛśāni*—touching; *smartuḥ*—by remembering them; *luṭhanti*—overwhelms; *hṛdayam*—heart and soul; *mama*—my; *mādhavasya*—of Mādhava (Kṛṣṇa).

TRANSLATION

O King! His jokings and frank talks were pleasing and beautifully decorated with smiles. His addresses unto me as "O son of Pṛthā, O friend, O son of the Kuru dynasty," and all

such heartiness are now remembered by me, and thus I am overwhelmed.

TEXT 19

शय्यासनाटनविकत्थनभोजनादि-
ष्वैक्याद्वयस्य ऋतवानिति विप्रलब्धः ।
सख्युः सखेव पितृवत्तनयस्य सर्वं
सेहे महान्महितया कुमतेरघं मे ॥१९॥

śayyāsanāṭana-vikatthana-bhojanādiṣv
aikyād vayasya ṛtavān iti vipra-labdhaḥ
sakhyuḥ sakheva pitṛvat tanayasya sarvaṁ
sehe mahān mahitayā kumater aghaṁ me

śayya—sleeping on one bed; *āsana*—sitting on one seat; *aṭana*—walking together; *vikatthana*—self-adoration; *bhojana*—dining together; *ādiṣu*—and in all such dealings; *aikyāt*—because of oneness; *vayasya*—O my friend; *ṛtavān*—truthful; *iti*—thus; *vipra-labdhaḥ*—misbehaved; *sakhyuḥ*—unto a friend; *sakhā iva*—just like a friend; *pitṛvat*—just like the father; *tanayasya*—of a child; *sarvam*—all; *sehe*—tolerated; *mahān*—great; *mahitayā*—by glories; *kumateḥ*—of one who is of low mentality; *agham*—offense; *me*—mine.

TRANSLATION

Generally both of us used to live together and sleep, sit and loiter together. And at the time of advertising oneself for acts of chivalry, sometimes, if there were any irregularity, I used to reproach Him by saying, "My friend, You are very truthful." Even in those hours when His value was minimized, He, being the Supreme Soul, used to tolerate all those utterings of mine, excusing me exactly as a true friend excuses his true friend, or a father excuses his son.

PURPORT

Since the Supreme Lord Śrī Kṛṣṇa is all-perfect, His transcendental pastimes with His pure devotees never lack anything in any respect, either as a friend, son or lover. The Lord relishes the reproaches of friends, parents or fiancées more than the Vedic hymns offered to Him by great learned scholars and religionists in an official fashion.

TEXT 20

सोऽहं नृपेन्द्र रहितः पुरुषोत्तमेन
सख्या प्रियेण सुहृदा हृदयेन शून्यः ।
अध्वन्युरुक्रमपरिग्रहमङ्ग रक्षन्
गोपैरसद्भिरबलेव विनिर्जितोऽस्मि ॥२०॥

so 'haṁ nṛpendra rahitaḥ puruṣottamena
sakhyā priyeṇa suhṛdā hṛdayena śūnyaḥ
adhvany urukrama-parigraham aṅga rakṣan
gopair asadbhir abaleva vinirjito 'smi

saḥ—that; *aham*—myself; *nṛpa-indra*—O Emperor; *rahitaḥ*—bereft of; *puruṣa-uttamena*—by the Supreme Lord; *sakhyā*—by my friend; *priyeṇa*—by my dearmost; *suhṛdā*—by the well-wisher; *hṛdayena*—by the heart and soul; *śūnyaḥ*—vacant; *adhvani*—recently; *urukrama-parigraham*—the wives of the all-powerful; *aṅga*—bodies; *rakṣan*—while protecting; *gopaiḥ*—by the cowherds; *asadbhiḥ*—by the infidels; *abalā iva*—like a weak woman; *vinirjitaḥ asmi*—I have been defeated.

TRANSLATION

O Emperor, now I am separated from my friend and dearmost well-wisher, the Supreme Personality of Godhead, and therefore my heart appears to be void of everything. In His absence I have been defeated by a number of infidel cowherd men while I was guarding the bodies of all the wives of Kṛṣṇa.

PURPORT

The important point in this verse is how it was possible that Arjuna could be defeated by a gang of ignoble cowherd men and how such mundane cowherd men could touch the bodies of the wives of Lord Kṛṣṇa, who were under the protection of Arjuna. Śrīla Viśvanātha Cakravartī Ṭhākura has justified the contradiction by research in the *Viṣṇu Purāṇa* and *Brahma Purāṇa.* In these *Purāṇas* it is said that once the fair denizens of heaven pleased Aṣṭāvakra Muni by their service and were blessed by the *muni* to have the Supreme Lord as their husband. Aṣṭāvakra Muni was curved in eight joints of his body, and thus he used to move in a peculiar curved manner. The daughters of the demigods could not check their laughter upon seeing the movements of the *muni,* and the *muni,* being angry at them, cursed them that they would be kidnapped by rogues, even if they would get the Lord as their husband. Later on, the girls again satisfied the *muni* by their prayers, and the *muni* blessed them that they would regain their husband even after being robbed by the rogues. So, in order to keep the words of the great *muni,* the Lord Himself kidnapped His wives from the protection of Arjuna, otherwise they would have at once vanished from the scene as soon as they were touched by the rogues. Besides that, some of the *gopīs* who prayed to become wives of the Lord returned to their respective positions after their desire was fulfilled. After the departure of Lord Kṛṣṇa, He wanted all His entourage back to Godhead, and they were called back under different conditions only.

TEXT 21

तद्वै धनुस्त इषवः स रथो हयास्ते
सोऽहं रथी नृपतयो यत आनमन्ति ।
सर्वं क्षणेन तदभूदसदीशरिक्तं
भस्मन् हुतं कुहकराद्धमिवोप्तमूष्याम् ॥२१॥

tad vai dhanus ta iṣavaḥ sa ratho hayās te
so 'haṁ rathī nṛpatayo yata ānamanti
sarvaṁ kṣaṇena tad abhūd asad īśa-riktaṁ
bhasman hutaṁ kuhaka-rāddham ivoptam ūṣyām

tat—the same; *vai*—certainly; *dhanuḥ te*—the same bow; *iṣavaḥ*—arrows; *saḥ*—the very same; *rathaḥ*—chariot; *hayāḥ te*—the very same horses; *saḥ aham*—I am the same Arjuna; *rathī*—the chariot-fighter; *nṛpatayaḥ*—all the kings; *yataḥ*—whom; *ānamanti*—offered their respects; *sarvam*—all; *kṣaṇena*—at a moment's notice; *tat*—all those; *abhūt*—became; *asat*—useless; *īśa*—because of the Lord; *riktam*—being void; *bhasman*—ashes; *hutam*—offering butter; *kuhaka-rāddham*—money created by magical feats; *iva*—like that; *uptam*—sown; *ūṣyām*—in barren land.

TRANSLATION

I have the very same Gāṇḍīva bow, the same arrows, the same chariot drawn by the same horses, and I use them as the same Arjuna to whom all the kings offered their due respects. But in the absence of Lord Kṛṣṇa, all of them, at a moment's notice, have become null and void. It is exactly like offering clarified butter on ashes, accumulating money with a magic wand or sowing seeds on barren land.

PURPORT

As we have discussed more than once, one should not be puffed up by borrowed plumes. All energies and powers are derived from the supreme source, Lord Kṛṣṇa, and they act as long as He desires and cease to function as soon as He withdraws. All electrical energies are received from the powerhouse, and as soon as the powerhouse stops supplying energy, the bulbs are of no use. In a moment's time such energies can be generated or withdrawn by the supreme will of the Lord. Material civilization without the blessing of the Lord is child's play only. As long as the parents allow the child to play, it is all right. As soon as the parents withdraw, the child has to stop. Human civilization and all activities thereof must be dovetailed with the supreme blessing of the Lord, and without this blessing all advancement of human civilization is like decoration on a dead body. It is said here that a dead civilization and its activities are something like clarified butter on ashes, the accumulation of money by a magic wand and the sowing of seeds in a barren land.

TEXTS 22–23

राजंस्त्वयानुपृष्टानां सुहृदां नः सुहृत्पुरे ।
विप्रशापविमूढानां निघ्नतां मुष्टिभिर्मिथः ॥२२॥

वारुणीं मदिरां पीत्वा मदोन्मथितचेतसाम् ।
अजानतामिवान्योन्यं चतुःपञ्चावशेषिताः ॥२३॥

rājaṁs tvayānupṛṣṭānāṁ
suhṛdāṁ naḥ suhṛt-pure
vipra-śāpa-vimūḍhānāṁ
nighnatāṁ muṣṭibhir mithaḥ

vāruṇīṁ madirāṁ pītvā
madonmathita-cetasām
ajānatām ivānyonyaṁ
catuḥ-pañcāvaśeṣitāḥ

rājan—O King; *tvayā*—by you; *anupṛṣṭānām*—as you inquired; *suhṛdām*—of friends and relatives; *naḥ*—our; *suhṛt-pure*—in the city of Dvārakā; *vipra*—the *brāhmaṇas; śāpa*—by the curse of; *vimūḍhānām*—of the befooled; *nighnatām*—of the killed; *muṣṭibhiḥ*—with bunches of sticks; *mithaḥ*—among themselves; *vāruṇīm*—fermented rice; *madirām*—wine; *pītvā*—having drunk; *madonmathita*—being intoxicated; *cetasām*—of that mental situation; *ajānatām*—of the unrecognized; *iva*—like; *anyonyam*—one another; *catuḥ*—four; *pañca*—five; *avaśeṣitāḥ*—now remaining.

TRANSLATION

O King, since you have asked me about our friends and relatives in the city of Dvārakā, I will inform you that all of them were cursed by the brāhmaṇas, and as a result they all became intoxicated with wine made of putrified rice and fought among themselves with sticks, not even recognizing one another. Now all but four or five of them are dead and gone.

TEXT 24

प्रायेणैतद् भगवत ईश्वरस्य विचेष्टितम् ।
मिथो निघ्नन्ति भूतानि भावयन्ति च यन्मिथः ॥२४॥

prāyeṇaitad bhagavata
īśvarasya viceṣṭitam
mitho nighnanti bhūtāni
bhāvayanti ca yan mithaḥ

prāyeṇa etat—it is almost by; *bhagavataḥ*—of the Personality of Godhead; *īśvarasya*—of the Lord; *viceṣṭitam*—by the will of; *mithaḥ*—one another; *nighnanti*—do kill; *bhūtāni*—the living beings; *bhāvayanti*—as also protect; *ca*—also; *yat*—of whom; *mithaḥ*—one another.

TRANSLATION

Factually this is all due to the supreme will of the Lord, the Personality of Godhead. Sometimes people kill one another, and at other times they protect one another.

PURPORT

According to the anthropologists, there is nature's law of struggle for existence and survival of the fittest. But they do not know that behind the law of nature is the supreme direction of the Supreme Personality of Godhead. In the *Bhagavad-gītā* it is confirmed that the law of nature is executed under the direction of the Lord. Whenever, therefore, there is peace in the world, it must be known that it is due to the good will of the Lord. And whenever there is upheaval in the world, it is also due to the supreme will of the Lord. Not a blade of grass moves without the will of the Lord. Whenever, therefore, there is disobedience of the established rules enacted by the Lord, there is war between men and nations. The surest way to the path of peace, therefore, is dovetailing everything to the established rule of the Lord. The established rule is that whatever we do, whatever we eat, whatever we sacrifice or whatever we give in charity must be done to the full satisfaction of the Lord. No one should do anything, eat anything, sacrifice anything or give anything in charity against the will of the Lord. Discretion is the better part of valor, and one must learn how to discriminate between actions which may be pleasing to the Lord and those which may not be pleasing to the Lord. An action is thus judged by the Lord's pleasure or displeasure. There is no room for personal whims; we must always be guided by the pleasure of the Lord. Such action is called *yogaḥ karmasu kauśalam*, or actions performed which are linked with the Supreme Lord. That is the art of doing a thing perfectly.

TEXTS 25–26

जलौकसां जले यद्वन्महान्तोऽदन्त्यणीयसः ।
दुर्बलान्बलिनो राजन्महान्तो बलिनो मिथः ॥२५॥
एवं बलिष्ठैर्यदुभिर्महद्भिरितरान् विभुः ।
यदून् यदुभिरन्योन्यं भूभारान् संजहार ह ॥२६॥

jalaukasāṁ jale yadvan
mahānto 'danty aṇīyasaḥ
durbalān balino rājan
mahānto balino mithaḥ

evaṁ baliṣṭhair yadubhir
mahadbhir itarān vibhuḥ
yadūn yadubhir anyonyaṁ
bhū-bhārān sañjahāra ha

jalaukasām—of the aquatics; *jale*—in the water; *yadvat*—as it is; *mahāntaḥ*—the larger one; *adanti*—swallows; *aṇīyasaḥ*—smaller ones; *durbalān*—the weak; *balinaḥ*—the stronger; *rājan*—O King; *mahāntaḥ*—the strongest; *balinaḥ*—less strong; *mithaḥ*—in a duel; *evam*—thus; *baliṣṭhaiḥ*—by the strongest; *yadubhiḥ*—by the descendants of Yadu; *mahadbhiḥ*—one who has greater strength; *itarān*—the common ones; *vibhuḥ*—the Supreme Personality of Godhead; *yadūn*—all the Yadus; *yadubhiḥ*—by the Yadus; *anyonyam*—among one another; *bhū-bhārān*—the burden of the world; *sañjahāra*—has unloaded; *ha*—in the past.

TRANSLATION

O King, as in the ocean the bigger and stronger aquatics swallow up the smaller and weaker ones, so also the Supreme Personality of Godhead, to lighten the burden of the earth, has engaged the stronger Yadu to kill the weaker, and the bigger Yadu to kill the smaller.

PURPORT

In the material world the struggle for existence and survival of the fittest are laws because in the material world there is disparity between conditioned souls due to everyone's desire to lord it over the material resources. This very mentality of lording it over the material nature is the root cause of conditioned life. And to give facility to such imitation lords, the illusory energy of the Lord has created a disparity between conditioned living beings by creating the stronger and the weaker in every species of life. The mentality of lording it over the material nature and the creation has naturally created a disparity and therefore the law of struggle for existence. In the spiritual world there is no such disparity, nor is there such a struggle for existence. In the spiritual world there is no struggle for existence because everyone there exists eternally. There is no disparity because everyone wants to render service to the Supreme Lord, and no one wants to imitate the Lord in becoming the beneficiary. The Lord, being creator of everything, including the living beings, factually is the proprietor and enjoyer of everything that be, but in the material world, by the spell of *māyā*, or illusion, this eternal relation with the Supreme Personality of Godhead is forgotten, and so the living being is conditioned under the law of struggle for existence and survival of the fittest.

TEXT 27

देशकालार्थयुक्तानि हृत्तापोपशमानि च ।
हरन्ति स्मरतश्चित्तं गोविन्दाभिहितानि मे ॥२७॥

deśa-kālārtha-yuktāni
hṛt-tāpopaśamāni ca
haranti smarataś cittaṁ
govindābhihitāni me

deśa—space; *kāla*—time; *artha*—importance; *yuktāni*—impregnated with; *hṛt*—the heart; *tāpa*—burning; *upaśamāni*—extinguishing; *ca*—and; *haranti*—are attracting; *smarataḥ*—by remembering; *cittam*—mind; *govinda*—the Supreme Personality of pleasure; *abhihitāni*—narrated by; *me*—unto me.

TRANSLATION

Now I am attracted to those instructions imparted to me by the Personality of Godhead [Govinda] because they are impregnated with instructions for relieving the burning heart in all circumstances of time and space.

PURPORT

Herein Arjuna refers to the instruction of the *Bhagavad-gītā*, which was imparted to him by the Lord on the Battlefield of Kurukṣetra. The Lord left behind Him the instructions of the *Bhagavad-gītā* not for the benefit of Arjuna alone, but also for all time and in all lands. The *Bhagavad-gītā*, being spoken by the Supreme Personality of Godhead, is the essence of all Vedic wisdom. It is nicely presented by the Lord Himself for all who have very little time to go through the vast Vedic literatures like the *Upaniṣads*, *Purāṇas* and *Vedānta-sūtras*. It is put within the study of the great historical epic *Mahābhārata*, which was especially prepared for the less intelligent class, namely the women, the laborers and those who are worthless descendants of the *brāhmaṇas*, *kṣatriyas* and higher sections of the *vaiśyas*. The problem which arose in the heart of Arjuna on the Battlefield of Kurukṣetra was solved by the teachings of the *Bhagavad-gītā*. Again, after the departure of the Lord from the vision of earthly people, when Arjuna was face to face with being vanquished in his acquired power and prominence, he wanted again to remember the great teachings of the *Bhagavad-gītā* just to teach all concerned that the *Bhagavad-gītā* can be consulted in all critical times, not only for solace from all kinds of mental agonies, but also for the way out of great entanglements which may embarrass one in some critical hour.

The merciful Lord left behind Him the great teachings of the *Bhagavad-gītā* so that one can take the instructions of the Lord even when He is not visible to material eyesight. Material senses cannot have any estimation of the Supreme Lord, but by His inconceivable power the Lord can incarnate Himself to the sense perception of the conditioned souls in a suitable manner through the agency of matter, which is also another form of the Lord's manifested energy. Thus the *Bhagavad-gītā*, or any authentic scriptural sound representation of the Lord, is also the incarnation of the Lord. There is no difference between the sound representation of the Lord and the Lord Himself. One can derive the same benefit from the *Bhagavad-gītā* as Arjuna did in the personal presence of the Lord.

The faithful human being who is desirous of being liberated from the clutches of material existence can very easily take advantage of the *Bhagavad-gītā*, and with this in view, the Lord instructed Arjuna as if Arjuna were in need of it. In the *Bhagavad-gītā*, five important factors of knowledge have been delineated pertaining to (1) the Supreme Lord, (2) the living being, (3) nature, (4) time and space and (5) the process of activity. Out of these, the Supreme Lord and the living being are qualitatively one. The difference between the two has been analyzed as the difference between the whole and the part and parcel. Nature is inert matter displaying the interaction of three different modes, and eternal time and unlimited space are considered to be beyond the existence of the material nature. Activities of the living being are different varieties of aptitudes which can entrap or liberate the living being within and without material nature. All these subject matters are concisely discussed in the *Bhagavad-gītā*, and later the subject matters are elaborated in the *Śrīmad-Bhāgavatam* for further enlightenment. Out of the five subjects, the Supreme Lord, the living entity, nature, and time and space are eternal, but the living entity, nature and time are under the direction of the Supreme Lord, who is absolute and completely independent of any other control. The Supreme Lord is the supreme controller. The material activity of the living being is beginningless, but it can be rectified by transferal into the spiritual quality. Thus it can cease its material qualitative reactions. Both the Lord and the living entity are cognizant, and both have the sense of identification, of being conscious as a living force. But the living being under the condition of material nature, called *mahat-tattva*, misidentifies himself as being different from the Lord. The whole scheme of Vedic wisdom is targeted to the aim of eradicating such a misconception and thus liberating the living being from the illusion of material identification. When such an illusion is eradicated by knowledge and renunciation, the living beings are responsible actors and enjoyers also. The sense of enjoyment in the Lord is real, but such a sense in the living being is a sort of wishful desire only. This difference in consciousness is the distinction of the two identities, namely the Lord and the living being. Otherwise there is no difference between the Lord and the living being. The living being is therefore eternally one and different simultaneously. The whole instruction of the *Bhagavad-gītā* stands on this principle.

In the *Bhagavad-gītā* the Lord and the living beings are both described as *sanātana*, or eternal, and the Lord's abode, far beyond the material sky, is also described as *sanātana.* The living being is invited to live in the *sanātana* existence of the Lord, and the process which can help a living being to approach the Lord's abode, where the liberated activity of the soul is exhibited, is called *sanātana-dharma.* One cannot, however, reach the eternal abode of the Lord without being free from the misconception of material identification, and the *Bhagavad-gītā* gives us the clue how to achieve this stage of perfection. The process of being liberated from the misconception of material identification is called, in different stages, fruitive activity, empiric philosophy and devotional service, up to transcendental realization. Such transcendental realization is made possible by dovetailing all the above items in relation with the Lord. Prescribed duties of the human being, as directed in the *Vedas*, can gradually purify the sinful mind of the conditioned soul and raise him to the stage of knowledge. The purified stage of acquiring knowledge becomes the basis of devotional service to the Lord. As long as one is engaged in researching the solution of the problems of life, his knowledge is called *jñāna*, or purified knowledge, but on realizing the actual solution of life, one becomes situated in the devotional service of the Lord. The *Bhagavad-gītā* begins with the problems of life by discriminating the soul from the elements of matter and proves by all reason and argument that the soul is indestructible in all circumstances and that the outer covering of matter, the body and the mind, change for another term of material existence which is full of miseries. The *Bhagavad-gītā* is therefore meant for terminating all different types of miseries, and Arjuna took shelter of this great knowledge, which had been imparted to him during the Kurukṣetra battle.

TEXT 28

सूत उवाच

एवं चिन्तयतो जिष्णोः कृष्णपादसरोरुहम् ।
सौहार्देनातिगाढेन शान्तासीद्विमला मतिः ॥२८॥

sūta uvāca
evaṁ cintayato jiṣṇoḥ
kṛṣṇa-pāda-saroruham
sauhārdenātigāḍhena
śāntāsīd vimalā matiḥ

sūtaḥ uvāca—Sūta Gosvāmī said; *evam*—thus; *cintayataḥ*—while thinking of the instructions; *jiṣṇoḥ*—of the Supreme Personality of Godhead; *kṛṣṇa-pāda*—the feet of Kṛṣṇa; *saroruham*—resembling lotuses; *sauhārdena*—by deep friendship; *ati-gāḍhena*—in great intimacy; *śāntā*—pacified; *āsīt*—it so became; *vimalā*—without any tinge of material contamination; *matiḥ*—mind.

TRANSLATION

Sūta Gosvāmī said: Thus being deeply absorbed in thinking of the instructions of the Lord, which were imparted in the great intimacy of friendship, and in thinking of His lotus feet, Arjuna's mind became pacified and free from all material contamination.

PURPORT

Since the Lord is absolute, deep meditation upon Him is as good as yogic trance. The Lord is nondifferent from His name, form, quality, pastimes, entourage and specific actions. Arjuna began to think of the Lord's instructions to him on the Battlefield of Kurukṣetra. Only those instructions began to eliminate the tinges of material contamination in the mind of Arjuna. The Lord is like the sun; the sun's appearance means immediate dissipation of darkness, or ignorance, and the Lord's appearance within the mind of the devotee can at once drive away the miserable material effects. Lord Caitanya has therefore recommended constant chanting of the name of the Lord for protection from all contamination of the material world. The feeling of separation from the Lord is undoubtedly painful to the devotee, but because it is in connection with the Lord, it has a specific transcendental effect which pacifies the heart. Feelings of separation are also sources of transcendental bliss, and they are never comparable to contaminated material feelings of separation.

TEXT 29

वासुदेवाङ्घ्र्यनुध्यानपरिबृंहितरंहसा ।
भक्त्या निर्मथिताशेषकषायधिषणोऽर्जुनः ॥२९॥

vāsudevāṅghry-anudhyāna-
paribṛṁhita-raṁhasā
bhaktyā nirmathitāśeṣa-
kaṣāya-dhiṣaṇo 'rjunaḥ

vāsudeva-aṅghri—the lotus feet of the Lord; *anudhyāna*—by constant remembrance; *paribṛṁhita*—expanded; *raṁhasā*—with great velocity; *bhaktyā*—in devotion; *nirmathita*—subsided; *aśeṣa*—unlimited; *kaṣāya*—dint; *dhiṣaṇaḥ*—conception; *arjunaḥ*—Arjuna.

TRANSLATION

Arjuna's constant remembrance of the lotus feet of Lord Śrī Kṛṣṇa rapidly increased his devotion, and as a result all the trash in his thoughts subsided.

PURPORT

Material desires in the mind are the trash of material contamination. By such contamination, the living being is faced with so many compatible and incompatible things that discourage the very existence of spiritual identity. Birth after birth the conditioned soul is entrapped with so many pleasing and displeasing elements, which are all false and temporary. They accumulate due to our reactions to material desires, but when we get in touch with the transcendental Lord in His variegated energies by devotional service, the naked forms of all material desires become manifest, and the intelligence of the living being is pacified in its true color. As soon as Arjuna turned his attention towards the instructions of the Lord, as they are inculcated in the *Bhagavad-gītā*, his true color of eternal association with the Lord became manifest, and thus he felt freed from all material contaminations.

TEXT 30

गीतं भगवता ज्ञानं यत् तत् सङ्ग्राममूर्धनि ।
कालकर्मतमोरुद्धं पुनरध्यगमत् प्रभुः ॥३०॥

gītaṁ bhagavatā jñānaṁ
yat tat saṅgrāma-mūrdhani
kāla-karma-tamo-ruddhaṁ
punar adhyagamat prabhuḥ

gītam—instructed; *bhagavatā*—by the Personality of Godhead; *jñānam*—transcendental knowledge; *yat*—which; *tat*—that; *saṅgrāma-mūrdhani*—in the midst of battle; *kāla-karma*—time and actions; *tamaḥ-ruddham*—enwrapped by such darkness; *punaḥ adhyagamat*—revived them again; *prabhuḥ*—the lord of his senses.

TRANSLATION

Because of the Lord's pastimes and activities and because of His absence, it appeared that Arjuna forgot the instructions left by the Personality of Godhead. But factually this was not the case, and again he became lord of his senses.

PURPORT

A conditioned soul is enwrapped in his fruitive activities by the force of eternal time. But the Supreme Lord, when He incarnates on the earth, is not influenced by *kāla*, or the material conception of past, present and future. The activities of the Lord are eternal, and they are manifestations of His *ātma-māyā*, or internal potency. All pastimes or activities of the Lord are spiritual in nature, but to the laymen they appear to be on the same level with material activities. It so appeared that Arjuna and the Lord were engaged in the Battle of Kurukṣetra as the other party was also engaged, but factually the Lord was executing His mission of incarnation and association with His eternal friend Arjuna. Therefore such apparently material activities of Arjuna did not drive him away from his transcendental position, but on the contrary revived his consciousness of the songs of the Lord, as He sang them personally. This revival of consciousness is assured by the Lord in the *Bhagavad-gītā* (18.65) as follows:

man-manā bhava mad-bhakto
mad-yājī māṁ namaskuru
mām evaiṣyasi satyaṁ te
pratijāne priyo 'si me

One should think of the Lord always; the mind should not forget Him. One should become a devotee of the Lord and offer obeisances unto Him. One who lives in that fashion becomes undoubtedly endowed with the blessing of the Lord by achieving the shelter of His lotus feet. There is nothing to doubt about this eternal truth. Because Arjuna was His confidential friend, the secret was disclosed to him.

Arjuna had no desire to fight with his relatives, but he fought for the mission of the Lord. He was always engaged in the execution of His mission only, and therefore after the Lord's departure he remained in the same transcendental position, even though it appeared that he forgot all the instructions of the *Bhagavad-gītā*. One should, therefore, adjust the activities of life in pace with the mission of the Lord, and by doing this one is sure to return back home, back to Godhead. This is the highest perfection of life.

TEXT 31

विशोको ब्रह्मसम्पत्त्या संछिन्नद्वैतसंशयः ।
लीनप्रकृतिनैर्गुण्यादलिङ्गत्वादसम्भवः ॥३१॥

viśoko brahma-sampattyā
sañchinna-dvaita-saṁśayaḥ
līna-prakṛti-nairguṇyād
aliṅgatvād asambhavaḥ

viśokaḥ—free from bereavement; *brahma-sampattyā*—by possession of spiritual assets; *sañchinna*—being completely cut off; *dvaita-saṁśayaḥ*—from the doubts of relativity; *līna*—merged in; *prakṛti*—material nature; *nairguṇyāt*—due to being in transcendence; *aliṅgat-vāt*—because of being devoid of a material body; *asambhavaḥ*—free from birth and death.

TRANSLATION

Because of his possessing spiritual assets, the doubts of duality were completely cut off. Thus he was freed from the three modes of material nature and placed in transcendence. There was no longer any chance of his becoming entangled in birth and death, for he was freed from material form.

PURPORT

Doubts of duality begin from the misconception of the material body, which is accepted as the self by less intelligent persons. The most foolish part of our ignorance is our identifying this material body with the self. Everything in relation with the body is ignorantly accepted as our own. Doubts due to misconceptions of myself and mine—in other words, my body, my relatives, my property, my wife, my children, my wealth, my country, my community, and hundreds and thousands of similar illusory contemplations—cause bewilderment for the conditioned soul. By assimilating the instructions of the *Bhagavad-gītā*, one is sure to be released from such bewilderment because real knowledge is knowledge that the Supreme Personality of Godhead, Vāsudeva, Lord Kṛṣṇa, is everything, including one's self. Everything is a manifestation of His potency as part and parcel. The potency and the potent are nondifferent, so the conception of duality is at once mitigated by attainment of perfect knowledge. As soon as Arjuna took up the instructions of the *Bhagavad-gītā*, expert as he was, he could at once eradicate the material conception of Lord Kṛṣṇa, his eternal friend. He could realize that the Lord was still present before him by His instruction, by His form, by His pastimes, by His qualities and everything else related to Him. He could realize that Lord Kṛṣṇa, his friend, was still present before him by His transcendental presence in different nondual energies, and there was no question of attainment of the association of the Lord by another change of body under the influence of time and space. By attainment of absolute knowledge, one can be in association with the Lord constantly, even in this present life, simply by hearing, chanting, thinking of and worshiping the Supreme Lord. One can see Him, one can feel His presence even in this present life simply by understanding the *advaya-jñāna* Lord, or the Absolute Lord, through the process of devotional service, which begins with hearing about Him. Lord Caitanya says that simply by chanting the holy name of the Lord one can at once wash off the dust on the mirror of pure consciousness, and as soon as the dust is removed, one is at once freed from all material conditions. To become free from material conditions means to liberate the soul. As soon as one is, therefore, situated in absolute knowledge, his material conception of life is removed or emerges from a false conception of life. Thus the function of the pure soul is revived in spiritual realization. This practical realization of the living being is made possible due to his becoming free from the reaction of the three modes of material nature, namely goodness, passion and ignorance. By the grace of the Lord, a pure devotee is at once raised to the place of the Absolute, and there is no chance of the devotee's becoming materially entangled again in conditioned life. One is not able to feel the presence of the Lord in all circumstances until one is endowed with the required transcendental vision made possible by devotional service prescribed in the revealed scriptures. Arjuna had attained this stage long before on the Battlefield of Kurukṣetra, and when he apparently felt the absence of the Lord, he at once took shelter of the instructions of the *Bhagavad-gītā*, and thus again he was placed in his original position. This is the position of *viśoka*, or the stage of being freed from all grief and anxieties.

TEXT 32

निशम्य भगवन्मार्गं संस्थां यदुकुलस्य च ।
स्वःपथाय मतिं चक्रे निभृतात्मा युधिष्ठिरः ॥३२॥

niśamya bhagavan-mārgaṁ
saṁsthāṁ yadu-kulasya ca
svaḥ-pathāya matiṁ cakre
nibhṛtātmā yudhiṣṭhiraḥ

niśamya—deliberating; *bhagavat*—regarding the Lord; *mārgam*—the ways of His appearance and disappearance; *saṁsthām*—end; *yadu-kulasya*—of the dynasty of King Yadu; *ca*—also; *svaḥ*—the abode of the Lord; *pathāya*—on the way of; *matim*—desire; *cakre*—gave attention; *nibhṛta-ātmā*—lonely and alone; *yudhiṣṭhiraḥ*—King Yudhiṣṭhira.

TRANSLATION

Upon hearing of Lord Kṛṣṇa's returning to His abode, and upon understanding the end of the Yadu dynasty's earthly manifestation, Mahārāja Yudhiṣṭhira decided to go back home, back to Godhead.

PURPORT

Mahārāja Yudhiṣṭhira also turned his attention to the instructions of the *Bhagavad-gītā* after hearing about the Lord's departure from the vision of earthly people. He began to deliberate on the Lord's way of appearance and departure. The mission of the Lord's appearance and disappearance in the mortal universe is completely dependent on His supreme will. He is not forced to appear or disappear by any superior energy, as the living beings appear and disappear, being forced by the laws of nature. Whenever the Lord likes, He can appear Himself from anywhere and everywhere without disturbing His appearance and disappearance in any other place. He is like the sun. The sun appears and disappears on its own accord at any place without disturbing its presence in other places. The sun appears in the morning in India without disappearing from the western hemisphere. The sun is present everywhere and anywhere all over the solar system, but it so appears that in a particular place the sun appears in the morning and also disappears at some fixed time in the evening. The time limitation even of the sun is of no concern, and so what to speak of the Supreme Lord who is the creator and controller of the sun. Therefore, in the *Bhagavad-gītā* it is stated that anyone who factually understands the transcendental appearance and disappearance of the Lord by His inconceivable energy becomes liberated from the laws of birth and death and is placed in the eternal spiritual sky where the Vaikuṇṭha planets are. There such liberated persons can eternally live without the pangs of birth, death, old age and disease. In the spiritual sky the Lord and those who are eternally engaged in the transcendental loving service of the Lord are all eternally young because there is no old age and disease and there is no death. Because there is no death there is no birth. It is concluded, therefore, that simply by understanding the Lord's appearance and disappearance in truth, one can attain the perfectional stage of eternal life. Therefore, Mahārāja Yudhiṣṭhira also began to consider going back to Godhead. The Lord appears on the earth or any other mortal planet along with His associates who live with Him eternally, and the members of the Yadu family who were engaged in supplementing the pastimes of the Lord are no other than His eternal associates, and so also Mahārāja Yudhiṣṭhira and his brothers and mother, etc. Since the appearance and disappearance of the Lord and His eternal associates are transcendental, one should not be bewildered by the external features of appearance and disappearance.

TEXT 33

पृथाप्यनुश्रुत्य धनञ्जयोदितं
नाशं यदूनां भगवद्गतिं च ताम् ।
एकान्तभक्त्या भगवत्यधोक्षजे
निवेशितात्मोपरराम संसृतेः ॥३३॥

pṛthāpy anuśrutya dhanañjayoditaṁ
nāśaṁ yadūnāṁ bhagavad-gatiṁ ca tām
ekānta-bhaktyā bhagavaty adhokṣaje
niveśitātmopararāma saṁsṛteḥ

pṛthā—Kuntī; *api*—also; *anuśrutya*—overhearing; *dhanañjaya*—Arjuna; *uditam*—uttered by; *nāśam*—end; *yadūnām*—of the Yadu dynasty; *bhagavat*—of the Personality of Godhead; *gatim*—disappearance; *ca*—also; *tām*—all those; *eka-anta*—unalloyed; *bhaktyā*—devotion; *bhagavati*—unto the Supreme Lord, Śrī Kṛṣṇa; *adhokṣaje*—transcendence; *niveśita-ātmā*—with full attention; *uparārama*—became released from; *saṁsṛteḥ*—material existence.

TRANSLATION

Kuntī, after overhearing Arjuna's telling of the end of the Yadu dynasty and disappearance of Lord Kṛṣṇa, engaged in the devotional service of the transcendental Personality of Godhead with full attention and thus gained release from the course of material existence.

PURPORT

The setting of the sun does not mean the end of the sun. It means that the sun is out of our sight. Similarly, the end of the mission of the Lord on a particular planet or universe only means that He is out of our sight. The end of the Yadu dynasty also does not mean that it is annihilated. It disappears, along with the Lord, out of our sight. As Mahārāja

Yudhiṣṭhira decided to prepare to go back to Godhead, so also Kuntī decided, and thus she fully engaged herself in the transcendental devotional service of the Lord which guarantees one a passport for going back to Godhead after quitting this present material body. The beginning of devotional service to the Lord is the beginning of spiritualizing the present body, and thus an unalloyed devotee of the Lord loses all material contact in the present body. The abode of the Lord is not a myth, as is thought by the unbelievers or ignorant people, but one cannot reach there by any material means like a sputnik or space capsule. But one can certainly reach there after leaving this present body, and one must prepare himself to go back to Godhead by practicing devotional service. That guarantees a passport for going back to Godhead, and Kuntī adopted it.

TEXT 34

ययाहरद् भुवो भारं तां तनुं विजहावजः ।
कण्टकं कण्टकेनेव द्वयं चापीशितुः समम् ॥३४॥

yayāharad bhuvo bhāraṁ
tāṁ tanuṁ vijahāv ajaḥ
kaṇṭakaṁ kaṇṭakeneva
dvayaṁ cāpīśituḥ samam

yayā—that by which; *aharat*—took away; *bhuvaḥ*—of the world; *bhāram*—burden; *tām*—that; *tanum*—body; *vijahau*—relinquished; *ajaḥ*—the unborn; *kaṇṭakam*—thorn; *kaṇṭakena*—by the thorn; *iva*—like that; *dvayam*—both; *ca*—also; *api*—although; *īśituḥ*—controlling; *samam*—equal.

TRANSLATION

The Supreme Unborn, Lord Śrī Kṛṣṇa, caused the members of the Yadu dynasty to relinquish their bodies, and thus He relieved the burden of the world. This action was like picking out a thorn with a thorn, though both are the same to the controller.

PURPORT

Śrīla Viśvanātha Cakravartī Ṭhākura suggests that the *ṛṣis* like Śaunaka and others who were hearing *Śrīmad-Bhāgavatam* from Sūta

Gosvāmī at Naimiṣāraṇya were not happy to hear about the Yadu's dying in the madness of intoxication. To give them relief from this mental agony, Sūta Gosvāmī assured them that the Lord caused the members of the Yadu dynasty to relinquish their bodies by which they had to take away the burden of the world. The Lord and His eternal associates appeared on earth to help the administrative demigods in eradicating the burden of the world. He therefore called for some of the confidential demigods to appear in the Yadu family and serve Him in His great mission. After the mission was fulfilled, the demigods, by the will of the Lord, relinquished their corporeal bodies by fighting amongst themselves in the madness of intoxication. The demigods are accustomed to drinking the *soma-rasa* beverage, and therefore the drinking of wine and intoxication are not unknown to them. Sometimes they were put into trouble for indulging in intoxication. Once the sons of Kuvera fell in the wrath of Nārada for being intoxicated, but afterwards they regained their original forms by the grace of the Lord Śrī Kṛṣṇa. We shall find this story in the Tenth Canto. For the Supreme Lord, both the *asuras* and the demigods are equal, but the demigods are obedient to the Lord, whereas the *asuras* are not. Therefore, the example of picking out a thorn by another thorn is quite befitting. One thorn, which causes pinpricks on the leg of the Lord, is certainly disturbing to the Lord, and the other thorn, which takes out the disturbing elements, certainly gives service to the Lord. So although every living being is a part and parcel of the Lord, still one who is a pinprick to the Lord is called an *asura*, and one who is a voluntary servitor of the Lord is called a *devatā*, or demigod. In the material world the *devatās* and *asuras* are always contending, and the *devatās* are always saved from the hands of the *asuras* by the Lord. Both of them are under the control of the Lord. The world is full of two kinds of living beings, and the Lord's mission is always to protect the *devatās* and destroy the *asuras*, whenever there is such a need in the world, and to do good to both of them.

TEXT 35

यथा मत्स्यादिरूपाणि धत्ते जह्याद् यथा नटः ।
भूभारः क्षपितो येन जहौ तच्च कलेवरम् ॥३५॥

yathā matsyādi-rūpāṇi
dhatte jahyād yathā naṭaḥ
bhū-bhāraḥ kṣapito yena
jahau tac ca kalevaram

yathā—as much as; *matsya-ādi*—incarnation as a fish, etc.; *rūpāṇi*—forms; *dhatte*—eternally accepts; *jahyāt*—apparently relinquishes; *yathā*—exactly like; *naṭaḥ*—magician; *bhū-bhāraḥ*—burden of the world; *kṣapitaḥ*—relieved; *yena*—by which; *jahau*—let go; *tat*—that; *ca*—also; *kalevaram*—body.

TRANSLATION

The Supreme Lord relinquished the body which He manifested to diminish the burden of the earth. Just like a magician, He relinquishes one body to accept different ones, like the fish incarnation and others.

PURPORT

The Supreme Lord Personality of Godhead is neither impersonal nor formless, but His body is nondifferent from Him, and therefore He is known as the embodiment of eternity, knowledge and bliss. In the *Bṛhad-vaiṣṇava Tantra* it is clearly mentioned that anyone who considers the form of Lord Kṛṣṇa to be made of material energy must be ostracized by all means. And if by chance the face of such an infidel is seen, one must clean himself by jumping in the river with his clothing. The Lord is described as *amṛta*, or deathless, because He has no material body. Under the circumstances, the Lord's dying or quitting His body is like the jugglery of a magician. The magician shows by his tricks that he is cut to pieces, burnt to ashes or made unconscious by hypnotic influences, but all are false shows only. Factually the magician himself is neither burnt to ashes nor cut to pieces, nor is he dead or unconscious at any stage of his magical demonstration. Similarly, the Lord has His eternal forms of unlimited variety, of which the fish incarnation, as was exhibited within this universe, is also one. Because there are innumerable universes, somewhere or other the fish incarnation must be manifesting His pastimes without cessation. In this verse, the particular word *dhatte*, eternally accepted, (and not the word *dhatvā*, accepted for the occasion) is used. The idea is that the Lord does not create the fish incarnation; He eternally has such a form, and the appearance and disappearance of such an incarnation serves particular purposes. In the *Bhagavad-gītā* (7.24–25) the Lord says, "The impersonalists think that I have no form, that I am formless, but that at present I have accepted a form to serve a purpose, and now I am manifested. But such speculators are factually without sharp intelligence. Though they may be good scholars in the Vedic literatures, they are practically ignorant of My inconceivable energies and My eternal forms of personality. The reason is that I reserve the power of not being exposed to the nondevotees by My mystic curtain. The less intelligent fools are therefore unaware of My eternal form, which is never to be vanquished and is unborn." In the *Padma Purāṇa* it is said that those who are envious and always angry at the Lord are unfit to know the actual and eternal form of the Lord. In the *Bhāgavatam* also it is said that the Lord appeared like a thunderbolt to those who were wrestlers. Śiśupāla, at the time of being killed by the Lord, could not see Him as Kṛṣṇa, being dazzled by the glare of the *brahmajyoti*. Therefore, the temporary manifestation of the Lord as a thunderbolt to the wrestlers appointed by Kaṁsa, or the glaring appearance of the Lord before Śiśupāla, was relinquished by the Lord, but the Lord as a magician is eternally existent and is never vanquished in any circumstance. Such forms are temporarily shown to the *asuras* only, and when such exhibitions are withdrawn, the *asuras* think that the Lord is no more existent, just as the foolish audience thinks the magician to be burnt to ashes or cut to pieces. The conclusion is that the Lord has no material body, and therefore He is never to be killed or changed by His transcendental body.

TEXT 36

यदा मुकुन्दो भगवानिमां महीं
जहौ स्वतन्वा श्रवणीयसत्कथः ।
तदाहरेवाप्रतिबुद्धचेतसा-
मभद्रहेतुः कलिरन्ववर्तत ॥३६॥

yadā mukundo bhagavān imāṁ mahīṁ
jahau sva-tanvā śravaṇīya-sat-kathaḥ
tadāhar evāprati-buddha-cetasām
abhadra-hetuḥ kalir anvavartata

yadā—when; *mukundaḥ*—Lord Kṛṣṇa; *bhagavān*—the Personality of Godhead; *imām*—this; *mahīm*—earth; *jahau*—left; *sva-tanvā*—with His selfsame body; *śravaṇīya-sat-kathaḥ*—hearing about Him is worthwhile; *tadā*—at that time; *ahaḥ eva*—from the very day; *aprati-buddha-cetasām*—of those whose minds are not sufficiently developed; *abhadra-hetuḥ*—cause of all ill fortune; *kaliḥ anvavartata*—Kali fully manifested.

TRANSLATION

When the Personality of Godhead, Lord Kṛṣṇa, left this earthly planet in His selfsame form, from that very day Kali, who had already partially appeared, became fully manifest to create inauspicious conditions for those who are endowed with a poor fund of knowledge.

PURPORT

The influence of Kali can be enforced only upon those who are not fully developed in God consciousness. One can neutralize the effects of Kali by keeping oneself fully under the supreme care of the Personality of Godhead. The age of Kali ensued just after the Battle of Kurukṣetra, but it could not exert its influence because of the presence of the Lord. The Lord, however, left this earthly planet in His own transcendental body, and as soon as He left, the symptoms of the Kali-yuga, as were envisioned by Mahārāja Yudhiṣṭhira prior to Arjuna's arrival from Dvārakā, began to manifest, and Mahārāja Yudhiṣṭhira rightly conjectured on the departure of the Lord from the earth. As we have already explained, the Lord left our sight just as when the sun sets it is out of our sight.

TEXT 37

युधिष्ठिरस्तत्परिसर्पणं बुधः
पुरे च राष्ट्रे च गृहे तथात्मनि ।

विभाव्य लोभानृतजिह्महिंसना-
द्यधर्मचक्रं गमनाय पर्यधात् ॥३७॥

yudhiṣṭhiras tat parisarpaṇaṁ budhaḥ
pure ca rāṣṭre ca gṛhe tathātmani
vibhāvya lobhānṛta-jihma-hiṁsanādy-
adharma-cakraṁ gamanāya paryadhāt

yudhiṣṭhiraḥ—Mahārāja Yudhiṣṭhira; *tat*—that; *parisarpaṇam*—expansion; *budhaḥ*—thoroughly experienced; *pure*—in the capital; *ca*—as also; *rāṣṭre*—in the state; *ca*—and; *gṛhe*—at home; *tathā*—as also; *ātmani*—in person; *vibhāvya*—observing; *lobha*—avarice; *anṛta*—untruth; *jihma*—diplomacy; *hiṁsana-ādi*—violence, envy; *adharma*—irreligion; *cakram*—a vicious circle; *gamanāya*—for departure; *paryadhāt*—dressed himself accordingly.

TRANSLATION

Mahārāja Yudhiṣṭhira was intelligent enough to understand the influence of the age of Kali, characterized by increasing avarice, falsehood, cheating and violence throughout the capital, state, home and among individuals. So he wisely prepared himself to leave home, and he dressed accordingly.

PURPORT

The present age is influenced by the specific qualities of Kali. Since the days of the Battle of Kurukṣetra, about 5,000 years ago, the influence of the age of Kali began manifesting, and from authentic scriptures it is learned that the age of Kali is still to run on for 427,000 years. The symptoms of the Kali-yuga, as mentioned above, namely avarice, falsehood, diplomacy, cheating, nepotism, violence and all such things, are already in vogue, and no one can imagine what is going to happen gradually with further increase of the influence of Kali till the day of annihilation. We have already come to know that the influence of the age of Kali is meant for godless so-called civilized man; those who are under the protection of the Lord have nothing to fear from this horrible age. Mahārāja Yudhiṣṭhira was a great devotee of the Lord, and there was no necessity of his being afraid of the age of Kali, but he preferred to retire from active household life and prepare himself to go back home, back to Godhead. The Pāṇḍavas are eternal companions of the Lord, and therefore they are more interested in the company of the Lord than anything else. Besides that, being an ideal king, Mahārāja Yudhiṣṭhira wanted to retire just to set an example for others. As soon as there is some young fellow to look after the household affairs, one should at once retire from family life to uplift oneself to spiritual realization. One should not rot in the dark well of household life till one is dragged out by the will of Yamarāja. Modern politicians should take lessons from Mahārāja Yudhiṣṭhira about voluntary retirement from active life and should make room for the younger generation. Also retired old gentlemen should take lessons from him and leave home for spiritual realization before forcefully dragged away to meet death.

TEXT 38

स्वराट् पौत्रं विनयिनमात्मनः सुसमं गुणैः ।
तोयनीव्याः पतिं भूमेरभ्यषिञ्चद्गजाह्वये ॥३८॥

sva-rāṭ pautraṁ vinayinam
ātmanaḥ susamaṁ guṇaiḥ
toya-nīvyāḥ patiṁ bhūmer
abhyaṣiñcad gajāhvaye

sva-rāṭ—the emperor; *pautram*—unto the grandson; *vinayinam*—properly trained; *ātmanaḥ*—his own self; *su-samam*—equal in all respects; *guṇaiḥ*—by the qualities; *toya-nīvyāḥ*—bordered by the seas; *patim*—master; *bhūmeḥ*—of the land; *abhyaṣiñcat*—enthroned; *gajāhvaye*—in the capital of Hastināpura.

TRANSLATION

Thereafter, in the capital of Hastināpura, he enthroned his grandson, who was trained and equally qualified, as the emperor and master of all land bordered by the seas.

PURPORT

The total land on the earth bordered by the seas was under the subjugation of the King of Hastināpura. Mahārāja Yudhiṣṭhira trained his grandson, Mahārāja Parīkṣit, who was equally qualified, in state administration in terms of the king's obligation to the citizens. Thus Parīkṣit was enthroned on the seat of Mahārāja Yudhiṣṭhira prior to his departure back to Godhead. Concerning Mahārāja Parīkṣit, the specific word used, *vinayinam*, is significant. Why was the King of Hastināpura, at least till the time of Mahārāja Parīkṣit, accepted as the Emperor of the world? The only reason is that the people of the world were happy because of the good administration of the Emperor. The happiness of the citizens was due to the ample production of natural produce such as grains, fruits, milk, herbs, valuable stones, minerals and everything that the people needed. They were even free from all bodily miseries, anxieties of mind, and disturbances caused by natural phenomena and other living beings. Because everyone was happy in all respects, there was no resentment, although there were sometimes battles between the state kings for political reasons and supremacy. Everyone was trained to attain the highest goal of life, and therefore the people were also enlightened enough not to quarrel over trivialities. The influence of the age of Kali gradually infiltrated the good qualities of both the kings and the citizens, and therefore a tense situation developed between the ruler and the ruled, but still even in this age of disparity between the ruler and the ruled, there can be spiritual emolument and God consciousness. That is a special prerogative.

TEXT 39

मथुरायां तथा वज्रं शूरसेनपतिं ततः ।
प्राजापत्यां निरूप्येष्टिमग्नीनपिबदीश्वरः ॥३९॥

mathurāyāṁ tathā vajraṁ
śūrasena-patiṁ tataḥ
prājāpatyāṁ nirūpyeṣṭim
agnīn apibad īśvaraḥ

mathurāyām—at Mathurā; *tathā*—also; *vajram*—Vajra; *śūrasena-patim*—King of the Śūrasenas; *tataḥ*—thereafter; *prājāpatyām*—

Prājāpatya sacrifice; *nirūpya*—having performed; *iṣṭim*—goal; *agnīn*—fire; *apibat*—placed in himself; *īśvaraḥ*—capable.

TRANSLATION

Then he posted Vajra, the son of Aniruddha [grandson of Lord Kṛṣṇa], at Mathurā as the King of Śūrasena. Afterwards Mahārāja Yudhiṣṭhira performed a Prājāpatya sacrifice and placed in himself the fire for quitting household life.

PURPORT

Mahārāja Yudhiṣṭhira, after placing Mahārāja Parīkṣit on the imperial throne of Hastināpura, and after posting Vajra, the great-grandson of Lord Kṛṣṇa, as the King of Mathurā, accepted the renounced order of life. The system of four orders of life and four castes in terms of quality and work, known as *varṇāśrama-dharma,* is the beginning of real human life, and Mahārāja Yudhiṣṭhira, as the protector of this system of human activities, timely retired from active life as a *sannyāsī,* handing over the charge of the administration to a trained prince, Mahārāja Parīkṣit. The scientific system of *varṇāśrama-dharma* divides the human life into four divisions of occupation and four orders of life. The four orders of life as *brahmacārī, gṛhastha, vānaprastha* and *sannyāsī* are to be followed by all, irrespective of the occupational division. Modern politicians do not wish to retire from active life, even if they are old enough, but Yudhiṣṭhira Mahārāja, as an ideal king, voluntarily retired from active administrative life to prepare himself for the next life. Everyone's life must be so arranged that the last stage of life, say at least the last fifteen to twenty years prior to death, can be absolutely devoted to the devotional service of the Lord to attain the highest perfection of life. It is really foolishness to engage oneself all the days of one's life in material enjoyment and fruitive activities, because as long as the mind remains absorbed in fruitive work for material enjoyment, there is no chance of getting out from conditioned life, or material bondage. No one should follow the suicidal policy of neglecting one's supreme task of attaining the highest perfection of life, namely going back home, back to Godhead.

TEXT 40

विसृज्य तत्र तत् सर्वं दुकूलवलयादिकम् ।
निर्ममो निरहंकारः संछिन्नाशेषबन्धनः ॥४०॥

visṛjya tatra tat sarvaṁ
dukūla-valayādikam
nirmamo nirhaṅkāraḥ
sañchinnāśeṣa-bandhanaḥ

visṛjya—relinquishing; *tatra*—all those; *tat*—that; *sarvam*—everything; *dukūla*—belt; *valaya-ādikam*—and bangles; *nirmamaḥ*—uninterested; *nirahaṅkāraḥ*—unattached; *sañchinna*—perfectly cut off; *aśeṣa-bandhanaḥ*—unlimited attachment.

TRANSLATION

Mahārāja Yudhiṣṭhira at once relinquished all his garments, belt and ornaments of the royal order and became completely disinterested and unattached to everything.

PURPORT

To become purified of material contamination is the necessary qualification for becoming one of the associates of the Lord. No one can become an associate of the Lord or can go back to Godhead without such purification. Mahārāja Yudhiṣṭhira, therefore, to become spiritually pure, at once gave up his royal opulence, relinquishing his royal dress and garments. The *kaṣāya*, or saffron loincloth of a *sannyāsī*, indicates freedom from all attractive material garments, and thus he changed his dress accordingly. He became disinterested in his kingdom and family and thus became free from all material contamination, or material designation. People are generally attached to various kinds of designations—the designations of family, society, country, occupation, wealth, position and many others. As long as one is attached to such designations, he is considered materially impure. The so-called leaders of men in the modern age are attached by national consciousness, but they do not know that such false consciousness is also another designation of the materially conditioned soul; one has to relinquish such designations before one can become eligible to go back to Godhead. Foolish people adore such men who die in national consciousness, but here is an example of Mahārāja Yudhiṣṭhira, a royal king who prepared himself to leave this world without such national consciousness. And yet he is remembered even today because he was a great pious king, almost on the same level with the Personality of Godhead Śrī Rāma. And because people of the world were dominated by such pious kings, they were happy in all respects, and it was quite possible for such great emperors to rule the world.

TEXT 41

वाचं जुहाव मनसि तत्प्राण इतरे च तम् ।
मृत्यावपानं सोत्सर्गं तं पञ्चत्वे ह्यजोहवीत् ॥४१॥

vācaṁ juhāva manasi
tat prāṇa itare ca tam
mṛtyāv apānaṁ sotsargaṁ
taṁ pañcatve hy ajohavīt

vācam—speeches; *juhāva*—relinquished; *manasi*—into the mind; *tat prāṇe*—mind into breathing; *itare ca*—other senses also; *tam*—into that; *mṛtyau*—into death; *apānam*—breathing; *sa-utsargam*—with all dedication; *tam*—that; *pañcatve*—into the body made of five elements; *hi*—certainly; *ajohavīt*—amalgamated it.

TRANSLATION

Then he amalgamated all the sense organs into the mind, then the mind into life, life into breathing, his total existence into the embodiment of the five elements, and his body into death. Then, as pure self, he became free from the material conception of life.

PURPORT

Mahārāja Yudhiṣṭhira, like his brother Arjuna, began to concentrate and gradually became freed from all material bondage. First he concentrated all the actions of the senses and amalgamated them into the mind, or in other words he turned his mind toward the transcendental service of the Lord. He prayed that since all material activities are performed by the mind in terms of actions and reactions of the material senses, and since he was going back to Godhead, the mind would wind up its material activities and be turned towards the transcendental service to the Lord. There was no longer a need for material activities. Actually the activities of the mind cannot be stopped, for they are the reflection of the eternal soul, but the quality of the activities can be changed from matter to the transcendental service of the Lord. The material color of the mind is changed when one washes it from contaminations of life-breathing and thereby frees it from the contamination of repeated births and deaths and situates it in pure spiritual life. All is manifested by the temporary embodiment of the material body, which is a production of the mind at the time of death, and if the mind is purified by practice of transcendental loving service to the Lord and is constantly engaged in the service of the lotus feet of the Lord, there is no more chance of the mind's producing another material body after death. It will be freed from absorption in material contamination. The pure soul will be able to return home, back to Godhead.

TEXT 42

त्रित्वे हुत्वा च पञ्चत्वं तच्चैकत्वेऽजुहोन्मुनिः ।
सर्वमात्मन्यजुहवीद्ब्रह्मण्यात्मानमव्यये ॥४२॥

tritve hutvā ca pañcatvaṁ
tac caikatve 'juhon muniḥ
sarvam ātmany ajuhavīd
brahmaṇy ātmānam avyaye

tritve—into the three qualities; *hutvā*—having offered; *ca*—also; *pañcatvam*—five elements; *tat*—that; *ca*—also; *ekatve*—in one nescience; *ajuhot*—amalgamated; *muniḥ*—the thoughtful; *sarvam*—the sum total; *ātmani*—in the soul; *ajuhavīt*—fixed; *brahmaṇi*—unto the spirit; *ātmānam*—the soul; *avyaye*—unto the inexhaustible.

TRANSLATION

Thus annihilating the gross body of five elements into the three qualitative modes of material nature, he merged them in one nescience and then absorbed that nescience in the self, Brahman, which is inexhaustible in all circumstances.

PURPORT

All that is manifested in the material world is the product of the *mahat-tattva-avyakta*, and things that are visible in our material vision are nothing but combinations and permutations of such variegated material products. But the living entity is different from such material products. It is due to the living entity's forgetfulness of his eternal nature as eternal servitor of the Lord, and his false conception of being a so-called lord of the material nature, that he is obliged to enter into the existence of false sense enjoyment. Thus a concomitant generation of material energies is the principal cause of the mind's being materially affected. Thus the gross body of five elements is produced. Mahārāja Yudhiṣṭhira reversed the action and merged the five elements of the body in the three modes of material nature. The qualitative distinction of the body as being good, bad or mediocre is extinguished, and again the qualitative manifestations become merged in the material energy, which is produced from a false sense of the pure living being. When one is thus inclined to become an associate of the Supreme Lord, the Personality of Godhead, in one of the innumerable planets of the spiritual sky, especially in Goloka Vṛndāvana, one has to think always that he is different from the material energy; he has nothing to do with it, and he has to realize himself as pure spirit, Brahman, qualitatively equal with the Supreme Brahman (Parameśvara). Mahārāja Yudhiṣṭhira, after distributing his kingdom to Parīkṣit and Vajra, did not think himself Emperor of the world or head of the Kuru dynasty. This sense of freedom from material relations, as well as freedom from the material encagement of the gross and subtle encirclement, makes one free to act as the servitor of the Lord, even though one is in the material world. This stage is called the *jīvanmukta* stage, or the liberated stage, even in the material world. That is the process of ending material existence. One must not only think that he is Brahman, but must act like Brahman. One who only thinks himself Brahman is an impersonalist. And one who acts like Brahman is the pure devotee.

TEXT 43

चीरवासा निराहारो बद्धवाङ् मुक्तमूर्धजः ।
दर्शयन्नात्मनो रूपं जडोन्मत्तपिशाचवत् ।
अनवेक्षमाणो निरगादशृण्वन् बधिरो यथा ॥४३॥

cīra-vāsā nirāhāro
baddha-vāṅ mukta-mūrdhajaḥ
darśayann ātmano rūpaṁ
jaḍonmatta-piśācavat
anavekṣamāṇo niragād
aśṛṇvan badhiro yathā

cīra-vāsāḥ—accepted torn clothing; *nirāhāraḥ*—gave up all solid foodstuff; *baddha-vāk*—stopped talking; *mukta-mūrdhajaḥ*—untied his hair; *darśayan*—began to show; *ātmanaḥ*—of himself; *rūpam*—bodily features; *jaḍa*—inert; *unmatta*—mad; *piśāca-vat*—just like an urchin; *anavekṣamāṇaḥ*—without waiting for; *niragāt*—was situated; *aśṛṇvan*—without hearing; *badhiraḥ*—just like a deaf man; *yathā*—as if.

TRANSLATION

After that, Mahārāja Yudhiṣṭhira dressed himself in torn clothing, gave up eating all solid foods, voluntarily became dumb and let his hair hang loose. All this combined to make him look like an urchin or madman with no occupation. He did not depend on his brothers for anything. And, just like a deaf man, he heard nothing.

PURPORT

Thus being freed from all external affairs, he had nothing to do with imperial life or family prestige, and for all practical purposes he posed himself exactly like an inert mad urchin and did not speak of material affairs. He had no dependence on his brothers, who had all along been helping him. This stage of complete independence from everything is also called the purified stage of fearlessness.

TEXT 44

उदीचीं प्रविवेशाशां गतपूर्वां महात्मभिः ।
हृदि ब्रह्म परं ध्यायन्नावर्तेत यतो गतः ॥४४॥

udīcīṁ praviveśāśāṁ
gata-pūrvāṁ mahātmabhiḥ
hṛdi brahma paraṁ dhyāyan
nāvarteta yato gataḥ

udīcīm—the northern side; *praviveśa-āśām*—those who wanted to enter there; *gata-pūrvām*—the path accepted by his forefathers; *mahā-ātmabhiḥ*—by the broad-minded; *hṛdi*—within the heart; *brahma*—the Supreme; *param*—Godhead; *dhyāyan*—constantly thinking of; *na āvarteta*—passed his days; *yataḥ*—wherever; *gataḥ*—went.

TRANSLATION

He then started towards the North, treading the path accepted by his forefathers and great men, to devote himself completely to the thought of the Supreme Personality of Godhead. And he lived in that way wherever he went.

PURPORT

It is understood from this verse that Mahārāja Yudhiṣṭhira followed in the footsteps of his forefathers and the great devotees of the Lord. We have discussed many times before that the system of *varṇāśrama-dharma*, as it was strictly followed by the inhabitants of the world, specifically by those who inhabited the Āryāvarta province of the world, emphasizes the importance of leaving all household connections at a certain stage of life. The training and education was so imparted, and thus a respectable person like Mahārāja Yudhiṣṭhira had to leave all family connection for self-realization and going back to Godhead. No king or respectable gentleman would continue family life till the end, because that was considered suicidal and against the interest of the perfection of human life. In order to be free from all family encumbrances and devote oneself cent percent in the devotional service of Lord Kṛṣṇa, this system is always recommended for everyone because it is the path of authority. The Lord instructs in the *Bhagavad-gītā* (18.62) that one must become a devotee of the Lord at least at the last stage of one's life. A sincere soul of the Lord like Mahārāja Yudhiṣṭhira must abide by this instruction of the Lord for his own interest.

The specific words *brahma param* indicate Lord Śrī Kṛṣṇa. This is corroborated in the *Bhagavad-gītā* (10.13) by Arjuna with reference to great authorities like Asita, Devala, Nārada and Vyāsa. Thus Mahārāja Yudhiṣṭhira, while leaving home for the North, constantly remembered Lord Śrī Kṛṣṇa within himself, following in the footsteps of his forefathers as well as the great devotees of all times.

TEXT 45

सर्वे तमनुनिर्जग्मुर्भ्रातरः कृतनिश्चयाः ।
कलिनाधर्ममित्रेण दृष्ट्वा स्पृष्टाः प्रजा भुवि ॥४५॥

sarve tam anunirjagmur
bhrātaraḥ kṛta-niścayāḥ
kalinādharma-mitreṇa
dṛṣṭvā spṛṣṭāḥ prajā bhuvi

sarve—all his younger brothers; *tam*—him; *anunirjagmuḥ*—left home by following the elder; *bhrātaraḥ*—brothers; *kṛta-niścayāḥ*—decidedly; *kalinā*—by the age of Kali; *adharma*—principle of irreligion; *mitreṇa*—by the friend; *dṛṣṭvā*—observing; *spṛṣṭāḥ*—having overtaken; *prajāḥ*—all citizens; *bhuvi*—on the earth.

TRANSLATION

The younger brothers of Mahārāja Yudhiṣṭhira observed that the age of Kali had already arrived throughout the world and that the citizens of the kingdom were already affected by irreligious practice. Therefore they decided to follow in the footsteps of their elder brother.

PURPORT

The younger brothers of Mahārāja Yudhiṣṭhira were already obedient followers of the great Emperor, and they had sufficiently been trained to know the ultimate goal of life. They therefore decidedly followed their eldest brother in rendering devotional service to Lord Śrī Kṛṣṇa. According to the principles of *sanātana-dharma,* one must retire from family life after half the duration of life is finished and must engage himself in self-realization. But the question of engaging oneself is not always decided. Sometimes retired men are bewildered about how to engage themselves for the last days of life. Here is a decision by authorities like the Pāṇḍavas. All of them engaged themselves in favorably culturing the devotional service of the Lord Śrī Kṛṣṇa, the Supreme Personality of Godhead. According to Svāmī Śrīdhara, *dharma, artha, kāma* and *mokṣa,* or fruitive activities, philosophical speculations and salvation, as conceived by several persons, are not the ultimate goal of life. They are more or less practiced by persons who have no information of the ultimate goal of life. The ultimate goal of life is already indicated by the Lord Himself in the *Bhagavad-gītā* (18.64), and the Pāṇḍavas were intelligent enough to follow it without hesitation.

TEXT 46

ते साधुकृतसर्वार्था ज्ञात्वात्यन्तिकमात्मनः ।
मनसा धारयामासुर्वैकुण्ठचरणाम्बुजम् ॥४६॥

te sādhu-kṛta-sarvārthā
jñātvātyantikam ātmanaḥ
manasā dhārayām āsur
vaikuṇṭha-caraṇāmbujam

te—all of them; *sādhu-kṛta*—having performed everything worthy of a saint; *sarva-arthāḥ*—that which includes everything worthy; *jñātvā*—knowing it well; *ātyantikam*—the ultimate; *ātmanaḥ*—of the living being; *manasā*—within the mind; *dhārayām āsuḥ*—sustained; *vaikuṇṭha*—the Lord of the spiritual sky; *caraṇa-ambujam*—the lotus feet.

TRANSLATION

They all had performed all the principles of religion and as a result rightly decided that the lotus feet of the Lord Śrī Kṛṣṇa are the supreme goal of all. Therefore they meditated upon His feet without interruption.

PURPORT

In the *Bhagavad-gītā* (7.28) the Lord says that only those who have done pious deeds in previous lives and have become freed from the results of all impious acts can concentrate upon the lotus feet of the Supreme Lord Śrī Kṛṣṇa. The Pāṇḍavas, not only in this life but also in their previous lives, had always performed the supreme pious work, and thus they are ever free from all the reactions of impious work. It is quite reasonable, therefore, that they concentrated their minds upon the lotus feet of the Supreme Lord Śrī Kṛṣṇa. According to Śrī Viśvanātha Cakravartī, *dharma, artha, kāma* and *mokṣa* principles are accepted by persons who are not free from the results of impious action. Such persons affected with the contaminations of the above four principles cannot at once accept the lotus feet of the Lord in the spiritual sky. The Vaikuṇṭha world is situated far beyond the material sky. The material sky is under the management of Durgā Devī, or the material energy of the Lord, but the Vaikuṇṭha world is managed by the personal energy of the Lord.

TEXTS 47–48

तद्ध्यानोद्रिक्तया भक्त्या विशुद्धधिषणाः परे ।
तस्मिन् नारायणपदे एकान्तमतयो गतिम् ॥४७॥
अवापुर्दुरवापां ते असद्भिर्विषयात्मभिः ।
विधूतकल्मषा स्थानं विरजेनात्मनैव हि ॥४८॥

tad-dhyānodriktayā bhaktyā
viśuddha-dhiṣaṇāḥ pare
tasmin nārāyaṇa-pade
ekānta-matayo gatim

avāpur duravāpāṁ te
asadbhir viṣayātmabhiḥ
vidhūta-kalmaṣā sthānaṁ
virajenātmanaiva hi

tat—that; *dhyāna*—positive meditation; *utriktayā*—being freed from; *bhaktyā*—by a devotional attitude; *viśuddha*—purified; *dhiṣaṇāḥ*—by intelligence; *pare*—unto the transcendence; *tasmin*—in that; *nārāyaṇa*—the Personality of Godhead Śrī Kṛṣṇa; *pade*—unto the lotus feet; *ekānta-matayaḥ*—of those who are fixed in the Supreme, who is one; *gatim*—destination; *avāpuḥ*—attained; *duravāpām*—very difficult to obtain; *te*—by them; *asadbhiḥ*—by the materialists; *viṣaya-ātmabhiḥ*—absorbed in material needs; *vidhūta*—washed off; *kalmaṣāḥ*—material contaminations; *sthānam*—abode; *virajena*—without material passion; *ātmanā eva*—by the selfsame body; *hi*—certainly.

TRANSLATION

Thus by pure consciousness due to constant devotional remembrance, they attained the spiritual sky, which is ruled over by the Supreme Nārāyaṇa, Lord Kṛṣṇa. This is attained only by those who meditate upon the one Supreme Lord without deviation. This abode of the Lord Śrī Kṛṣṇa, known as Goloka Vṛndāvana, cannot be attained by persons who are absorbed in the material conception of life. But the Pāṇḍavas, being completely washed of all material contamination, attained that abode in their very same bodies.

PURPORT

According to Śrīla Jīva Gosvāmī, a person freed from the three modes of material qualities, namely goodness, passion and ignorance, and situated in transcendence can reach the highest perfection of life without change of body. Śrīla Sanātana Gosvāmī in his *Hari-bhakti-vilāsa* says that a person, whatever he may be, can attain the perfection of a twice-born *brāhmaṇa* by undergoing the spiritual disciplinary actions under the guidance of a bona fide spiritual master, exactly as a chemist can turn gun metal into gold by chemical manipulation. It is therefore the actual guidance that matters in the process of becoming a *brāhmaṇa,* even without change of body, or in going back to Godhead without change of body. Śrīla Jīva Gosvāmī remarks that the word "*hi*" used in this connection positively affirms this truth, and there is no doubt about this factual position. The *Bhagavad-gītā* (14.26) also affirms this statement of Śrīla Jīva Gosvāmī when the Lord says that anyone who executes devotional service systematically without deviation can attain the perfection of Brahman by surpassing the contamination of the three modes of material nature, and when the Brahman perfection is still more advanced by the selfsame execution of devotional service, there is no doubt at all that one can attain the supreme spiritual planet, Goloka Vṛndāvana, without change of body, as we have already discussed in connection with the Lord's returning to His abode without a change of body.

TEXT 49

विदुरोऽपि परित्यज्य प्रभासे देहमात्मनः ।
कृष्णावेशेन तच्चित्तः पितृभिः स्वक्षयं ययौ ॥४९॥

viduro 'pi parityajya
prabhāse deham ātmanaḥ
kṛṣṇāveśena tac-cittaḥ
pitṛbhiḥ sva-kṣayaṁ yayau

viduraḥ—Vidura (the uncle of Mahārāja Yudhiṣṭhira); *api*—also; *parityajya*—after quitting the body; *prabhāse*—in the place of pilgrimage at Prabhāsa; *deham ātmanaḥ*—his body; *kṛṣṇa*—the Personality of Godhead; *āveśena*—being absorbed in that thought; *tat*—his; *cittaḥ*—thoughts and actions; *pitṛbhiḥ*—along with the residents of Pitṛloka; *sva-kṣayam*—his own abode; *yayau*—departed.

TRANSLATION

Vidura, while on pilgrimage, left his body at Prabhāsa. Because he was absorbed in thought of Lord Kṛṣṇa, he was received by the denizens of Pitṛloka planet, where he returned to his original post.

PURPORT

The difference between the Pāṇḍavas and Vidura is that the Pāṇḍavas are eternal associates of the Lord, the Personality of Godhead, whereas Vidura is one of the administrative demigods in charge of the Pitṛloka planet and is known as Yamarāja. Men are afraid of Yamarāja because it is he only who awards punishment to the miscreants of the material world, but those who are devotees of the Lord have nothing to fear from him. To the devotees he is a cordial friend, but to the nondevotees he is fear personified. As we have already discussed, it is understood that Yamarāja was cursed by Maṇḍūka Muni to be degraded as a *śūdra*, and therefore Vidura was an incarnation of Yamarāja. As an eternal servitor of the Lord, he displayed his devotional activities very ardently and lived a life of a pious man, so much so that a materialistic man like Dhṛtarāṣṭra also got salvation by his instruction. So by his pious activities in the devotional service of the Lord he was able to always remember the lotus feet of the Lord, and thus he became washed of all contamination of a *śūdra*-born life. At the end he was again received by the denizens of Pitṛloka and posted in his original position. The demigods are also associates of the Lord without personal touch, whereas the direct associates of the Lord are in constant personal touch with Him. The Lord and His personal associates incarnate in many universes without cessation. The Lord remembers them all, whereas the associates forget due to their being very minute parts and parcels of the Lord; they are apt to forget such incidents due to being infinitesimal. This is corroborated in the *Bhagavad-gītā* (4.5).

TEXT 50

द्रौपदी च तदाज्ञाय पतीनामनपेक्षताम् ।
वासुदेवे भगवति ह्येकान्तमतिराप तम् ॥५०॥

draupadī ca tadājñāya
patīnām anapekṣatām
vāsudeve bhagavati
hy ekānta-matir āpa tam

draupadī—Draupadī (the wife of the Pāṇḍavas); *ca*—and; *tadā*—at that time; *ājñāya*—knowing Lord Kṛṣṇa fully well; *patīnām*—of the husbands; *anapekṣatām*—who did not care for her; *vāsudeve*—unto Lord Vāsudeva (Kṛṣṇa); *bhagavati*—the Personality of Godhead; *hi*—exactly; *eka-anta*—absolutely; *matiḥ*—concentration; *āpa*—got; *tam*—Him (the Lord).

TRANSLATION

Draupadī also saw that her husbands, without caring for her, were leaving home. She knew well about Lord Vāsudeva, Kṛṣṇa, the Personality of Godhead. Both she and Subhadrā became absorbed in thoughts of Kṛṣṇa and attained the same results as their husbands.

PURPORT

When flying an airplane, one cannot take care of other planes. Everyone has to take care of his own plane, and if there is any danger, no other plane can help another in that condition. Similarly, at the end of life, when one has to go back home, back to Godhead, everyone has to take care of himself without help rendered by another. The help is, however, offered on the ground before flying in space. Similarly, the spiritual master, the father, the mother, the relatives, the husband and others can all render help during one's lifetime, but while crossing the sea one has to take care of himself and utilize the instructions formerly received. Draupadī had five husbands, and no one asked Draupadī to come; Draupadī had to take care of herself without waiting for her great husbands. And because she was already trained, she at once took to concentration upon the lotus feet of Lord Vāsudeva, Kṛṣṇa, the Personality of Godhead. The wives also got the same result as their husbands, in the same manner; that is to say, without changing their bodies they reached the destination of Godhead. Śrīla Viśvanātha Cakravartī Ṭhākura suggests that both Draupadī and Subhadrā, although her name is not mentioned herein, got the same result. None of them had to quit the body.

TEXT 51

यः श्रद्धयैतद् भगवत्प्रियाणां
पाण्डोः सुतानामिति सम्प्रयाणम् ।
शृणोत्यलं स्वस्त्ययनं पवित्रं
लब्ध्वा हरौ भक्तिमुपैति सिद्धिम् ॥५१॥

yaḥ śraddhayaitad bhagavat-priyāṇāṁ
pāṇḍoḥ sutānām iti samprayāṇam
śṛṇoty alaṁ svastyayanaṁ pavitraṁ
labdhvā harau bhaktim upaiti siddhim

yaḥ—anyone who; *śraddhayā*—with devotion; *etat*—this; *bhagavat-priyāṇām*—of those who are very dear to the Personality of Godhead; *pāṇḍoḥ*—of Pāṇḍu; *sutānām*—of the sons; *iti*—thus; *samprayāṇam*—departure for the ultimate goal; *śṛṇoti*—hears; *alam*—only; *svastyayanam*—good fortune; *pavitram*—perfectly pure; *labdhvā*—by obtaining; *harau*—unto the Supreme Lord; *bhaktim*—devotional service; *upaiti*—gains; *siddhim*—perfection.

TRANSLATION

The subject of the departure of the sons of Pāṇḍu for the ultimate goal of life, back to Godhead, is fully auspicious and is perfectly pure. Therefore anyone who hears this narration with devotional faith certainly gains the devotional service of the Lord, the highest perfection of life.

PURPORT

Śrīmad-Bhāgavatam is a narration about the Personality of Godhead and the devotees of the Lord like the Pāṇḍavas. The narration of the Personality of Godhead and His devotees is absolute in itself, and thus to hear it with a devotional attitude is to associate with the Lord and constant companions of the Lord. By the process of hearing *Śrīmad-Bhāgavatam* one can attain the highest perfection of life, namely going back home, back to Godhead, without failure.

Thus end the Bhaktivedanta purports of the Fifteenth Chapter, First Canto, of the Śrīmad-Bhāgavatam, *entitled "The Pāṇḍavas Retire Timely."*

CHAPTER SIXTEEN

How Parīkṣit Received the Age of Kali

TEXT 1

सूत उवाच
ततः परीक्षिद् द्विजवर्यशिक्षया
महीं महाभागवतः शशास ह ।
यथा हि सूत्यामभिजातकोविदाः
समादिशन् विप्र महद्गुणस्तथा ॥ १ ॥

sūta uvāca
tataḥ parīkṣid dvija-varya-śikṣayā
mahīṁ mahā-bhāgavataḥ śaśāsa ha
yathā hi sūtyām abhijāta-kovidāḥ
samādiśan vipra mahad-guṇas tathā

sūtaḥ uvāca—Sūta Gosvāmī said; *tataḥ*—thereafter; *parīkṣit*—Mahārāja Parīkṣit; *dvija-varya*—the great twice-born *brāhmaṇas; śikṣayā*—by their instructions; *mahīm*—the earth; *mahā-bhāgavataḥ*—the great devotee; *śaśāsa*—ruled; *ha*—in the past; *yathā*—as they told it; *hi*—certainly; *sūtyām*—at the time of his birth; *abhijāta-kovidāḥ*—expert astrologers at the time of birth; *samādiśan*—gave their opinions; *vipra*—O *brāhmaṇas; mahat-guṇaḥ*—great qualities; *tathā*—true to that.

TRANSLATION

Sūta Gosvāmī said: O learned brāhmaṇas, Mahārāja Parīkṣit then began to rule over the world as a great devotee of the Lord under the instructions of the best of the twice-born brāhmaṇas. He ruled by those great qualities which were foretold by expert astrologers at the time of his birth.

PURPORT

At the time of Mahārāja Parīkṣit's birth, the expert astrologer-*brāhmaṇas* foretold some of his qualities. Mahārāja Parīkṣit developed all those qualities, being a great devotee of the Lord. The real qualification is to become a devotee of the Lord, and gradually all the good qualities worthy of possession develop. Mahārāja Parīkṣit was a *mahā-bhāgavata*, or a first-class devotee, who was not only well versed in the science of devotion but also able to convert others to become devotees by his transcendental instructions. Mahārāja Parīkṣit was, therefore, a devotee of the first order, and thus he used to consult great sages and learned *brāhmaṇas*, who could advise him by the *śāstras* how to execute the state administration. Such great kings were more responsible than modern elected executive heads because they obliged the great authorities by following their instructions left in Vedic literatures. There was no need for impractical fools to enact daily a new legislative bill and to conveniently alter it again and again to serve some purpose. The rules and regulations were already set forth by great sages like Manu, Yājñavalkya, Parāśara and other liberated sages, and the enactments were all suitable for all ages in all places. Therefore the rules and regulations were standard and without flaw or defect. Kings like Mahārāja Parīkṣit had their council of advisers, and all the members of that council were either great sages or *brāhmaṇas* of the first order. They did not accept any salary, nor had they any necessity for such salaries. *The state would get the best advice without expenditure.* They were themselves *samadarśī*, equal to everyone, both man and animal. They would not advise the king to give protection to man and instruct him to kill the poor animals. Such council members were not fools or representatives to compose a fool's paradise. They were all self-realized souls, and they knew perfectly well how all living beings in the state would be happy, both in this life and in the next. They were not concerned with the hedonistic philosophy of eat, drink, be merry and enjoy. They were philosophers in the real sense, and they knew well what is the mission of human life. Under all these obligations, the advisory council of the king would give correct directions, and the king or executive head, being himself a qualified devotee of the Lord, would scrutinizingly follow them for the welfare of the state. The state in the days of Mahārāja Yudhiṣṭhira or Mahārāja Parīkṣit was a welfare state in the real sense of the term because no one was unhappy in that state, be he man or animal. Mahārāja Parīkṣit was an ideal king for a welfare state of the world.

TEXT 2

स उत्तरस्य तनयामुपयेम इरावतीम् ।
जनमेजयादींश्चतुरस्तस्यामुत्पादयत् सुतान् ॥ २ ॥

sa uttarasya tanayām
upayema irāvatīm
janamejayādīṁś caturas
tasyām utpādayat sutān

saḥ—he; *uttarasya*—of King Uttara; *tanayām*—daughter; *upayeme*—married; *irāvatīm*—Irāvatī; *janamejaya-ādīn*—headed by Mahārāja Janamejaya; *caturaḥ*—four; *tasyām*—in her; *utpādayat*—begot; *sutān*—sons.

TRANSLATION

King Parīkṣit married the daughter of King Uttara and begot four sons, headed by Mahārāja Janamejaya.

PURPORT

Mahārāja Uttara was the son of Virāṭa and maternal uncle of Mahārāja Parīkṣit. Irāvatī, being the daughter of Mahārāja Uttara, was the cousin-sister of Mahārāja Parīkṣit, but cousin-brothers and sisters were allowed to get married if they did not belong to the same *gotra*, or family. In the Vedic system of marriage, the importance of the *gotra*, or family, was stressed. Arjuna also married Subhadrā, although she was his maternal cousin-sister.

Janamejaya: One of the *rājarṣi* kings and the famous son of Mahārāja Parīkṣit. His mother's name was Irāvatī, or according to some, Mādravatī. Mahārāja Janamejaya begot two sons of the names Jñātānīka and Śaṅkukarṇa. He celebrated several sacrifices in the Kurukṣetra pilgrimage site, and he had three younger brothers named Śrutasena, Ugrasena and Bhīmasena II. He invaded Takṣalā (Ajanta), and he decided to avenge the unlawful curse upon his great father, Mahārāja

Parīkṣit. He performed a great sacrifice called Sarpa-yajña, to kill the race of serpents, including the *takṣaka*, which had bitten his father to death. On request from many influential demigods and sages, he had to change his decision to kill the race of snakes, but despite stopping the sacrifice, he satisfied everyone concerned in the sacrifice by rewarding them properly. In the ceremony, Mahāmuni Vyāsadeva also was present, and he personally narrated the history of the Battle of Kurukṣetra before the King. Later on by the order of Vyāsadeva, his disciple Vaiśampāyana narrated before the King the subject matter of *Mahābhārata*. He was much affected by his great father's untimely death and was very anxious to see him again, and he expressed his desire before the great sage Vyāsadeva. Vyāsadeva also fulfilled his desire. His father was present before him, and he worshiped both his father and Vyāsadeva with great respect and pomp. Being fully satisfied, he most munificently gave charities to the *brāhmaṇas* present at the sacrifice.

TEXT 3

आजहाराश्वमेधांस्त्रीन् गङ्गायां भूरिदक्षिणान् ।
शारद्वतं गुरुं कृत्वा देवा यत्राक्षिगोचराः ॥ ३ ॥

ājahārāśva-medhāṁs trīn
gaṅgāyāṁ bhūri-dakṣiṇān
śāradvataṁ guruṁ kṛtvā
devā yatrākṣi-gocarāḥ

ājahāra—performed; *aśva-medhān*—horse sacrifices; *trīn*—three; *gaṅgāyām*—the bank of the Ganges; *bhūri*—sufficiently; *dakṣiṇān*—rewards; *śāradvatam*—unto Kṛpācārya; *gurum*—spiritual master; *kṛtvā*—having selected; *devāḥ*—the demigods; *yatra*—wherein; *akṣi*—eyes; *gocarāḥ*—within the purview.

TRANSLATION

Mahārāja Parīkṣit, after having selected Kṛpācārya for guidance as his spiritual master, performed three horse sacrifices on the banks of the Ganges. These were executed with sufficient rewards

for the attendants. And at these sacrifices, even the comman man could see demigods.

PURPORT

It appears from this verse that interplanetary travel by the denizens of higher planets is easy. In many statements in *Bhāgavatam*, we have observed that the demigods from heaven used to visit this earth to attend sacrifices performed by influential kings and emperors. Herein also we find that during the time of the horse sacrifice ceremony of Mahārāja Parīkṣit, the demigods from other planets were visible even to the common man, due to the sacrificial ceremony. The demigods are not generally visible to common men, as the Lord is not visible. But as the Lord, by His causeless mercy, descends to be visible to the common man, similarly the demigods also become visible to the common man by their own grace. Although celestial beings are not visible to the naked eyes of the inhabitants of this earth, it was due to the influence of Mahārāja Parīkṣit that the demigods also agreed to be visible. The kings used to spend lavishly during such sacrifices, as a cloud distributes rains. A cloud is nothing but another form of water, or, in other words, the waters of the earth transform into clouds. Similarly, the charity made by the kings in such sacrifices are but another form of the taxes collected from the citizens. But, as the rains fall down very lavishly and appear to be more than necessary, the charity made by such kings also seems to be more than what the citizen needs. Satisfied citizens will never organize agitation against the king, and thus there was no need in changing the monarchial state.

Even for a king like Mahārāja Parīkṣit there was need of a spiritual master for guidance. Without such guidance one cannot make progress in spiritual life. The spiritual master must be bona fide, and one who wants to have self-realization must approach and take shelter of a bona fide spiritual master to achieve real success.

TEXT 4

निजग्राहौजसा वीरः कलिं दिग्विजये क्वचित् ।
नृपलिङ्गधरं शूद्रं घ्नन्तं गोमिथुनं पदा ॥ ४ ॥

nijagrāhaujasā vīraḥ
kaliṁ digvijaye kvacit
nṛpa-liṅga-dharaṁ śūdraṁ
ghnantaṁ go-mithunaṁ padā

nijagrāha—sufficiently punished; *ojasā*—by prowess; *vīraḥ*—valiant hero; *kalim*—unto Kali, the master of the age; *digvijaye*—on his way to conquer the world; *kvacit*—once upon a time; *nṛpa-liṅga-dharam*—one who passes in the dress of a king; *śūdram*—the lower class; *ghnantam*—hurting; *go-mithunam*—a cow and bull; *padā*—on the leg.

TRANSLATION

Once, when Mahārāja Parīkṣit was on his way to conquer the world, he saw the master of Kali-yuga, who was lower than a śūdra, disguised as a king and hurting the legs of a cow and bull. The King at once caught hold of him to deal sufficient punishment.

PURPORT

The purpose of a king's going out to conquer the world is not for self-aggrandizement. Mahārāja Parīkṣit went out to conquer the world after his ascendance on the throne, but this was not for the purpose of aggression on other states. He was the Emperor of the world, and all small states were already under his regime. His purpose in going out was to see how things were going on in terms of the godly state. The king, being the representative of the Lord, has to execute the will of the Lord duly. There is no question of self-aggrandizement. Thus as soon as Mahārāja Parīkṣit saw that a lower-class man in the dress of a king was hurting the legs of a cow and a bull, at once he arrested and punished him. The king cannot tolerate insults to the most important animal, the cow, nor can he tolerate disrespect for the most important man, the *brāhmaṇa*. Human civilization means to advance the cause of brahminical culture, and to maintain it, cow protection is essential. There is a miracle in milk, for it contains all the necessary vitamins to sustain human physiological conditions for higher achievements. Brahminical culture can advance only when man is educated to develop the quality of goodness, and for this there is a prime necessity of food prepared with milk, fruits and grains. Mahārāja Parīkṣit was astonished to see that a black *śūdra*, dressed like a ruler, was mistreating a cow, the most important animal in human society.

The age of Kali means mismanagement and quarrel. And the root cause of all mismanagement and quarrel is that worthless men with the modes of lower-class men, who have no higher ambition in life, come to the helm of the state management. Such men at the post of a king are sure to first hurt the cow and the brahminical culture, thereby pushing all society towards hell. Mahārāja Parīkṣit, trained as he was, got the scent of this root cause of all quarrel in the world. Thus he wanted to stop it in the very beginning.

TEXT 5

शौनक उवाच

कस्य हेतोर्निजग्राह कलिं दिग्विजये नृपः ।
नृदेवचिह्नधृक् शूद्रकोऽसौ गां यः पदाहनत् ।
तत्कथ्यतां महाभाग यदि कृष्णकथाश्रयम् ॥ ५ ॥

śaunaka uvāca
kasya hetor nijagrāha
kaliṁ digvijaye nṛpaḥ
nṛdeva-cihna-dhṛk śūdra-
ko 'sau gāṁ yaḥ padāhanat
tat kathyatāṁ mahā-bhāga
yadi kṛṣṇa-kathāśrayam

śaunakaḥ uvāca—Śaunaka Ṛṣi said; *kasya*—for what; *hetoḥ*—reason; *nijagrāha*—sufficiently punished; *kalim*—the master of the age of Kali; *digvijaye*—during the time of his world tour; *nṛpaḥ*—the king; *nṛ-deva*—royal person; *cihna-dhṛk*—decorated like; *śūdrakaḥ*—lowest of the *śūdras; asau*—he; *gām*—cow; *yaḥ*—one who; *padā ahanat*—struck with his leg; *tat*—all that; *kathyatām*—please describe; *mahā-bhāga*—O greatly fortunate one; *yadi*—if, however; *kṛṣṇa*—about Kṛṣṇa; *kathā-āśrayam*—related with His topics.

TRANSLATION

Śaunaka Ṛṣi inquired: Why did Mahārāja Parīkṣit simply punish him, since he was the lowest of the śūdras, having dressed as a king and having struck a cow with his leg? Please describe all these incidents if they relate to the topics of Lord Kṛṣṇa.

PURPORT

Śaunaka and the *ṛṣis* were astonished to hear that the pious Mahārāja Parīkṣit simply punished the culprit and did not kill him. This suggests that a pious king like Mahārāja Parīkṣit should have at once killed an offender who wanted to cheat the public by dressing like a king and at the same time daring to insult the purest of the animals, a cow. The *ṛṣis* in those days, however, could not even imagine that in the advanced days of the age of Kali the lowest of the *śūdras* will be elected as administrators and will open organized slaughterhouses for killing cows. Anyway, although hearing about a *śūdraka* who was a cheat and insulter of a cow was not very interesting to the great *ṛṣis*, they nevertheless wanted to hear about it to see if the event had any connection with Lord Kṛṣṇa. They were simply interested in the topics of Lord Kṛṣṇa, for anything that is dovetailed with the narration of Kṛṣṇa is worth hearing. There are many topics in the *Bhāgavatam* about sociology, politics, economics, cultural affairs, etc., but all of them are in relation with Kṛṣṇa, and therefore all of them are worth hearing. Kṛṣṇa is the purifying ingredient in all matters, regardless of what they are. In the mundane world, everything is impure due to its being a product of the three mundane qualities. The purifying agent, however, is Kṛṣṇa.

TEXT 6

अथवास्य पदाम्भोजमकरन्दलिहां सताम् ।
किमन्यैरसदालापैरायुषो यदसद्व्ययः ॥ ६ ॥

athavāsya padāmbhoja-
makaranda-lihāṁ satām
kim anyair asad-ālāpair
āyuṣo yad asad-vyayaḥ

athavā—otherwise; *asya*—of His (Lord Kṛṣṇa's); *pada-ambhoja*—lotus feet; *makaranda-lihām*—of those who lick the honey from such a lotus flower; *satām*—of those who are to exist eternally; *kim anyaiḥ*—what is the use of anything else; *asat*—illusory; *ālāpaiḥ*—topics; *āyuṣaḥ*—of the duration of life; *yat*—that which is; *asat-vyayaḥ*—unnecessary waste of life.

TRANSLATION

The devotees of the Lord are accustomed to licking up the honey available from the lotus feet of the Lord. What is the use of topics which simply waste one's valuable life?

PURPORT

Lord Kṛṣṇa and His devotees are both on the transcendental plane; therefore the topics of Lord Kṛṣṇa and of His pure devotees are equally good. The Battle of Kurukṣetra is full of politics and diplomacy, but because the topics are related with Lord Kṛṣṇa, the *Bhagavad-gītā* is therefore adored all over the world. There is no need to eradicate politics, economics, sociology, etc., which are mundane to the mundaners. To a pure devotee, who is actually related with the Lord, such mundane things are transcendental if dovetailed with the Lord or with His pure devotees. We have heard and talked about the activities of the Pāṇḍavas, and we now are dealing with the topics of Mahārāja Parīkṣit, but because all these topics are related to the Lord Śrī Kṛṣṇa, they are all transcendental, and pure devotees have great interest in hearing them. We have already discussed this matter in connection with the prayers of Bhīṣmadeva.

Our duration of life is not very long, and there is no certainty of when we shall be ordered to leave everything for the next stage. Thus it is our duty to see that not a moment of our life is wasted in topics which are not related with Lord Kṛṣṇa. Any topic, however pleasant, is not worth hearing if it is devoid of its relation to Kṛṣṇa.

The spiritual planet, Goloka Vṛndāvana, the eternal abode of Lord Kṛṣṇa, is shaped like the whorl of a lotus flower. Even when the Lord descends to any one of the mundane planets, He does so by manifesting His own abode as it is. Thus His feet remain always on the same big whorl of the lotus flower. His feet are also as beautiful as the lotus flower. Therefore it is said that Lord Kṛṣṇa has lotus feet.

A living being is eternal by constitution. He is, so to speak, in the whirlpool of birth and death due to his contact with material energy. Freed from such material energy, a living entity is liberated and is eligible to return home, back to Godhead. Those who want to live forever without changing their material bodies should not waste valuable time with topics other than those relating to Lord Kṛṣṇa and His devotees.

TEXT 7

क्षुद्रायुषां नृणामङ्ग मर्त्यानामृतमिच्छताम् ।
इहोपहूतो भगवान् मृत्युः शामित्रकर्मणि ॥ ७ ॥

kṣudrāyuṣāṁ nṛṇām aṅga
martyānām ṛtam icchatām
ihopahūto bhagavān
mṛtyuḥ śāmitra-karmaṇi

kṣudra—very small; *āyuṣām*—of the duration of life; *nṛṇām*—of the human beings; *aṅga*—O Sūta Gosvāmī; *martyānām*—of those who are sure to meet death; *ṛtam*—eternal life; *icchatām*—of those who desire it; *iha*—herein; *upahūtaḥ*—called for being present; *bhagavān*—representing the Lord; *mṛtyuḥ*—the controller of death, Yamarāja; *śāmitra*—suppressing; *karmaṇi*—performances.

TRANSLATION

O Sūta Gosvāmī, there are those amongst men who desire freedom from death and get eternal life. They escape the slaughtering process by calling the controller of death, Yamarāja.

PURPORT

The living entity, as he develops from lower animal life to a higher human being and gradually to higher intelligence, becomes anxious to get free from the clutches of death. Modern scientists try to avoid death by physiochemical advancement of knowledge, but alas, the controller of death, Yamarāja, is so cruel that he does not spare even the very life of the scientist himself. The scientist, who puts forward the theory of stopping death by advancement of scientific knowledge, becomes himself a victim of death when he is called by Yamarāja. What to speak of stopping death, no one can enhance the short period of life even by a fraction of a moment. The only hope of suspending the cruel slaughtering process of Yamarāja is to call him to hear and chant the holy name of the Lord. Yamarāja is a great devotee of the Lord, and he likes to be invited to *kīrtanas* and sacrifices by the pure devotees, who are constantly engaged in the devotional service of the Lord. Thus the great sages, headed by Śaunaka and others, invited Yamarāja to attend the sacrifice performed at Naimiṣāraṇya. This was good for those who did not want to die.

TEXT 8

न कश्चिन्म्रियते तावद् यावदास्त इहान्तकः ।
एतदर्थं हि भगवानाहूतः परमर्षिभिः ।
अहो नृलोके पीयेत हरिलीलामृतं वचः ॥ ८ ॥

na kaścin mriyate tāvad
yāvad āsta ihāntakaḥ
etad-arthaṁ hi bhagavān
āhūtaḥ paramarṣibhiḥ
aho nṛ-loke pīyeta
hari-līlāmṛtaṁ vacaḥ

na—not; *kaścit*—anyone; *mriyate*—will die; *tāvat*—so long; *yāvat*—as long as; *āste*—is present; *iha*—herein; *antakaḥ*—one who causes the end of life; *etat*—this; *artham*—reason; *hi*—certainly; *bhagavān*—the representative of the Lord; *āhūtaḥ*—invited; *parama-ṛṣibhiḥ*—by the great sages; *aho*—alas; *nṛ-loke*—in human society; *pīyeta*—let them drink; *hari-līlā*—transcendental pastimes of the Lord; *amṛtam*—nectar for eternal life; *vacaḥ*—narrations.

TRANSLATION

As long as Yamarāja, who causes everyone's death, is present here, no one shall meet with death. The great sages have invited

the controller of death, Yamarāja, who is the representative of the Lord. Living beings who are under his grip should take advantage by hearing the deathless nectar in the form of this narration of the transcendental pastimes of the Lord.

PURPORT

Every human being dislikes meeting death, but he does not know how to get rid of death. The surest remedy for avoiding death is to accustom oneself to hearing the nectarean pastimes of the Lord as they are systematically narrated in the text of *Śrīmad-Bhāgavatam.* It is advised herein, therefore, that any human being who desires freedom from death should take to this course of life as recommended by the *ṛṣis* headed by Śaunaka.

TEXT 9

मन्दस्य मन्दप्रज्ञस्य वयो मन्दायुषश्च वै ।
निद्रया ह्रियते नक्तं दिवा च व्यर्थकर्मभिः ॥ ९ ॥

mandasya manda-prajñasya
vayo mandāyuṣaś ca vai
nidrayā hriyate naktaṁ
divā ca vyartha-karmabhiḥ

mandasya—of the lazy; *manda*—paltry; *prajñasya*—of intelligence; *vayaḥ*—age; *manda*—short; *āyuṣaḥ*—of duration of life; *ca*—and; *vai*—exactly; *nidrayā*—by sleeping; *hriyate*—passes away; *naktam*—night; *divā*—daytime; *ca*—also; *vyartha*—for nothing; *karmabhiḥ*—by activities.

TRANSLATION

Lazy human beings with paltry intelligence and a short duration of life pass the night sleeping and the day performing activities that are for naught.

PURPORT

The less intelligent do not know the real value of the human form of life. The human form is a special gift of material nature in the course of her enforcing stringent laws of miseries upon the living being. It is a chance to achieve the highest boon of life, namely to get out of the entanglement of repeated birth and death. The intelligent take care of this important gift by strenuously endeavoring to get out of the entanglement. But the less intelligent are lazy and unable to evaluate the gift of the human body to achieve liberation from the material bondage; they become more interested in so-called economic development and work very hard throughout life simply for the sense enjoyment of the temporary body. Sense enjoyment is also allowed to the lower animals by the law of nature, and thus a human being is also destined to a certain amount of sense enjoyment according to his past or present life. But one should definitely try to understand that sense enjoyment is not the ultimate goal of human life. Herein it is said that during the daytime one works "for nothing" because the aim is nothing but sense enjoyment. We can particularly observe how the human being is engaged for nothing in the great cities and industrial towns. There are so many things manufactured by human energy, but they are all meant for sense enjoyment, and not for getting out of material bondage. And after working hard during the daytime, a tired man either sleeps or engages in sex habits at night. That is the program of materialistic civilized life for the less intelligent. Therefore they are designated herein as lazy, unfortunate and short-lived.

TEXT 10

सूत उवाच
यदा परीक्षित् कुरुजाङ्गलेऽवसत्
कलिं प्रविष्टं निजचक्रवर्तिते ।
निशम्य वार्तामनतिप्रियां ततः
शरासनं संयुगशौण्डिराददे ॥१०॥

sūta uvāca
yadā parīkṣit kuru-jāṅgale 'vasat
kaliṁ praviṣṭaṁ nija-cakravartite
niśamya vārtām anatipriyāṁ tataḥ
śarāsanaṁ saṁyuga-śauṇḍir ādade

sūtaḥ uvāca—Sūta Gosvāmī said; *yadā*—when; *parīkṣit*—Mahārāja Parīkṣit; *kuru-jāṅgale*—in the capital of Kuru's empire; *avasat*—was residing; *kalim*—the symptoms of the age of Kali; *praviṣṭam*—entered; *nija-cakravartite*—within his jurisdiction; *niśamya*—thus hearing; *vārtām*—news; *anati-priyām*—not very palatable; *tataḥ*—thereafter; *śarāsanam*—arrows and bow; *saṁyuga*—having gotten a chance for; *śauṇḍiḥ*—martial activities; *ādade*—took up.

TRANSLATION

Sūta Gosvāmī said: While Mahārāja Parīkṣit was residing in the capital of the Kuru empire, the symptoms of the age of Kali began to infiltrate within the jurisdiction of his state. When he learned about this, he did not think the matter very palatable. This did, however, give him a chance to fight. He took up his bow and arrows and prepared himself for military activities.

PURPORT

The state administration of Mahārāja Parīkṣit was so perfect that he was sitting in his capital peacefully. But he got the news that the symptoms of the age of Kali had already infiltrated into the jurisdiction of his state, and he did not like this news. What are the symptoms of the age of Kali? They are (1) illicit connection with women, (2) indulgence in meat-eating, (3) intoxication and (4) taking pleasure in gambling. The age of Kali literally means the age of quarrel, and the above-mentioned four symptoms in human society are the root causes for all kinds of quarrel. Mahārāja Parīkṣit heard that some of the people of the state had already taken to those symptoms, and he wanted to take immediate steps against such causes of unrest. This means that at least up to the regime of Mahārāja Parīkṣit, such symptoms of public life were practically unknown, and as soon as they were slightly detected, he wanted to root them out. The news was not palatable for him, but in a way it was because Mahārāja Parīkṣit got a chance to fight. There was no need to fight with small states because everyone was peacefully under his subordination, but the Kali-yuga miscreants gave his fighting spirit a chance for exhibition. A perfect *kṣatriya* king is always jubilant as soon as he gets a chance to fight, just as a sportsman is eager when there is a chance for a sporting match. It is no argument that in the age of Kali such symptoms are predestined. If so, then why was there preparation for fighting out such symptoms? Such arguments are offered by lazy and unfortunate men. In the rainy season, rain is predestined, and yet people take precautions to protect themselves. Similarly, in the age of Kali the symptoms as above mentioned are sure to infiltrate into social life, but it is the duty of the state to save the citizens from the association of the agents of the age of Kali. Mahārāja Parīkṣit wanted to punish the miscreants indulging in the symptoms of Kali, and thus save the innocent citizens who were pure in habit by culture of religion. It is the duty of the king to give such protection, and Mahārāja Parīkṣit was perfectly right when he prepared himself to fight.

TEXT 11

स्वलंकृतं श्यामतुरङ्गयोजितं
रथं मृगेन्द्रध्वजमाश्रितः पुरात् ।
वृतो रथाश्वद्विपपत्तियुक्तया
स्वसेनया दिग्विजयाय निर्गतः ॥११॥

svalaṅkṛtaṁ śyāma-turaṅga-yojitaṁ
rathaṁ mṛgendra-dhvajam āśritaḥ purāt
vṛto rathāśva-dvipapatti-yuktayā
sva-senayā digvijayāya nirgataḥ

su-alaṅkṛtam—very well decorated; *śyāma*—black; *turaṅga*—horses; *yojitam*—tackled; *ratham*—chariot; *mṛga-indra*—lion; *dhvajam*—flagged; *āśritaḥ*—under the protection; *purāt*—from the capital; *vṛtaḥ*—surrounded by; *ratha*—charioteers; *aśva*—cavalry; *dvipapatti*—elephants; *yuktayā*—thus being equipped; *sva-senayā*—along with infantry; *digvijayāya*—for the purpose of conquering; *nirgataḥ*—went out.

TRANSLATION

Mahārāja Parīkṣit sat on a chariot drawn by black horses. His flag was marked with the sign of a lion. Being so decorated and

surrounded by charioteers, cavalry, elephants and infantry soldiers, he left the capital to conquer in all directions.

PURPORT

Mahārāja Parīkṣit is distinguished from his grandfather Arjuna, for black horses pulled his chariot instead of white horses. He marked his flag with the mark of a lion, and his grandfather marked his with the mark of Hanumānjī. A royal procession like that of Mahārāja Parīkṣit surrounded by well-decorated chariots, cavalry, elephants, infantry and band not only is pleasing to the eyes, but also is a sign of a civilization that is aesthetic even on the fighting front.

TEXT 12

भद्राश्वं केतुमालं च भारतं चोत्तरान् कुरून् ।
किम्पुरुषादीनि वर्षाणि विजित्य जगृहे बलिम् ॥१२॥

bhadrāśvaṁ ketumālaṁ ca
bhārataṁ cottarān kurūn
kimpuruṣādīni varṣāṇi
vijitya jagṛhe balim

bhadrāśvam—Bhadrāśva; *ketumālam*—Ketumāla; *ca*—also; *bhāratam*—Bhārata; *ca*—and; *uttarān*—the northern countries; *kurūn*—the kingdom of the Kuru dynasty; *kimpuruṣa-ādīni*—a country beyond the northern side of the Himalayas; *varṣāṇi*—parts of the earth planet; *vijitya*—conquering; *jagṛhe*—exacted; *balim*—strength.

TRANSLATION

Mahārāja Parīkṣit then conquered all parts of the earthly planet—Bhadrāśva, Ketumāla, Bhārata, the northern portion of Kurujāṅgala, Kimpuruṣa, etc.—and exacted tributes from their respective rulers.

PURPORT

Bhadrāśva: It is an island near Meru Parvata. There is a description of this island in the *Mahābhārata* (*Bhīṣma Parva* 7.16–18). The description was narrated by Sañjaya to Dhṛtarāṣṭra.

Mahārāja Yudhiṣṭhira also conquered this island, and thus the province was included within the jurisdiction of his empire. Mahārāja Parīkṣit was formerly declared to be the emperor of all lands ruled by his grandfather, but still he had to establish his supremacy while he was out of his capital to exact tribute from such states.

Ketumāla: This earth planet is divided into seven parts, and according to others it is divided into nine parts. This earth is called Jambūdvīpa and is divided into nine *varṣas*. Bhārata-varṣa is one of the above mentioned nine *varṣas*. Such *varṣas* are known as continents in the modern geographical context. Ketumāla is described as one of the above *varṣas*. It is said that in this *varṣa*, women are the most beautiful. This *varṣa* was conquered by Arjuna also. A description of this part of the world is available in the *Mahābhārata* (*Sabhā Parva* 286.32–33).

It is said that this part of the world is situated on the western side of the Meru Parvata, and the inhabitants of this province used to live up to ten thousands of years (*Bhīṣma Parva* 6.16.31–32). Human beings living in this part of the globe are of golden color, and the women resemble the angels of heaven. The inhabitants are free from all kinds of diseases and grief.

Bhārata-varṣa: This part of the world is also one of the nine *varṣas* of the Jambūdvīpa, or earthly planet. Each planet is also sometimes called a *dvīpa* because of its being an island in the fathomless outer space. Each planet is factually an island in the airy ocean of outer space. Jambūdvīpa is only one of such countless islands in this airy ocean of space. A description of Bhārata-varṣa is given in the *Mahābhārata* (*Bhīṣma Parva*, Chapters 9–10).

Uttarāḥ: According to Śrīdhara Svāmī these parts of the world are called Ilāvṛta-varṣa, or the Mediterranean countries of Europe. The description of the Ilāvṛta-varṣa is given in the *Mahābhārata* (*Sabhā Parva* 28.7–8) as follows:

nagarāṁś ca vanāṁś caiva
nadīś ca vimalodakāḥ
puruṣān deva-kalpāṁś ca
nārīś ca priya-darśanāḥ

adṛṣṭa-pūrvān subhagān
sa dadarśa dhanañjayaḥ

sadanāni ca śubhrāṇi
nārīś cāpsarasāṁ nibhāḥ

It is twice mentioned here that the women are beautiful, and some of them are equal to the *apsarās*, or heavenly women. Therefore the countries mentioned are round about the Mediterranean coast.

Kimpuruṣa-varṣa: It is stated to be situated beyond the northern side of Darjelling Dhavala Giri and probably may be a country like Nepal, Bhutan, Tibet and China. These parts of the world were also conquered by Arjuna (*Sabhā Parva* 28.1–2). The Kimpuruṣas are descendants of the daughter of Dakṣa. When Mahārāja Yudhiṣṭhira performed a horse sacrifice, the inhabitants of these countries were also present to take part in the festival, and they paid tributes to the Emperor. This part of the world is called Kimpuruṣa-varṣa, or sometimes the Himalayan provinces (Himavatī). It is said that Śukadeva Gosvāmī was born in these Himalayan provinces, and he came to Bhārata-varṣa after crossing the Himalayan countries.

In other words, Mahārāja Parīkṣit conquered all the world, namely all the continents adjoining all the seas and oceans in all directions, namely the eastern, western, northern and southern parts of the world.

TEXTS 13–15

तत्र तत्रोपशृण्वानः स्वपूर्वेषां महात्मनाम् ।
प्रगीयमाणं च यशः कृष्णमाहात्म्यसूचकम् ॥१३॥
आत्मानं च परित्रातमश्वत्थाम्नोऽस्त्रतेजसः ।
स्नेहं च वृष्णिपार्थानां तेषां भक्तिं च केशवे ॥१४॥
तेभ्यः परमसंतुष्टः प्रीत्युज्जृम्भितलोचनः ।
महाधनानि वासांसि ददौ हारान् महामनाः ॥१५॥

tatra tatropaśṛṇvānaḥ
sva-pūrveṣāṁ mahātmanām
pragīyamāṇaṁ ca yaśaḥ
kṛṣṇa-māhātmya-sūcakam

ātmānaṁ ca paritrātam
aśvatthāmno 'stra-tejasaḥ

snehaṁ ca vṛṣṇi-pārthānāṁ
teṣāṁ bhaktiṁ ca keśave

tebhyaḥ parama-santuṣṭaḥ
prīty-ujjṛmbhita-locanaḥ
mahā-dhanāni vāsāṁsi
dadau hārān mahā-manāḥ

tatra tatra—everywhere the King visited; *upaśṛṇvānaḥ*—continuously he heard; *sva-pūrveṣām*—about his own forefathers; *mahā-ātmanām*—who were all great devotees of the Lord; *pragīyamāṇam*—unto those who were thus addressing; *ca*—also; *yaśaḥ*—glories; *kṛṣṇa*—Lord Kṛṣṇa; *māhātmya*—glorious acts; *sūcakam*—indicating; *ātmānam*—his personal self; *ca*—also; *paritrātam*—delivered; *aśvatthāmnaḥ*—of Aśvatthāmā; *astra*—weapon; *tejasaḥ*—powerful rays; *sneham*—affection; *ca*—also; *vṛṣṇi-pārthānām*—between descendants of Vṛṣṇi and that of Pṛthā; *teṣām*—of all of them; *bhaktim*—devotion; *ca*—also; *keśave*—unto Lord Kṛṣṇa; *tebhyaḥ*—unto them; *parama*—extremely; *santuṣṭaḥ*—pleased; *prīti*—attraction; *ujjṛmbhita*—pleasingly open; *locanaḥ*—one who has such eyes; *mahā-dhanāni*—valuable riches; *vāsāṁsi*—clothing; *dadau*—gave in charity; *hārān*—necklace; *mahā-manāḥ*—one who has a broader outlook.

TRANSLATION

Wherever the King visited, he continuously heard the glories of his great forefathers, who were all devotees of the Lord, and also of the glorious acts of Lord Kṛṣṇa. He also heard how he himself had been protected by the Lord from the powerful heat of the weapon of Aśvatthāmā. People also mentioned the great affection between the descendants of Vṛṣṇi and Pṛthā due to the latter's great devotion to Lord Keśava. The King, being very pleased with the singers of such glories, opened his eyes in great satisfaction. Out of magnanimity he was pleased to award them very valuable necklaces and clothing.

PURPORT

Kings and great personalities of the state are presented with welcome addresses. This is a system from time immemorial, and Mahārāja

Parīkṣit, since he was one of the well-known emperors of the world, was also presented with addresses of welcome in all parts of the world as he visited those places. The subject matter of those welcome addresses was Kṛṣṇa. Kṛṣṇa means Kṛṣṇa and His eternal devotees, as the king means the king and his confidential associates.

Kṛṣṇa and His unalloyed devotees cannot be separated, and therefore glorifying the devotee means glorifying the Lord and vice versa. Mahārāja Parīkṣit would not have been glad to hear about the glories of his forefathers like Mahārāja Yudhiṣṭhira and Arjuna had they not been connected with the acts of Lord Kṛṣṇa. The Lord descends specifically to deliver His devotees (*paritrāṇāya sādhūnām*). The devotees are glorified by the presence of the Lord because they cannot live for a moment without the presence of the Lord and His different energies. The Lord is present for the devotee by His acts and glories, and therefore Mahārāja Parīkṣit felt the presence of the Lord when He was glorified by His acts, especially when he was saved by the Lord in the womb of his mother. The devotees of the Lord are never in danger, but in the material world which is full of dangers at every step, the devotees are apparently placed into dangerous positions, and when they are saved by the Lord, the Lord is glorified. Lord Kṛṣṇa would not have been glorified as the speaker of the *Bhagavad-gītā* had His devotees like the Pāṇḍavas not been entangled in the Battlefield of Kurukṣetra. All such acts of the Lord were mentioned in the addresses of welcome, and Mahārāja Parīkṣit, in full satisfaction, rewarded those who presented such addresses. The difference between the presentation of welcome addresses today and in those days is that formerly the welcome addresses were presented to a person like Mahārāja Parīkṣit. The welcome addresses were full of facts and figures, and those who presented such addresses were sufficiently rewarded, whereas in the present days the welcome address is presented not always with factual statements but to please the postholder, and often they are full of flattering lies. And rarely are those who present such welcome addresses rewarded by the poor receiver.

TEXT 16

सारथ्यपारषदसेवनसख्यदौत्य-
वीरासनानुगमनस्तवनप्रणामान् ।

स्निग्धेषु पाण्डुषु जगत्प्रणतिं चविष्णो-
र्भक्तिं करोति नृपतिश्चरणारविन्दे ॥१६॥

sārathya-pāraṣada-sevana-sakhya-dautya-
vīrāsanānugamana-stavana-praṇāmān
snigdheṣu pāṇḍuṣu jagat-praṇatiṁ ca viṣṇor
bhaktiṁ karoti nṛ-patiś caraṇāravinde

sārathya—acceptance of the post of a chariot driver; *pāraṣada*—acceptance of the presidency in the assembly of the Rājasūya sacrifice; *sevana*—engaging the mind constantly in the service of the Lord; *sakhya*—to think of the Lord as a friend; *dautya*—acceptance of the post of a messenger; *vīra-āsana*—acceptance of the post of a watchman with a drawn sword at night; *anugamana*—following in the footsteps; *stavana*—offering of prayers; *praṇāmān*—offering obeisances; *snigdheṣu*—unto them who are malleable to the will of the Lord; *pāṇḍuṣu*—unto the sons of Pāṇḍu; *jagat*—the universal; *praṇatim*—one who is obeyed; *ca*—and; *viṣṇoḥ*—of Viṣṇu; *bhaktim*—devotion; *karoti*—does; *nṛ-patiḥ*—the King; *caraṇa-aravinde*—unto His lotus feet.

TRANSLATION

Mahārāja Parīkṣit heard that out of His causeless mercy Lord Kṛṣṇa [Viṣṇu], who is universally obeyed, rendered all kinds of service to the malleable sons of Pāṇḍu by accepting posts ranging from chariot driver to president to messenger, friend, night watchman, etc., according to the will of the Pāṇḍavas, obeying them like a servant and offering obeisances like one younger in years. When he heard this, Mahārāja Parīkṣit became overwhelmed with devotion to the lotus feet of the Lord.

PURPORT

Lord Kṛṣṇa is everything to the unalloyed devotees like the Pāṇḍavas. The Lord was for them the Supreme Lord, the spiritual master, the worshipable Deity, the guide, the chariot driver, the friend, the servant, the messenger and everything they could conceive of. And thus the Lord also reciprocated the feelings of the Pāṇḍavas. Mahārāja Parīkṣit, as a pure devotee of the Lord, could appreciate the Lord's transcendental reciprocation of the feelings of His devotees, and thus he himself also was overwhelmed with the dealings of the Lord. Simply by appreciating the dealings of the Lord with His pure devotees, one can attain salvation. The Lord's dealings with His devotees appear to be ordinary human dealings, but one who knows them in truth becomes at once eligible to go back home, back to Godhead. The Pāṇḍavas were so malleable to the will of the Lord that they could sacrifice any amount of energy for the service of the Lord, and by such unalloyed determination they could secure the Lord's mercy in any shape they desired.

TEXT 17

तस्यैवं वर्तमानस्य पूर्वेषां वृत्तिमन्वहम् ।
नातिदूरे किलाश्चर्यं यदासीत् तन्निबोध मे ॥१७॥

tasyaivaṁ vartamānasya
pūrveṣāṁ vṛttim anvaham
nātidūre kilāścaryaṁ
yad āsīt tan nibodha me

tasya—of Mahārāja Parīkṣit; *evam*—thus; *vartamānasya*—remaining absorbed in such thought; *pūrveṣām*—of his forefathers; *vṛttim*—good engagement; *anvaham*—day after day; *na*—not; *ati-dūre*—far off; *kila*—verily; *āścaryam*—astonishing; *yat*—that; *āsīt*—was; *tat*—which; *nibodha*—know it; *me*—from me.

TRANSLATION

Now you may hear from me of what happened while Mahārāja Parīkṣit was passing his days hearing of the good occupations of his forefathers and being absorbed in thought of them.

TEXT 18

धर्मः पदैकेन चरन् विच्छायामुपलभ्य गाम् ।
पृच्छति स्माश्रुवदनां विवत्सामिव मातरम् ॥१८॥

dharmaḥ padaikena caran
vicchāyām upalabhya gām
pṛcchati smāśru-vadanāṁ
vivatsām iva mātaram

dharmaḥ—the personality of religious principles; *padā*—leg; *ekena*—on one only; *caran*—wandering; *vicchāyām*—overtaken by the shadow of grief; *upalabhya*—having met; *gām*—the cow; *pṛcchati*—asking; *sma*—with; *aśru-vadanām*—with tears on the face; *vivatsām*—one who has lost her offspring; *iva*—like; *mātaram*—the mother.

TRANSLATION

The personality of religious principles, Dharma, was wandering about in the form of a bull. And he met the personality of earth in the form of a cow who appeared to grieve like a mother who had lost her child. She had tears in her eyes, and the beauty of her body was lost. Thus Dharma questioned the earth as follows.

PURPORT

The bull is the emblem of the moral principle, and the cow is the representative of the earth. When the bull and the cow are in a joyful mood, it is to be understood that the people of the world are also in a joyful mood. The reason is that the bull helps production of grains in the agricultural field, and the cow delivers milk, the miracle of aggregate food values. The human society, therefore, maintains these two important animals very carefully so that they can wander everywhere in cheerfulness. But at the present moment in this age of Kali both the bull and the cow are now being slaughtered and eaten up as foodstuff by a class of men who do not know the brahminical culture. The bull and the cow can be protected for the good of all human society simply by the spreading of brahminical culture as the topmost perfection of all cultural affairs. By advancement of such culture, the morale of society is properly maintained, and so peace and prosperity are also attained without extraneous effort. When brahminical culture deteriorates, the cow and bull are mistreated, and the resultant actions are prominent by the following symptoms.

TEXT 19

धर्म उवाच
कच्चिद्भद्रेऽनामयमात्मनस्ते
विच्छायासि म्लायतेषन्मुखेन ।
आलक्षये भवतीमन्तराधिं
दूरे बन्धुं शोचसि कञ्चनाम्ब ॥१९॥

dharma uvāca
kaccid bhadre 'nāmayam ātmanas te
vicchāyāsi mlāyateṣan mukhena
ālakṣaye bhavatīṁ antarādhiṁ
dūre bandhuṁ śocasi kañcanāmba

dharmaḥ uvāca—Dharma inquired; *kaccit*—whether; *bhadre*—madam; *anāmayam*—quite hail and hearty; *ātmanaḥ*—self; *te*—unto you; *vicchāyā asi*—appear to be covered with the shadow of grief; *mlāyatā*—which darkens; *īṣat*—slightly; *mukhena*—by the face; *ālakṣaye*—you look; *bhavatīm*—unto yourself; *antarādhim*—some disease within; *dūre*—long distant; *bandhum*—friend; *śocasi*—thinking of; *kañcana*—someone; *amba*—O mother.

TRANSLATION

Dharma [in the form of a bull] asked: Madam, are you not hale and hearty? Why are you covered with the shadow of grief? It appears by your face that you have become black. Are you suffering from some internal disease, or are you thinking of some relative who is away in a distant place?

PURPORT

The people of the world in this age of Kali are always full of anxieties. Everyone is diseased with some kind of ailment. From the very faces of the people of this age, one can find out the index of the mind. Everyone feels the absence of his relative who is away from home. The particular symptom of the age of Kali is that no family is now blessed to live together. To earn a livelihood, the father lives at a place far away from the son, or the wife lives far away from the husband and so on. There are sufferings from internal diseases, separation from those near and dear, and anxieties for maintaining the status quo. These are but some important factors which make the people of this age always unhappy.

TEXT 20

पादैर्न्यूनं शोचसि मैकपाद-
मात्मानं वा वृषलैर्भोक्ष्यमाणम् ।
आहो सुरादीन् हृतयज्ञभागान्
प्रजा उत स्विन्मघवत्यवर्षति ॥२०॥

pādair nyūnaṁ śocasi maika-pādam
ātmānaṁ vā vṛṣalair bhokṣyamāṇam
āho surādīn hṛta-yajña-bhāgān
prajā uta svin maghavaty avarṣati

pādaiḥ—by three legs; *nyūnam*—diminished; *śocasi*—if you are lamenting for that; *mā*—my; *eka-pādam*—only one leg; *ātmānam*—own body; *vā*—or; *vṛṣalaiḥ*—by the unlawful meat-eaters; *bhokṣyamāṇam*—to be exploited; *āhoḥ*—in sacrifice; *sura-ādīn*—the authorized demigods; *hṛta-yajña*—devoid of sacrificial; *bhāgān*—share; *prajāḥ*—the living beings; *uta*—increasing; *svit*—whether; *maghavati*—in famine and scarcity; *avarṣati*—because of rainlessness.

TRANSLATION

I have lost my three legs and am now standing on one only. Are you lamenting for my state of existence? Or are you in great anxiety because henceforward the unlawful meat-eaters will exploit you? Or are you in a sorry plight because the demigods are now bereft of their share of sacrificial offerings because no sacrifices are being performed at present? Or are you grieving for living beings because of their sufferings due to famine and drought?

PURPORT

With the progress of the age of Kali, four things particularly, namely the duration of life, mercy, the power of recollection, and moral or religious principles will gradually diminish. Since Dharma, or the principles of religion, would be lost in the proportion of three out of four, the symbolic bull was standing on one leg only. When three fourths of the population of the whole world become irreligious, the situation is converted into hell for the animals. In the age of Kali, godless civilizations will create so many so-called religious societies in which the Personality of Godhead will be directly or indirectly defied. And thus faithless societies of men will make the world uninhabitable for the saner section of people. There are gradations of human beings in terms of proportionate faith in the Supreme Personality of Godhead. The first-class faithful men are the Vaiṣṇavas and the *brāhmaṇas*, then the *kṣatriyas*, then the *vaiśyas*, then the *śūdras*, then the *mlecchas*, the *yavanas* and at last the *caṇḍālas*. The degradation of the human instinct begins from the *mlecchas*, and the *caṇḍāla* state of life is the last word in human degradation. All the above terms mentioned in the Vedic literatures are never meant for any particular community or birth. They are different qualifications of human beings in general. There is no question of birthright or community. One can acquire the respective qualifications by one's own efforts, and thus the son of a Vaiṣṇava can become a *mleccha*, or the son of a *caṇḍāla* can become more than a *brāhmaṇa*, all in terms of their association and intimate relation with the Supreme Lord.

The meat-eaters are generally called *mlecchas*. But all meat-eaters are not *mlecchas*. Those who accept meat in terms of scriptural injunctions are not *mlecchas*, but those who accept meat without restriction are called *mlecchas*. Beef is forbidden in the scriptures, and the bulls and cows are offered special protection by followers of the *Vedas*. But in this age of Kali, people will exploit the body of the bull and the cow as they like, and thus they will invite sufferings of various types.

The people of this age will not perform any sacrifice. The *mleccha* population will care very little for performances of sacrifices, although performance of sacrifice is essential for persons who are materially engaged in sense enjoyment. In the *Bhagavad-gītā* performance of sacrifices is strongly recommended (Bg. 3.14–16).

The living beings are created by the creator Brahmā, and just to maintain the created living being progressively towards the path back to Godhead, the system of performing sacrifice is also created by him. The system is that living beings live on the produce of grains and vegetables, and by eating such foodstuff they get vital power of the body in the shape of blood and semina, and from blood and semina one living being is able to create other living beings. But the production of grains, grass, etc., becomes possible by rain, and this rain is made to shower properly by performance of recommended sacrifices. Such sacrifices are directed by the rites of the *Vedas*, namely *Sāma, Yajur, Ṛg* and *Atharva*. In the *Manu-smṛti* it is recommended that by offerings of sacrifice on the altar of the fire, the sun-god is pleased. When the sun-god is pleased, he properly collects water from the sea, and thus sufficient clouds collect on the horizon and rains fall. After sufficient rains fall, there is sufficient production of grains for men and all animals, and thus there is energy in the living being for progressive activity. The *mlecchas*, however, make plans to install slaughterhouses for killing bulls and cows along with other animals, thinking that they will prosper by increasing the number of factories and live on animal food without caring for performance of sacrifices and production of grains. But they must know that even for the animals they must produce grass and vegetables, otherwise the animals cannot live. And to produce grass for the animals, they require sufficient rains. Therefore they have to depend ultimately on the mercy of the demigods like the sun-god, Indra and Candra, and such demigods must be satisfied by performances of sacrifice.

This material world is a sort of prison house, as we have several times mentioned. The demigods are the servants of the Lord who see to the proper upkeep of the prison house. These demigods want to see that the rebel living beings, who want to survive faithlessly, are gradually turned towards the supreme power of the Lord. Therefore, the system of offering sacrifice is recommended in the scriptures.

The materialistic men want to work hard and enjoy fruitive results for sense enjoyment. Thus they are committing many types of sins at every step of life. Those, however, who are consciously engaged in the devotional service of the Lord are transcendental to all varieties of sin and virtue. Their activities are free from the contamination of the three modes of material nature. For the devotees there is no need for performance of prescribed sacrifices because the very life of the devotee is a symbol of sacrifice. But persons who are engaged in fruitive activities for sense enjoyment must perform the prescribed sacrifices because that is the only means to get free from the reaction of all sins committed by fruitive workers. Sacrifice is the means for counteracting such accumulated sins. The demigods are pleased when such sacrifices are performed, just as prison officers are satisfied when the prisoners are turned into obedient subjects. Lord Caitanya, however, has recommended only one *yajña*, or sacrifice, called the *saṅkīrtana-yajña*, the chanting of Hare Kṛṣṇa, in which everyone can take part. Thus both devotees and fruitive workers can derive equal benefit from the performances of *saṅkīrtana-yajña*.

TEXT 21

अरक्ष्यमाणाः स्त्रिय उर्वि बालान्
शोचस्यथो पुरुषादैरिवार्तान् ।
वाचं देवीं ब्रह्मकुले कुकर्म-
ण्यब्रह्मण्ये राजकुले कुलाग्र्यान् ॥२१॥

arakṣyamāṇāḥ striya urvi bālān
śocasy atho puruṣādair ivārtān
vācaṁ devīṁ brahma-kule kukarmaṇy
abrahmaṇye rāja-kule kulāgryān

arakṣyamāṇāḥ—unprotected; *striyaḥ*—women; *urvi*—on the earth; *bālān*—children; *śocasi*—you are feeling compassion; *atho*—as such; *puruṣa-ādaiḥ*—by men; *iva*—like that; *ārtān*—those who are unhappy; *vācam*—vocabulary; *devīm*—the goddess; *brahma-kule*—in the family of the *brāhmaṇa; kukarmaṇi*—acts against the principles of religion; *abrahmaṇye*—persons against the brahminical culture; *rāja-kule*—in the administrative family; *kula-agryān*—most of all the families (the *brāhmaṇas*).

TRANSLATION

Are you feeling compunction for the unhappy women and children who are left forlorn by unscrupulous persons? Or are you unhappy because the goddess of learning is being handled by brāhmaṇas addicted to acts against the principles of religion? Or are you sorry to see that the brāhmaṇas have taken shelter of administrative families that do not respect brahminical culture?

PURPORT

In the age of Kali, the women and the children, along with *brāhmaṇas* and cows, will be grossly neglected and left unprotected. In this age illicit connection with women will render many women and children uncared for. Circumstantially, the women will try to become independent of the protection of men, and marriage will be performed as a matter of formal agreement between man and woman. In most cases, the children will not be taken care of properly. The *brāhmaṇas* are traditionally intelligent men, and thus they will be able to pick up modern education to the topmost rank, but as far as moral and religious principles are concerned, they shall be the most fallen. Education and bad character go ill together, but such things will run parallel. The administrative heads as a class will condemn the tenets of Vedic wisdom and will prefer to conduct a so-called secular state, and the so-called educated *brāhmaṇas* will be purchased by such unscrupulous administrators. Even a philosopher and writer of many books on religious principles may also accept an exalted post in a government which denies all the moral codes of the *śāstras*. The *brāhmaṇas* are specifically restricted from accepting such service. But in this age they will not only accept service, but they will do so even if it is of the meanest quality. These are some of the symptoms of the Kali age which are harmful to the general welfare of human society.

TEXT 22

किं क्षत्रबन्धून् कलिनोपसृष्टान्
राष्ट्राणि वा तैरवरोपितानि ।
इतस्ततो वाशनपानवासः-
स्नानव्यवायोन्मुखजीवलोकम् ॥२२॥

kiṁ kṣatra-bandhūn kalinopasṛṣṭān
rāṣṭrāṇi vā tair avaropitāni
itas tato vāśana-pāna-vāsaḥ-
snāna-vyavāyonmukha-jīva-lokam

kim—whether; *kṣatra-bandhūn*—the unworthy administrators; *kalinā*—by the influence of the age of Kali; *upasṛṣṭān*—bewildered; *rāṣṭrāṇi*—state affairs; *vā*—or; *taiḥ*—by them; *avaropitāni*—put into disorder; *itaḥ*—here; *tataḥ*—there; *vā*—or; *aśana*—accepting foodstuff; *pāna*—drink; *vāsaḥ*—residence; *snāna*—bath; *vyavāya*—sexual intercourse; *unmukha*—inclined; *jīva-lokam*—human society.

TRANSLATION

The so-called administrators are now bewildered by the influence of this age of Kali, and thus they have put all state affairs into disorder. Are you now lamenting this disorder? Now the general populace does not follow the rules and regulations for eating, sleeping, drinking, mating, etc., and they are inclined to perform such anywhere and everywhere. Are you unhappy because of this?

PURPORT

There are some necessities of life on a par with those of the lower animals, and they are eating, sleeping, fearing and mating. These bodily demands are for both the human beings and the animals. But the human being has to fulfill such desires not like animals, but like a human being. A dog can mate with a bitch before the public eyes without hesitation, but if a human being does so the act will be considered a public nuisance, and the person will be criminally prosecuted. Therefore for the human being there are some rules and regulations, even for fulfilling common demands. The human society avoids such rules and regulations when it is bewildered by the influence of the age of Kali. In this age, people are indulging in such necessities of life without following the rules and regulations, and this deterioration of social and moral rules is certainly lamentable because of the harmful effects of such beastly behavior. In this age, the fathers and the guardians are not happy with the behavior or their wards. They should know that so many innocent children are victims of bad association awarded by the influence of this age of Kali. We know from *Śrīmad-Bhāgavatam* that Ajāmila, an innocent son of a *brāhmaṇa*, was walking down a road and saw a *śūdra* pair sexually embracing. This attracted the boy, and later on the boy became a victim of all debaucheries. From a pure *brāhmaṇa*, he fell down to the position of a wretched urchin, and it was all due to bad association. There was but one victim like Ajāmila in those days, but in this age of Kali the poor innocent students are daily victims of cinemas which attract men only for sex indulgence. The so-called administrators are all untrained in the affairs of a *kṣatriya*. The *kṣatriyas* are meant for administration, as the *brāhmaṇas* are meant for knowledge and guidance. The word *kṣatra-bandhu* refers to the so-called administrators or persons promoted to the post of the administrator without proper training by culture and tradition. Nowadays they are promoted to such exalted posts by the votes of the people who are themselves fallen in the rules and regulations of life. How can such people select a proper man when they are themselves fallen in the standard of life? Therefore, by the influence of the age of Kali, everywhere, politically, socially or religiously, everything is topsy-turvy, and therefore for the sane man it is all regrettable.

TEXT 23

यद्वाम्ब ते भूरिभरावतार-
कृतावतारस्य हरेर्धरित्रि ।
अन्तर्हितस्य स्मरती विसृष्टा
कर्माणि निर्वाणविलम्बितानि ॥२३॥

yadvāmba te bhūri-bharāvatāra-
kṛtāvatārasya harer dharitri
antarhitasya smaratī visṛṣṭā
karmāṇi nirvāṇa-vilambitāni

yadvā—that may be; *amba*—O mother; *te*—your; *bhūri*—heavy; *bhara*—load; *avatāra*—decreasing the load; *kṛta*—done; *avatārasya*—one who incarnated; *hareḥ*—of Lord Śrī Kṛṣṇa; *dharitri*—O earth; *antaḥ-hitasya*—of Him who is now out of sight; *smaratī*—while thinking of; *visṛṣṭā*—all that were performed; *karmāṇi*—activities; *nirvāṇa*—salvation; *vilambitāni*—that which entails.

TRANSLATION

O mother earth, the Supreme Personality of Godhead, Hari, incarnated Himself as Lord Śrī Kṛṣṇa just to unload your heavy burden. All His activities here are transcendental, and they cement

the path of liberation. You are now bereft of His presence. You are probably now thinking of those activities and feeling sorry in their absence.

PURPORT

The activities of the Lord include liberation, but they are more relishable than the pleasure derived from *nirvāṇa*, or liberation. According to Śrīla Jīva Gosvāmī and Viśvanātha Cakravartī Ṭhākura, the word used here is *nirvāṇa-vilambitāni*, that which minimizes the value of liberation. To attain *nirvāṇa*, liberation, one has to undergo a severe type of *tapasya*, austerities, but the Lord is so merciful that He incarnates to diminish the burden of the earth. Simply by remembering such activities, one can defy the pleasure derived from *nirvāṇa* and reach the transcendental abode of the Lord to associate with Hím, eternally engaged in His blissful loving service.

TEXT 24

इदं ममाचक्ष्व तवाधिमूलं
वसुन्धरे येन विकर्शितासि ।
कालेन वा ते बलिनां बलीयसा
सुरार्चितं किं हृतमम्ब सौभगम् ॥२४॥

idaṁ mamācakṣva tavādhimūlaṁ
vasundhare yena vikarśitāsi
kālena vā te balināṁ balīyasā
surārcitaṁ kiṁ hṛtam amba saubhagam

idam—this; *mama*—unto me; *ācakṣva*—kindly inform; *tava*—your; *ādhimūlam*—the root cause of your tribulations; *vasundhare*—O reservoir of all riches; *yena*—by which; *vikarśitā asi*—reduced to much weakness; *kālena*—by the influence of time; *vā*—or; *te*—your; *balinām*—very powerful; *balīyasā*—more powerful; *sura-arcitam*—adored by the demigods; *kim*—whether; *hṛtam*—taken away; *amba*—mother; *saubhagam*—fortune.

TRANSLATION

Mother, you are the reservoir of all riches. Please inform me of the root cause of your tribulations by which you have been reduced to such a weak state. I think that the powerful influence of time, which conquers the most powerful, might have forcibly taken away all your fortune, which was adored even by the demigods.

PURPORT

By the grace of the Lord, each and every planet is created fully equipped. So not only is this earth fully equipped with all the riches for the maintenance of its inhabitants, but also when the Lord descends on the earth the whole earth becomes so enriched with all kinds of opulences that even the denizens of heaven worship it with all affection. But by the will of the Lord, the whole earth can at once be changed. He can do and undo a thing by His sweet will. Therefore no one should consider himself to be self-sufficient or independent of the Lord.

TEXT 25

धरण्युवाच

भवान् हि वेद तत्सर्वं यन्मां धर्मानुपृच्छसि ।
चतुर्भिर्वर्तसे येन पादैर्लोकसुखावहैः ॥२५॥

dharaṇy uvāca
bhavān hi veda tat sarvaṁ
yan māṁ dharmānupṛcchasi
caturbhir vartase yena
pādair loka-sukhāvahaiḥ

dharaṇī uvāca—mother earth replied; *bhavān*—your good self; *hi*—certainly; *veda*—know; *tat sarvam*—all that you have inquired from me; *yat*—that; *mām*—from me; *dharma*—O personality of religious principles; *anupṛcchasi*—you have inquired one after another; *caturbhiḥ*—by four; *vartase*—you exist; *yena*—by which; *pādaiḥ*—by the legs; *loka*—in each and every planet; *sukha-āvahaiḥ*—increasing the happiness.

TRANSLATION

The earthly deity [in the form of a cow] thus replied to the personality of religious principles [in the form of a bull]: O Dharma, whatever you have inquired from me shall be known to you. I shall try to reply to all those questions. Once you too were maintained by your four legs, and you increased happiness all over the universe by the mercy of the Lord.

PURPORT

The principles of religion are laid down by the Lord Himself, and the executor of such laws is Dharmarāja, or Yamarāja. Such principles work fully in the age of Satya-yuga; in the Tretā-yuga they are reduced by a fraction of one fourth; in the Dvāpara-yuga they are reduced to one half, and in the Kali-yuga they are reduced to one fourth, gradually diminishing to the zero point, and then devastation takes place. Happiness in the world depends proportionately on the maintenance of the religious principles, individually or collectively. The best part of valor is to maintain the principles despite all kinds of odds. Thus one can be happy during the span of life and ultimately return to Godhead.

TEXTS 26–30

सत्यं शौचं दया क्षान्तिस्त्यागः सन्तोष आर्जवम् ।
शमो दमस्तपः साम्यं तितिक्षोपरतिः श्रुतम् ॥२६॥
ज्ञानं विरक्तिरैश्वर्यं शौर्यं तेजो बलं स्मृतिः ।
स्वातन्त्र्यं कौशलं कान्तिर्धैर्यं मार्दवमेव च ॥२७॥
प्रागल्भ्यं प्रश्रयः शीलं सह ओजो बलं भगः ।
गाम्भीर्यं स्थैर्यमास्तिक्यं कीर्तिर्मानोऽनहंकृतिः ॥२८॥
एते चान्ये च भगवन्नित्या यत्र महागुणाः ।
प्रार्थ्या महत्त्वमिच्छद्भिर्न वियन्ति स्म कर्हिचित् ॥२९॥
तेनाहं गुणपात्रेण श्रीनिवासेन साम्प्रतम् ।
शोचामि रहितं लोकं पाप्मना कलिनेक्षितम् ॥३०॥

satyaṁ śaucaṁ dayā kṣāntis
tyāgaḥ santoṣa ārjavam
śamo damas tapaḥ sāmyaṁ
titikṣoparatiḥ śrutam

jñānaṁ viraktir aiśvaryaṁ
śauryaṁ tejo balaṁ smṛtiḥ
svātantryaṁ kauśalaṁ kāntir
dhairyaṁ mārdavam eva ca

prāgalbhyaṁ praśrayaḥ śīlaṁ
saha ojo balaṁ bhagaḥ
gāmbhīryaṁ sthairyam āstikyaṁ
kīrtir māno 'nahaṅkṛtiḥ

ete cānye ca bhagavan
nityā yatra mahā-guṇāḥ
prārthyā mahattvam icchadbhir
na viyanti sma karhicit

tenāhaṁ guṇa-pātreṇa
śrī-nivāsena sāmpratam
śocāmi rahitaṁ lokaṁ
pāpmanā kalinekṣitam

satyam—truthfulness; *śaucam*—cleanliness; *dayā*—intolerance of others' unhappiness; *kṣāntiḥ*—self-control even if there is cause of anger; *tyāgaḥ*—magnanimity; *santoṣaḥ*—self-satisfaction; *ārjavam*—straightforwardness; *śamaḥ*—fixing of the mind; *damaḥ*—control of the sense organs; *tapaḥ*—trueness to one's responsibility; *sāmyam*—indiscrimination between friend and foe; *titikṣā*—tolerance of the offenses of others; *uparatiḥ*—indifference to loss and gain; *śrutam*—following scriptural injunctions; *jñānam*—knowledge (self-realization); *viraktiḥ*—detachment from sense enjoyment; *aiśvaryam*—leadership; *śauryam*—chivalry; *tejaḥ*—influence; *balam*—to render possible that which is impossible; *smṛtiḥ*—to find one's proper duty; *svātantryam*—not to depend on others; *kauśalam*—dexterity in all activities; *kāntiḥ*—

beauty; *dhairyam*—freedom from disturbance; *mārdavam*—kindheartedness; *eva*—thus; *ca*—also; *prāgalbhyam*—ingenuity; *praśrayaḥ*—gentility; *śīlam*—mannerliness; *sahaḥ*—determination; *ojaḥ*—perfect knowledge; *balam*—proper execution; *bhagaḥ*—object of enjoyment; *gāmbhīryam*—joyfulness; *sthairyam*—immovability; *āstikyam*—faithfulness; *kīrtiḥ*—fame; *mānaḥ*—worthy of being worshiped; *anahaṅkṛtiḥ*—pridelessness; *ete*—all these; *ca anye*—also many others; *ca*—and; *bhagavan*—the Personality of Godhead; *nityāḥ*—everlasting; *yatra*—where; *mahā-guṇāḥ*—great qualities; *prārthyāḥ*—worthy to possess; *mahattvam*—greatness; *icchadbhiḥ*—those who desire so; *na*—never; *viyanti*—deteriorates; *sma*—ever; *karhicit*—at any time; *tena*—by Him; *aham*—myself; *guṇa-pātreṇa*—the reservoir of all qualities; *śrī*—the goddess of fortune; *nivāsena*—by the resting place; *sāmpratam*—very recently; *śocāmi*—I am thinking of; *rahitam*—bereft of; *lokam*—planets; *pāpmanā*—by the store of all sins; *kalinā*—by Kali; *īkṣitam*—is seen.

TRANSLATION

In Him reside (1) truthfulness, (2) cleanliness, (3) intolerance of another's unhappiness, (4) the power to control anger, (5) self-satisfaction, (6) straight-forwardness, (7) steadiness of mind, (8) control of the sense organs, (9) responsibility, (10) equality, (11) tolerance, (12) equanimity, (13) faithfulness, (14) knowledge, (15) absence of sense enjoyment, (16) leadership, (17) chivalry, (18) influence, (19) the power to make everything possible, (20) the discharge of proper duty, (21) complete independence, (22) dexterity, (23) fullness of all beauty, (24) serenity, (25) kindheartedness, (26) ingenuity, (27) gentility, (28) magnanimity, (29) determination, (30) perfection in all knowledge, (31) proper execution, (32) possession of all objects of enjoyment, (33) joyfulness, (34) immovability, (35) fidelity, (36) fame, (37) worship, (38) pridelessness, (39) being (as the Personality of Godhead), (40) eternity, and many other transcendental qualities which are eternally present and never to be separated from Him. That Personality of Godhead, the reservoir of all goodness and beauty, Lord Śrī Kṛṣṇa, has now closed His transcendental pastimes on the face of the earth. In His

absence the age of Kali has spread its influence everywhere, so I am sorry to see this condition of existence.

PURPORT

Even if it were possible to count the atoms after smashing the earth into powder, still it would not be possible to estimate the unfathomable transcendental qualities of the Lord. It is said that Lord Anantadeva has tried to expound the transcendental qualities of the Supreme Lord with His numberless tongues, and that for numberless years together it has been impossible to estimate the qualities of the Lord. The above statement of the qualities of the Lord is just to estimate His qualities as far as a human being is able to see Him. But even if it is so, the above qualities can be divided into many subheadings. According to Śrīla Jīva Gosvāmī, the third quality, intolerance of another's unhappiness, can be subdivided into (1) protection of the surrendered souls and (2) well wishes for the devotees. In the *Bhagavad-gītā* the Lord states that He wants every soul to surrender unto Him only, and He assures everyone that if one does so He will give protection from the reactions of all sins. Unsurrendered souls are not devotees of the Lord, and thus there is no particular protection for everyone in general. For the devotees He has all good wishes, and for those who are actually engaged in loving transcendental service of the Lord, He gives particular attention. He gives direction to such pure devotees to help them discharge their responsibilities on the path back to Godhead. By equality (10), the Lord is equally kind to everyone, as the sun is equal in distributing its rays over everyone. Yet there are many who are unable to take advantage of the sun's rays. Similarly, the Lord says that surrendering unto Him is the guarantee for all protection from Him, but unfortunate persons are unable to accept this proposition, and therefore they suffer from all material miseries. So even though the Lord is equally well-wishing to everyone, the unfortunate living being, due to bad association only, is unable to accept His instructions in toto, and for this the Lord is never to be blamed. He is called the well-wisher for the devotees only. He appears to be partial to His devotees, but factually the matter rests on the living being to accept or reject equal treatment by the Lord.

The Lord never deviates from His word of honor. When He gives assurance for protection, the promise is executed in all circumstances. It is the duty of the pure devotee to be fixed in the discharge of the duty entrusted to him by the Lord or the Lord's bona fide representative, the spiritual master. The rest is carried on by the Lord without a break.

The responsibility of the Lord is also unique. The Lord has no responsibility because all His work is done by His different appointed energies. But still He accepts voluntary responsibilities in displaying different roles in His transcendental pastimes. As a boy, He was playing the part of a cowboy. As the son of Nanda Mahārāja, He discharged responsibility perfectly. Similarly, when He was playing the part of a *kṣatriya* as the son of Mahārāja Vasudeva, He displayed all the skill of a martially spirited *kṣatriya.* In almost all cases, the *kṣatriya* king has to secure a wife by fighting or kidnapping. This sort of behavior for a *kṣatriya* is praiseworthy in the sense that a *kṣatriya* must show his power of chivalry to his would-be wife so that the daughter of a *kṣatriya* can see the valor of her would-be husband. Even the Personality of Godhead Śrī Rāma displayed such a spirit of chivalry during His marriage. He broke the strongest bow, called Haradhanur, and achieved the hand of Sītādevī, the mother of all opulence. The *kṣatriya* spirit is displayed during marriage festivals, and there is nothing wrong in such fighting. Lord Śrī Kṛṣṇa discharged such responsibility fully because although He had more than sixteen thousand wives, in each and every case He fought like a chivalrous *kṣatriya* and thus secured a wife. To fight sixteen thousand times to secure sixteen thousand wives is certainly possible only for the Supreme Personality of Godhead. Similarly, He displayed full responsibility in every action of His different transcendental pastimes.

The fourteenth quality, knowledge, can be further extended into five subheadings, namely (1) intelligence, (2) gratefulness, (3) power of understanding the circumstantial environments of place, object and time, (4) perfect knowledge of everything, and (5) knowledge of the self. Only fools are ungrateful to their benefactors. The Lord, however, does not require benefit from anyone besides Himself because He is full in Himself; still He feels benefited by the unalloyed services of His devotees. The Lord feels grateful to His devotees for such unsophisticated, unconditional service and tries to reciprocate it by rendering service, although the devotee also has no such desire in his heart. The transcendental service of the Lord is itself a transcendental benefit for the devotee, and therefore the devotee has nothing to expect from the Lord.

On the assertion of the Vedic aphorism *sarvaṁ khalv idaṁ brahma*, we can understand that the Lord, by the omnipresent rays of His effulgence, called *brahmajyoti*, is all-pervading inside or outside of everything, like the omnipresent material sky, and thus He is also omniscient.

As far as beauty of the Lord is concerned, He has some special features that distinguish Him from all other living beings, and over and above that He has some special attractive beautiful features by which He attracts the mind of even Rādhārāṇī, the supermost beautiful creation of the Lord. He is known, therefore, as Madana-mohana, or one who attracts the mind of even Cupid. Śrīla Jīva Gosvāmī Prabhu has scrutinizingly analyzed other transcendental qualities of the Lord and affirms that Lord Śrī Kṛṣṇa is the Absolute Supreme Personality of Godhead (Parabrahman). He is omnipotent by His inconceivable energies, and therefore He is the Yogeśvara, or the supreme master of all mystic powers. Being the Yogeśvara, His eternal form is spiritual, a combination of eternity, bliss and knowledge. The nondevotee class cannot understand the dynamic nature of His knowledge because they are satisfied to reach up to His eternal form of knowledge. All great souls aspire to be equal in knowledge with Him. This means that all other knowledge is ever insufficient, flexible and measurable, whereas the knowledge of the Lord is ever fixed and unfathomable. Śrīla Sūta Gosvāmī affirms in the *Bhāgavatam* that although He was observed by the citizens of Dvārakā every day, they were ever increasingly anxious to see Him again and again. The living beings can appreciate the qualities of the Lord as the ultimate goal, but they cannot attain the status quo of such equality. This material world is a product of the *mahat-tattva*, which is a state of the Lord's dreaming condition in His *yoga-nidrā* mystic slumber in the Causal Ocean, and yet the whole creation appears to be a factual presentation of His creation. This means that the Lord's dreaming conditions are also factual manifestations. He can therefore bring everything under His transcendental control, and thus whenever and wherever He does appear, He does so in His fullness.

The Lord, being all that is described above, maintains the affairs of the creation, and by His so doing He gives salvation even to His enemies who are killed by Him. He is attractive even to the topmost liberated soul, and thus He is worshipable even by Brahmā and Śiva, the greatest of all demigods. Even in His incarnation of *puruṣa-avatāra* He is the Lord of the creative energy. The creative material energy is working under His direction, as confirmed in the *Bhagavad-gītā* (9.10). He is the control switch of the material energy, and to control the material energy in the innumerable universes, He is the root cause of innumerable incarnations in all the universes. There are more than five hundred thousand incarnations of Manu in only one universe, besides other incarnations in different universes. In the spiritual world, however, beyond the *mahat-tattva,* there is no question of incarnations, but there are plenary expansions of the Lord in different Vaikuṇṭhas. The planets in the spiritual sky are at least three times the number of those within the innumerable universes in the *mahat-tattva.* And all the Nārāyaṇa forms of the Lord are but expansions of His Vāsudeva feature, and thus He is Vāsudeva, Nārāyaṇa and Kṛṣṇa simultaneously. He is *śrī-kṛṣṇa govinda hare murāre, he nātha nārāyaṇa vāsudeva,* all in one. His qualities, therefore, cannot be counted by anyone, however great one may be.

TEXT 31

आत्मानं चानुशोचामि भवन्तं चामरोत्तमम् ।
देवान् पितॄनृषीन् साधून् सर्वान् वर्णांस्तथाश्रमान् ॥ ३१ ॥

ātmānaṁ cānuśocāmi
bhavantaṁ cāmarottamam
devān pitṝn ṛṣīn sādhūn
sarvān varṇāṁs tathāśramān

ātmānam—myself; *ca*—also; *anuśocāmi*—lamenting; *bhavantam*—yourself; *ca*—as well as; *amara-uttamam*—the best amongst the demigods; *devān*—about the demigods; *pitṝn*—about the denizens of the Pitṛloka planet; *ṛṣīn*—about the sages; *sādhūn*—about the devotees; *sarvān*—all of them; *varṇān*—sections; *tathā*—as also; *āśramān*—orders of human society.

TRANSLATION

I am thinking about myself and also, O best amongst the demigods, about you, as well as about all the demigods, sages, denizens of Pitṛloka, devotees of the Lord and all men obedient to the system of varṇa and āśrama in human society.

PURPORT

To effect the perfection of human life there is cooperation between men and demigods, sages, denizens of the Pitṛloka, devotees of the Lord and the scientific system of *varṇa* and *āśrama* orders of life. The distinction between human life and animal life therefore begins with the scientific system of *varṇa* and *āśrama,* guided by the experience of the sages in relation with the demigods, gradually rising to the summit of reestablishing our eternal relation with the Supreme Absolute Truth, the Personality of Godhead, Lord Śrī Kṛṣṇa. When God-made *varṇāśrama-dharma,* which is strictly meant for developing animal consciousness into human consciousness and human consciousness into godly consciousness, is broken by advancement of foolishness, the whole system of peaceful and progressive life is at once disturbed. In the age of Kali, the first attack of the venomous snake strikes against the God-made *varṇāśrama-dharma,* and thus a person properly qualified as a *brāhmaṇa* is called a *śūdra,* and a *śūdra* by qualification is passing as a *brāhmaṇa,* all on a false birthright claim. To become a *brāhmaṇa* by a birthright claim is not at all bona fide, although it may be a fulfillment of one of the conditions. But the real qualification of a *brāhmaṇa* is to control the mind and the senses, and to cultivate tolerance, simplicity, cleanliness, knowledge, truthfulness, devotion and faith in the Vedic wisdom. In the present age, consideration of the necessary qualification is being neglected, and the false birthright claim is being supported even by a popular, sophisticated poet, the author of *Rāma-carita-mānasa.*

This is all due to the influence of the age of Kali. Thus mother earth, represented as a cow, was lamenting the regrettable condition.

TEXTS 32–33

ब्रह्मादयो बहु तिथं यदपाङ्गमोक्ष-
कामास्तपः समचरन् भगवत्प्रपन्नाः ।
सा श्रीः स्ववासमरविन्दवनं विहाय
यत्पादसौभगमलं भजतेऽनुरक्ता ॥३२॥
तस्याहमब्जकुलिशाङ्कुशकेतुकेतैः
श्रीमत्पदैर्भगवतः समलंकृताङ्गी ।

त्रीनत्यरोच उपलभ्य ततो विभूतिं
लोकान् स मां व्यसृजदुत्स्मयतीं तदन्ते ॥३३॥

brahmādayo bahu-titham yad-apāṅga-mokṣa-
kāmās tapaḥ samacaran bhagavat-prapannāḥ
sā śrīḥ sva-vāsam aravinda-vanaṁ vihāya
yat-pāda-saubhagam alaṁ bhajate 'nuraktā

tasyāham abja-kuliśāṅkuśa-ketu-ketaiḥ
śrīmat-padair bhagavataḥ samalaṅkṛtāṅgī
trīn atyaroca upalabhya tato vibhūtiṁ
lokān sa māṁ vyasṛjad utsmayatīṁ tad-ante

brahma-ādayaḥ—demigods such as Brahmā; *bahu-titham*—for many days; *yat*—of Lakṣmī, the goddess of fortune; *apāṅga-mokṣa*—glance of grace; *kāmāḥ*—being desirous of; *tapaḥ*—penances; *samacaran*—executing; *bhagavat*—unto the Personality of Godhead; *prapannāḥ*—surrendered; *sā*—she (the goddess of fortune); *śrīḥ*—Lakṣmījī; *sva-vāsam*—her own abode; *aravinda-vanam*—the forest of lotus flowers; *vihāya*—leaving aside; *yat*—whose; *pāda*—feet; *saubhagam*—all-blissful; *alam*—without hesitation; *bhajate*—worships; *anuraktā*—being attached; *tasya*—His; *aham*—myself; *abja*—lotus flower; *kuliśa*—thunderbolt; *aṅkuśa*—rod for driving elephants; *ketu*—flag; *ketaiḥ*—impressions; *śrīmat*—the owner of all opulence; *padaiḥ*—by the soles of the feet; *bhagavataḥ*—of the Personality of Godhead; *samalaṅkṛta-aṅgī*—one whose body is so decorated; *trīn*—three; *ati*—superseding; *aroce*—beautifully decorated; *upalabhya*—having obtained; *tataḥ*—thereafter; *vibhūtim*—specific powers; *lokān*—planetary systems; *saḥ*—He; *mām*—me; *vyasṛjat*—gave up; *utsmayatīm*—while feeling proud; *tat-ante*—at the end.

TRANSLATION

Lakṣmījī, the goddess of fortune, whose glance of grace was sought by demigods like Brahmā and for whom they surrendered many a day unto the Personality of Godhead, gave up her own abode in the forest of lotus flowers and engaged herself in the ser-

vice of the lotus feet of the Lord. I was endowed with specific powers to supersede the fortune of all the three planetary systems by being decorated with the impressions of the flag, thunderbolt, elephant-driving rod and lotus flower, which are signs of the lotus feet of the Lord. But at the end, when I felt I was so fortunate, the Lord left me.

PURPORT

The beauty and opulence of the world can be enhanced by the grace of the Lord and not by any manmade planning. When the Lord Śrī Kṛṣṇa was present on this earth, the impressions of the special signs of His lotus feet were stamped on the dust, and as a result of this specific grace, the whole earth was made as perfect as possible. In other words, the rivers, the seas, the forests, the hills and the mines, which are the supplying agents for the necessities of men and animals, were fully discharging their respective duties. Therefore the riches of the world surpassed all the riches of all other planets in the three planetary systems of the universe. One should, therefore, ask that the grace of the Lord always be present on earth so that we may be favored with His causeless mercy and be happy, having all necessities of life. One may ask how we can detain the Supreme Lord on this earth after His mission is fulfilled and He has left this earth for His own abode. The answer is that there is no need to detain the Lord. The Lord, being omnipresent, can be present with us if we want Him at all. By His omnipresence, He can always be with us if we are attached to His devotional service by hearing, chanting, remembering, etc.

There is nothing in the world with which the Lord is disconnected. The only thing we must learn is to excavate the source of connection and thus be linked with Him by offenseless service. We can be connected with Him by the transcendental sound representation of the Lord. The holy name of the Lord and the Lord Himself are identical, and one who chants the holy name of the Lord in an offenseless manner can at once realize that the Lord is present before him. Even by the vibration of radio sound, we can partially realize sound relativity, and by resounding the sound of transcendence we can verily feel the presence of the Lord. In this age, when everything is polluted by the contamination of Kali, it is instructed in the scriptures and preached by Lord Śrī Caitanya

Mahāprabhu that by chanting the holy name of the Lord, we can at once be free from contamination and gradually rise to the status of transcendence and go back to Godhead. The offenseless chanter of the holy name of the Lord is as auspicious as the Lord Himself, and the movement of pure devotees of the Lord all over the world can at once change the troublesome face of the world. Only by the propagation of the chanting of the holy name of the Lord can we be immune from all effects of the age of Kali.

TEXT 34

यो वै ममातिभरमासुरवंशराज्ञा-
मक्षौहिणीशतमपानुददात्मतन्त्रः ।
त्वां दुःस्थमूनपदमात्मनि पौरुषेण
सम्पादयन् यदुषु रम्यमबिभ्रदङ्गम् ॥३४॥

yo vai mamātibharam āsura-vaṁśa-rājñām
akṣauhiṇī-śatam apānudad ātma-tantraḥ
tvāṁ duḥstham ūna-padam ātmani pauruṣeṇa
sampādayan yaduṣu ramyam abibhrad aṅgam

yaḥ—He who; *vai*—certainly; *mama*—mine; *ati-bharam*—too burdensome; *āsura-vaṁśa*—unbelievers; *rājñām*—of the kings; *akṣauhiṇī*—one military division;* *śatam*—hundreds of such divisions; *apānudat*—extirpated; *ātma-tantraḥ*—self-sufficient; *tvām*—unto you; *duḥstham*—put into difficulty; *ūna-padam*—devoid of strength to stand; *ātmani*—internal; *pauruṣeṇa*—by dint of energy; *sampādayan*—for executing; *yaduṣu*—in the Yadu dynasty; *ramyam*—transcendentally beautiful; *abibhrat*—accepted; *aṅgam*—body.

TRANSLATION

O personality of religion, I was greatly overburdened by the undue military phalanxes arranged by atheistic kings, and I was relieved by the grace of the Personality of Godhead. Similarly you

*An *akṣauhiṇī* phalanx consists of 21,870 chariots, 21,870 elephants, 106,950 infantrymen, and 65,600 cavalrymen.

were also in a distressed condition, weakened in your standing strength, and thus He also incarnated by His internal energy in the family of the Yadus to relieve you.

PURPORT

The *asuras* want to enjoy a life of sense gratification, even at the cost of others' happiness. In order to fulfill this ambition, the *asuras*, especially atheistic kings or state executive heads, try to equip themselves with all kinds of deadly weapons to bring about a war in a peaceful society. They have no ambition other than personal aggrandizement, and thus mother earth feels overburdened by such undue increases of military strength. By increase of the asuric population, those who follow the principles of religion become unhappy, especially the devotees, or *devas*.

In such a situation, the Personality of Godhead incarnates to vanquish the unwanted *asuras* and to reestablish the true principles of religion. This was the mission of Lord Śrī Kṛṣṇa, and He fulfilled it.

TEXT 35

का वा सहेत विरहं पुरुषोत्तमस्य
प्रेमावलोकरुचिरस्मितवल्गुजल्पैः ।
स्थैर्यं समानमहरन्मधुमानिनीनां
रोमोत्सवो मम यदङ्घ्रिविटङ्किताया: ॥३५॥

kā vā saheta virahaṁ puruṣottamasya
premāvaloka-rucira-smita-valgu-jalpaiḥ
sthairyaṁ samānam aharan madhu-māninīnāṁ
romotsavo mama yad-aṅghri-viṭaṅkitāyāḥ

kā—who; *vā*—either; *saheta*—can tolerate; *viraham*—separation; *puruṣa-uttamasya*—of the Supreme Personality of Godhead; *prema*—loving; *avaloka*—glancing; *rucira-smita*—pleasing smile; *valgu-jalpaiḥ*—hearty appeals; *sthairyam*—gravity; *samānam*—along with passionate wrath; *aharat*—conquered; *madhu*—sweethearts; *māninīnām*—women such as Satyabhāmā; *roma-utsavaḥ*—hair standing on end out of pleasure; *mama*—mine; *yat*—whose; *aṅghri*—feet; *viṭaṅkitāyāḥ*—imprinted with.

TRANSLATION

Who, therefore, can tolerate the pangs of separation from that Supreme Personality of Godhead? He could conquer the gravity and passionate wrath of His sweethearts like Satyabhāmā by His sweet smile of love, pleasing glance and hearty appeals. When He traversed my [earth's] surface, I would be immersed in the dust of His lotus feet and thus would be sumptuously covered with grass which appeared like hairs standing on me out of pleasure.

PURPORT

There were chances of separation between the Lord and His thousands of queens because of the Lord's being absent from home, but as far as His connection with earth was concerned, the Lord would traverse the earth with His lotus feet, and therefore there was no chance of separation. When the Lord left the surface of the earth to return to His spiritual abode, the earth's feelings of separation were therefore more acute.

TEXT 36

तयोरेवं कथयतोः पृथिवीधर्मयोस्तदा ।
परीक्षिन्नाम राजर्षिः प्राप्तः प्राचीं सरस्वतीम् ॥३६॥

tayor evaṁ kathayatoḥ
pṛthivī-dharmayos tadā
parīkṣin nāma rājarṣiḥ
prāptaḥ prācīṁ sarasvatīm

tayoḥ—between them; *evam*—thus; *kathayatoḥ*—engaged in conversation; *pṛthivī*—earth; *dharmayoḥ*—and the personality of religion; *tadā*—at that time; *parīkṣit*—King Parīkṣit; *nāma*—of the name; *rājarṣiḥ*—a saint amongst kings; *prāptaḥ*—arrived; *prācīm*—flowing towards the east; *sarasvatīm*—River Sarasvatī.

TRANSLATION

While the earth and the personality of religion were thus engaged in conversation, the saintly King Parīkṣit reached the shore of the Sarasvatī River, which flowed towards the east.

Thus end the Bhaktivedanta purports of the First Canto, Sixteenth Chapter, of the Śrīmad-Bhāgavatam, *entitled "How Parīkṣit Received the Age of Kali."*

CHAPTER SEVENTEEN

Punishment and Reward of Kali

TEXT 1

सूत उवाच
तत्र गोमिथुनं राजा हन्यमानमनाथवत् ।
दण्डहस्तं च वृषलं ददृशे नृपलाञ्छनम् ॥ १ ॥

sūta uvāca
tatra go-mithunaṁ rājā
hanyamānam anāthavat
daṇḍa-hastaṁ ca vṛṣalaṁ
dadṛśe nṛpa-lāñchanam

sūtaḥ uvāca—Śrī Sūta Gosvāmī said; *tatra*—thereupon; *go-mithunam*—a cow and a bull; *rājā*—the King; *hanyamānam*—being beaten; *anātha-vat*—appearing to be bereft of their owner; *daṇḍa-hastam*—with a club in hand; *ca*—also; *vṛṣalam*—lower caste *śūdra;* *dadṛśe*—observed; *nṛpa*—a king; *lāñchanam*—dressed like.

TRANSLATION

Sūta Gosvāmī said: After reaching that place, Mahārāja Parīkṣit observed that a lower caste śūdra, dressed like a king, was beating a cow and a bull with a club, as if they had no owner.

PURPORT

The principal sign of the age of Kali is that lower caste *śūdras*, i.e., men without brahminical culture and spiritual initiation, will be dressed like administrators or kings, and the principal business of such non-*kṣatriya* rulers will be to kill the innocent animals, especially the cows and the bulls, who shall be unprotected by their masters, the bona fide *vaiśyas*, the mercantile community. In the *Bhagavad-gītā* (18.44), it is said that the *vaiśyas* are meant to deal in agriculture, cow protection and trade. In the age of Kali, the degraded *vaiśyas*, the mercantile men, are engaged in supplying cows to slaughterhouses. The *kṣatriyas* are meant to protect the citizens of the state, whereas the *vaiśyas* are meant to protect the cows and bulls and utilize them to produce grains and milk. The cow is meant to deliver milk, and the bull is meant to produce grains. But in the age of Kali, the *śūdra* class of men are in the posts of administrators, and the cows and bulls, or the mothers and the fathers, unprotected by the *vaiśyas*, are subjected to the slaughterhouses organized by the *śūdra* administrators.

TEXT 2

वृषं मृणालधवलं मेहन्तमिव बिभ्यतम् ।
वेपमानं पदैकेन सीदन्तं शूद्रताडितम् ॥ २ ॥

vṛṣaṁ mṛṇāla-dhavalaṁ
mehantam iva bibhyatam
vepamānaṁ padaikena
sīdantaṁ śūdra-tāḍitam

vṛṣam—the bull; *mṛṇāla-dhavalam*—as white as a white lotus; *mehantam*—urinating; *iva*—as if; *bibhyatam*—being too afraid; *vepamānam*—trembling; *padā ekena*—standing on only one leg; *sīdantam*—terrified; *śūdra-tāḍitam*—being beaten by a *śūdra*.

TRANSLATION

The bull was as white as a white lotus flower. He was terrified of the śūdra who was beating him, and he was so afraid that he was standing on one leg, trembling and urinating.

PURPORT

The next symptom of the age of Kali is that principles of religion, which are all spotlessly white, like the white lotus flower, will be attacked by the uncultured *śūdra* population of the age. They may be descendants of *brāhmaṇa* or *kṣatriya* forefathers, but in the age of Kali, for want of sufficient education and culture of Vedic wisdom, such a *śūdra*-like population will defy the principles of religion, and persons who are religiously endowed will be terrified by such men. They will declare themselves as adherents of no religious principles, and many "isms" and cults will spring up in Kali-yuga only to kill the spotless bull of religion. The state will be declared to be secular, or without any particular principle of religion, and as a result there will be total indifference to the principles of religion. The citizens will be free to act as they like, without respect for *sādhu*, *śāstra* and *guru*. The bull standing on one leg indicates that the principles of religion are gradually diminishing. Even the fragmental existence of religious principles will be embarrassed by so many obstacles as if in the trembling condition of falling down at any time.

TEXT 3

गां च धर्मदुघां दीनां भृशं शूद्रपदाहताम् ।
विवत्सामाश्रुवदनां क्षामां यवसमिच्छतीम् ॥ ३ ॥

gāṁ ca dharma-dughāṁ dīnāṁ
bhṛśaṁ śūdra-padāhatām
vivatsām āśru-vadanāṁ
kṣāmāṁ yavasam icchatīm

gām—the cow; *ca*—also; *dharma-dughām*—beneficial because one can draw religion from her; *dīnām*—now rendered poor; *bhṛśam*—distressed; *śūdra*—the lower caste; *pada-āhatām*—beaten on the legs; *vivatsām*—without any calf; *āśru-vadanām*—with tears in her eyes; *kṣāmām*—very weak; *yavasam*—grass; *icchatīm*—as if desiring to have some grass to eat.

TRANSLATION

Although the cow is beneficial because one can draw religious principles from her, she was now rendered poor and calfless. Her legs were being beaten by a śūdra. There were tears in her eyes, and she was distressed and weak. She was hankering after some grass in the field.

PURPORT

The next symptom of the age of Kali is the distressed condition of the cow. Milking the cow means drawing the principles of religion in a liquid form. The great *ṛṣis* and *munis* would live only on milk. Śrīla Śukadeva Gosvāmī would go to a householder while he was milking a cow, and he would simply take a little quantity of it for subsistence. Even fifty years ago, no one would deprive a *sādhu* of a quart or two of milk, and every householder would give milk like water. For a Sanātanist (a follower of Vedic principles) it is the duty of every householder to have cows and bulls as household paraphernalia, not only for drinking milk, but also for deriving religious principles. The Sanātanist worships cows on religious principles and respects *brāhmaṇas.* The cow's milk is required for the sacrificial fire, and by performing sacrifices the householder can be happy. The cow's calf not only is beautiful to look at, but also gives satisfaction to the cow, and so she delivers as much milk as possible. But in the Kali-yuga, the calves are separated from the cows as early as possible for purposes which may not be mentioned in these pages of *Śrīmad-Bhāgavatam.* The cow stands with tears in her eyes, the *śūdra* milkman draws milk from the cow artificially, and when there is no milk the cow is sent to be slaughtered. These greatly sinful acts are responsible for all the troubles in present society. People do not know what they are doing in the name of economic development. The influence of Kali will keep them in the darkness of ignorance. Despite all endeavors for peace and prosperity, they must try to see the cows and the bulls happy in all respects. Foolish people do not know how one earns happiness by making the cows and bulls happy, but it is a fact by the law of nature. Let us take it from the authority of *Śrīmad-Bhāgavatam* and adopt the principles for the total happiness of humanity.

TEXT 4

पप्रच्छ रथमारूढः कार्तस्वरपरिच्छदम् ।
मेघगम्भीरया वाचा समारोपितकार्मुकः ॥ ४ ॥

papraccha ratham ārūḍhaḥ
kārtasvara-paricchadam
megha-gambhīrayā vācā
samāropita-kārmukaḥ

papraccha—inquired; *ratham*—chariot; *ārūḍhaḥ*—seated on; *kārtasvara*—gold; *paricchadam*—embossed with; *megha*—cloud;

gambhīrayā—exonerating; *vācā*—sound; *samāropita*—well equipped; *kārmukaḥ*—arrows and bow.

TRANSLATION

Mahārāja Parīkṣit, well equipped with arrows and bow and seated on a gold-embossed chariot, spoke to him [the śūdra] with a deep voice sounding like thunder.

PURPORT

An administrative head or king like Mahārāja Parīkṣit, with full majestic authority, well equipped with weapons to chastise miscreants, can challenge the agents of the age of Kali. Then only will it be possible to counteract the degraded age. And in the absence of such strong executive heads, there is always disruption of tranquility. The elected show bottle executive head, as representative of a degraded public, cannot be equal with a strong king like Mahārāja Parīkṣit. The dress or style of royal order does not count. It is one's actions which are counted.

TEXT 5

कस्त्वं मच्छरणे लोके बलाद्धंस्यबलान् बली ।
नरदेवोऽसि वेषेण नटवत्कर्मणाद्विजः ॥ ५ ॥

kas tvaṁ mac-charaṇe loke
balād dhaṁsy abalān balī
nara-devo 'si veṣeṇa
naṭavat karmaṇā 'dvijaḥ

kaḥ—who are; *tvam*—you; *mat*—my; *śaraṇe*—under protection; *loke*—in this world; *balāt*—by force; *haṁsi*—killing; *abalān*—those who are helpless; *balī*—although full of strength; *nara-devaḥ*—man-god; *asi*—appear to be; *veṣeṇa*—by your dress; *naṭa-vat*—like a theatrical player; *karmaṇā*—by deeds; *advi-jaḥ*—a man not twice-born by culture.

TRANSLATION

Oh, who are you? You appear to be strong and yet you dare kill, within my protection, those who are helpless! By your dress you

pose yourself to be a godly man [king], but by your deeds you are opposing the principles of the twice-born kṣatriyas.

PURPORT

The *brāhmaṇas, kṣatriyas* and *vaiśyas* are called twice-born because for these higher classes of men there is one birth by parental conjugation and there is another birth of cultural rejuvenation by spiritual initiation from the bona fide *ācārya,* or spiritual master. So a *kṣatriya* is also twice-born like a *brāhmaṇa,* and his duty is to give protection to the helpless. The *kṣatriya* king is considered to be the representative of God to give protection to the helpless and chastise the miscreants. Whenever there are anomalies in this routine work by the administrators, there is an incarnation of the Lord to reestablish the principles of a godly kingdom. In the age of Kali, the poor helpless animals, especially the cows, which are meant to receive all sorts of protection from the administrative heads, are killed without restriction. Thus the administrative heads under whose noses such things happen are representatives of God in name only. Such powerful administrators are rulers of the poor citizens by dress or office, but factually they are worthless, lower-class men without the cultural assets of the twice-born. No one can expect justice or equality of treatment from once-born (spiritually uncultured) lower-class men. Therefore in the age of Kali everyone is unhappy due to the maladministration of the state. The modern human society is not twice-born by spiritual culture. Therefore the people's government, by the people who are not twice-born, must be a government of Kali in which everyone is unhappy.

TEXT 6

यस्त्वं कृष्णे गते दूरं सहगाण्डीवधन्वना ।
शोच्योऽस्यशोच्यान् रहसि प्रहरन् वधमर्हसि ॥ ६ ॥

yas tvaṁ kṛṣṇe gate dūraṁ
saha-gāṇḍīva-dhanvanā
śocyo 'sy aśocyān rahasi
praharan vadham arhasi

yaḥ—on account of; *tvam*—you rogue; *kṛṣṇe*—Lord Kṛṣṇa; *gate*—having gone away; *dūram*—out of sight; *saha*—along with; *gāṇḍīva*—the bow named Gāṇḍīva; *dhanvanā*—the carrier, Arjuna; *śocyaḥ*—culprit; *asi*—you are considered; *aśocyān*—innocent; *rahasi*—in a secluded place; *praharan*—beating; *vadham*—to be killed; *arhasi*—deserve.

TRANSLATION

You rogue, do you dare beat an innocent cow because Lord Kṛṣṇa and Arjuna, the carrier of the Gāṇḍīva bow, are out of sight? Since you are beating the innocent in a secluded place, you are considered a culprit and therefore deserve to be killed.

PURPORT

In a civilization where God is conspicuously banished, and there is no devotee-warrior like Arjuna, the associates of the age of Kali take advantage of this lawless kingdom and arrange to kill innocent animals like the cow in secluded slaughterhouses. Such murderers of animals stand to be condemned to death by the order of a pious king like Mahārāja Parīkṣit. For a pious king, the culprit who kills an animal in a secluded place is punishable by the death penalty, exactly like a murderer who kills an innocent child in a secluded place.

TEXT 7

त्वं वा मृणालधवलः पादैर्न्यूनः पदा चरन् ।
वृषरूपेण किं कश्चिद् देवो नः परिखेदयन् ॥ ७ ॥

tvaṁ vā mṛṇāla-dhavalaḥ
pādair nyūnaḥ padā caran
vṛṣa-rūpeṇa kiṁ kaścid
devo naḥ parikhedayan

tvam—you; *vā*—either; *mṛṇāla-dhavalaḥ*—as white as a lotus; *pādaiḥ*—of three legs; *nyūnaḥ*—being deprived; *padā*—on one leg; *caran*—moving; *vṛṣa*—bull; *rūpeṇa*—in the form of; *kim*—whether; *kaścit*—someone; *devaḥ*—demigod; *naḥ*—us; *parikhedayan*—causing grief.

TRANSLATION

Then he [Mahārāja Parīkṣit] asked the bull: Oh, who are you? Are you a bull as white as a white lotus, or are you a demigod? You have lost three of your legs and are moving on only one. Are you some demigod causing us grief in the form of a bull?

PURPORT

At least up to the time of Mahārāja Parīkṣit, no one could imagine the wretched conditions of the cow and the bull. Mahārāja Parīkṣit, therefore, was astonished to see such a horrible scene. He inquired whether the bull was not a demigod assuming such a wretched condition to indicate the future of the cow and the bull.

TEXT 8

न जातु कौरवेन्द्राणां दोर्दण्डपरिरम्भिते ।
भूतलेऽनुपतन्त्यस्मिन् विना ते प्राणिनां शुचः ॥ ८ ॥

na jātu kauravendrāṇāṁ
dordaṇḍa-parirambhite
bhū-tale 'nupatanty asmin
vinā te prāṇināṁ śucaḥ

na—not; *jātu*—at any time; *kaurava-indrāṇām*—of the kings in the Kuru dynasty; *dordaṇḍa*—strength of arms; *parirambhite*—protected by; *bhū-tale*—on the surface of the earth; *anupatanti*—grieving; *asmin*—up till now; *vinā*—save and except; *te*—you; *prāṇinām*—of the living being; *śucaḥ*—tears in the eyes.

TRANSLATION

Now for the first time in a kingdom well protected by the arms of the kings of the Kuru dynasty, I see you grieving with tears in your eyes. Up till now no one on earth has ever shed tears because of royal negligence.

PURPORT

The protection of the lives of both the human beings and the animals is the first and foremost duty of a government. A government must not discriminate in such principles. It is simply horrible for a pure-hearted soul to see organized animal killing by the state in this age of Kali. Mahārāja Parīkṣit was lamenting for the tears in the eyes of the bull, and he was astonished to see such an unprecedented thing in his good kingdom. Men and animals were equally protected as far as life was concerned. That is the way in God's kingdom.

TEXT 9

मा सौरभेयात्रशुचो व्येतु ते वृषलाद् भयम् ।
मा रोदीरम्ब भद्रं ते खलानां मयि शास्तरि ॥ ९ ॥

mā saurabheyātra śuco
vyetu te vṛṣalād bhayam
mā rodīr amba bhadraṁ te
khalānāṁ mayi śāstari

mā—do not; *saurabheya*—O son of *surabhi; atra*—in my kingdom; *śucaḥ*—lamentation; *vyetu*—let there be; *te*—your; *vṛṣalāt*—by the *śūdra; bhayam*—cause of fear; *mā*—do not; *rodīḥ*—cry; *amba*—mother cow; *bhadram*—all good; *te*—unto you; *khalānām*—of the envious; *mayi*—while I am living; *śāstari*—the ruler or subduer.

TRANSLATION

O son of surabhi, you need lament no longer now. There is no need to fear this low-class śūdra. And, O mother cow, as long as I am living as the ruler and subduer of all envious men, there is no cause for you to cry. Everything will be good for you.

PURPORT

Protection of bulls and cows and all other animals can be possible only when there is a state ruled by an executive head like Mahārāja Parīkṣit. Mahārāja Parīkṣit addresses the cow as mother, for he is a cultured, twice-born, *kṣatriya* king. *Surabhi* is the name of the cows which exist in the spiritual planets and are especially reared by Lord Śrī Kṛṣṇa Himself. As men are made after the form and features of the Supreme Lord, so also the cows are made after the form and features of the *surabhi* cows in the spiritual kingdom. In the material world the human society gives all protection to the human being, but there is no law to protect the descendants of *surabhi,* who can give all protection to men by supplying the miracle food, milk. But Mahārāja Parīsķit and the Pāṇḍavas were fully conscious of the importance of the cow and bull, and they were prepared to punish the cow-killer with all chastisement, including death. There has sometimes been agitation for the protection of the cow, but for want of pious executive heads and suitable laws, the cow and the bull are not given protection. The human society should recognize the importance of the cow and the bull and thus give all protection to these important animals, following in the footsteps of Mahārāja Parīkṣit. For protecting the cows and brahminical culture, the Lord, who is very kind to the cow and the *brāhmaṇas* (*go-brāhmaṇa-hitāya*), will be pleased with us and will bestow upon us real peace.

TEXTS 10–11

यस्य राष्ट्रे प्रजाः सर्वास्त्रस्यन्ते साध्व्यसाधुभिः ।
तस्य मत्तस्य नश्यन्ति कीर्तिरायुर्भगो गतिः ॥१०॥
एष राज्ञां परो धर्मो ह्यार्तानामार्तिनिग्रहः ।
अत एनं वधिष्यामि भूतद्रुहमसत्तमम् ॥११॥

yasya rāṣṭre prajāḥ sarvās
trasyante sādhvy asādhubhiḥ
tasya mattasya naśyanti
kīrtir āyur bhago gatiḥ

eṣa rājñāṁ paro dharmo
hy ārtānām ārti-nigrahaḥ
ata enaṁ vadhiṣyāmi
bhūta-druham asattamam

yasya—one whose; *rāṣṭre*—in the state; *prajāḥ*—living beings; *sarvāḥ*—one and all; *trasyante*—are terrified; *sādhvi*—O chaste one; *asādhubhiḥ*—by the miscreants; *tasya*—his; *mattasya*—of the illusioned; *naśyanti*—vanishes; *kīrtiḥ*—fame; *āyuḥ*—duration of life;

bhagaḥ—fortune; *gatiḥ*—good rebirth; *eṣaḥ*—these are; *rājñām*—of the kings; *paraḥ*—superior; *dharmaḥ*—occupation; *hi*—certainly; *ārtānām*—of the sufferers; *ārti*—sufferings; *nigrahaḥ*—subduing; *ataḥ*—therefore; *enam*—this man; *vadhiṣyāmi*—I shall kill; *bhūta-druham*—revolter against other living beings; *asat-tamam*—the most wretched.

TRANSLATION

O chaste one, the king's good name, duration of life and good rebirth vanish when all kinds of living beings are terrified by miscreants in his kingdom. It is certainly the prime duty of the king to subdue first the sufferings of those who suffer. Therefore I must kill this most wretched man because he is violent against other living beings.

PURPORT

When there is some disturbance caused by wild animals in a village or town, the police or others take action to kill them. Similarly, it is the duty of the government to kill at once all bad social elements such as thieves, dacoits and murderers. The same punishment is also due to animal-killers because the animals of the state are also the *prajā. Prajā* means one who has taken birth in the state, and this includes both men and animals. Any living being who takes birth in a state has the primary right to live under the protection of the king. The jungle animals are also subject to the king, and they also have a right to live. So what to speak of domestic animals like the cows and bulls.

Any living being, if he terrifies other living beings, is a most wretched subject, and the king should at once kill such a disturbing element. As the wild animal is killed when it creates disturbances, similarly any man who unnecessarily kills or terrifies the jungle animals or other animals must be punished at once. By the law of the Supreme Lord, all living beings, in whatever shape they may be, are the sons of the Lord, and no one has any right to kill another animal, unless it is so ordered by the codes of natural law. The tiger can kill a lower animal for his subsistence, but a man cannot kill an animal for his subsistence. That is the law of God, who has created the law that a living being subsists by eating another living being. Thus the vegetarians are also living by eating other living beings. Therefore, the law is that one should live only by eating specific living beings, as ordained by the law of God. The *Īśopaniṣad* directs that one should live by the direction of the Lord and not at one's sweet will. A man can subsist on varieties of grains, fruits and milk ordained by God, and there is no need of animal food, save and except in particular cases.

The illusioned king or executive head, even though sometimes advertised as a great philosopher and learned scholar, will allow slaughterhouses in the state without knowing that torturing poor animals clears the way to hell for such foolish kings or executive heads. The executive head must always be alert to the safety of the *prajās,* both man and animal, and inquire whether a particular living being is harassed at any place by another living being. The harassing living being must at once be caught and put to death, as shown by Mahārāja Parīkṣit.

The people's government, or government by the people, should not allow killing of innocent animals by the sweet will of foolish government men. They must know the codes of God, as mentioned in the revealed scriptures. Mahārāja Parīkṣit quotes here that according to the codes of God the irresponsible king or state executive jeopardizes his good name, duration of life, power and strength and ultimately his progressive march towards a better life and salvation after death. Such foolish men do not even believe in the existence of a next life.

While commenting on this particular verse, we have in our presence the statement of a great modern politician who has recently died and left his will, which discloses his poor fund of knowledge of the codes of God mentioned by Mahārāja Parīkṣit. The politician was so ignorant of the codes of God that he writes: "I do not believe in any such ceremonies, and to submit to them, even as a matter of form, would be hypocrisy and an attempt to delude ourselves and others . . . I have no religious sentiment in the matter."

Contrasting these statements of a great politician in the modern age with those of Mahārāja Parīkṣit, we find a vast difference. Mahārāja Parīkṣit was pious according to the scriptural codes, whereas the modern politician goes by his personal belief and sentiments. Any great man of the material world is, after all, a conditioned soul. He is bound by his hands and feet by the ropes of material nature, and still the foolish conditioned soul thinks of himself as free to act by his whimsical sentiments. The conclusion is that people in the time of Mahārāja Parīkṣit were happy, and the animals were given proper protection because the executive head was not whimsical or ignorant of God's law. Foolish, faithless creatures try to avoid the existence of the Lord and proclaim themselves secular at the cost of valuable human life. The human life is especially meant for knowing the science of God, but foolish creatures, especially in this age of Kali, instead of knowing God scientifically, make propaganda against religious belief as well as the existence of God, even though they are always bound by the laws of God by the symptoms of birth, death, old age and disease.

TEXT 12

कोऽवृश्चत् तव पादांस्त्रीन् सौरभेय चतुष्पद ।
मा भूवंस्त्वादृशा राष्ट्रे राज्ञां कृष्णानुवर्तिनाम् ॥१२॥

ko 'vṛścat tava pādāṁs trīn
saurabheya catuṣ-pada
mā bhūvaṁs tvādṛśā rāṣṭre
rājñāṁ kṛṣṇānuvartinām

kaḥ—who is he; *avṛścat*—cut off; *tava*—your; *pādān*—legs; *trīn*—three; *saurabheya*—O son of *surabhi; catuḥ-pada*—you are four-legged; *mā*—never to be; *bhūvan*—it so happened; *tvādṛśāḥ*—as yourself; *rāṣṭre*—in the state; *rājñām*—of the kings; *kṛṣṇa-anuvartinām*—those who follow the codes of Kṛṣṇa, the Supreme Personality of Godhead.

TRANSLATION

He [Mahārāja Parīkṣit] repeatedly addressed and questioned the bull thus: O son of surabhi, who has cut off your three legs? In the state of the kings who are obedient to the laws of the Supreme Personality of Godhead, Kṛṣṇa, there is no one as unhappy as you.

PURPORT

The kings or the executive heads of all states must know the codes of Lord Kṛṣṇa (generally *Bhagavad-gītā* and *Śrīmad-Bhāgavatam*) and must act accordingly in order to fulfill the mission of human life, which is to make an end to all miseries of material conditions. One who knows the codes of Lord Kṛṣṇa can achieve this end without any difficulty. In the *Bhagavad-gītā*, in a synopsis, we can understand the codes of Godhead, and in the *Śrīmad-Bhāgavatam* the same codes are explained further.

In a state where the codes of Kṛṣṇa are followed, no one is unhappy. Where such codes are not followed, the first sign is that three legs of the representative of religion are cut off, and thereby all miseries follow. When Kṛṣṇa was personally present, the codes of Kṛṣṇa were being followed without question, but in His absence such codes are presented in the pages of *Śrīmad-Bhāgavatam* for the guidance of the blind persons who happen to be at the helm of all affairs.

TEXT 13

आख्याहि वृष भद्रं वः साधूनामकृतागसाम् ।
आत्मवैरूप्यकर्तारं पार्थानां कीर्तिदूषणम् ॥१३॥

ākhyāhi vṛṣa bhadraṁ vaḥ
sādhūnām akṛtāgasām
ātma-vairūpya-kartāraṁ
pārthānāṁ kīrti-dūṣaṇam

ākhyāhi—just let me know; *vṛṣa*—O bull; *bhadram*—good; *vaḥ*—for you; *sādhūnām*—of the honest; *akṛta-āgasām*—of those who are offenseless; *ātma-vairūpya*—deformation of the self; *kartāram*—the doer; *pārthānām*—of the sons of Pṛthā; *kīrti-dūṣaṇam*—blackmailing the reputation.

TRANSLATION

O bull, you are offenseless and thoroughly honest; therefore I wish all good to you. Please tell me of the perpetrator of these mutilations, which blackmail the reputation of the sons of Pṛthā.

PURPORT

The reputation of the reign of Mahārāja Rāmacandra and that of the kings who followed in the footsteps of Mahārāja Rāmacandra, like the

Pāṇḍavas and their descendants, are never to be forgotten because in their kingdom offenseless and honest living beings were never in trouble. The bull and the cow are the symbols of the most offenseless living beings because even the stool and urine of these animals are utilized to benefit human society. The descendants of the sons of Pṛthā, like Mahārāja Parīkṣit, were afraid of losing their reputations, but in the modern days the leaders are not even afraid of killing such offenseless animals. Herein lies the difference between the reign of those pious kings and the modern states ruled by irresponsible executive heads without knowledge of the codes of God.

TEXT 14

जनेऽनागस्यघं युञ्जन् सर्वतोऽस्य च मद्भयम् ।
साधूनां भद्रमेव स्यादसाधुदमने कृते ॥१४॥

jane 'nāgasy aghaṁ yuñjan
sarvato 'sya ca mad-bhayam
sādhūnāṁ bhadram eva syād
asādhu-damane kṛte

jane—to the living beings; *anāgasi*—those who are offenseless; *agham*—sufferings; *yuñjan*—by applying; *sarvataḥ*—anywhere and everywhere; *asya*—of such offenders; *ca*—and; *mat-bhayam*—fear me; *sādhūnām*—of the honest persons; *bhadram*—good fortune; *eva*—certainly; *syāt*—will take place; *asādhu*—dishonest miscreants; *damane*—curbed; *kṛte*—being so done.

TRANSLATION

Whoever causes offenseless living beings to suffer must fear me anywhere and everywhere in the world. By curbing dishonest miscreants, one automatically benefits the offenseless.

PURPORT

Dishonest miscreants flourish because of cowardly and impotent executive heads of state. But when the executive heads are strong enough to curb all sorts of dishonest miscreants, in any part of the state, certainly they cannot flourish. When the miscreants are punished in an exemplary manner, automatically all good fortune follows. As said before, it is the prime duty of the king or the executive head to give protection in all respects to the peaceful, offenseless citizens of the state. The devotees of the Lord are by nature peaceful and offenseless, and therefore it is the prime duty of the state to arrange to convert everyone to become a devotee of the Lord. Thus automatically there will be peaceful, offenseless citizens. Then the only duty of the king will be to curb the dishonest miscreants. That will bring about peace and harmony all over human society.

TEXT 15

अनागःस्विह भूतेषु य आगस्कृन्निरङ्कुशः ।
आहर्तास्मि भुजं साक्षादमर्त्यस्यापि साङ्गदम् ॥१५॥

anāgaḥsv iha bhūteṣu
ya āgas-kṛn niraṅkuśaḥ
āhartāsmi bhujaṁ sākṣād
amartyasyāpi sāṅgadam

anāgaḥsu iha—to the offenseless; *bhūteṣu*—living beings; *yaḥ*—the person; *āgaḥ-kṛt*—commits offense; *niraṅkuśaḥ*—upstart; *āhartā asmi*—I shall bring forth; *bhujam*—arms; *sākṣāt*—directly; *amartyasya api*—even one who is a demigod; *sa-aṅgadam*—with decorations and armor.

TRANSLATION

An upstart living being who commits offenses by torturing those who are offenseless shall be directly uprooted by me, even though he be a denizen of heaven with armor and decorations.

PURPORT

The denizens of the heavenly kingdom are called *amara,* or deathless, due to their possessing a long span of life, far greater than that of the human beings. For a human being, who has only a maximum one-hundred-year duration of life, a span of life spreading over millions of years is certainly considered to be deathless. For example, from the *Bhagavad-gītā* we learn that on the Brahmaloka planet the duration of one day is calculated to be 4,300,000 *x* 1,000 solar years. Similarly, in other heavenly planets one day is calculated to be six months of this planet, and the inhabitants get a life of ten million of their years. Therefore, in all higher planets, since the span of life is far greater than that of the human being, the denizens are called deathless by imagination, although actually no one within the material universe is deathless.

Mahārāja Parīkṣit challenges even such denizens of heaven if they torture the offenseless. This means that the state executive head must be as strong as Mahārāja Parīkṣit so that he may be determined to punish the strongest offenders. It should be the principle of a state executive head that the offender of the codes of God is always punished.

TEXT 16

राज्ञो हि परमो धर्मः स्वधर्मस्थानुपालनम् ।
शासतोऽन्यान् यथाशास्त्रमनापद्युत्पथानिह ॥१६॥

rājño hi paramo dharmaḥ
sva-dharma-sthānupālanam
śāsato 'nyān yathā-śāstram
anāpady utpathān iha

rājñaḥ—of the king or the executive head; *hi*—certainly; *paramaḥ*—supreme; *dharmaḥ*—occupational duty; *sva-dharma-stha*—one who is faithful to his prescribed duty; *anupālanam*—giving protection always; *śāsataḥ*—while ruling; *anyān*—others; *yathā*—according to; *śāstram*—rulings of scriptures; *anāpadi*—without danger; *utpathān*—persons going astray; *iha*—as a matter of fact.

TRANSLATION

The supreme duty of the ruling king is to give all protection to law-abiding persons and to chastise those who stray from the ordinances of the scriptures in ordinary times, when there is no emergency.

PURPORT

In the scriptures there is mention of *āpad-dharma*, or occupational duty at times of extraordinary happenings. It is said that sometimes the great sage Viśvāmitra had to live on the flesh of dogs in some extraordinary dangerous position. In cases of emergency, one may be allowed to live on the flesh of animals of all description, but that does not mean that there should be regular slaughterhouses to feed the animal-eaters and that this system should be encouraged by the state. No one should try to live on flesh in ordinary times simply for the sake of the palate. If anyone does so, the king or the executive head should punish him for gross enjoyment.

There are regular scriptural injunctions for different persons engaged in different occupational duties, and one who follows them is called *sva-dharma-stha*, or faithful in one's prescribed duties. In the *Bhagavad-gītā* (18.48) it is advised that one should not give up his occupational prescribed duties, even if they are not always flawless. Such *sva-dharma* might be violated in cases of emergency, if one is forced by circumstances, but they cannot be violated in ordinary times. The state executive head is to see that such *sva-dharma* is not changed by the follower, whatever it may be, and he should give all protection to the follower of *sva-dharma*. The violater is subject to punishment in terms of the *śāstra*, and the duty of the king is to see that everyone strictly follows his occupational duty, as prescribed in the scripture.

TEXT 17

धर्म उवाच

एतद् वः पाण्डवेयानां युक्तमार्तभयं वचः ।
येषां गुणगणैः कृष्णो दौत्यादौ भगवान् कृतः ॥१७॥

dharma uvāca
etad vaḥ pāṇḍaveyānāṁ
yuktam ārtābhayaṁ vacaḥ
yeṣāṁ guṇa-gaṇaiḥ kṛṣṇo
dautyādau bhagavān kṛtaḥ

dharmaḥ uvāca—the personality of religion said; *etat*—all these; *vaḥ*—by you; *pāṇḍaveyānām*—of those who are in the Pāṇḍava dynasty; *yuktam*—just befitting; *ārta*—the sufferer; *abhayam*—freedom from all fears; *vacaḥ*—speeches; *yeṣām*—those; *guṇa-gaṇaiḥ*—by the qualifications; *kṛṣṇaḥ*—even Lord Kṛṣṇa; *dautya-ādau*—the duty of a messenger, etc.; *bhagavān*—the Personality of Godhead; *kṛtaḥ*—performed.

TRANSLATION

The personality of religion said: These words just spoken by you befit a person of the Pāṇḍava dynasty. Captivated by the devotional qualities of the Pāṇḍavas, even Lord Kṛṣṇa, the Personality of Godhead, performed duties as a messenger.

PURPORT

The assurances and challenges made by Mahārāja Parīkṣit are never exaggerations of his real power. The Mahārāja said that even the denizens of heaven could not escape his stringent government if they were violators of religious principles. He was not falsely proud, for a devotee of the Lord is equally as powerful as the Lord or sometimes more powerful by His grace, and any promise made by a devotee, though it may be ordinarily very difficult to fulfill, is properly executed by the grace of the Lord. The Pāṇḍavas, by their unalloyed devotional service and full surrender unto the Lord, made it possible for the Lord to become a chariot driver or sometimes their letter messenger. Such duties executed by the Lord for His devotee are always very pleasing to the Lord because the Lord wants to render service to His unalloyed devotee, whose life has no other engagement than to serve the Lord will full love and devotion. Mahārāja Parīkṣit, grandson of Arjuna, the celebrated friendly servitor of the Lord, was a pure devotee of the Lord like his grandfather, and therefore the Lord was always with him, even from the time when he was helplessly lying in the womb of his mother and was attacked by the blazing *brahmāstra* weapon of Aśvatthāmā. A devotee is always under the protection of the Lord, and therefore the assurance of protection by Mahārāja Parīkṣit could never be without meaning. The personality of religion accepted this fact and thus thanked the King for his being true to his exalted position.

TEXT 18

न वयं क्लेशबीजानि यतः स्युः पुरुषर्षभ ।
पुरुषं तं विजानीमो वाक्यभेदविमोहिताः ॥१८॥

na vayaṁ kleśa-bījāni
yataḥ syuḥ puruṣarṣabha
puruṣaṁ taṁ vijānīmo
vākya-bheda-vimohitāḥ

na—not; *vayam*—we; *kleśa-bījāni*—the root cause of sufferings; *yataḥ*—wherefrom; *syuḥ*—it so happens; *puruṣa-ṛṣabha*—O greatest of all human beings; *puruṣam*—the person; *tam*—that; *vijānīmaḥ*—know; *vākya-bheda*—difference of opinion; *vimohitāḥ*—bewildered by.

TRANSLATION

O greatest among human beings, it is very difficult to ascertain the particular miscreant who has caused our sufferings, because we are bewildered by all the different opinions of theoretical philosophers.

PURPORT

There are many theoretical philosophers in the world who put forward their own theories of cause and effect especially about the cause of suffering and its effect on different living beings. Generally there are six great philosophers: Kaṇāda, the author of Vaiśeṣika philosophy; Gautama, the author of logic; Patañjali, the author of mystic *yoga;* Kapila, the author of Sāṅkhya philosophy; Jaimini, the author of Karma-mīmāṁsā; and Vyāsadeva, the author of Vedānta-darśana.

Although the bull, or the personality of religion, and the cow, the personality of the earth, knew perfectly well that the personality of Kali was the direct cause of their sufferings, still, as devotees of the Lord, they knew well also that without the sanction of the Lord no one could inflict trouble upon them. According to the *Padma Purāṇa,* our present trouble is due to the fructifying of seedling sins, but even those seedling sins also gradually fade away by execution of pure devotional service. Thus even if the devotees see the mischief-mongers, they do not accuse them for the sufferings inflicted. They take it for granted that the mischief-monger is made to act by some indirect cause, and therefore they tolerate the sufferings, thinking them to be God-given in small doses, for otherwise the sufferings should have been greater.

Mahārāja Parīkṣit wanted to get a statement of accusation against the direct mischief-monger, but they declined to give it on the above-mentioned grounds. Speculative philosophers, however, do not recognize the sanction of the Lord; they try to find out the cause of sufferings in their own way, as will be described in the following verses. According to Śrīla Jīva Gosvāmī, such speculators are themselves bewildered, and thus they cannot know that the ultimate cause of all causes is the Supreme Lord, the Personality of Godhead.

TEXT 19

केचिद् विकल्पवसना आहुरात्मानमात्मनः ।
दैवमन्येऽपरे कर्म स्वभावमपरे प्रभुम् ॥१९॥

kecid vikalpa-vasanā
āhur ātmānam ātmanaḥ
daivam anye 'pare karma
svabhāvam apare prabhum

kecit—some of them; *vikalpa-vasanāḥ*—those who deny all kinds of duality; *āhuḥ*—declare; *ātmānam*—own self; *ātmanaḥ*—of the self; *daivam*—superhuman; *anye*—others; *apare*—someone else; *karma*—activity; *svabhāvam*—material nature; *apare*—many other; *prabhum*—authorities.

TRANSLATION

Some of the philosophers, who deny all sorts of duality, declare that one's own self is responsible for his personal happiness and distress. Others say that superhuman powers are responsible, while yet others say that activity is responsible, and the gross materialists maintain that nature is the ultimate cause.

PURPORT

As referred to above, philosophers like Jaimini and his followers establish that fruitive activity is the root cause of all distress and happiness, and that even if there is a superior authority, some superhuman powerful God or gods, He or they are also under the influence of fruitive activity because they reward result according to one's action. They say that action is not independent because action is performed by some performer; therefore, the performer himself is the cause of his own happiness or distress. In the *Bhagavad-gītā* (6.5) also it is confirmed that by one's mind, freed from material affection, one can deliver himself from the sufferings of material pangs. So one should not entangle oneself in matter by the mind's material affections. Thus one's own mind is one's friend or enemy in one's material happiness and distress.

Atheistic, materialistic Sāṅkhyaites conclude that material nature is the cause of all causes. According to them, combinations of material elements are the causes of material happiness and distress, and disintegration of matter is the cause of freedom from all material pangs. Gautama and Kaṇāda find that atomic combination is the cause of everything, and impersonalists like Aṣṭāvakra discover that the spiritual effulgence of Brahman is the cause of all causes. But in the *Bhagavad-gītā* the Lord Himself declares that He is the source of impersonal Brahman, and therefore He, the Personality of Godhead, is the ultimate cause of all causes. It is also confirmed in the *Brahma-saṁhitā* that Lord Kṛṣṇa is the ultimate cause of all causes.

TEXT 20

अप्रतर्क्यादनिर्देश्यादिति केष्वपि निश्चयः ।
अत्रानुरूपं राजर्षे विमृश स्वमनीषया ॥२०॥

apratarkyād anirdeśyād
iti keṣv api niścayaḥ
atrānurūpaṁ rājarṣe
vimṛśa sva-manīṣayā

apratarkyāt—beyond the power of reasoning; *anirdeśyāt*—beyond the power of thinking; *iti*—thus; *keṣu*—someone; *api*—also;

niścayaḥ—definitely concluded; *atra*—herein; *anurūpam*—which of them is right; *rāja-ṛṣe*—O sage amongst the kings; *vimṛśa*—judge yourself; *sva*—by your own; *manīṣayā*—power of intelligence.

TRANSLATION

There are also some thinkers who believe that no one can ascertain the cause of distress by argumentation, nor know it by imagination, nor express it by words. O sage amongst kings, judge for yourself by thinking over all this with your own intelligence.

PURPORT

The Vaiṣṇavites, the devotees of the Lord, do believe, as above explained, that nothing can take place without the sanction of the Supreme Lord. He is the supreme director, for He confirms in the *Bhagavad-gītā* (15.15) that He, as all-pervading Paramātmā, stays in everyone's heart and keeps vigilance over all actions and witnesses all activities. The argument of the atheist that one cannot be punished for one's misdeeds unless proved before a qualified justice is refuted herein, for we accept the perpetual witness and constant companion of the living being. A living being may forget all that he might have done in his past or present life, but one must know that in the same tree of the material body, the individual soul and the Supreme Soul as Paramātmā are sitting like two birds. One of them, the living being, is enjoying the fruits of the tree, whereas the Supreme Being is there to witness the activities. Therefore the Paramātmā feature, the Supreme Soul, is actually the witness of all activities of the living being, and only by His direction can the living being remember or forget what he might have done in the past. He is, therefore, both the all-pervading impersonal Brahman and the localized Paramātmā in everyone's heart. He is the knower of all past, present and future, and nothing can be concealed from Him. The devotees know this truth, and therefore they discharge their duties sincerely, without being overly anxious for rewards. Besides that, one cannot estimate the Lord's reactions, either by speculation or by scholarship. Why does He put some into difficulty and not others? He is the supreme knower of the Vedic knowledge, and thus He is the factual Vedāntist. At the same time He is the compiler of the *Vedānta.* No one is independent of Him, and everyone is engaged in His service in different ways. In the conditioned state, such services are rendered by the living being under force of the material nature, whereas in the liberated state the living being is helped by the spiritual nature in the voluntary loving service of the Lord. There is no incongruity or inebriety in His actions. All are on the path of Absolute Truth. Bhīṣmadeva correctly estimated the inconceivable actions of the Lord. The conclusion is, therefore, that the sufferings of the representative of religion and the representative of the earth, as present before Mahārāja Parīkṣit, were planned to prove that Mahārāja Parīkṣit was the ideal executive head because he knew well how to give protection to the cows (the earth) and the *brāhmaṇas* (religious principles), the two pillars of spiritual advancement. Everyone is under the full control of the Lord. He is quite correct in His action when He desires something to be done by someone, irrespective of the consideration of the particular case. Mahārāja Parīkṣit was thus put to test for his greatness. Now let us see how he solves it by his sagacious mind.

TEXT 21

सूत उवाच

एवं धर्मे प्रवदति स सम्राड् द्विजसत्तमाः ।
समाहितेन मनसा विखेदः पर्यचष्ट तम् ॥२१॥

sūta uvāca
evaṁ dharme pravadati
sa samrāḍ dvija-sattamāḥ
samāhitena manasā
vikhedaḥ paryacaṣṭa tam

sūtaḥ uvāca—Sūta Gosvāmī said; *evam*—so; *dharme*—the personality of religion; *pravadati*—thus having spoken; *saḥ*—he; *samrāṭ*—the Emperor; *dvija-sattamāḥ*—O best among the *brāhmaṇas; samāhitena*—with proper attention; *manasā*—by the mind; *vikhedaḥ*—without any mistake; *paryacaṣṭa*—counterreplied; *tam*—unto him.

TRANSLATION

Sūta Gosvāmī said: O best among the brāhmaṇas, the Emperor Parīkṣit, thus hearing the personality of religion speak, was fully satisfied, and without mistake or regret he gave his reply.

PURPORT

The statement of the bull, the personality of religion, was full of philosophy and knowledge, and the King was satisfied, since he could understand that the suffering bull was not an ordinary one. Unless one is perfectly conversant with the law of the Supreme Lord, one cannot speak such things touching philosophical truths. The Emperor, being also on an equal level of sagacity, replied to the point, without doubts or mistakes.

TEXT 22

राजोवाच
धर्मं ब्रवीषि धर्मज्ञ धर्मोऽसि वृषरूपधृक् ।
यदधर्मकृतः स्थानं सूचकस्यापि तद्भवेत् ॥२२॥

rājovāca
dharmaṁ bravīṣi dharma-jña
dharmo 'si vṛṣa-rūpa-dhṛk
yad adharma-kṛtaḥ sthānaṁ
sūcakasyāpi tad bhavet

rājā uvāca—the King said; *dharmam*—religion; *bravīṣi*—as you speak; *dharma-jña*—O one who knows the codes of religion; *dharmaḥ*—the personality of religion; *asi*—you are; *vṛṣa-rūpa-dhṛk*—in the disguise of a bull; *yat*—whatever; *adharma-kṛtaḥ*—one who acts irreligiously; *sthānam*—place; *sūcakasya*—of the identifier; *api*—also; *tat*—that; *bhavet*—becomes.

TRANSLATION

The King said: O you, who are in the form of a bull! You know the truth of religion, and you are speaking according to the

principle that the destination intended for the perpetrator of irreligious acts is also intended for one who identifies the perpetrator. You are no other than the personality of religion.

PURPORT

A devotee's conclusion is that no one is directly responsible for being a benefactor or mischief-monger without the sanction of the Lord; therefore he does not consider anyone to be directly responsible for such action. But in both the cases he takes it for granted that either benefit or loss is God-sent, and thus it is His grace. In case of benefit, no one will deny that it is God-sent, but in case of loss or reverses one becomes doubtful about how the Lord could be so unkind to His devotee as to put him in great difficulty. Jesus Christ was seemingly put into such great difficulty, being crucified by the ignorant, but he was never angry at the mischief-mongers. That is the way of accepting a thing, either favorable or unfavorable. Thus for a devotee the identifier is equally a sinner, like the mischief-monger. By God's grace, the devotee tolerates all reverses. Mahārāja Parīkṣit observed this, and therefore he could understand that the bull was no other than the personality of religion himself. In other words, a devotee has no suffering at all because so-called suffering is also God's grace for a devotee who sees God in everything. The cow and bull never placed any complaint before the King for being tortured by the personality of Kali, although everyone lodges such complaints before the state authorities. The extraordinary behavior of the bull made the King conclude that the bull was certainly the personality of religion, for no one else could understand the finer intricacies of the codes of religion.

TEXT 23

अथवा देवमायाया नूनं गतिरगोचरा ।
चेतसो वचसश्चापि भूतानामिति निश्चयः ॥२३॥

athavā deva-māyāyā
nūnaṁ gatir agocarā
cetaso vacasaś cāpi
bhūtānām iti niścayaḥ

athavā—alternatively; *deva*—the Lord; *māyāyāḥ*—energies; *nūnam*—very little; *gatiḥ*—movement; *agocarā*—inconceivable; *cetasaḥ*—either by the mind; *vacasaḥ*—by words; *ca*—or; *api*—also; *bhūtānām*—of all living beings; *iti*—thus; *niścayaḥ*—concluded.

TRANSLATION

Thus it is concluded that the Lord's energies are inconceivable. No one can estimate them by mental speculation or by word jugglery.

PURPORT

A question may be raised as to why a devotee should refrain from identifying an actor, although he knows definitely that the Lord is the ultimate doer of everything. Knowing the ultimate doer, one should not pose himself as ignorant of the actual performer. To answer this doubt, the reply is that the Lord is also not directly responsible, for everything is done by His deputed *māyā-śakti,* or material energy. The material energy is always provoking doubts about the supreme authority of the Lord. The personality of religion knew perfectly well that nothing can take place without the sanction of the Supreme Lord, and still he was put into doubts by the deluding energy, and thus he refrained from mentioning the supreme cause. This doubtfulness was due to the contamination of both Kali and the material energy. The whole atmosphere of the age of Kali is magnified by the deluding energy, and the proportion of measurement is inexplicable.

TEXT 24

तपः शौचं दया सत्यमिति पादाः कृते कृताः ।
अधर्मांशैस्त्रयो भग्नाः स्मयसङ्गमदैस्तव ॥२४॥

tapaḥ śaucaṁ dayā satyam
iti pādāḥ kṛte kṛtāḥ
adharmāṁśais trayo bhagnāḥ
smaya-saṅga-madais tava

tapaḥ—austerity; *śaucam*—cleanliness; *dayā*—mercy; *satyam*—truthfulness; *iti*—thus; *pādāḥ*—legs; *kṛte*—in the age of Satya; *kṛtāḥ*—

established; *adharma*—irreligiosity; *aṁśaiḥ*—by the parts; *trayaḥ*—three combined; *bhagnāḥ*—broken; *smaya*—pride; *saṅga*—too much association with women; *madaiḥ*—intoxication; *tava*—your.

TRANSLATION

In the age of Satya [truthfulness] your four legs were established by the four principles of austerity, cleanliness, mercy and truthfulness. But it appears that three of your legs are broken due to rampant irreligion in the form of pride, lust for women, and intoxication.

PURPORT

The deluding energy, or material nature, can act upon the living beings proportionately in terms of the living beings' falling prey to the deluding attraction of *māyā*. Moths are captivated by the glaring brightness of light, and thus they become prey to the fire. Similarly, the deluding energy is always captivating the conditioned souls to become prey to the fire of delusion, and the Vedic scriptures warn the conditioned souls not to become prey to delusion but to get rid of it. The *Vedas* warn us to go not to the darkness of ignorance but to the progressive path of light. The Lord Himself also warns that the deluding power of material energy is too powerful to overcome, but one who completely surrenders unto the Lord can easily do so. But to surrender unto the lotus feet of the Lord is also not very easy. Such surrender is possible by persons of austerity, cleanliness, mercy and truthfulness. These four principles of advanced civilization were remarkable features in the age of Satya. In that age, every human being was practically a qualified *brāhmaṇa* of the highest order, and in the social orders of life they were all *paramahaṁsas*, or the topmost in the renounced order. By cultural standing, the human beings were not at all subjected to the deluding energy. Such strong men of character were competent enough to get away from the clutches of *māyā*. But gradually, as the basic principles of brahminical culture, namely austerity, cleanliness, mercy and truthfulness, became curtailed by proportionate development of pride, attachment for women and intoxication, the path of salvation or the path of transcendental bliss retreated far, far away from human society.

With the progression of the age of Kali, people are becoming very proud, and attached to women and intoxication. By the influence of the age of Kali, even a pauper is proud of his penny, the women are always dressed in an overly attractive fashion to victimize the minds of men, and the man is addicted to drinking wine, smoking, drinking tea and chewing tobacco, etc. All these habits, or so-called advancement of civilization, are the root causes of all irreligiosities, and therefore it is not possible to check corruption, bribery and nepotism. Man cannot check all these evils simply by statutory acts and police vigilance, but he can cure the disease of the mind by the proper medicine, namely advocating the principles of brahminical culture or the principles of austerity, cleanliness, mercy and truthfulness. Modern civilization and economic development are creating a new situation of poverty and scarcity with the result of blackmailing the consumer's commodities. If the leaders and the rich men of the society spend fifty percent of their accumulated wealth mercifully for the misled mass of people and educate them in God consciousness, the knowledge of *Bhāgavatam*, certainly the age of Kali will be defeated in its attempt to entrap the conditioned souls. We must always remember that false pride, or too high an estimation of one's own values of life, undue attachment to women or association with them, and intoxication will divert human civilization from the path of peace, however much the people clamor for peace in the world. The preaching of the *Bhāgavatam* principles will automatically render all men austere, clean both inside and outside, merciful to the suffering, and truthful in daily behavior. That is the way of correcting the flaws of human society, which are very prominently exhibited at the present moment.

TEXT 25

इदानीं धर्म पादस्ते सत्यं निर्वर्तयेद्यतः ।
तं जिघृक्षत्यधर्मोऽयमनृतेनैधितः कलिः ॥२५॥

idānīṁ dharma pādas te
satyaṁ nirvartayed yataḥ
taṁ jighṛkṣaty adharmo 'yam
anṛtenaidhitaḥ kaliḥ

idānīm—at the present moment; *dharma*—O personality of religion; *pādaḥ*—leg; *te*—of you; *satyam*—truthfulness; *nirvartayet*—hobbling along somehow or other; *yataḥ*—whereby; *tam*—that; *jighṛkṣati*—trying to destroy; *adharmaḥ*—the personality of irreligion; *ayam*—this; *anṛtena*—by deceit; *edhitaḥ*—flourishing; *kaliḥ*—quarrel personified.

TRANSLATION

You are now standing on one leg only, which is your truthfulness, and you are somehow or other hobbling along. But quarrel personified [Kali], flourishing by deceit, is also trying to destroy that leg.

PURPORT

The principles of religion do not stand on some dogmas or manmade formulas, but they stand on four primary regulative observances, namely austerity, cleanliness, mercy and truthfulness. The mass of people must be taught to practice these principles from childhood. Austerity means to accept voluntarily things which may not be very comfortable for the body but are conducive for spiritual realization, for example, fasting. Fasting twice or four times a month is a sort of austerity which may be voluntarily accepted for spiritual realization only, and not for any other purposes, political or otherwise. Fastings which are meant not for self-realization but for some other purposes are condemned in the *Bhagavad-gītā* (17.5–6). Similarly, cleanliness is necessary both for the mind and for the body. Simply bodily cleanliness may help to some extent, but cleanliness of the mind is necessary, and it is effected by glorifying the Supreme Lord. No one can cleanse the accumulated mental dust without glorifying the Supreme Lord. A godless civilization cannot cleanse the mind because it has no idea of God, and for this simple reason people under such a civilization cannot have good qualifications, however they may be materially equipped. We have to see things by their resultant action. The resultant action of human civilization in the age of Kali is dissatisfaction, so everyone is anxious to get peace of mind. This peace of mind was complete in the Satya age because of the existence of the above-mentioned attributes of the human beings. Gradually these attributes have diminished in the Tretā-yuga to three fourths, in the Dvāpara to half, and in this age of Kali to one fourth, which is also gradually diminishing on account of prevailing untruthfulness. By pride, either artificial or real, the resultant action of austerity is spoiled; by too much affection for female association, cleanliness is spoiled; by too much addiction to intoxication, mercy is spoiled; and by too much lying propaganda, truthfulness is spoiled. The revival of *bhāgavata-dharma* can save human civilization from falling prey to evils of all description.

TEXT 26

इयं च भूमिर्भगवता न्यासितोरुभरा सती ।
श्रीमद्भिस्तत्पदन्यासैः सर्वतः कृतकौतुका ॥२६॥

iyaṁ ca bhūmir bhagavatā
nyāsitoru-bharā satī
śrīmadbhis tat-pada-nyāsaiḥ
sarvataḥ kṛta-kautukā

iyam—this; *ca*—and; *bhūmiḥ*—surface of the earth; *bhagavatā*—by the Personality of Godhead; *nyāsita*—being performed personally as well as by others; *uru*—great; *bharā*—burden; *satī*—being so done; *śrīmadbhiḥ*—by the all-auspicious; *tat*—that; *pada-nyāsaiḥ*—footprints; *sarvataḥ*—all around; *kṛta*—done; *kautukā*—good fortune.

TRANSLATION

The burden of the earth was certainly diminished by the Personality of Godhead and by others as well. When He was present as an incarnation, all good was performed because of His auspicious footprints.

TEXT 27

शोचत्यश्रुकला साध्वी दुर्भगेवोज्झितासती ।
अब्रह्मण्या नृपव्याजाः शूद्रा भोक्ष्यन्ति मामिति ॥२७॥

śocaty aśru-kalā sādhvī
durbhagevojjhitā satī
abrahmaṇyā nṛpa-vyājāḥ
śūdrā bhokṣyanti mām iti

śocati—lamenting; *aśru-kalā*—with tears in the eyes; *sādhvī*—the chaste; *durbhagā*—as if the most unfortunate; *iva*—like; *ujjhitā*—forlorn; *satī*—being so done; *abrahmaṇyāḥ*—devoid of brahminical culture; *nṛpa-vyājāḥ*—posed as the ruler; *śūdrāḥ*—lower class; *bhokṣyanti*—would enjoy; *mām*—me; *iti*—thus.

TRANSLATION

Now she, the chaste one, being unfortunately forsaken by the Personality of Godhead, laments her future with tears in her eyes, for now she is being ruled and enjoyed by lower-class men who pose as rulers.

PURPORT

The *kṣatriya,* or the man who is qualified to protect the sufferers, is meant to rule the state. Untrained lower-class men, or men without ambition to protect the sufferers, cannot be placed on the seat of an administrator. Unfortunately, in the age of Kali the lower-class men, without training, occupy the post of a ruler by strength of popular votes, and instead of protecting the sufferers, such men create a situation quite intolerable for everyone. Such rulers illegally gratify themselves at the cost of all comforts of the citizens, and thus the chaste mother earth cries to see the pitiable condition of her sons, both men and animals. That is the future of the world in the age of Kali, when irreligiosity prevails most prominently. And in the absence of a suitable King to curb irreligious tendencies, educating the people systematically in the teaching of *Śrīmad-Bhāgavatam* will clear up the hazy atmosphere of corruption, bribery, blackmail, etc.

TEXT 28

इति धर्मं महीं चैव सान्त्वयित्वा महारथः ।
निशातमाददे खड्गं कलयेऽधर्महेतवे ॥२८॥

iti dharmaṁ mahīṁ caiva
sāntvayitvā mahā-rathaḥ

niśātam ādade khaḍgaṁ
kalaye 'dharma-hetave

iti—thus; *dharmam*—the personality of religion; *mahīm*—the earth; *ca*—also; *eva*—as; *sāntvayitvā*—after pacifying; *mahā-rathaḥ*—the general who could fight alone with thousands of enemies; *niśātam*—sharp; *ādade*—took up; *khaḍgam*—sword; *kalaye*—to kill the personified Kali; *adharma*—irreligion; *hetave*—the root cause.

TRANSLATION

Mahārāja Parīkṣit, who could fight one thousand enemies singlehandedly, thus pacified the personality of religion and the earth. Then he took up his sharp sword to kill the personality of Kali, who is the cause of all irreligion.

PURPORT

As described above, the personality of Kali is he who deliberately commits all kinds of sinful acts which are forbidden in the revealed scriptures. This age of Kali will certainly be full of all activities of Kali, but this does not mean that the leaders of society, the executive heads, the learned and intelligent men, or above all the devotees of the Lord should sit down tightly and become callous to the reactions of the age of Kali. In the rainy season certainly there will be profuse rainfalls, but that does not mean that men should not take means to protect themselves from the rains. It is the duty of the executive heads of state and others to take all necessary actions against the activities of Kali or the persons influenced by the age of Kali; and Mahārāja Parīkṣit is the ideal executive head of the state, for at once he was ready to kill the personality of Kali with his sharp sword. The administrators should not simply pass resolutions for anticorruptional steps, but they must be ready with sharp swords to kill the persons creating corruptions from the angle of vision of the recognized *śāstras.* The administrators cannot prevent corrupt activities by allowing wine shops. They must at once close all shops of intoxicating drugs and wine and force punishment even by death for those who indulge in habits of intoxication of all description. That is the way of stopping the activities of Kali, as exhibited herein by Mahārāja Parīkṣit, the *mahā-ratha.*

TEXT 29

तं जिघांसुमभिप्रेत्य विहाय नृपलाञ्छनम् ।
तत्पादमूलं शिरसा समगाद् भयविह्वलः ॥२९॥

taṁ jighāṁsum abhipretya
vihāya nṛpa-lāñchanam
tat-pāda-mūlaṁ śirasā
samagād bhaya-vihvalaḥ

tam—him; *jighāṁsum*—willing to kill; *abhipretya*—knowing it well; *vihāya*—leaving aside; *nṛpa-lāñchanam*—the dress of a king; *tat-pāda-mūlam*—at his feet; *śirasā*—by the head; *samagāt*—fully surrendered; *bhaya-vihvalaḥ*—under pressure of fearfulness.

TRANSLATION

When the personality of Kali understood that the King was willing to kill him, he at once abandoned the dress of a king and, under pressure of fear, completely surrendered to him, bowing his head.

PURPORT

The royal dress of the personality of Kali is artificial. The royal dress is suitable for a king or *kṣatriya,* but when a lower-class man artificially dresses himself as a king, his real identity is disclosed by the challenge of a bona fide *kṣatriya* like Mahārāja Parīkṣit. A real *kṣatriya* never surrenders. He accepts the challenge of his rival *kṣatriya,* and he fights either to die or to win. Surrender is unknown to a real *kṣatriya.* In the age of Kali there are so many pretenders dressed and posed like administrators or executive heads, but their real identity is disclosed when they are challenged by a real *kṣatriya.* Therefore when the artificially dressed personality of Kali saw that to fight Mahārāja Parīkṣit was beyond his ability, he bowed down his head like a subordinate and gave up his royal dress.

TEXT 30

पतितं पादयोर्वीरः कृपया दीनवत्सलः ।
शरण्यो नावधीच्छ्लोक्य आह चेदं हसन्निव ॥३०॥

patitaṁ pādayor vīraḥ
kṛpayā dīna-vatsalaḥ
śaraṇyo nāvadhīc chlokya
āha cedaṁ hasann iva

patitam—fallen; *pādayoḥ*—at the feet; *vīraḥ*—the hero; *kṛpayā*—out of compassion; *dīna-vatsalaḥ*—kind to the poor; *śaraṇyaḥ*—one who is qualified to accept surrender; *na*—not; *avadhīt*—did kill; *ślokyaḥ*—one who is worthy of being sung; *āha*—said; *ca*—also; *idam*—this; *hasan*—smiling; *iva*—like.

TRANSLATION

Mahārāja Parīkṣit, who was qualified to accept surrender and worthy of being sung in history, did not kill the poor surrendered and fallen Kali, but smiled compassionately, for he was kind to the poor.

PURPORT

Even an ordinary *kṣatriya* does not kill a surrendered person, and what to speak of Mahārāja Parīkṣit, who was by nature compassionate and kind to the poor. He was smiling because the artificially dressed Kali had disclosed his identity as a lower-class man, and he was thinking how ironic it was that although no one was saved from his sharp sword when he desired to kill, the poor lower-class Kali was spared by his timely surrender. Mahārāja Parīkṣit's glory and kindness are therefore sung in history. He was a kind and compassionate emperor, fully worthy of accepting surrender even from his enemy. Thus the personality of Kali was saved by the will of Providence.

TEXT 31

राजोवाच

न ते गुडाकेशयशोधराणां
बद्धाञ्जलेर्वै भयमस्ति किंचित् ।

न वर्तितव्यं भवता कथंचन
क्षेत्रे मदीये त्वमधर्मबन्धुः ॥३१॥

rājovāca
na te guḍākeśa-yaśo-dharāṇāṁ
baddhāñjaler vai bhayam asti kiñcit
na vartitavyaṁ bhavatā kathañcana
kṣetre madīye tvam adharma-bandhuḥ

rājā uvāca—the King said; *na*—not; *te*—your; *guḍākeśa*—Arjuna; *yaśaḥ-dharāṇām*—of us who inherited the fame; *baddha-añjaleḥ*—one with folded hands; *vai*—certainly; *bhayam*—fear; *asti*—there is; *kiñcit*—even a slight; *na*—neither; *vartitavyam*—can be allowed to live; *bhavatā*—by you; *kathañcana*—by all means; *kṣetre*—in the land; *madīye*—in my kingdom; *tvam*—you; *adharma-bandhuḥ*—the friend of irreligion.

TRANSLATION

The King thus said: We have inherited the fame of Arjuna; therefore since you have surrendered yourself with folded hands you need not fear for your life. But you cannot remain in my kingdom, for you are the friend of irreligion.

PURPORT

The personality of Kali, who is the friend of all kinds of irreligiosities, may be excused if he surrenders, but in all circumstances he cannot be allowed to live as a citizen in any part of a welfare state. The Pāṇḍavas were entrusted representatives of the Personality of Godhead, Lord Kṛṣṇa, who practically brought into being the Battle of Kurukṣetra, but not for any personal interest. He wanted an ideal king like Mahārāja Yudhiṣṭhira and his descendants like Mahārāja Parīkṣit to rule the world, and therefore a responsible king like Mahārāja Parīkṣit could not allow the friend of irreligiosity to flourish in his kingdom at the cost of the good fame of the Pāṇḍavas. That is the way of wiping out corruption in the state, and not otherwise. The friends of irreligiosity should be banished from the state, and that will save the state from corruption.

TEXT 32

त्वां वर्तमानं नरदेवदेहे-
ष्वनुप्रवृत्तोऽयमधर्मपूगः ।
लोभोऽनृतं चौर्यमनार्यमंहो
ज्येष्ठा च माया कलहश्च दम्भः ॥३२॥

tvāṁ vartamānaṁ nara-deva-deheṣv
anupravṛtto 'yam adharma-pūgaḥ
lobho 'nṛtaṁ cauryam anāryam aṁho
jyeṣṭhā ca māyā kalahaś ca dambhaḥ

tvām—you; *vartamānam*—while present; *nara-deva*—a man-god, or a king; *deheṣu*—in the body; *anupravṛttaḥ*—taking place everywhere; *ayam*—all these; *adharma*—irreligious principles; *pūgaḥ*—in the masses; *lobhaḥ*—greed; *anṛtam*—falsity; *cauryam*—robbery; *anāryam*—incivility; *aṁhaḥ*—treachery; *jyeṣṭhā*—misfortune; *ca*—and; *māyā*—cheating; *kalahaḥ*—quarrel; *ca*—and; *dambhaḥ*—vanity.

TRANSLATION

If the personality of Kali, irreligion, is allowed to act as a man-god or an executive head, certainly irreligious principles like greed, falsehood, robbery, incivility, treachery, misfortune, cheating, quarrel and vanity will abound.

PURPORT

The principles of religion, namely *austerity, cleanliness, mercy and truthfulness,* as we have already discussed, may be followed by the follower of any faith. There is no need to turn from Hindu to Mohammedan to Christian or some other faith and thus become a renegade and not follow the principles of religion. The *Bhāgavatam religion* urges following the *principles of religion.* The principles of religion are not the dogmas or regulative principles of a certain faith. Such regulative principles may be different in terms of the time and place concerned. One has to see whether the aims of religion have been achieved. Sticking to the dogmas and formulas without attaining the real principles is not good. A secular state may be impartial to any particular type of faith, but the state cannot be indifferent to the principles of religion as above mentioned. But in the age of Kali, the executive heads of state will be indifferent to such religious principles, and therefore under their patronage the opponents of religious principles, such as greed, falsehood, cheating and pilfery, will naturally follow, and so there will be no meaning to propaganda crying to stop corruption in the state.

TEXT 33

न वर्तितव्यं तदधर्मबन्धो
धर्मेण सत्येन च वर्तितव्ये ।
ब्रह्मावर्ते यत्र यजन्ति यज्ञै-
र्यज्ञेश्वरं यज्ञवितानविज्ञाः ॥३३॥

na vartitavyaṁ tad adharma-bandho
dharmeṇa satyena ca vartitavye
brahmāvarte yatra yajanti yajñair
yajñeśvaraṁ yajña-vitāna-vijñāḥ

na—not; *vartitavyam*—deserve to remain; *tat*—therefore; *adharma*—irreligiosity; *bandho*—friend; *dharmeṇa*—with religion; *satyena*—with truth; *ca*—also; *vartitavye*—being situated in; *brahma-āvarte*—place where sacrifice is performed; *yatra*—where; *yajanti*—duly perform; *yajñaiḥ*—by sacrifices or devotional services; *yajña-īśvaram*—unto the Supreme Lord, the Personality of Godhead; *yajña*—sacrifice; *vitāna*—spreading; *vijñāḥ*—experts.

TRANSLATION

Therefore, O friend of irreligion, you do not deserve to remain in a place where experts perform sacrifices according to truth and religious principles for the satisfaction of the Supreme Personality of Godhead.

PURPORT

Yajñeśvara, or the Supreme Personality of Godhead, is the beneficiary of all kinds of sacrificial ceremonies. Such sacrificial ceremonies are prescribed differently in the scriptures for different ages. In other words, sacrifice means to accept the supremacy of the Lord and thereby perform acts by which the Lord may be satisfied in all respects. The atheists do not believe in the existence of God, and they do not perform any sacrifice for the satisfaction of the Lord. Any place or country where the supremacy of the Lord is accepted and thus sacrifice is performed is called *brahmāvarta.* There are different countries in different parts of the world, and each and every country may have different types of sacrifice to please the Supreme Lord, but the central point in pleasing Him is ascertained in the *Bhāgavatam,* and it is truthfulness. The basic principle of religion is truthfulness, and the ultimate goal of all religions is to satisfy the Lord. In this age of Kali, the greatest common formula of sacrifice is the *saṅkīrtana-yajña.* That is the opinion of the experts who know how to propagate the process of *yajña.* Lord Caitanya preached this method of *yajña,* and it is understood from this verse that the sacrificial method of *saṅkīrtana-yajña* may be performed anywhere and everywhere in order to drive away the personality of Kali and save human society from falling prey to the influence of the age.

TEXT 34

यस्मिन् हरिर्भगवानिज्यमान
इज्यात्ममूर्तिर्यजतां शं तनोति ।
कामानमोघान् स्थिरजङ्गमाना-
मन्तर्बहिर्वायुरिवैष आत्मा ॥३४॥

yasmin harir bhagavān ijyamāna
ijyātma-mūrtir yajatāṁ śaṁ tanoti
kāmān amoghān sthira-jaṅgamānām
antar bahir vāyur ivaiṣa ātmā

yasmin—in such sacrificial ceremonies; *hariḥ*—the Supreme Lord; *bhagavān*—the Personality of Godhead; *ijyamānaḥ*—being worshiped; *ijya-ātma*—the soul of all worshipable deities; *mūrtiḥ*—in the forms; *yajatām*—those who worship; *śam*—welfare; *tanoti*—spreads; *kāmān*—desires; *amoghān*—inviolable; *sthira-jaṅgamānām*—of all the moving and nonmoving; *antaḥ*—within; *bahiḥ*—outside; *vāyuḥ*—air; *iva*—like; *eṣaḥ*—of all of them; *ātmā*—spirit soul.

TRANSLATION

In all sacrificial ceremonies, although sometimes a demigod is worshiped, the Supreme Lord Personality of Godhead is worshiped because He is the Supersoul of everyone, and exists both inside and outside like the air. Thus it is He only who awards all welfare to the worshiper.

PURPORT

It is even sometimes seen that demigods like Indra and Candra are worshiped and offered sacrificial awards, yet the rewards of all such sacrifices are awarded to the worshiper by the Supreme Lord, and it is the Lord only who can offer all welfare to the worshiper. The demigods, although worshiped, cannot do anything without the sanction of the Lord because the Lord is the Supersoul of everyone, both moving and nonmoving.

In *Bhagavad-gītā* (9.23) the Lord Himself confirms this in the following *śloka:*

ye 'py anya-devatā-bhaktā
yajante śraddhayānvitāḥ
te 'pi mām eva kaunteya
yajanty avidhi-pūrvakam

"Whatever a man may sacrifice to other gods, O son of Kuntī, is really meant for Me alone, but it is offered without true understanding."

The fact is that the Supreme Lord is one without a second. There is no God other than the Lord Himself. Thus the Supreme Lord is eternally transcendental to the material creation. But there are many who worship the demigods like the sun, the moon and Indra, who are only material representatives of the Supreme Lord. These demigods are indirect, qualitative representations of the Supreme Lord. A learned scholar or devotee, however, knows who is who. Therefore he directly worships the Supreme Lord and is not diverted by the material, qualitative representations. Those who are not so learned worship such qualitative, material representations, but their worship is unceremonious because it is irregular.

TEXT 35

सूत उवाच

परीक्षितैवमादिष्टः स कलिर्जातवेपथुः ।
तमुद्यतासिमाहेदं दण्डपाणिमिवोद्यतम् ॥३५॥

sūta uvāca
parīkṣitaivam ādiṣṭaḥ
sa kalir jāta-vepathuḥ
tam udyatāsim āhedaṁ
daṇḍa-pāṇim ivodyatam

sūtaḥ uvāca—Śrī Sūta Gosvāmī said; *parīkṣitā*—by Mahārāja Parīkṣit; *evam*—thus; *ādiṣṭaḥ*—being ordered; *saḥ*—he; *kaliḥ*—the personality of Kali; *jāta*—there was; *vepathuḥ*—trembling; *tam*—him; *udyata*—raised; *asim*—sword; *āha*—said; *idam*—thus; *daṇḍa-pāṇim*—Yamarāja, the personality of death; *iva*—like; *udyatam*—almost ready.

TRANSLATION

Śrī Sūta Gosvāmī said: The personality of Kali, thus being ordered by Mahārāja Parīkṣit, began to tremble in fear. Seeing the King before him like Yamarāja, ready to kill him, Kali spoke to the King as follows.

PURPORT

The King was ready to kill the personality of Kali at once, as soon as he disobeyed his order. Otherwise the King had no objection to allowing him to prolong his life. The personality of Kali also, after attempting to get rid of the punishment in various ways, decided that he must surrender unto him, and thus he began to tremble in fear of his life. The king, or the executive head, must be so strong as to stand before the personality of Kali like the personality of death, Yamarāja. The King's order must be obeyed, otherwise the culprit's life is in risk. That is the way to rule the personalities of Kali who create disturbance in the normal life of the state citizens.

TEXT 36

कलिरुवाच
यत्र क्वाथ वत्स्यामि सार्वभौम तवाज्ञया ।
लक्षये तत्र तत्रापि त्वामात्तेषुशरासनम् ॥३६॥

kalir uvāca
yatra kva vātha vatsyāmi
sārva-bhauma tavājñayā
lakṣaye tatra tatrāpi
tvām ātteṣu-śarāsanam

kaliḥ uvāca—the personality of Kali said; *yatra*—anywhere; *kva*—and everywhere; *vā*—either; *atha*—thereof; *vatsyāmi*—I shall reside; *sārva-bhauma*—O Lord (or Emperor) of the earth; *tava*—your; *ājñayā*—by the order; *lakṣaye*—I see; *tatra tatra*—anywhere and everywhere; *api*—also; *tvām*—Your Majesty; *ātta*—taken over; *iṣu*—arrows; *śarāsanam*—bows.

TRANSLATION

O Your Majesty, though I may live anywhere and everywhere under your order, I shall but see you with bow and arrows wherever I look.

PURPORT

The personality of Kali could see that Mahārāja Parīkṣit was the emperor of all lands all over the world, and thus anywhere he might live he would have to meet with the same mood of the King. The personality of Kali was meant for mischief, and Mahārāja Parīkṣit was meant for subduing all kinds of mischief-mongers, especially the personality of Kali. It was better, therefore, for the personality of Kali to have been killed by the King then and there instead of being killed elsewhere. He was, after all, a surrendered soul before the King, and it was for the King to do what was required.

TEXT 37

तन्मे धर्मभृतां श्रेष्ठ स्थानं निर्देष्टुमर्हसि ।
यत्रैव नियतो वत्स्य आतिष्ठंस्तेऽनुशासनम् ॥३७॥

tan me dharma-bhṛtāṁ śreṣṭha
sthānaṁ nirdeṣṭum arhasi
yatraiva niyato vatsya
ātiṣṭhaṁs te 'nuśāsanam

tat—therefore; *me*—me; *dharma-bhṛtām*—of all the protectors of religion; *śreṣṭha*—O chief; *sthānam*—place; *nirdeṣṭum*—fix; *arhasi*—may you do so; *yatra*—where; *eva*—certainly; *nityataḥ*—always; *vatsye*—can reside; *ātiṣṭhan*—permanently situated; *te*—your; *anuśāsanam*—under your rule.

TRANSLATION

Therefore, O chief amongst the protectors of religion, please fix some place for me where I can live permanently under the protection of your government.

PURPORT

The personality of Kali addressed Mahārāja Parīkṣit as the chief amongst the protectors of religiosity because the King refrained from killing a person who surrendered unto him. A surrendered soul should be given all protection, even though he may be an enemy. That is the principle of religion. And we can just imagine what sort of protection is given by the Personality of Godhead to the person who surrenders unto Him, not as an enemy but as a devoted servitor. The Lord protects the surrendered soul from all sins and all resultant reactions of sinful acts (Bg. 18.66).

TEXT 38

सूत उवाच
अभ्यर्थितस्तदा तस्मै स्थानानि कलये ददौ ।
द्यूतं पानं स्त्रियः सूना यत्राधर्मश्चतुर्विधः ॥३८॥

sūta uvāca
abhyarthitas tadā tasmai
sthānāni kalaye dadau
dyūtaṁ pānaṁ striyaḥ sūnā
yatrādharmaś catur-vidhaḥ

sūtaḥ uvāca—Sūta Gosvāmī said; *abhyarthitaḥ*—thus being petitioned; *tadā*—at that time; *tasmai*—unto him; *sthānāni*—places; *kalaye*—to the personality of Kali; *dadau*—gave him permission; *dyūtam*—gambling; *pānam*—drinking; *striyaḥ*—illicit association with women; *sūnā*—animal slaughter; *yatra*—wherever; *adharmaḥ*—sinful activities; *catuḥ-vidhaḥ*—four kinds of.

TRANSLATION

Sūta Gosvāmī said: Mahārāja Parīkṣit, thus being petitioned by the personality of Kali, gave him permission to reside in places where gambling, drinking, prostitution and animal slaughter were performed.

PURPORT

The basic principles of irreligiosity, such as pride, prostitution, intoxication and falsehood, counteract the four principles of religion, namely austerity, cleanliness, mercy and truthfulness. The personality of Kali was given permission to live in four places particularly mentioned by the King, namely the place of gambling, the place of prostitution, the place of drinking and the place of animal slaughter.

Śrīla Jīva Gosvāmī directs that drinking against the principles of scriptures, such as the *sautrāmaṇī-yajña*, association with women outside marriage, and killing animals against the injunctions of scriptures are irreligious. In the *Vedas* two different types of injunctions are there for the *pravṛttas*, or those who are engaged in material enjoyment, and for the *nivṛttas*, or those who are liberated from material bondage. The Vedic injunction for the *pravṛttas* is to gradually regulate their activities towards the path of liberation. Therefore, for those who are in the lowest stage of ignorance and who indulge in wine, women and flesh, drinking by performing *sautrāmaṇī-yajña*, association of women by marriage and flesh-eating by sacrifices are sometimes recommended. Such recommendations in the Vedic literature are meant for a particular class of men, and not for all. But because they are injunctions of the *Vedas* for particular types of persons, such activities by the *pravṛttas* are not considered *adharma*. One man's food may be poison for others; similarly, what is recommended for those in the mode of ignorance may be poison for those in the mode of goodness. Śrīla Jīva Gosvāmī Prabhu, therefore, affirms that recommendations in the scriptures for a certain class of men are never to be considered *adharma*, or irreligious. But such activities are factually *adharma*, and they are never to be encouraged. The recommendations in the scriptures are not meant for the encouragement of such *adharma*, but for regulating the necessary *adharma* gradually toward the path of *dharma*.

Following in the footsteps of Mahārāja Parīkṣit, it is the duty of all executive heads of states to see that the principles of religion, namely austerity, cleanliness, mercy and truthfulness, are established in the state, and that the principles of irreligion, namely pride, illicit female association or prostitution, intoxication and falsity, are checked by all means. And to make the best use of a bad bargain, the personality of Kali may be transferred to places of gambling, drinking, prostitution and slaughterhouses, if there are any places like that. Those who are addicted to these irreligious habits may be regulated by the injunctions of the scripture. In no circumstances should they be encouraged by any state. In other words, the state should categorically stop all sorts of gambling, drinking, prostitution and falsity. The state which wants to eradicate corruption by majority may introduce the principles of religion in the following manner:

1. Two compulsory fasting days in a month, if not more (austerity). Even from the economic point of view, such two fasting days in a month in the state will save tons of food, and the system will also act very favorably on the general health of the citizens.

2. There must be compulsory marriage of young boys and girls attaining twenty-four years of age and sixteen years of age respectively. There is no harm in coeducation in the schools and colleges, provided the boys and girls are duly married, and in case there is any intimate connection between a male and female student, they should be married properly without illicit relation. The divorce act is encouraging prostitution, and this should be abolished.

3. The citizens of the state must give in charity up to fifty percent of their income for the purpose of creating a spiritual atmosphere in the state or in human society, both individually and collectively. They should preach the principles of *Bhāgavatam* by (a) *karma-yoga*, or doing everything for the satisfaction of the Lord, (b) regular hearing of the *Śrīmad-Bhāgavatam* from authorized persons or realized souls,

(c) chanting of the glories of the Lord congregationally at home or at places of worship, (d) rendering all kinds of service to *bhāgavatas* engaged in preaching *Śrīmad-Bhāgavatam* and (e) residing in a place where the atmosphere is saturated with God consciousness. If the state is regulated by the above process, naturally there will be God consciousness everywhere.

Gambling of all description, even speculative business enterprise, is considered to be degrading, and when gambling is encouraged in the state, there is a complete disappearance of truthfulness. Allowing young boys and girls to remain unmarried more than the above-mentioned ages and licensing animal slaughterhouses of all description should be at once prohibited. The flesh-eaters may be allowed to take flesh as mentioned in the scriptures, and not otherwise. Intoxication of all description—even smoking cigarettes, chewing tobacco or the drinking of tea—must be prohibited.

TEXT 39

पुनश्च याचमानाय जातरूपमदात्प्रभुः ।
ततोऽनृतं मदं कामं रजो वैरं च पञ्चमम् ॥३९॥

punaś ca yācamānāya
jāta-rūpam adāt prabhuḥ
tato 'nṛtaṁ madaṁ kāmaṁ
rajo vairaṁ ca pañcamam

punaḥ—again; *ca*—also; *yācamānāya*—to the beggar; *jāta-rūpam*—gold; *adāt*—gave away; *prabhuḥ*—the king; *tataḥ*—whereby; *anṛtam*—falsehood; *madam*—intoxication; *kāmam*—lust; *rajaḥ*—on account of a passionate mood; *vairam*—enmity; *ca*—also; *pañcamam*—the fifth one.

TRANSLATION

The personality of Kali asked for something more, and because of his begging, the King gave him permission to live where there is gold because wherever there is gold there is also falsity, intoxication, lust, envy and enmity.

PURPORT

Although Mahārāja Parīkṣit gave Kali permission to live in four places, it was very difficult for him to find the places because during the reign of Mahārāja Parīkṣit there were no such places. Therefore Kali asked the King to give him something practical which could be utilized for his nefarious purposes. Mahārāja Parīkṣit thus gave him permission to live in a place where there is gold, because wherever there is gold there are all the above-mentioned four things, and over and above them there is enmity also. So the personality of Kali became gold-standardized. According to *Śrīmad-Bhāgavatam,* gold encourages falsity, intoxication, prostitution, envy and enmity. Even a gold-standard exchange and currency is bad. Gold-standard currency is based on falsehood because the currency is not on a par with the reserved gold. The basic principle is falsity because currency notes are issued in value beyond that of the actual reserved gold. This artificial inflation of currency by the authorities encourages prostitution of the state economy. The price of commodities becomes artificially inflated because of bad money, or artificial currency notes. Bad money drives away good money. Instead of paper currency, actual gold coins should be used for exchange, and this will stop prostitution of gold. Gold ornaments for women may be allowed by control, not by quality, but by quantity. This will discourage lust, envy and enmity. When there is actual gold currency in the form of coins, the influence of gold in producing falsity, prostitution, etc., will automatically cease. There will be no need of an anticorruption ministry for another term of prostitution and falsity of purpose.

TEXT 40

अमूनि पञ्च स्थानानि ह्यधर्मप्रभवः कलिः ।
औत्तरेयेण दत्तानि न्यवसत् तन्निदेशकृत् ॥४०॥

amūni pañca sthānāni
hy adharma-prabhavaḥ kaliḥ
auttareyeṇa dattāni
nyavasat tan-nideśa-kṛt

amūni—all those; *pañca*—five; *sthānāni*—places; *hi*—certainly; *adharma*—irreligious principles; *prabhavaḥ*—encouraging; *kaliḥ*—the age of Kali; *auttareyeṇa*—by the son of Uttarā; *dattāni*—delivered; *nyavasat*—dwelt; *tat*—by him; *nideśa-kṛt*—directed.

TRANSLATION

Thus the personality of Kali, by the directions of Mahārāja Parīkṣit, the son of Uttarā, was allowed to live in those five places.

PURPORT

Thus the age of Kali began with gold standardization, and therefore falsity, intoxication, animal slaughter and prostitution are rampant all over the world, and the saner section is eager to drive out corruption. The counteracting process is suggested above, and everyone can take advantage of this suggestion.

TEXT 41

अथैतानि न सेवेत बुभूषुः पुरुषः क्वचित् ।
विशेषतो धर्मशीलो राजा लोकपतिर्गुरुः ॥४१॥

athaitāni na seveta
bubhūṣuḥ puruṣaḥ kvacit
viśeṣato dharma-śīlo
rājā loka-patir guruḥ

atha—therefore; *etāni*—all these; *na*—never; *seveta*—come in contact; *bubhūṣuḥ*—those who desire well-being; *puruṣaḥ*—person; *kvacit*—in any circumstances; *viśeṣataḥ*—specifically; *dharma-śīlaḥ*—those who are on the progressive path of liberation; *rājā*—the king; *loka-patiḥ*—public leader; *guruḥ*—the *brāhmaṇas* and the *sannyāsīs*.

TRANSLATION

Therefore, whoever desires progressive well-being, especially kings, religionists, public leaders, brāhmaṇas and sannyāsīs, should never come in contact with the four above-mentioned irreligious principles.

PURPORT

The *brāhmaṇas* are the religious preceptors for all other castes, and the *sannyāsīs* are the spiritual masters for all the castes and orders of society. So also are the king and the public leaders who are responsible for the material welfare of all people. The progressive religionists and those who are responsible human beings or those who do not want to spoil their valuable human lives should refrain from all the principles of irreligiosity, especially illicit connection with women. If a *brāhmaṇa* is not truthful, all his claims as a *brāhmaṇa* at once become null and void. If a *sannyāsī* is illicitly connected with women, all his claims as a *sannyāsī* at once become false. Similarly, if the king and the public leader are unnecessarily proud or habituated to drinking and smoking, certainly they become disqualified to discharge public welfare activities. Truthfulness is the basic principle for all religions. The four leaders of the human society, namely the *sannyāsīs*, the *brāhmaṇa*, the king and the public leader, must be tested crucially by their character and qualification. Before one can be accepted as a spiritual or material master of society, he must be tested by the above-mentioned criteria of character. Such public leaders may be less qualified in academic qualifications, but it is necessary primarily that they be free from the contamination of the four disqualifications, namely gambling, drinking, prostitution and animal slaughter.

TEXT 42

वृषस्य नष्टांस्त्रीन् पादान् तपः शौचं दयामिति ।
प्रतिसंदध आश्वास्य महीं च समवर्धयत् ॥४२॥

vṛṣasya naṣṭāṁs trīn pādān
tapaḥ śaucaṁ dayām iti
pratisandadha āśvāsya
mahīṁ ca samavardhayat

vṛṣasya—of the bull (the personality of religion); *naṣṭān*—lost; *trīn*—three; *pādān*—legs; *tapaḥ*—austerity; *śaucam*—cleanliness; *dayām*—mercy; *iti*—thus; *pratisandadhe*—reestablished; *āśvāsya*—by encouraging activities; *mahīm*—the earth; *ca*—and; *samavardhayat*—perfectly improved.

TRANSLATION

Thereafter the King reestablished the lost legs of the personality of religion [the bull], and by encouraging activities he sufficiently improved the condition of the earth.

PURPORT

By designating particular places for the personality of Kali, Mahārāja Parīkṣit practically cheated Kali. In the presence of Kali, Dharma (in the shape of a bull), and the earth (in the shape of a cow), he could actually estimate the general condition of his kingdom, and therefore he at once took proper steps to reestablish the legs of the bull, namely austerity, cleanliness and mercy. And for the general benefit of the people of the world, he saw that the gold stock might be employed for stabilization. Gold is certainly a generator of falsity, intoxication, prostitution, enmity and violence, but under the guidance of a proper king or public leader, or a *brāhmaṇa* or *sannyāsī*, the same gold can be properly utilized to reestablish the lost legs of the bull, the personality of religion.

Mahārāja Parīkṣit, therefore, like his grandfather Arjuna, collected all illicit gold kept for the propensities of Kali and employed it in the *saṅkīrtana-yajña*, as per instruction of the *Śrīmad-Bhāgavatam.* As we have suggested before, one's accumulated wealth may be divided into three parts for distribution, namely fifty percent for the service of the Lord, twenty-five percent for the family members and twenty-five percent for personal necessities. Spending fifty percent for the service of the Lord or for propagation of spiritual knowledge in society by way of the *saṅkīrtana-yajña* is the maximum display of human mercy. People of the world are generally in darkness regarding spiritual knowledge, especially in regard to the devotional service of the Lord, and therefore to propagate the systematic transcendental knowledge of devotional service is the greatest mercy that one can show in this world. When everyone is taught to sacrifice fifty percent of his accumulated gold for the Lord's service, certainly austerity, cleanliness and mercy automatically ensue, and thus the lost three legs of the personality of religion are automatically established. When there is sufficient austerity, cleanliness, mercy and truthfulness, naturally mother earth is completely satisfied, and there is very little chance for Kali to infiltrate the structure of human society.

TEXTS 43–44

स एष एतर्ह्यध्यास्त आसनं पार्थिवोचितम् ।
पितामहेनोपन्यस्तं राज्ञारण्यं विविक्षता ॥४३॥
आस्तेऽधुना स राजर्षिः कौरवेन्द्रश्रियोल्लसन् ।
गजाह्वये महाभागश्चक्रवर्ती बृहच्छ्रवाः ॥४४॥

sa eṣa etarhy adhyāsta
āsanaṁ pārthivocitam
pitāmahenopanyastaṁ
rājñāraṇyaṁ vivikṣatā

āste 'dhunā sa rājarṣiḥ
kauravendra-śriyollasan
gajāhvaye mahā-bhāgaś
cakravartī bṛhac-chravāḥ

saḥ—he; *eṣaḥ*—this; *etarhi*—at the present; *adhyāste*—is ruling over; *āsanam*—the throne; *pārthiva-ucitam*—just befitting a king; *pitāmahena*—by the grandfather; *upanyastam*—being handed over; *rājñā*—by the King; *araṇyam*—forest; *vivikṣatā*—desiring; *āste*—is there; *adhunā*—at present; *saḥ*—that; *rāja-ṛṣiḥ*—the sage amongst the kings; *kaurava-indra*—the chief amongst the Kuru kings; *śriyā*—glories; *ullasan*—spreading; *gajāhvaye*—in Hastināpura; *mahā-bhāgaḥ*—the most fortunate; *cakravartī*—the Emperor; *bṛhat-śravāḥ*—highly famous.

TRANSLATION

The most fortunate Emperor Mahārāja Parīkṣit, who was entrusted with the kingdom of Hastināpura by Mahārāja Yudhiṣṭhira when he desired to retire to the forest, is now ruling the world with great success due to his being glorified by the deeds of the kings of the Kuru dynasty.

PURPORT

The prolonged sacrificial ceremonies undertaken by the sages of Naimiṣāraṇya were begun shortly after the demise of Mahārāja Parīkṣit. The sacrifice was to continue for one thousand years, and it is understood that in the beginning some of the contemporaries of Baladeva, the elder brother of Lord Kṛṣṇa, also visited the sacrificial place. According to some authorities, the present tense is also used to indicate the nearest margin of time from the past. In that sense, the present tense is applied to the reign of Mahārāja Parīkṣit here. For a continuous fact, also, present tense can be used. The principles of Mahārāja Parīkṣit can be still continued, and human society can still be improved if there is determination by the authorities. We can still purge out from the state all the activities of immorality introduced by the personality of Kali if we are determined to take action like Mahārāja Parīkṣit. He allotted some place for Kali, but in fact Kali could not find such places in the world at all because Mahārāja Parīkṣit was strictly vigilant to see that there were no places for gambling, drinking, prostitution and animal slaughter. Modern administrators want to banish corruption from the state, but fools as they are, they do not know how to do it. They want to issue licenses for gambling houses, wine and other intoxicating drug houses, brothels, hotel prostitution and cinema houses, and falsity in every dealing, even in their own, and they want at the same time to drive out corruption from the state. They want the kingdom of God without God consciousness. How can it be possible to adjust two contradictory matters? If we want to drive out corruption from the state, we must first of all organize society to accept the principles of religion, namely austerity, cleanliness, mercy and truthfulness, and to make the condition favorable we must close all places of gambling, drinking, prostitution and falsity. These are some of the practical lessons from the pages of *Śrīmad-Bhāgavatam.*

TEXT 45

इत्थम्भूतानुभावोऽयमभिमन्युसुतो नृपः ।
यस्य पालयतः क्षौणीं यूयं सत्राय दीक्षिताः ॥४५॥

ittham-bhūtānubhāvo 'yam
abhimanyu-suto nṛpaḥ

yasya pālayataḥ kṣauṇīṁ
yūyaṁ satrāya dīkṣitāḥ

ittham-bhūta—being thus; *anubhāvaḥ*—experience; *ayam*—of this; *abhimanyu-sutaḥ*—son of Abhimanyu; *nṛpaḥ*—the king; *yasya*—whose; *pālayataḥ*—on account of his ruling; *kṣauṇīm*—on the earth; *yūyam*—you all; *satrāya*—in performing sacrifices; *dīkṣitāḥ*—initiated.

TRANSLATION

Mahārāja Parīkṣit, the son of Abhimanyu, is so experienced that by dint of his expert administration and patronage, it has been possible for you to perform a sacrifice such as this.

PURPORT

The *brāhmaṇas* and the *sannyāsīs* are expert in the spiritual advancement of society, whereas the *kṣatriyas* or the administrators are expert in the material peace and prosperity of human society. Both of them are the pillars of all happiness, and therefore they are meant for full cooperation for common welfare. Mahārāja Parīkṣit was experienced enough to drive away Kali from his field of activities and thereby make the state receptive to spiritual enlightenment. If the common people are not receptive, it is very difficult to impress upon them the necessity of spiritual enlightenment. Austerity, cleanliness, mercy and truthfulness, the basic principles of religion, prepare the ground for the reception of advancement in spiritual knowledge, and Mahārāja Parīkṣit made this favorable condition possible. Thus the *ṛṣis* of Naimiṣāraṇya were able to perform the sacrifices for a thousand years. In other words, without state support, no doctrines of philosophy or religious principles can progressively advance. There should be complete cooperation between the *brāhmaṇas* and the *kṣatriyas* for this common good. Even up to Mahārāja Aśoka, the same spirit was prevailing. Lord Buddha was sufficiently supported by King Aśoka, and thus his particular cult of knowledge was spread all over the world.

Thus end the Bhaktivedanta purports of the First Canto, Seventeenth Chapter, of the Śrīmad-Bhāgavatam, *entitled "Punishment and Reward of Kali."*

CHAPTER EIGHTEEN

Mahārāja Parīkṣit Cursed by a Brāhmaṇa Boy

TEXT 1

सूत उवाच
यो वै द्रौण्यस्त्रविप्लुष्टो न मातुरुदरे मृतः ।
अनुग्रहाद् भगवतः कृष्णस्याद्भुतकर्मणः ॥ १ ॥

sūta uvāca
yo vai drauṇy-astra-vipluṣṭo
na mātur udare mṛtaḥ
anugrahād bhagavataḥ
kṛṣṇasyādbhuta-karmaṇaḥ

sūtaḥ uvāca—Śrī Sūta Gosvāmī said; *yaḥ*—one who; *vai*—certainly; *drauṇi-astra*—by the weapon of the son of Droṇa; *vipluṣṭaḥ*—burned by; *na*—never; *mātuḥ*—of the mother; *udare*—in the womb; *mṛtaḥ*—met his death; *anugrahāt*—by the mercy; *bhagavataḥ*—of the Personality of Godhead; *kṛṣṇasya*—Kṛṣṇa; *adbhuta-karmaṇaḥ*—who acts wonderfully.

TRANSLATION

Śrī Sūta Gosvāmī said: Due to the mercy of the Personality of Godhead, Śrī Kṛṣṇa, who acts wonderfully, Mahārāja Parīkṣit, though struck by the weapon of the son of Droṇa in his mother's womb, could not be burned.

PURPORT

The sages of Naimiṣāraṇya became struck with wonder after hearing about the wonderful administration of Mahārāja Parīkṣit, especially in reference to his punishing the personality of Kali and making him completely unable to do any harm within the kingdom. Sūta Gosvāmī was equally anxious to describe Mahārāja Parīkṣit's wonderful birth and death, and this verse is stated by Sūta Gosvāmī to increase the interest of the sages of Naimiṣāraṇya.

TEXT 2

ब्रह्मकोपोत्थिताद् यस्तु तक्षकात्प्राणविप्लवात् ।
न सम्मुमोहोरुभयाद् भगवत्यर्पिताशयः ॥ २ ॥

brahma-kopotthitād yas tu
takṣakāt prāṇa-viplavāt
na sammumohorubhayād
bhagavaty arpitāśayaḥ

brahma-kopa—fury of a *brāhmaṇa; utthitāt*—caused by; *yaḥ*—what was; *tu*—but; *takṣakāt*—by the snake-bird; *prāṇa-viplavāt*—from dissolution of life; *na*—never; *sammumoha*—was overwhelmed; *uru-bhayāt*—great fear; *bhagavati*—unto the Personality of Godhead; *arpita*—surrendered; *āśayaḥ*—consciousness.

TRANSLATION

Furthermore, Mahārāja Parīkṣit was always consciously surrendered to the Personality of Godhead, and therefore he was neither afraid nor overwhelmed by fear due to a snake-bird which was to bite him because of the fury of a brāhmaṇa boy.

PURPORT

A self-surrendered devotee of the Lord is called *nārāyaṇa-parāyaṇa.* Such a person is never afraid of any place or person, not even of death. For him nothing is as important as the Supreme Lord, and thus he gives equal importance to heaven and hell. He knows well that both heaven and hell are creations of the Lord, and similarly life and death are different conditions of existence created by the Lord. But in all conditions and in all circumstances, remembrance of Nārāyaṇa is essential. The *nārāyaṇa-parāyaṇa* practices this constantly. Mahārāja Parīkṣit was such a pure devotee. He was wrongfully cursed by an inexperienced son of a *brāhmaṇa*, who was under the influence of Kali, and Mahārāja Parīkṣit took this to be sent by Nārāyaṇa. He knew that Nārāyaṇa (Lord Kṛṣṇa) had saved him when he was burned in the womb of his mother, and if he were to be killed by a snake bite, it would also take place by the will of the Lord. The devotee never goes against the will of the Lord; anything sent by God is a blessing for the devotee. Therefore Mahārāja Parīkṣit was neither afraid of nor bewildered by such things. That is the sign of a pure devotee of the Lord.

TEXT 3

उत्सृज्य सर्वतः सङ्गं विज्ञाताजितसंस्थितिः ।
वैयासकेर्जहौ शिष्यो गङ्गायां स्वं कलेवरम् ॥ ३ ॥

utsṛjya sarvataḥ saṅgaṁ
vijñātājita-saṁsthitiḥ
vaiyāsaker jahau śiṣyo
gaṅgāyāṁ svaṁ kalevaram

utsṛjya—after leaving aside; *sarvataḥ*—all around; *saṅgam*—association; *vijñāta*—being understood; *ajita*—one who is never conquered (the Personality of Godhead); *saṁsthitiḥ*—actual position; *vaiyāsakeḥ*—unto the son of Vyāsa; *jahau*—gave up; *śiṣyaḥ*—as a disciple; *gaṅgāyām*—on the bank of the Ganges; *svam*—his own; *kalevaram*—material body.

TRANSLATION

Furthermore, after leaving all his associates, the King surrendered himself as a disciple to the son of Vyāsa [Śukadeva Gosvāmī], and thus he was able to understand the actual position of the Personality of Godhead.

PURPORT

The word *ajita* is significant here. The Personality of Godhead, Śrī Kṛṣṇa, is known as Ajita, or unconquerable, and He is so in every respect. No one can know His actual position. He is unconquerable by knowledge also. We have heard about His *dhāma*, or place, eternal

Goloka Vṛndāvana, but there are many scholars who interpret this abode in different ways. But by the grace of a spiritual master like Śukadeva Gosvāmī, unto whom the King gave himself up as a most humble disciple, one is able to understand the actual position of the Lord, His eternal abode, and His transcendental paraphernalia in that *dhāma*, or abode. Knowing the transcendental position of the Lord and the transcendental method by which one can approach that transcendental *dhāma*, the King was confident about His ultimate destination, and by knowing this he could leave aside everything material, even his own body, without any difficulty of attachment. In the *Bhagavad-gītā*, it is stated, *paraṁ dṛṣṭvā nivartate:* one can give up all connection with material attachment when one is able to see the *param*, or the superior quality of things. From *Bhagavad-gītā* we understand the quality of the Lord's energy that is superior to the material quality of energy, and by the grace of a bona fide spiritual master like Śukadeva Gosvāmī, it is quite possible to know everything of the superior energy of the Lord by which the Lord manifests His eternal name, quality, pastimes, paraphernalia and variegatedness. Unless one thoroughly understands this superior or eternal energy of the Lord, it is not possible to leave the material energy, however one may theoretically speculate on the true nature of the Absolute Truth. By the grace of Lord Kṛṣṇa, Mahārāja Parīkṣit was able to receive the mercy of such a personality as Śukadeva Gosvāmī, and thus he was able to know the actual position of the unconquerable Lord. It is very difficult to find the Lord from the Vedic literatures, but it is very easy to know Him by the mercy of a liberated devotee like Śukadeva Gosvāmī.

TEXT 4

नोत्तमश्लोकवार्तानां जुषतां तत्कथामृतम् ।
स्यात्सम्भ्रमोऽन्तकालेऽपि स्मरतां तत्पदाम्बुजम् ॥४॥

nottamaśloka-vārtānāṁ
juṣatāṁ tat-kathāmṛtam
syāt sambhramo 'nta-kāle 'pi
smaratāṁ tat-padāmbujam

na—never; *uttama-śloka*—the Personality of Godhead, of whom the Vedic hymns sing; *vārtānām*—of those who live on them;

juṣatām—of those who are engaged in; *tat*—His; *kathā-amṛtam*—transcendental topics about Him; *syāt*—it so happens; *sambhramaḥ*—misconception; *anta*—at the end; *kāle*—in time; *api*—also; *smaratām*—remembering; *tat*—His; *pada-ambujam*—lotus feet.

TRANSLATION

This was so because those who have dedicated their lives to the transcendental topics of the Personality of Godhead, of whom the Vedic hymns sing, and who are constantly engaged in remembering the lotus feet of the Lord, do not run the risk of having misconceptions even at the last moment of their lives.

PURPORT

The highest perfection of life is attained by remembering the transcendental nature of the Lord at the last moment of one's life. This perfection of life is made possible by one who has learned the actual transcendental nature of the Lord from the Vedic hymns sung by a liberated soul like Śukadeva Gosvāmī or someone in that line of disciplic succession. There is no gain in hearing the Vedic hymns from some mental speculator. When the same is heard from an actual self-realized soul and is properly understood by service and submission, everything becomes transparently clear. Thus a submissive disciple is able to live transcendentally and continue to the end of life. By scientific adaptation, one is able to remember the Lord even at the end of life, when the power of remembrance is slackened due to derangement of bodily membranes. For a common man, it is very difficult to remember things as they are at the time of death, but by the grace of the Lord and His bona fide devotees, the spiritual masters, one can get this opportunity without difficulty. And it was done in the case of Mahārāja Parīkṣit.

TEXT 5

तावत्कलिर्न प्रभवेत् प्रविष्टोऽपीह सर्वतः ।
यावदीशो महानुर्व्यामाभिमन्यव एकराट् ॥ ५ ॥

tāvat kalir na prabhavet
praviṣṭo 'pīha sarvataḥ

yāvad īśo mahān urvyām
ābhimanyava eka-rāṭ

tāvat—so long; *kaliḥ*—the personality of Kali; *na*—cannot; *prabhavet*—flourish; *praviṣṭaḥ*—entered in; *api*—even though; *iha*—here; *sarvataḥ*—everywhere; *yāvat*—as long as; *īśaḥ*—the lord; *mahān*—great; *urvyām*—powerful; *ābhimanyavaḥ*—the son of Abhimanyu; *eka-rāṭ*—the one emperor.

TRANSLATION

As long as the great, powerful son of Abhimanyu remains the Emperor of the world, there is no chance that the personality of Kali will flourish.

PURPORT

As we have already explained, the personality of Kali had entered the jurisdiction of this earth long ago, and he was looking for an opportunity to spread his influence all over the world. But he could not do so satisfactorily due to the presence of Mahārāja Parīkṣit. That is the way of good government. The disturbing elements like the personality of Kali will always try to extend their nefarious activities, but it is the duty of the able state to check them by all means. Although Mahārāja Parīkṣit allotted places for the personality of Kali, at the same time he gave no chance for the citizens to be swayed by the personality of Kali.

TEXT 6

यस्मिन्नहनि यर्ह्येव भगवानुत्ससर्ज गाम् ।
तदैवेहानुवृत्तोऽसावधर्मप्रभवः कलिः ॥ ६ ॥

yasminn ahani yarhy eva
bhagavān utsasarja gām
tadaivehānuvṛtto 'sāv
adharma-prabhavaḥ kaliḥ

yasmin—on that; *ahani*—very day; *yarhi eva*—in the very moment; *bhagavān*—the Personality of Godhead; *utsasarja*—left aside; *gām*—

the earth; *tadā*—at that time; *eva*—certainly; *iha*—in this world; *anuvṛttaḥ*—followed; *asau*—he; *adharma*—irreligion; *prabhavaḥ*—accelerating; *kaliḥ*—the personality of quarrel.

TRANSLATION

The very day and moment the Personality of Godhead, Lord Śrī Kṛṣṇa, left this earth, the personality of Kali, who promotes all kinds of irreligious activities, came into this world.

PURPORT

The Personality of Godhead and His holy name, qualities, etc., are all identical. The personality of Kali was not able to enter the jurisdiction of the earth due to the presence of the Personality of Godhead. And similarly, if there is an arrangement for the constant chanting of the holy names, qualities, etc., of the Supreme Personality of Godhead, there is no chance at all for the personality of Kali to enter. That is the technique of driving away the personality of Kali from the world. In modernized human society there are great advancements of material science, and they have invented the radio to distribute sound in the air. So instead of vibrating some nuisance sound for sense enjoyment, if the state arranges to distribute transcendental sound by resounding the holy name, fame and activities of the Lord, as they are authorized in the *Bhagavad-gītā* or *Śrīmad-Bhāgavatam*, then a favorable condition will be created, the principles of religion in the world will be reestablished, and thus the executive heads, who are so anxious to drive away corruption from the world, will be successful. Nothing is bad if properly used for the service of the Lord.

TEXT 7

नानुद्वेष्टि कलिं सम्राट् सारङ्ग इव सारभुक् ।
कुशलान्याशु सिद्ध्यन्ति नेतराणि कृतानि यत्॥ ७॥

nānudveṣṭi kaliṁ samrāṭ
sāraṅga iva sāra-bhuk
kuśalāny āśu siddhyanti
netarāṇi kṛtāni yat

na—never; *anudveṣṭi*—envious; *kalim*—unto the personality of Kali; *samrāṭ*—the Emperor; *sāram-ga*—realist, like the bees; *iva*—like; *sāra-bhuk*—one who accepts the substance; *kuśalāni*—auspicious objects; *āśu*—immediately; *siddhyanti*—become successful; *na*—never; *itarāṇi*—which are inauspicious; *kṛtāni*—being performed; *yat*—as much as.

TRANSLATION

Mahārāja Parīkṣit was a realist, like the bees who only accept the essence [of a flower]. He knew perfectly well that in this age of Kali, auspicious things produce good effects immediately, whereas inauspicious acts must be actually performed [to render effects]. So he was never envious of the personality of Kali.

PURPORT

The age of Kali is called the fallen age. In this fallen age, because the living beings are in an awkward position, the Supreme Lord has given some special facilities to them. So by the will of the Lord, a living being does not become a victim of a sinful act until the act is actually performed. In other ages, simply by thinking of performing a sinful act, one used to become a victim of the act. On the contrary, a living being in this age is awarded with the results of pious acts simply by thinking of them. Mahārāja Parīkṣit, being the most learned and experienced king by the grace of the Lord, was not unnecessarily envious of the personality of Kali because he did not intend to give him any chance to perform any sinful act. He protected his subjects from falling prey to the sinful acts of the age of Kali, and at the same time he gave full facility to the age of Kali by allotting him some particular places. At the end of the *Śrīmad-Bhāgavatam* it is said that even though all nefarious activities of the personality of Kali are present, there is a great advantage in the age of Kali. One can attain salvation simply by chanting the holy name of the Lord. Thus Mahārāja Parīkṣit made an organized effort to propagate the chanting of the Lord's holy name, and thus he saved the citizens from the clutches of Kali. It is for this advantage only that great sages sometimes wish all good for the age of Kali. In the *Vedas* also it is said that by discourse on Lord Kṛṣṇa's activities, one can get rid of all the disadvantages of the age of Kali. In the beginning of the *Śrīmad-Bhāgavatam* it is also said that by the recitation of *Śrīmad-Bhāgavatam,* the Supreme Lord becomes at once arrested within one's heart. These are some of the great advantages of the age of Kali, and Mahārāja Parīkṣit took all the advantages and did not think any ill of the age of Kali, true to his Vaiṣṇavite cult.

TEXT 8

किं नु बालेषु शूरेण कलिना धीरभीरुणा ।
अप्रमत्तः प्रमत्तेषु यो वृको नृषु वर्तते ॥ ८ ॥

kiṁ nu bāleṣu śūreṇa
kalinā dhīra-bhīruṇā
apramattaḥ pramatteṣu
yo vṛko nṛṣu vartate

kim—what; *nu*—may be; *bāleṣu*—among the less intelligent persons; *śūreṇa*—by the powerful; *kalinā*—by the personality of Kali; *dhīra*—self-controlled; *bhīruṇā*—by one who is afraid of; *apramattaḥ*—one who is careful; *pramatteṣu*—among the careless; *yaḥ*—one who; *vṛkaḥ*—tiger; *nṛṣu*—among men; *vartate*—exists.

TRANSLATION

Mahārāja Parīkṣit considered that less intelligent men might find the personality of Kali to be very powerful, but that those who are self-controlled would have nothing to fear. The King was powerful like a tiger and took care for the foolish, careless persons.

PURPORT

Those who are not devotees of the Lord are careless and unintelligent. Unless one is thoroughly intelligent, one cannot be a devotee of the Lord. Those who are not devotees of the Lord fall prey to the actions of Kali. It will not be possible to bring about a saner condition in society unless we are prepared to accept the modes of action adopted by Mahārāja Parīskit, i.e., propagation of the devotional service of the Lord to the common man.

TEXT 9

उपवर्णितमेतद्वः पुण्यं पारीक्षितं मया ।
वासुदेवकथोपेतमाख्यानं यदपृच्छत ॥ ९ ॥

upavarṇitam etad vaḥ
puṇyaṁ pārīkṣitaṁ mayā
vāsudeva-kathopetam
ākhyānaṁ yad apṛcchata

upavarṇitam—almost everything described; *etat*—all these; *vaḥ*—unto you; *puṇyam*—pious; *pārīkṣitam*—about Mahārāja Parīskit; *mayā*—by me; *vāsudeva*—of Lord Kṛṣṇa; *kathā*—narrations; *upetam*—in connection with; *ākhyānam*—statements; *yat*—what; *apṛcchata*—you asked from me.

TRANSLATION

O sages, as you did ask me, now I have described almost everything regarding the narrations about Lord Kṛṣṇa in connection with the history of the pious Mahārāja Parīkṣit.

PURPORT

Śrīmad-Bhāgavatam is the history of the activities of the Lord. And the activities of the Lord are performed in relation with the devotees of the Lord. Therefore, the history of the devotees is not different from the history of Lord Kṛṣṇa's activities. A devotee of the Lord regards both the activities of the Lord and those of His pure devotees on an equal level, for they are all transcendental.

TEXT 10

या याः कथा भगवतः कथनीयोरुकर्मणः ।
गुणकर्माश्रयाः पुम्भिः संसेव्यास्ता बुभूषुभिः ॥१०॥

yā yāḥ kathā bhagavataḥ
kathanīyoru-karmaṇaḥ

guṇa-karmāśrayāḥ pumbhiḥ
saṁsevyās tā bubhūṣubhiḥ

yāḥ—whatever; *yāḥ*—and whatsoever; *kathāḥ*—topics; *bhagavataḥ* —about the Personality of Godhead; *kathanīya*—were to be spoken by me; *uru-karmaṇaḥ*—of Him who acts wonderfully; *guṇa*—transcendental qualities; *karma*—uncommon deeds; *āśrayāḥ*—involving; *pumbhiḥ*—by persons; *saṁsevyāḥ*—ought to be heard; *tāḥ*—all of them; *bubhūṣubhiḥ*—by those who want their own welfare.

TRANSLATION

Those who are desirous of achieving complete perfection in life must submissively hear all topics that are connected with the transcendental activities and qualities of the Personality of Godhead, who acts wonderfully.

PURPORT

The systematic hearing of the transcendental activities, qualities and names of Lord Śrī Kṛṣṇa pushes one towards eternal life. Systematic hearing means knowing Him gradually in truth and fact, and this knowing Him in truth and fact means attaining eternal life, as stated in the *Bhagavad-gītā.* Such transcendental, glorified activities of Lord Śrī Kṛṣṇa are the prescribed remedy for counteracting the process of birth, death, old age and disease, which are considered to be material awards for the conditioned living being. The culmination of such a perfectional stage of life is the goal of human life and the attainment of transcendental bliss.

TEXT 11

ऋषय ऊचुः

सूत जीव समाः सौम्य शाश्वतीर्विशदं यशः ।
यस्त्वं शंससि कृष्णस्य मर्त्यानाममृतं हि नः ॥११॥

ṛṣaya ūcuḥ
sūta jīva samāḥ saumya
śāśvatīr viśadaṁ yaśaḥ

yas tvaṁ śaṁsasi kṛṣṇasya
martyānām amṛtaṁ hi naḥ

ṛṣayaḥ ūcuḥ—the good sages said; *sūta*—O Sūta Gosvāmī; *jīva*—we wish you life for; *samāḥ*—many years; *saumya*—grave; *śāśvatīḥ*—eternal; *viśadam*—particularly; *yaśaḥ*—in fame; *yaḥ tvam*—because you; *śaṁsasi*—speaking nicely; *kṛṣṇasya*—of Lord Śrī Kṛṣṇa; *martyānām*—of those who die; *amṛtam*—eternity of life; *hi*—certainly; *naḥ*—our.

TRANSLATION

The good sages said: O grave Sūta Gosvāmī! May you live many years and have eternal fame, for you are speaking very nicely about the activities of Lord Kṛṣṇa, the Personality of Godhead. This is just like nectar for mortal beings like us.

PURPORT

When we hear about the transcendental qualities and activities of the Personality of Godhead, we may always remember what has been spoken by the Lord Himself in the *Bhagavad-gītā* (4.9). His acts, even when He acts in human society, are all transcendental, for they are all accentuated by the spiritual energy of the Lord, which is distinguished from His material energy. As stated in the *Bhagavad-gītā*, such acts are called *divyam.* This means that He does not act or take His birth like an ordinary living being under the custody of material energy. Nor is His body material or changeable like that of ordinary living beings. And one who understands this fact, either from the Lord or from authorized sources, is not reborn after leaving the present material body. Such an enlightened soul is admitted into the spiritual realm of the Lord and engages in the transcendental loving service of the Lord. Therefore, the more we hear about the transcendental activities of the Lord, as they are stated in the *Bhagavad-gītā* and *Śrīmad-Bhāgavatam*, the more we can know about His transcendental nature and thus make definite progress on the path back to Godhead.

TEXT 12

कर्मण्यस्मिन्ननाश्वासे धूमधूम्रात्मनां भवान् ।
आपाययति गोविन्दपादपद्मासवं मधु ॥१२॥

karmaṇy asminn anāśvāse
dhūma-dhūmrātmanāṁ bhavān
āpāyayati govinda-
pāda-padmāsavaṁ madhu

karmaṇi—performance of; *asmin*—in this; *anāśvāse*—without certainty; *dhūma*—smoke; *dhūmra-ātmanām*—tinged body and mind; *bhavān*—your good self; *āpāyayati*—very much pleasing; *govinda*—the Personality of Godhead; *pāda*—feet; *padma-āsavam*—nectar of the lotus flower; *madhu*—honey.

TRANSLATION

We have just begun the performance of this fruitive activity, a sacrificial fire, without certainty of its result due to the many imperfections in our action. Our bodies have become black from the smoke, but we are factually pleased by the nectar of the lotus feet of the Personality of Godhead, Govinda, which you are distributing.

PURPORT

The sacrificial fire kindled by the sages of Naimiṣāraṇya was certainly full of smoke and doubts because of so many flaws. The first flaw is that there is an acute scarcity of expert *brāhmaṇas* able to carry out such performances successfully in this age of Kali. Any discrepancy in such sacrifices spoils the whole show, and the result is uncertain, like agricultural enterprises. The good result of tilling the paddy field depends on providential rain, and therefore the result is uncertain. Similarly, performance of any kind of sacrifice in this age of Kali is also uncertain. Unscrupulous greedy *brāhmaṇas* of the age of Kali induce the innocent public to such uncertain sacrificial shows without disclosing the scriptural injunction that in the age of Kali there is no fruitful sacrificial performance but the sacrifice of the congregational chanting of the holy name of the Lord. Sūta Gosvāmī was narrating the transcendental activities of the Lord before the congregation of sages, and they were factually perceiving the result of hearing these transcendental activities. One can feel this practically, as one can feel the result of eating food. Spiritual realization acts in that way.

The sages of Naimiṣāraṇya were practically sufferers from the smoke of a sacrificial fire and were doubtful about the result, but by hearing from a realized person like Sūta Gosvāmī, they were fully satisfied. In the *Brahma-vaivarta Purāṇa,* Viṣṇu tells Śiva that in the age of Kali, men full of anxieties of various kinds can vainly labor in fruitive activity and philosophical speculations, but when they are engaged in devotional service, the result is sure and certain, and there is no loss of energy. In other words, nothing performed for spiritual realization or for material benefit can be successful without the devotional service to the Lord.

TEXT 13

तुलयाम लवेनापि न स्वर्गं नापुनर्भवम् ।
भगवत्सङ्गिसङ्गस्य मर्त्यानां किमुताशिषः ॥१३॥

tulayāma lavenāpi
na svargaṁ nāpunar-bhavam
bhagavat-saṅgi-saṅgasya
martyānāṁ kim utāśiṣaḥ

tulayāma—to be balanced with; *lavena*—by a moment; *api*—even; *na*—never; *svargam*—heavenly planets; *na*—nor; *apunaḥ-bhavam*—liberation from matter; *bhagavat-saṅgi*—devotee of the Lord; *saṅgasya*—of the association; *martyānām*—those who are meant for death; *kim*—what is there; *uta*—to speak of; *āśiṣaḥ*—worldly benediction.

TRANSLATION

The value of a moment's association with the devotee of the Lord cannot even be compared to the attainment of heavenly planets or liberation from matter, and what to speak of worldly benedictions in the form of material prosperity, which are for those who are meant for death.

PURPORT

When there are some similar points, it is possible to compare one thing to another. One cannot compare the association of a pure devotee to anything material. Men who are addicted to material happiness aspire to reach the heavenly planets like the moon, Venus and Indraloka, and those who are advanced in material philosophical speculations aspire after liberation from all material bondage. When one becomes frustrated with all kinds of material advancement, one desires the opposite type of liberation, which is called *apunar-bhava,* or no rebirth. But the pure devotees of the Lord do not aspire after the happiness obtained in the heavenly kingdom, nor do they aspire after liberation from material bondage. In other words, for the pure devotees of the Lord the material pleasures obtainable in the heavenly planets are like phantasmagoria, and because they are already liberated from all material conceptions of pleasure and distress, they are factually liberated even in the material world. This means that the pure devotees of the Lord are engaged in a transcendental existence, namely in the loving service of the Lord, both in the material world and in the spiritual world. As a government servant is always the same, either in the office or at home or at any place, so a devotee has nothing to do with anything material, for he is exclusively engaged in the transcendental service of the Lord. Since he has nothing to do with anything material, what pleasure can he derive from material benedictions like kingship or other overlordships, which are finished quickly with the end of the body? Devotional service is eternal; it has no end, because it is spiritual. Therefore, since the assets of a pure devotee are completely different from material assets, there is no comparison between the two. Sūta Gosvāmī was a pure devotee of the Lord, and therefore his association with the *ṛṣis* in Naimiṣāraṇya is unique. In the material world, association with gross materialists is veritably condemned. The materialist is called *yoṣit-saṅgī,* or one who is much attached to material entanglement (women and other paraphernalia). Such attachment is conditioned because it drives away the benedictions of life and prosperity. And just the opposite is *bhāgavata-saṅgī,* or one who is always in the association with the Lord's name, form, qualities, etc. Such association is always desirable; it is worshipable, it is praiseworthy, and one may accept it as the highest goal of life.

TEXT 14

को नाम तृप्येद् रसवित्कथायां
महत्तमैकान्तपरायणस्य ।

नान्तं गुणानामगुणस्य जग्मु-
र्योगेश्वरा ये भवपाद्ममुख्याः ॥१४॥

ko nāma tṛpyed rasavit kathāyāṁ
mahattamaikānta-parāyaṇasya
nāntaṁ guṇānām aguṇasya jagmur
yogeśvarā ye bhava-pādma-mukhyāḥ

kaḥ—who is he; *nāma*—specifically; *tṛpyet*—get full satisfaction; *rasa-vit*—expert in relishing mellow nectar; *kathāyām*—in the topics of; *mahat-tama*—the greatest amongst the living beings; *ekānta*—exclusively; *parāyaṇasya*—of one who is the shelter of; *na*—never; *antam*—end; *guṇānām*—of attributes; *aguṇasya*—of the Transcendence; *jagmuḥ*—could ascertain; *yoga-īśvarāḥ*—the lords of mystic power; *ye*—all they; *bhava*—Lord Śiva; *pādma*—Lord Brahmā; *mukhyāḥ*—heads.

TRANSLATION

The Personality of Godhead, Lord Kṛṣṇa [Govinda], is the exclusive shelter for all great living beings, and His transcendental attributes cannot even be measured by such masters of mystic powers as Lord Śiva and Lord Brahmā. Can anyone who is expert in relishing nectar [rasa] ever be fully satiated by hearing topics about Him?

PURPORT

Lord Śiva and Lord Brahmā are two chiefs of the demigods. They are full of mystic powers. For example, Lord Śiva drank an ocean of poison of which one drop was sufficient to kill an ordinary living being. Similarly, Brahmā could create many powerful demigods, including Lord Śiva. So they are *īśvaras*, or lords of the universe. But they are not the supreme powerful. The supreme powerful is Govinda, Lord Kṛṣṇa. He is Transcendence, and His transcendental attributes cannot be measured even by such powerful *īśvaras* as Śiva and Brahmā. Therefore Lord Kṛṣṇa is the exclusive shelter of the greatest of all living beings. Brahmā is counted amongst the living beings, but he is the greatest of all of us. And why is the greatest of all the living beings so much attached to the transcendental topics of Lord Kṛṣṇa? Because He is the reservoir of all enjoyment. Everyone wants to relish some kind of taste in everything, but one who is engaged in the transcendental loving service of the Lord can derive unlimited pleasure from such engagement. The Lord is unlimited, and His name, attributes, pastimes, entourage, variegatedness, etc., are unlimited, and those who relish them can do so unlimitedly and still not feel satiated. This fact is confirmed in the *Padma Purāṇa:*

ramante yogino 'nante satyānanda-cid-ātmani
iti rāma-padenāsau paraṁ brahmābhidhīyate

"The mystics derive unlimited transcendental pleasures from the Absolute Truth, and therefore the Supreme Absolute Truth, the Personality of Godhead, is also known as Rāma."

There is no end to such transcendental discourses. In mundane affairs there is the law of satiation, but in transcendence there is no such satiation. Sūta Gosvāmī desired to continue the topics of Lord Kṛṣṇa before the sages of Naimiṣāraṇya, and the sages also expressed their readiness to hear from him continuously. Since the Lord is transcendence and His attributes are transcendental, such discourses increase the receptive mood of the purified audience.

TEXT 15

तन्नो भवान् वै भगवत्प्रधानो
महत्तमैकान्तपरायणस्य ।
हरेरुदारं चरितं विशुद्धं
शुश्रूषतां नो वितनोतु विद्वन् ॥१५॥

tan no bhavān vai bhagavat-pradhāno
mahattamaikānta-parāyaṇasya
harer udāraṁ caritaṁ viśuddhaṁ
śuśrūṣatāṁ no vitanotu vidvan

tat—therefore; *naḥ*—of us; *bhavān*—your good self; *vai*—certainly; *bhagavat*—in relation with the Personality of Godhead; *pradhānaḥ*—chiefly; *mahat-tama*—the greatest of all greats; *ekānta*—exclusively; *parāyaṇasya*—of the shelter; *hareḥ*—of the Lord; *udāram*—impartial;

caritam—activities; *viśuddham*—transcendental; *śuśrūṣatām*—those who are receptive; *naḥ*—ourselves; *vitanotu*—kindly describe; *vidvan*—O learned one.

TRANSLATION

O Sūta Gosvāmī, you are a learned and pure devotee of the Lord because the Personality of Godhead is your chief object of service. Therefore please describe to us the pastimes of the Lord, which are above all material conception, for we are anxious to receive such messages.

PURPORT

The speaker on the transcendental activities of the Lord should have only one object of worship and service, Lord Kṛṣṇa, the Supreme Personality of Godhead. And the audience for such topics should be anxious to hear about Him. When such a combination is possible, namely a qualified speaker and a qualified audience, it is then and there very much congenial to continue discourses on the Transcendence. Professional speakers and a materially absorbed audience cannot derive real benefit from such discourses. Professional speakers make a show of *Bhāgavata-saptāha* for the sake of family maintenance, and the materially disposed audience hears such discourses of *Bhāgavata-saptāha* for some material benefit, namely religiosity, wealth, gratification of the senses, or liberation. Such *Bhāgavatam* discourses are not purified from the contamination of the material qualities. But the discourses between the saints of Naimiṣāraṇya and Śrī Sūta Gosvāmī are on the transcendental level. There is no motive for material gain. In such discourses, unlimited transcendental pleasure is relished both by the audience and by the speaker, and therefore they can continue the topics for many thousands of years. Now *Bhāgavata-saptāhas* are held for seven days only, and after finishing the show, both the audience and the speaker become engaged in material activities as usual. They can do so because the speaker is not *bhagavat-pradhāna* and the audience is not *śuśrūṣatām*, as explained above.

TEXT 16

स वै महाभागवतः परीक्षिद्
येनापवर्गाख्यमदभ्रबुद्धिः ।

ज्ञानेन वैयासकिशब्दितेन
भेजे खगेन्द्रध्वजपादमूलम् ॥१६॥

sa vai mahā-bhāgavataḥ parīkṣid
yenāpavargākhyam adabhra-buddhiḥ
jñānena vaiyāsaki-śabditena
bheje khagendra-dhvaja-pāda-mūlam

saḥ—he; *vai*—certainly; *mahā-bhāgavataḥ*—first-class devotee; *parīkṣit*—the King; *yena*—by which; *apavarga-ākhyam*—by the name of liberation; *adabhra*—fixed; *buddhiḥ*—intelligence; *jñānena*—by knowledge; *vaiyāsaki*—the son of Vyāsa; *śabditena*—vibrated by; *bheje*—taken to; *khaga-indra*—Garuḍa, the King of the birds; *dhvaja*—flag; *pāda-mūlam*—soles of the feet.

TRANSLATION

O Sūta Gosvāmī, please describe those topics of the Lord by which Mahārāja Parīkṣit, whose intelligence was fixed on liberation, attained the lotus feet of the Lord, who is the shelter of Garuḍa, the King of birds. Those topics were vibrated by the son of Vyāsa [Śrīla Śukadeva].

PURPORT

There is some controversy amongst the students on the path of liberation. Such transcendental students are known as impersonalists and devotees of the Lord. The devotee of the Lord worships the transcendental form of the Lord, whereas the impersonalist meditates upon the glaring effulgence, or the bodily rays of the Lord, known as the *brahmajyoti.* Here in this verse it is said that Mahārāja Parīkṣit attained the lotus feet of the Lord by instructions in knowledge delivered by the son of Vyāsadeva, Śrīla Śukadeva Gosvāmī. Śukadeva Gosvāmī was also an impersonalist in the beginning, as he himself has admitted in the *Bhāgavatam* (2.1.9), but later on he was attracted by the transcendental pastimes of the Lord and thus became a devotee. Such devotees with perfect knowledge are called *mahā-bhāgavatas,* or first-class devotees. There are three classes of devotees, namely the *prākṛta, madhyama,* and *mahā-bhāgavata.* The *prākṛta,* or third-class devotees, are temple worshipers without specific knowledge of the Lord and the Lord's devotees. The *madhyama*, or the second-class devotee, knows well the Lord, the Lord's devotees, the neophytes, and the nondevotees also. But the *mahā-bhāgavata*, or the first-class devotee, sees everything in relation with the Lord and the Lord present in everyone's relation. The *mahā-bhāgavata*, therefore, does not make any distinction, particularly between a devotee and nondevotee. Mahārāja Parīkṣit was such a *mahā-bhāgavata* devotee because he was initiated by a *mahā-bhāgavata* devotee, Śukadeva Gosvāmī. He was equally kind, even to the personality of Kali, and what to speak of others.

So there are many instances in the transcendental histories of the world of an impersonalist who has later become a devotee. But a devotee has never become an impersonalist. This very fact proves that on the transcendental steps, the step occupied by a devotee is higher than the step occupied by an impersonalist. It is also stated in the *Bhagavad-gītā* (12.5) that persons stuck on the impersonal step undergo more sufferings than achievement of reality. Therefore knowledge imparted by Śukadeva Gosvāmī unto Mahārāja Parīkṣit helped him attain the service of the Lord. And this stage of perfection is called *apavarga*, or the perfect stage of liberation. Simple knowledge of liberation is material knowledge. Actual freedom from material bondage is called liberation, but attainment of the transcendental service of the Lord is called the perfect stage of liberation. Such a stage is attained by knowledge and renunciation, as we have already explained (*Bhāg*. 1.2.12), and perfect knowledge, as delivered by Śrīla Śukadeva Gosvāmī, results in the attainment of the transcendental service of the Lord.

TEXT 17

तन्नः परं पुण्यमसंवृतार्थ-
मारख्यानमत्यद्भुतयोगनिष्ठम् ।
आख्याह्यनन्ताचरितोपपन्नं
पारीक्षितं भागवताभिरामम् ॥१७॥

tan naḥ paraṁ puṇyam asaṁvṛtārtham
ākhyānam atyadbhuta-yoga-niṣṭham

ākhyāhy anantācaritopapannaṁ
pārīkṣitaṁ bhāgavatābhirāmam

tat—therefore; *naḥ*—unto us; *param*—supreme; *puṇyam*—purifying; *asaṁvṛta-artham*—as it is; *ākhyānam*—narration; *ati*—very; *adbhuta*—wonderful; *yoga-niṣṭham*—compact in *bhakti-yoga; ākhyāhi*—describe; *ananta*—the Unlimited; *ācarita*—activities; *upapannam*—full of; *pārīkṣitam*—spoken to Mahārāja Parīkṣit; *bhāgavata*—of the pure devotees; *abhirāmam*—particularly very dear.

TRANSLATION

Thus please narrate to us the narrations of the Unlimited, for they are purifying and supreme. They were spoken to Mahārāja Parīkṣit, and they are very dear to the pure devotees, being full of bhakti-yoga.

PURPORT

What was spoken to Mahārāja Parīkṣit and what is very dear to the pure devotees is *Śrīmad-Bhāgavatam. Śrīmad-Bhāgavatam* is mainly full of the narrations of the activities of the Supreme Unlimited, and therefore it is the science of *bhakti-yoga*, or the devotional service of the Lord. Thus it is *para*, or supreme, because although it is enriched with all knowledge and religion, it is specifically enriched with the devotional service of the Lord.

TEXT 18

सूत उवाच
अहो वयं जन्मभृतोऽद्य हास्म
वृद्धानुवृत्त्यापि विलोमजाताः ।
दौष्कुल्यमाधिं विधुनोति शीघ्रं
महत्तमानामभिधानयोगः ॥१८॥

sūta uvāca
aho vayaṁ janma-bhṛto 'dya hāsma
vṛddhānuvṛttyāpi viloma-jātāḥ
dauṣkulyam ādhiṁ vidhunoti śīghraṁ
mahattamānām abhidhāna-yogaḥ

sūtaḥ uvāca—Sūta Gosvāmī said; *aho*—how; *vayam*—we; *janma-bhṛtaḥ*—promoted in birth; *adya*—today; *ha*—clearly; *āsma*—have become; *vṛddha-anuvṛttyā*—by serving those who are advanced in knowledge; *api*—although; *viloma-jātāḥ*—born in a mixed caste; *dauṣkulyam*—disqualification of birth; *ādhim*—sufferings; *vidhunoti*—purifies; *śīghram*—very soon; *mahat-tamānām*—of those who are great; *abhidhāna*—conversation; *yogaḥ*—connection.

TRANSLATION

Śrī Sūta Gosvāmī said: O God, although we are born in a mixed caste, we are still promoted in birthright simply by serving and following the great who are advanced in knowledge. Even by conversing with such great souls, one can without delay cleanse oneself of all disqualifications resulting from lower births.

PURPORT

Sūta Gosvāmī did not take his birth in a *brāhmaṇa* family. He was born in a family of mixed caste, or an uncultured low family. But because of higher association, like Śrī Śukadeva Gosvāmī and the great *ṛṣis* of Naimiṣāraṇya, certainly the disqualification of inferior birth was washed off. Lord Śrī Caitanya Mahāprabhu followed this principle in pursuance of the Vedic usages, and by His transcendental association He elevated many lowborn, or those disqualified by birth or action, to the status of devotional service and established them in the position of *ācāryas*, or authorities. He clearly stated that any man, whatever he may be, whether a *brāhmaṇa* or *śūdra* by birth, or a householder or mendicant in the order of society, if he is conversant with the science of Kṛṣṇa, he can be accepted as an *ācārya* or *guru*, a spiritual master.

Sūta Gosvāmī learned the science of Kṛṣṇa from great *ṛṣis* and authorities like Śukadeva and Vyāsadeva and he was so qualified that even the sages of Naimiṣāraṇya eagerly wanted to hear from him the science of Kṛṣṇa in the form of *Śrīmad-Bhāgavatam.* So he had the double association of great souls by hearing and preaching. Transcendental science, or the science of Kṛṣṇa, has to be learned from the authorities, and when one preaches the science, he becomes still more qualified. So Sūta Gosvāmī had both the advantages, and thus undoubtedly he was completely freed from all disqualifications of low birth and mental agonies. This verse definitely proves that Śrīla Śukadeva Gosvāmī did not refuse to teach Sūta Gosvāmī about the transcendental science nor did the sages of Naimiṣāraṇya refuse to hear lessons from him because of his inferior birth. This means that thousands of years ago there was no bar to learning or preaching the transcendental science because of inferior birth. The rigidity of the so-called caste system in Hindu society became prominent within only one hundred years or so when the number of *dvija-bandhus*, or disqualified men in the families of higher castes, increased. Lord Śrī Caitanya revived the original Vedic system, and He elevated Ṭhākura Haridāsa to the position of *nāmācārya*, or the authority in preaching the glories of the holy name of the Lord, although His Holiness Śrīla Haridāsa Ṭhākura was pleased to appear in a family of Mohammedans.

Such is the power of pure devotees of the Lord. The Ganges water is accepted as pure, and one can become purified after taking a bath in the waters of the Ganges. But as far as the great devotees of the Lord are concerned, they can purify a degraded soul even by being seen by the lowborn, and what to speak of association. Lord Śrī Caitanya Mahāprabhu wanted to purify the whole atmosphere of the polluted world by sending qualified preachers all over the world, and it remains with the Indians to take up this task scientifically and thus do the best kind of humanitarian work. The mental diseases of the present generation are more acute than bodily diseases; it is quite fit and proper to take up the preaching of *Śrīmad-Bhāgavatam* all over the world without delay. *Mahattamānām abhidhāna* also means dictionary of great devotees, or a book full of the words of great devotees. Such a dictionary of the words of great devotees and those of the Lord are in the *Vedas* and allied literatures, specifically the *Śrīmad-Bhāgavatam.*

TEXT 19

कुतः पुनर्गृणतो नाम तस्य
महत्तमैकान्तपरायणस्य ।
योऽनन्तशक्तिर्भगवाननन्तो
महद्गुणत्वाद् यमनन्तमाहुः ॥१९॥

kutaḥ punar gṛṇato nāma tasya
mahattamaikānta-parāyaṇasya
yo 'nanta-śaktir bhagavān ananto
mahad-guṇatvād yam anantam āhuḥ

kutaḥ—what to say; *punaḥ*—again; *gṛṇataḥ*—one who chants; *nāma*—holy name; *tasya*—His; *mahat-tama*—great devotees; *ekānta*—exclusive; *parāyaṇasya*—of one who takes shelter of; *yaḥ*—He who; *ananta*—is the Unlimited; *śaktiḥ*—potency; *bhagavān*—the Personality of Godhead; *anantaḥ*—immeasurable; *mahat*—great; *guṇatvāt*—on account of such attributes; *yam*—whom; *anantam*—by the name *ananta; āhuḥ*—is called.

TRANSLATION

And what to speak of those who are under the direction of the great devotees, chanting the holy name of the Unlimited, who has unlimited potency? The Personality of Godhead, unlimited in potency and transcendental by attributes, is called the ananta [Unlimited].

PURPORT

The *dvija-bandhu,* or the less intelligent, uncultured men born of higher castes, put forward many arguments against the lower caste men becoming *brāhmaṇas* in this life. They argue that birth in a family of *śūdras* or less than *śūdras* is made possible by one's previous sinful acts and that one therefore has to complete the terms of disadvantages due to lower birth. And to answer these false logicians, *Śrīmad-Bhāgavatam* asserts that one who chants the holy name of the Lord under the direction of a pure devotee can at once get free from the disadvantages due to a lower-caste birth. A pure devotee of the Lord does not commit any offense while chanting the holy name of the Lord. There are ten different offenses in the chanting of the holy name of the Lord. To chant the holy name under the direction of a pure devotee is offenseless chanting. Offenseless chanting of the holy name of the Lord is transcendental, and, therefore, such chanting can at once purify one from the effects of all kinds of previous sins. This offenseless chanting indicates that one has fully understood the transcendental nature of the holy name and has thus surrendered unto the Lord. Transcendentally the holy name of the Lord and the Lord Himself are identical, being absolute. The holy name of the Lord is as powerful as the Lord. The Lord is the all-powerful Personality of Godhead, and He has innumerable names, which are all non-different from Him and are equally powerful also. In the last word of the *Bhagavad-gītā* the Lord asserts that one who surrenders fully unto Him is protected from all sins by the grace of the Lord. Since His name and He Himself are identical, the holy name of the Lord can protect the devotee from all effects of sins. The chanting of the holy name of the Lord can undoubtedly deliver one from the disadvantages of a lower caste birth. The Lord's unlimited power is extended on and on by the unlimited expansion of the devotees and incarnations, and thus every devotee of the Lord and incarnations also can be equally surcharged with the potency of the Lord. Since the devotee is surcharged with the potency of the Lord, even fractionally, the disqualification due to lower birth cannot stand in the way.

TEXT 20

एतावतालं ननु सूचितेन
गुणैरसाम्यानतिशायनस्य ।
हित्वेतरान् प्रार्थयतो विभूति-
र्यस्याङ्घ्रिरेणुं जुषतेऽनभीप्सोः ॥२०॥

etāvatālaṁ nanu sūcitena
guṇair asāmyānatiśāyanasya
hitvetarān prārthayato vibhūtir
yasyāṅghri-reṇuṁ juṣate 'nabhīpsoḥ

etāvatā—so far; *alam*—unnecessary; *nanu*—if at all; *sūcitena*—by description; *guṇaiḥ*—by attributes; *asāmya*—immeasurable; *anatiśāyanasya*—of one who is unexcelled; *hitvā*—leaving aside; *itarān*—others; *prārthayataḥ*—of those who ask for; *vibhūtiḥ*—favor of the goddess of fortune; *yasya*—one whose; *aṅghri*—feet; *reṇum*—dust; *juṣate*—serves; *anabhīpsoḥ*—of one who is unwilling.

TRANSLATION

It is now ascertained that He [the Personality of Godhead] is unlimited and there is none equal to Him. Consequently no one can speak of Him adequately. Great demigods cannot obtain the favor of the goddess of fortune even by prayers, but this very goddess renders service unto the Lord, although He is unwilling to have such service.

PURPORT

The Personality of Godhead, or the Parameśvara Parabrahman, according to the *śrutis*, has nothing to do. He has no equal. Nor does anyone excel Him. He has unlimited potencies, and His every action is carried out systematically in His natural and perfect ways. Thus the Supreme Personality of Godhead is full in Himself, and He has nothing to accept from anyone else, including the great demigods like Brahmā. Others ask for the favor of the goddess of fortune, and despite such prayers she declines to award such favors. But still she renders service unto the Supreme Personality of Godhead, although He has nothing to accept from her. The Personality of Godhead in His Garbhodakaśāyī Viṣṇu feature begets Brahmā, the first created person in the material world, from His navel lotus stem and not in the womb of the goddess of fortune, who is eternally engaged in His service. These are some of the instances of His complete independence and perfection. That He has nothing to do does not mean that He is impersonal. He is transcendentally so full of inconceivable potencies that simply by His willing, everything is done without physical or personal endeavor. He is called, therefore, Yogeśvara, or the Lord of all mystic powers.

TEXT 21

अथापि यत्पादनखावसृष्टं
जगद्विरिञ्चोपहृतार्हणाम्भः ।
सेशं पुनात्यन्यतमो मुकुन्दात्
को नाम लोके भगवत्पदार्थः ॥२१॥

athāpi yat-pāda-nakhāvasṛṣṭaṁ
jagad viriñcopahṛtārhaṇāmbhaḥ

seśaṁ punāty anyatamo mukundāt
ko nāma loke bhagavat-padārthaḥ

atha—therefore; *api*—certainly; *yat*—whose; *pāda-nakha*—nails of the feet; *avasṛṣṭam*—emanating; *jagat*—the whole universe; *viriñca*—Brahmājī; *upahṛta*—collected; *arhaṇa*—worship; *ambhaḥ*—water; *sa*—along with; *īśam*—Lord Śiva; *punāti*—purifies; *anyatamaḥ*—who else; *mukundāt*—besides the Personality of Godhead Śrī Kṛṣṇa; *kaḥ*—who; *nāma*—name; *loke*—within the world; *bhagavat*—Supreme Lord; *pada*—position; *arthaḥ*—worth.

TRANSLATION

Who can be worthy of the name of the Supreme Lord but the Personality of Godhead Śrī Kṛṣṇa? Brahmājī collected the water emanating from the nails of His feet in order to award it to Lord Śiva as a worshipful welcome. This very water [the Ganges] is purifying the whole universe, including Lord Śiva.

PURPORT

The conception of many gods in the Vedic literatures by the ignorant is completely wrong. The Lord is one without a second, but He expands Himself in many ways, and this is confirmed in the *Vedas.* Such expansions of the Lord are limitless, but some of them are the living entities. The living entities are not as powerful as the Lord's plenary expansions, and therefore there are two different types of expansions. Lord Brahmā is generally one of the living entities, and Lord Śiva is the via medium between the Lord and the living entities. In other words, even demigods like Lord Brahmā and Lord Śiva, who are the chief amongst all demigods, are never equal to or greater than Lord Viṣṇu, the Supreme Personality of Godhead. The goddess of fortune, Lakṣmī, and all-powerful demigods like Brahmā and Śiva are engaged in the worship of Viṣṇu or Lord Kṛṣṇa; therefore who can be more powerful than Mukunda (Lord Kṛṣṇa) to be factually called the Supreme Personality of Godhead? The goddess of fortune, Lakṣmījī, Lord Brahmā and Lord Śiva are not independently powerful; they are powerful as expansions of the Supreme Lord, and all of them are engaged in the transcendental loving service of the Lord, and so also are the living entities. There are four sects of worshipful devotees of the Lord, and the chief amongst them are the Brahma-sampradāya, Rudra-sampradāya and Śrī-sampradāya, descending directly from Lord Brahmā, Lord Śiva and the goddess of fortune, Lakṣmī, respectively. Besides the above-mentioned three *sampradāyas*, there is the Kumāra-sampradāya, descending from Sanatkumāra. All of the four original *sampradāyas* are still scrupulously engaged in the transcendental service of the Lord up to date, and they all declare that Lord Kṛṣṇa, Mukunda, is the Supreme Personality of Godhead, and no other personality is equal to Him or greater than Him.

TEXT 22

यत्रानुरक्ताः सहसैव धीरा
व्यपोह्य देहादिषु सङ्गमूढम् ।
व्रजन्ति तत्पारमहंस्यमन्त्यं
यस्मिन्नहिंसोपशमः स्वधर्मः ॥२२॥

yatrānuraktāḥ sahasaiva dhīrā
vyapohya dehādiṣu saṅgam ūḍham
vrajanti tat pārama-haṁsyam antyaṁ
yasminn ahiṁsopaśamaḥ sva-dharmaḥ

yatra—unto whom; *anuraktāḥ*—firmly attached; *sahasā*—all of a sudden; *eva*—certainly; *dhīrāḥ*—self-controlled; *vyapohya*—leaving aside; *deha*—the gross body and subtle mind; *ādiṣu*—relating to; *saṅgam*—attachment; *ūḍham*—taken to; *vrajanti*—go away; *tat*—that; *pārama-haṁsyam*—the highest stage of perfection; *antyam*—and beyond that; *yasmin*—in which; *ahiṁsā*—nonviolence; *upaśamaḥ*—and renunciation; *sva-dharmaḥ*—consequential occupation.

TRANSLATION

Self-controlled persons who are attached to the Supreme Lord Śrī Kṛṣṇa can all of a sudden give up the world of material attachment, including the gross body and subtle mind, and go away to attain the highest perfection of the renounced order of life, by which nonviolence and renunciation are consequential.

PURPORT

Only the self-controlled can gradually be attached to the Supreme Personality of Godhead. Self-controlled means not indulging in sense enjoyment more than is necessary. And those who are not self-controlled are given over to sense enjoyment. Dry philosophical speculation is a subtle sense enjoyment of the mind. Sense enjoyment leads one to the path of darkness. Those who are self-controlled can make progress on the path of liberation from the conditional life of material existence. The *Vedas*, therefore, enjoin that one should not go on the path of darkness but should make a progressive march towards the path of light or liberation. Self-control is actually achieved not by artificially stopping the senses from material enjoyment, but by becoming factually attached to the Supreme Lord by engaging one's unalloyed senses in the transcendental service of the Lord. The senses cannot be forcibly curbed, but they can be given proper engagement. Purified senses, therefore, are always engaged in the transcendental service of the Lord. This perfectional stage of sense engagement is called *bhakti-yoga*. So those who are attached to the means of *bhakti-yoga* are factually self-controlled and can all of a sudden give up their homely or bodily attachment for the service of the Lord. This is called the *paramahaṁsa* stage. *Haṁsas*, or swans, accept only milk out of a mixture of milk and water. Similarly, those who accept the service of the Lord instead of *māyā's* service are called the *paramahaṁsas*. They are naturally qualified with all the good attributes, such as pridelessness, freedom from vanity, nonviolence, tolerance, simplicity, respectability, worship, devotion and sincerity. All these godly qualities exist in the devotee of the Lord spontaneously. Such *paramahaṁsas*, who are completely given up to the service of the Lord, are very rare. They are very rare even amongst the liberated souls. Real nonviolence means freedom from envy. In this world everyone is envious of his fellow being. But a perfect *paramahaṁsa*, being completely given up to the service of the Lord, is perfectly nonenvious. He loves every living being in relation with the Supreme Lord. Real renunciation means perfect dependence on God. Every living being is dependent on someone else because he is so made. Actually everyone is dependent on the mercy of the Supreme Lord, but when one forgets his relation with the Lord, he becomes dependent on the conditions of material nature. Renunciation means renouncing ones dependence on the conditions of material nature and thus becoming completely dependent on the mercy of the Lord. Real independence means complete faith in the mercy of the Lord without dependence on the conditions of matter. This *paramahaṁsa* stage is the highest perfectional stage in *bhakti-yoga*, the process of devotional service to the Supreme Lord.

TEXT 23

अहं हि पृष्टोऽर्यमणो भवद्भि-
राचक्ष आत्मावगमोऽत्र यावान् ।
नभः पतन्त्यात्मसमं पतत्त्रिण-
स्तथा समं विष्णुगतिं विपश्चितः ॥२३॥

ahaṁ hi pṛṣṭo 'ryamaṇo bhavadbhir
ācakṣa ātmāvagamo 'tra yāvān
nabhaḥ patanty ātma-samaṁ patattriṇas
tathā samaṁ viṣṇu-gatiṁ vipaścitaḥ

aham—my humble self; *hi*—certainly; *pṛṣṭaḥ*—asked by you; *aryamaṇaḥ*—as powerful as the sun; *bhavadbhiḥ*—by you; *ācakṣe*—may describe; *ātma-avagamaḥ*—as far as my knowledge is concerned; *atra*—herein; *yāvān*—so far; *nabhaḥ*—sky; *patanti*—fly; *ātma-samam*—as far as it can; *patattriṇaḥ*—the birds; *tathā*—thus; *samam*—similarly; *viṣṇu-gatim*—knowledge of Viṣṇu; *vipaścitaḥ*—even though learned.

TRANSLATION

O ṛṣis, who are as powerfully pure as the sun, I shall try to describe to you the transcendental pastimes of Viṣṇu as far as my knowledge is concerned. As the birds fly in the sky as far as their capacity allows, so do the learned devotees describe the Lord as far as their realization allows.

PURPORT

The Supreme Absolute Truth is unlimited. No living being can know about the unlimited by his limited capacity. The Lord is impersonal, personal and localized. By His impersonal feature He is all-pervading Brahman, by His localized feature He is present in everyone's heart as the Supreme Soul, and by His ultimate personal feature He is the object of transcendental loving service by His fortunate associates the pure devotees. The pastimes of the Lord in different features can only be estimated partly by the great learned devotees. So Śrīla Sūta Gosvāmī has rightly taken this position in describing the pastimes of the Lord as far as he has realized. Factually only the Lord Himself can describe Himself, and His learned devotee also can describe Him as far as the Lord gives him the power of description.

TEXTS 24–25

एकदा धनुरुद्यम्य विचरन् मृगयां वने ।
मृगाननुगतः श्रान्तः क्षुधितस्तृषितो भृशम् ॥२४॥
जलाशयमचक्षाणः प्रविवेश तमाश्रमम् ।
ददर्श मुनिमासीनं शान्तं मीलितलोचनम् ॥२५॥

ekadā dhanur udyamya
vicaran mṛgayāṁ vane
mṛgān anugataḥ śrāntaḥ
kṣudhitas tṛṣito bhṛśam

jalāśayam acakṣāṇaḥ
praviveśa tam āśramam
dadarśa munim āsīnaṁ
śāntaṁ mīlita-locanam

ekadā—once upon a time; *dhanuḥ*—arrows and bow; *udyamya*—taking firmly; *vicaran*—following; *mṛgayām*—hunting excursion; *vane*—in the forest; *mṛgān*—stags; *anugataḥ*—while following; *śrāntaḥ*—fatigued; *kṣudhitaḥ*—hungry; *tṛṣitaḥ*—being thirsty; *bhṛśam*—extremely; *jala-āśayam*—reservoir of water; *acakṣāṇaḥ*—while searching for; *praviveśa*—entered into; *tam*—that famous; *āśramam*—hermitage of Śamīka Ṛṣi; *dadarśa*—saw; *munim*—the sage; *āsīnam*—seated; *śāntam*—all silent; *mīlita*—closed; *locanam*—eyes.

TRANSLATION

Once upon a time Mahārāja Parīkṣit, while engaged in hunting in the forest with bow and arrows, became extremely fatigued, hungry and thirsty while following the stags. While searching for a reservoir of water, he entered the hermitage of the well-known Śamīka Ṛṣi and saw the sage sitting silently with closed eyes.

PURPORT

The Supreme Lord is so kind to His pure devotees that in proper time He calls such devotees up to Him and thus creates an auspicious circumstance for the devotee. Mahārāja Parīkṣit was a pure devotee of the Lord, and there was no reason for him to become extremely fatigued, hungry and thirsty because a devotee of the Lord never becomes perturbed by such bodily demands. But by the desire of the Lord, even such a devotee can become apparently fatigued and thirsty just to create a situation favorable for his renunciation of worldly activities. One has to give up all attachment for worldly relations before one is able to go back to Godhead, and thus when a devotee is too much absorbed in worldly affairs, the Lord creates a situation to cause indifference. The Supreme Lord never forgets His pure devotee, even though he may be engaged in so-called worldly affairs. Sometimes He creates an awkward situation, and the devotee becomes obliged to renounce all worldly affairs. The devotee can understand by the signal of the Lord, but others take it to be unfavorable and frustrating. Mahārāja Parīskit was to become the medium for the revelation of *Śrīmad-Bhāgavatam* by Lord Śrī Kṛṣṇa, as his grandfather Arjuna was the medium for the *Bhagavad-gītā*. Had Arjuna not been taken up with an illusion of family affection by the will of the Lord, the *Bhagavad-gītā* would not have been spoken by the Lord Himself for the good of all concerned. Similarly, had Mahārāja Parīkṣit not been fatigued, hungry and thirsty at this time, *Śrīmad-Bhāgavatam* would not have been spoken by Śrīla Śukadeva Gosvāmī, the prime authority of *Śrīmad-Bhāgavatam*. So this is a prelude to the circumstances under which *Śrīmad-Bhāgavatam* was spoken for the benefit of all concerned. The prelude, therefore, begins with the words "once upon a time."

TEXT 26

प्रतिरुद्धेन्द्रियप्राणमनोबुद्धिमुपारतम् ।
स्थानत्रयात्परं प्राप्तं ब्रह्मभूतमविक्रियम् ॥२६॥

pratiruddhendriya-prāṇa-
mano-buddhim upāratam
sthāna-trayāt paraṁ prāptaṁ
brahma-bhūtam avikriyam

pratiruddha—restrained; *indriya*—the sense organs; *prāṇa*—air of respiration; *manaḥ*—the mind; *buddhim*—intelligence; *upāratam*—inactive; *sthāna*—places; *trayāt*—from the three; *param*—transcendental; *prāptam*—achieved; *brahma-bhūtam*—qualitatively equal with the Supreme Absolute; *avikriyam*—unaffected.

TRANSLATION

The muni's sense organs, breath, mind and intelligence were all restrained from material activities, and he was situated in a trance apart from the three [wakefulness, dream and unconsciousness], having achieved a transcendental position qualitatively equal with the Supreme Absolute.

PURPORT

It appears that the *muni*, in whose hermitage the King entered, was in yogic trance. The transcendental position is attained by three processes, namely the process of *jñāna*, or theoretical knowledge of transcendence, the process of *yoga*, or factual realization of trance by manipulation of the physiological and psychological functions of the body, and the most approved process of *bhakti-yoga*, or the engagement of senses in the devotional service of the Lord. In the *Bhagavad-gītā* also we have the information of the gradual development of perception from matter to a living entity. Our material mind and body develop from the living entity, the soul, and being influenced by the three qualities of matter, we forget our real identity. The *jñāna* process theoretically speculates about the reality of the soul. But *bhakti-yoga* factually engages the spirit soul in activities. The perception of matter is transcended to still subtler states of the senses. The senses are transcended to the subtler mind, and then to breathing activities and gradually to intelligence. Beyond the intelligence, the living soul is realized by the mechanical activities of the *yoga* system, or practice of meditation restraining the senses, regulating the breathing system and applying intelligence to rise to the transcendental position. This trance stops all material activities of the body. The King saw the *muni* in that position. He also saw the *muni* as follows.

TEXT 27

विप्रकीर्णजटाच्छन्नं रौरवेणाजिनेन च ।
विशुष्यत्तालुरुदकं तथाभूतमयाचत ॥२७॥

viprakīrṇa-jaṭācchannaṁ
rauraveṇājinena ca
viśuṣyat-tālur udakaṁ
tathā-bhūtam ayācata

viprakīrṇa—all scattered; *jaṭa-ācchannam*—covered with compressed, long hair; *rauraveṇa*—by the skin of a stag; *ajinena*—by the skin; *ca*—also; *viśuṣyat*—dried up; *tāluḥ*—palate; *udakam*—water; *tathā-bhūtam*—in that state; *ayācata*—asked for.

TRANSLATION

The sage, in meditation, was covered by the skin of a stag, and long, compressed hair was scattered all over him. The King, whose palate was dry from thirst, asked him for water.

PURPORT

The King, being thirsty, asked the sage for water. That such a great devotee and king asked for water from a sage absorbed in trance was certainly providential. Otherwise there was no chance of such a unique happening. Mahārāja Parīkṣit was thus placed in an awkward position so that gradually *Śrīmad-Bhāgavatam* could be revealed.

TEXT 28

अलब्धतृणभूम्यादिरसम्प्राप्तार्घ्यसूनृतः ।
अवज्ञातमिवात्मानं मन्यमानश्चुकोप ह ॥२८॥

alabdha-tṛṇa-bhūmy-ādir
asamprāptārghya-sūnṛtaḥ
avajñātam ivātmānaṁ
manyamānaś cukopa ha

alabdha—having not received; *tṛṇa*—seat of straw; *bhūmi*—place; *ādiḥ*—and so on; *asamprāpta*—not properly received; *arghya*—water for reception; *sūnṛtaḥ*—sweet words; *avajñātam*—thus being neglected; *iva*—like that; *ātmānam*—personally; *manyamānaḥ*—thinking like that; *cukopa*—became angry; *ha*—in that way.

TRANSLATION

The King, not received by any formal welcome by means of being offered a seat, place, water and sweet addresses, considered himself neglected, and so thinking he became angry.

PURPORT

The law of reception in the codes of the Vedic principles states that even if an enemy is received at home, he must be received with all respects. He should not be given a chance to understand that he has come into the house of an enemy. When Lord Kṛṣṇa, accompanied by Arjuna and Bhīma, approached Jarāsandha in Magadha, the respectable enemies were given a royal reception by King Jarāsandha. The guest enemy, namely Bhīma, was to fight with Jarāsandha, and yet they were given a grand reception. At night they used to sit down together as friends and guests, and in the day they used to fight, risking life and death. That was the law of reception. The reception law enjoins that a poor man, who has nothing to offer his guest, should be good enough to offer a straw mat for sitting, a glass of water for drinking and some sweet words. Therefore, to receive a guest, either friend or foe, there is no expense. It is only a question of good manners.

When Mahārāja Parīkṣit entered the door of Śamīka Ṛṣi, he did not expect a royal reception by the Ṛṣi because he knew that saints and *ṛṣis* are not materially rich men. But he never expected that a seat of straw, a glass of water and some sweet words would be denied to him. He was not an ordinary guest, nor was he an enemy of the Ṛṣi, and therefore the cold reception by the Ṛṣi astonished the King greatly. As a matter of fact, the King was right to get angry with the Ṛṣi when he needed a glass of water very badly. To become angry in such a grave situation was not unnatural for the King, but because the King himself was not less than a great saint, his becoming angry and taking action were astonishing. So it must be accepted that it was so ordained by the supreme will of the Lord. The King was a great devotee of the Lord, and the saint was also as good as the King. But by the will of the Lord, the circumstances were so created that they became ways to the King's becoming unattached to family connection and governmental activities and thus becoming a completely surrendered soul unto the lotus feet of Lord Kṛṣṇa. The merciful Lord sometimes creates such awkward positions for his pure devotees in order to drag them towards Himself from the mire of material existence. But outwardly the situations appear to be frustrating to the devotees. The devotees of the Lord are always under the protection of the Lord, and in any condition, frustration or success, the Lord is the supreme guide for the devotees. The pure devotees, therefore, accept all conditions of frustration as blessings from the Lord.

TEXT 29

अभूतपूर्वः सहसा क्षुत्तृड्भ्यामर्दितात्मनः ।
ब्राह्मणं प्रत्यभूद्ब्रह्मन् मत्सरो मन्युरेव च ॥२९॥

abhūta-pūrvaḥ sahasā
kṣut-tṛḍbhyām arditātmanaḥ
brāhmaṇaṁ praty abhūd brahman
matsaro manyur eva ca

abhūta-pūrvaḥ—unprecedented; *sahasā*—circumstantially; *kṣut*—hunger; *tṛḍbhyām*—as well as by thirst; *ardita*—being distressed; *ātmanaḥ*—of his self; *brāhmaṇam*—unto a *brāhmaṇa; prati*—against;

abhūt—became; *brahman*—O *brāhmaṇas; matsaraḥ*—envious; *manyuḥ*—angry; *eva*—thus; *ca*—and.

TRANSLATION

O brāhmaṇas, the King's anger and envy, directed toward the brāhmaṇa sage, were unprecedented, being that circumstances had made him hungry and thirsty.

PURPORT

For a king like Mahārāja Parīkṣit to become angry and envious, especially at a sage and *brāhmaṇa,* was undoubtedly unprecedented. The King knew well that *brāhmaṇas,* sages, children, women and old men are always beyond the jurisdiction of punishment. Similarly, the king, even though he commits a great mistake, is never to be considered a wrongdoer. But in this case, Mahārāja Parīkṣit became angry and envious at the sage due to his thirst and hunger, by the will of the Lord. The King was right to punish his subject for coldly receiving him or neglecting him, but because the culprit was a sage and a *brāhmaṇa,* it was unprecedented. As the Lord is never envious of anyone, so also the Lord's devotee is never envious of anyone. The only justification for Mahārāja Parīkṣit's behavior is that it was ordained by the Lord.

TEXT 30

स तु ब्रह्मऋषेरंसे गतासुमुरगं रुषा ।
विनिर्गच्छन्धनुष्कोट्या निधाय पुरमागतः ॥३०॥

sa tu brahma-ṛṣer aṁse
gatāsum uragaṁ ruṣā
vinirgacchan dhanuṣ-koṭyā
nidhāya puram āgataḥ

saḥ—the King; *tu*—however; *brahma-ṛṣeḥ*—of the *brāhmaṇa* sage; *aṁse*—on the shoulder; *gatāsum*—lifeless; *uragam*—snake; *ruṣā*—in anger; *vinirgacchan*—while leaving; *dhanuḥ-koṭyā*—with the front of the bow; *nidhāya*—by placing it; *puram*—palace; *āgataḥ*—returned.

TRANSLATION

While leaving, the King, being so insulted, picked up a lifeless snake with his bow and angrily placed it on the shoulder of the sage. Then he returned to his palace.

PURPORT

The King thus treated the sage tit for tat, although he was never accustomed to such silly actions. By the will of the Lord, the King, while going away, found a dead snake in front of him, and he thought that the sage, who had coldly received him, thus might be coldly rewarded by being offered a garland of a dead snake. In the ordinary course of dealing, this was not very unnatural, but in the case of Mahārāja Parīkṣit's dealing with a *brāhmaṇa* sage, this was certainly unprecedented. It so happened by the will of the Lord.

TEXT 31

एष किं निभृताशेषकरणो मीलितेक्षणः ।
मृषासमाधिराहोस्वित्किं नु स्यात्क्षत्रबन्धुभिः ॥३१॥

eṣa kiṁ nibhṛtāśeṣa-
karaṇo mīlitekṣaṇaḥ
mṛṣā-samādhir āhosvit
kiṁ nu syāt kṣatra-bandhubhiḥ

eṣaḥ—this; *kim*—whether; *nibhṛta-aśeṣa*—meditative mood; *karaṇaḥ*—senses; *mīlita*—closed; *īkṣaṇaḥ*—eyes; *mṛṣā*—false; *samādhiḥ*—trance; *āho*—remains; *svit*—if it is so; *kim*—either; *nu*—but; *syāt*—may be; *kṣatra-bandhubhiḥ*—by the lower *kṣatriya.*

TRANSLATION

Upon returning, he began to contemplate and argue within himself whether the sage had actually been in meditation, with senses concentrated and eyes closed or whether he had just been feigning trance just to avoid receiving a lower kṣatriya.

PURPORT

The King, being a devotee of the Lord, did not approve of his own action, and thus he began to wonder whether the sage was really in a trance or was just pretending in order to avoid receiving the King, who was a *kṣatriya* and therefore lower in rank. Repentance comes in the mind of a good soul as soon as he commits something wrong. Śrīla Viśvanātha Cakravartī Ṭhākura and Śrīla Jīva Gosvāmī do not believe that the King's action was due to his past misdeeds. The arrangement was so made by the Lord just to call the King back home, back to Godhead.

According to Śrīla Viśvanātha Cakravartī, the plan was made by the will of the Lord, and by the will of the Lord the situation of frustration was created. The plan was that for his so-called misdeed the King could be cursed by an inexperienced *brāhmaṇa* boy infected by the influence of Kali, and thus the King would leave his hearth and home for good. His connections with Śrīla Śukadeva Gosvāmī would enable the presentation of the great *Śrīmad-Bhāgavatam*, which is considered to be the book incarnation of the Lord. This book incarnation of the Lord gives much fascinating information of the transcendental pastimes of the Lord, like His *rāsa-līlā* with the spiritual cowherd damsels of Vrajabhūmi. This specific pastime of the Lord has a special significance because anyone who properly learns about this particular pastime of the Lord will certainly be dissuaded from mundane sex desire and be placed on the path of sublime devotional service to the Lord. The pure devotee's mundane frustration is meant to elevate the devotee to a higher transcendental position. By placing Arjuna and the Pāṇḍavas in frustration due to the intrigue of their cousin-brothers, the prelude of the Battle of Kurukṣetra was created by the Lord. This was to incarnate the sound representative of the Lord, *Bhagavad-gītā*. So by placing King Parīkṣit in an awkward position, the incarnation of *Śrīmad-Bhāgavatam* was created by the will of the Lord. Being distressed by hunger and thirst was only a show, because the King endured much, even in the womb of his mother. He was never disturbed by the glaring heat of the *brahmāstra* released by Aśvatthāmā. The King's distressed condition was certainly unprecedented. The devotees like Mahārāja Parīkṣit are powerful enough to forbear such distresses, by the will of the Lord, and they are never disturbed. The situation, in this case, was therefore all planned by the Lord.

TEXT 32

तस्य पुत्रोऽतितेजस्वी विहरन् बालकोऽर्भकैः ।
राज्ञाघं प्रापितं तातं श्रुत्वा तत्रेदमब्रवीत् ॥३२॥

tasya putro 'titejasvī
viharan bālako 'rbhakaiḥ
rājñāghaṁ prāpitaṁ tātaṁ
śrutvā tatredam abravīt

tasya—his (the sage's); *putraḥ*—son; *ati*—extremely; *tejasvī*—powerful; *viharan*—while playing; *bālakaḥ*—with boys; *arbhakaiḥ*—who were all childish; *rājñā*—by the King; *agham*—distress; *prāpitam*—made to have; *tātam*—the father; *śrutvā*—by hearing; *tatra*—then and there; *idam*—this; *abravīt*—spoke.

TRANSLATION

The sage had a son who was very powerful, being a brāhmaṇa's son. While he was playing with inexperienced boys, he heard of his father's distress, which was occasioned by the King. Then and there the boy spoke as follows.

PURPORT

Due to Mahārāja Parīkṣit's good government, even a boy of tender age, who was playing with other inexperienced boys, could become as powerful as a qualified *brāhmaṇa*. This boy was known as Śṛṅgi, and he achieved good training in *brahmacarya* by his father so that he could be as powerful as a *brāhmaṇa*, even at that age. But because the age of Kali was seeking an opportunity to spoil the cultural heritage of the four orders of life, the inexperienced boy gave a chance for the age of Kali to enter into the field of Vedic culture. Hatred of the lower orders of life began from this *brāhmaṇa* boy, under the influence of Kali, and thus cultural life began to dwindle day after day. The first victim of brahminical injustice was Mahārāja Parīkṣit, and thus the protection given by the King against the onslaught of Kali was slackened.

TEXT 33

अहो अधर्मः पालानां पीव्नां बलिभुजामिव ।
स्वामिन्यघं यद् दासानां द्वारपानां शुनामिव ॥३३॥

aho adharmaḥ pālānāṁ
pīvnāṁ bali-bhujām iva
svāminy aghaṁ yad dāsānāṁ
dvāra-pānāṁ śunām iva

aho—just look at; *adharmaḥ*—irreligion; *pālānām*—of the rulers; *pīvnām*—of one who is brought up; *bali-bhujām*—like the crows; *iva*—like; *svāmini*—unto the master; *agham*—sin; *yat*—what is; *dāsānām*—of the servants; *dvāra-pānām*—keeping watch at the door; *śunām*—of the dogs; *iva*—like.

TRANSLATION

[The brāhmaṇa's son, Śṛṅgi, said] O just look at the sins of the rulers who, like crows and watchdogs at the door, perpetrate sins against their masters, contrary to the principles governing servants.

PURPORT

The *brāhmaṇas* are considered to be the head and brains of the social body, and the *kṣatriyas* are considered to be the arms of the social body. The arms are required to protect the body from all harm, but the arms must act according to the directions of the head and brain. That is a natural arrangement made by the supreme order, for it is confirmed in the *Bhagavad-gītā* that four social orders or castes, namely the *brāhmaṇas*, the *kṣatriyas*, the *vaiśyas* and the *śūdras*, are set up according to quality and work done by them. Naturally the son of a *brāhmaṇa* has a good chance to become a *brāhmaṇa* by the direction of his qualified father, as a son of a medical practitioner has a very good chance to become a qualified medical practitioner. So the caste system is quite scientific. The son must take advantage of the father's qualification and thus become a *brāhmaṇa* or medical practitioner, and not otherwise.

Without being qualified, one cannot become a *brāhmaṇa* or medical practitioner, and that is the verdict of all scriptures and social orders. Herein Śṛṅgi, a qualified son of a great *brāhmaṇa*, attained the required brahminical power both by birth and by training, but he was lacking in culture because he was an inexperienced boy. By the influence of Kali, the son of a *brāhmaṇa* became puffed up with brahminical power and thus wrongly compared Mahārāja Parīkṣit to crows and watchdogs. The King is certainly the watchdog of the state in the sense that he keeps vigilant eyes over the border of the state for its protection and defense, but to address him as a watchdog is the sign of a less cultured boy. Thus the downfall of the brahminical powers began as they gave importance to birthright without culture. The downfall of the *brāhmaṇa* caste began in the age of Kali. And since *brāhmaṇas* are the heads of the social order, all other orders of society also began to deteriorate. This beginning of brahminical deterioration was highly deplored by the father of Śṛṅgi, as we will find.

TEXT 34

ब्राह्मणैः क्षत्रबन्धुर्हि गृहपालो निरूपितः ।
स कथं तद्गृहे द्वाःस्थः सभाण्डं भोक्तुमर्हति ॥३४॥

brāhmaṇaiḥ kṣatra-bandhur hi
gṛha-pālo nirūpitaḥ
sa kathaṁ tad-gṛhe dvāḥ-sthaḥ
sabhāṇḍaṁ bhoktum arhati

brāhmaṇaiḥ—by the brahminical order; *kṣatra-bandhuḥ*—the sons of the *kṣatriyas; hi*—certainly; *gṛha-pālaḥ*—the watchdog; *nirūpitaḥ*—designated; *saḥ*—he; *katham*—on what grounds; *tat-gṛhe*—in the home of him (the master); *dvāḥ-sthaḥ*—keeping at the door; *sa-bhāṇḍam*—in the same pot; *bhoktum*—to eat; *arhati*—deserves.

TRANSLATION

The descendants of the kingly orders are definitely designated as watchdogs, and they must keep themselves at the door. On what grounds can dogs enter the house and claim to dine with the master on the same plate?

PURPORT

The inexperienced *brāhmaṇa* boy certainly knew that the King asked for water from his father and the father did not respond. He tried to explain away his father's inhospitality in an impertinent manner befitting an uncultured boy. He was not at all sorry for the King's not being well received. On the contrary, he justified the wrong act in a way characteristic of the *brāhmaṇas* of Kali-yuga. He compared the King to a watchdog, and so it was wrong for the King to enter the home of a *brāhmaṇa* and ask for water from the same pot. The dog is certainly reared by its master, but that does not mean that the dog shall claim to dine and drink from the same pot. This mentality of false prestige is the cause of downfall of the perfect social order, and we can see that in the beginning it was started by the inexperienced son of a *brāhmaṇa.* As the dog is never allowed to enter within the room and hearth, although it is reared by the master, similarly, according to Śṛṅgi, the King had no right to enter the house of Śamīka Ṛṣi. According to the boy's opinion, the King was on the wrong side and not his father, and thus he justified his silent father.

TEXT 35

कृष्णे गते भगवति शास्तर्युत्पथगामिनाम् ।
तद्भिन्नसेतूनद्याहं शास्मि पश्यत मे बलम् ॥३५॥

kṛṣṇe gate bhagavati
śāstary utpatha-gāminām
tad bhinna-setūn adhyāhaṁ
śāsmi paśyata me balam

kṛṣṇe—Lord Kṛṣṇa; *gate*—having departed from this world; *bhagavati*—the Personality of Godhead; *śāstari*—the supreme ruler; *utpatha-gāminām*—of those who are upstarts; *tat bhinna*—being separated; *setūn*—the protector; *adya*—today; *aham*—myself; *śāsmi*—shall punish; *paśyata*—just see; *me*—my; *balam*—prowess.

TRANSLATION

After the departure of Lord Śrī Kṛṣṇa, the Personality of Godhead and supreme ruler of everyone, these upstarts have

flourished, our protector being gone. Therefore I myself shall take up this matter and punish them. Just witness my power.

PURPORT

The inexperienced *brāhmaṇa*, puffed up by a little *brahma-tejas*, became influenced by the spell of Kali-yuga. Mahārāja Parīkṣit gave license to Kali to live in four places as mentioned hereinbefore, but by his very expert government the personality of Kali could hardly find the places allotted him. The personality of Kali-yuga, therefore, was seeking the opportunity to establish authority, and by the grace of the Lord he found a hole in the puffed-up, inexperienced son of a *brāhmaṇa*. The little *brāhmaṇa* wanted to show his prowess in destruction, and he had the audacity to punish such a great king as Mahārāja Parīkṣit. He wanted to take the place of Lord Kṛṣṇa after His departure. These are the principal signs of upstarts who want to take the place of Śrī Kṛṣṇa under the influence of the age of Kali. An upstart with a little power wants to become an incarnation of the Lord. There are many false incarnations after the departure of Lord Kṛṣṇa from the face of the globe, and they are misleading the innocent public by accepting the spiritual obedience of the general mass of people to maintain false prestige. In other words, the personality of Kali got the opportunity to reign through this son of a *brāhmaṇa*, Śṛṅgi.

TEXT 36

इत्युक्त्वा रोषताम्राक्षो वयस्यानृषिबालकः ।
कौशिक्याप उपस्पृश्य वाग्वज्रं विससर्ज ह ॥३६॥

ity uktvā roṣa-tāmrākṣo
vayasyān ṛṣi-bālakaḥ
kauśiky-āpa upaspṛśya
vāg-vajraṁ visasarja ha

iti—thus; *uktvā*—saying; *roṣa-tāmra-akṣaḥ*—with red-hot eyes due to being angry; *vayasyān*—unto the playmates; *ṛṣi-bālakaḥ*—the son of a *ṛṣi; kauśiki*—the river Kauśika; *āpaḥ*—water; *upaspṛśya*—by touching; *vāk*—words; *vajram*—thunderbolt; *visasarja*—threw; *ha*—in the past.

TRANSLATION

The son of the ṛṣi, his eyes red-hot with anger, touched the water of the River Kauśika while speaking to his playmates and discharged the following thunderbolt of words.

PURPORT

The circumstances under which Mahārāja Parīkṣit was cursed were simply childish, as it appears from this verse. Śṛṅgi was showing his impudency amongst his playmates, who were innocent. Any sane man would have prevented him from doing such great harm to all human society. By killing a king like Mahārāja Parīkṣit, just to make a show of acquired brahminical power, the inexperienced son of a *brāhmaṇa* committed a great mistake.

TEXT 37

इति लङ्घितमर्यादं तक्षकः सप्तमेऽहनि ।
दङ्क्ष्यति स्म कुलाङ्गारं चोदितो मे ततद्रुहम् ॥३७॥

iti laṅghita-maryādaṁ
takṣakaḥ saptame 'hani
daṅkṣyati sma kulāṅgāraṁ
codito me tata-druham

iti—thus; *laṅghita*—surpassing; *maryādam*—etiquette; *takṣakaḥ*—snake-bird; *saptame*—on the seventh; *ahani*—day; *daṅkṣyati*—will bite; *sma*—certainly; *kula-aṅgāram*—the wretched of the dynasty; *coditaḥ*—having done; *me*—my; *tata-druham*—enmity towards the father.

TRANSLATION

The brāhmaṇa's son cursed the King thus: On the seventh day from today a snake-bird will bite the most wretched one of that dynasty [Mahārāja Parīkṣit] because of his having broken the laws of etiquette by insulting my father.

PURPORT

Thus the beginning of the misuse of brahminical power began, and gradually the *brāhmaṇas* in the age of Kali became devoid of both brahminical powers and culture. The *brāhmaṇa* boy considered Mahārāja Parīkṣit to be *kulāṅgāra*, or the wretched of the dynasty, but factually the *brāhmaṇa* boy himself was so because only from him did the *brāhmaṇa* caste become powerless, like the snake whose poisoned teeth are broken. The snake is fearful as long as his poison teeth are there, otherwise he is fearful only to children. The personality of Kali conquered the *brāhmaṇa* boy first, and gradually the other castes. Thus the whole scientific system of the orders of society in this age has assumed the form of a vitiated caste system, which is now being uprooted by another class of men similarly influenced by the age of Kali. One should see to the root cause of vitiation and not try to condemn the system as it is, without knowledge of its scientific value.

TEXT 38

ततोऽभ्येत्याश्रमं बालो गले सर्पकलेवरम् ।
पितरं वीक्ष्य दुःखार्तो मुक्तकण्ठो रुरोद ह ॥३८॥

tato 'bhyetyāśramaṁ bālo
gale sarpa-kalevaram
pitaraṁ vīkṣya duḥkhārto
mukta-kaṇṭho ruroda ha

tataḥ—thereafter; *abhyetya*—after entering into; *āśramam*—the hermitage; *bālaḥ*—boy; *gale sarpa*—the snake on the shoulder; *kalevaram*—body; *pitaram*—unto the father; *vīkṣya*—having seen; *duḥkha-ārtaḥ*—in a sorry plight; *mukta-kaṇṭhaḥ*—loudly; *ruroda*—cried; *ha*—in the past.

TRANSLATION

Thereafter, when the boy returned to the hermitage, he saw a snake on his father's shoulder, and out of his grief he cried very loudly.

PURPORT

The boy was not happy because he committed a great mistake, and he wanted to be relieved of the burden on his heart by crying. So after entering the hermitage and seeing his father in that condition, he cried loudly so that he might be relieved. But it was too late. The father regretted the whole incident.

TEXT 39

स वा आङ्गिरसो ब्रह्मन् श्रुत्वा सुतविलापनम् ।
उन्मील्य शनकैर्नेत्रे दृष्ट्वा चांसे मृतोरगम् ॥३९॥

sa vā āṅgiraso brahman
śrutvā suta-vilāpanam
unmīlya śanakair netre
dṛṣṭvā cāṁse mṛtoragam

saḥ—he; *vai*—also; *āṅgirasaḥ*—the *ṛṣi* born in the family of Aṅgirā; *brahman*—O Śaunaka; *śrutvā*—on hearing; *suta*—his son; *vilāpanam*—crying in distress; *unmīlya*—opening; *śanakaiḥ*—gradually; *netre*—by the eyes; *dṛṣṭvā*—by seeing; *ca*—also; *aṁse*—on the shoulder; *mṛta*—dead; *uragam*—snake.

TRANSLATION

O brāhmaṇas, the ṛṣi, who was born in the family of Aṅgirā Muni, hearing his son crying, gradually opened his eyes and saw the dead snake around his neck.

TEXT 40

विसृज्य तञ्च पप्रच्छ वत्स कस्माद्धि रोदिषि ।
केन वा तेऽपकृतमित्युक्तः स न्यवेदयत् ॥४०॥

visṛjya taṁ ca papraccha
vatsa kasmād dhi rodiṣi
kena vā te 'pakṛtam
ity uktaḥ sa nyavedayat

visṛjya—throwing aside; *tam*—that; *ca*—also; *papraccha*—asked; *vatsa*—my dear son; *kasmāt*—what for; *hi*—certainly; *rodiṣi*—crying;

kena—by whom; *vā*—otherwise; *te*—they; *apakṛtam*—misbehaved; *iti*—thus; *uktaḥ*—being asked; *saḥ*—the boy; *nyavedayat*—informed of everything.

TRANSLATION

He threw the dead snake aside and asked his son why he was crying, whether anyone had done him harm. On hearing this, the son explained to him what had happened.

PURPORT

The father did not take the dead snake on his neck very seriously. He simply threw it away. Actually there was nothing seriously wrong in Mahārāja Parīkṣit's act, but the foolish son took it very seriously, and being influenced by Kali he cursed the King and thus ended a chapter of happy history.

TEXT 41

निशम्य शप्तमतदर्हं नरेन्द्रं
स ब्राह्मणो नात्मजमभ्यनन्दत् ।
अहो बतांहो महदद्य ते कृत-
मल्पीयसि द्रोह उरुर्दमो धृतः ॥४१॥

niśamya śaptam atad-arhaṁ narendraṁ
sa brāhmaṇo nātmajam abhyanandat
aho batāṁho mahad adya te kṛtam
alpīyasi droha urur damo dhṛtaḥ

niśamya—after hearing; *śaptam*—cursed; *atat-arham*—never to be condemned; *nara-indram*—unto the King, best of humankind; *saḥ*—that; *brāhmaṇaḥ*—*brāhmaṇa-ṛṣi;* *na*—not; *ātma-jam*—his own son; *abhyanandat*—congratulated; *aho*—alas; *bata*—distressing; *aṁhaḥ*—sins; *mahat*—great; *adya*—today; *te*—yourself; *kṛtam*—performed; *alpīyasi*—insignificant; *drohe*—offense; *uruḥ*—very great; *damaḥ*—punishment; *dhṛtaḥ*—awarded.

TRANSLATION

The father heard from his son that the King had been cursed, although he should never have been condemned, for he was the best

amongst all human beings. The ṛṣi did not congratulate his son, but, on the contrary, began to repent, saying: Alas! What a great sinful act was performed by my son. He has awarded heavy punishment for an insignificant offense.

PURPORT

The king is the best of all human beings. He is the representative of God, and he is never to be condemned for any of his actions. In other words, the king can do no wrong. The king may order hanging of a culprit son of a *brāhmaṇa*, but he does not become sinful for killing a *brāhmaṇa*. Even if there is something wrong with the king, he is never to be condemned. A medical practitioner may kill a patient by mistaken treatment, but such a killer is never condemned to death. So what to speak of a good and pious king like Mahārāja Parīkṣit? In the Vedic way of life, the king is trained to become a *rājarṣi*, or a great saint, although he is ruling as king. It is the king only by whose good government the citizens can live peacefully and without any fear. The *rājarṣis* would manage their kingdoms so nicely and piously that their subjects would respect them as if they were the Lord. That is the instruction of the *Vedas*. The king is called *narendra*, or the best amongst the human beings. How then could a king like Mahārāja Parīkṣit be condemned by an inexperienced, puffed-up son of a *brāhmaṇa*, even though he had attained the powers of a qualified *brāhmaṇa?*

Since Śamīka Ṛṣi was an experienced, good *brāhmaṇa*, he did not approve of the actions of his condemned son. He began to lament for all that his son had done. The king was beyond the jurisdiction of curses as a general rule, and what to speak of a good king like Mahārāja Parīkṣit. The offense of the King was most insignificant, and his being condemned to death was certainly a very great sin for Śṛṅgi. Therefore Ṛṣi Śamīka regretted the whole incident.

TEXT 42

न वै नृभिर्नरदेवं पराख्यं
सम्मातुमर्हस्यविपक्वबुद्धे ।
यत्तेजसा दुर्विषहेण गुप्ता
विन्दन्ति भद्राण्यकुतोभयाः प्रजाः ॥४२॥

na vai nṛbhir nara-devaṁ parākhyaṁ
sammātum arhasy avipakva-buddhe
yat-tejasā durviṣaheṇa guptā
vindanti bhadrāṇy akutobhayāḥ prajāḥ

na—never; *vai*—as a matter of fact; *nṛbhiḥ*—by any man; *nara-devam*—unto a man-god; *para-ākhyam*—who is transcendental; *sammātum*—place on equal footing; *arhasi*—by the prowess; *avipakva*—unripe or immature; *buddhe*—intelligence; *yat*—of whom; *tejasā*—by the prowess; *durviṣaheṇa*—unsurpassable; *guptāḥ*—protected; *vindanti*—enjoys; *bhadrāṇi*—all prosperity; *akutaḥ-bhayāḥ*—completely defended; *prajāḥ*—the subjects.

TRANSLATION

O my boy, your intelligence is immature, and therefore you have no knowledge that the king, who is the best amongst human beings, is as good as the Personality of Godhead. He is never to be placed on an equal footing with common men. The citizens of the state live in prosperity, being protected by his unsurpassable prowess.

TEXT 43

अलक्ष्यमाणे नरदेवनाम्नि
रथाङ्गपाणावयमङ्ग लोकः ।
तदा हि चौरप्रचुरो विनङ्क्ष्य-
त्यरक्ष्यमाणोऽविवरूथवत् क्षणात् ॥४३॥

alakṣyamāṇe nara-deva-nāmni
rathāṅga-pāṇāv ayam aṅga lokaḥ
tadā hi caura-pracuro vinaṅkṣyaty
arakṣyamāṇo 'vivarūthavat kṣaṇāt

alakṣyamāṇe—being abolished; *nara-deva*—monarchical; *nāmni*—of the name; *ratha-aṅga-pāṇau*—the representative of the Lord; *ayam*—this; *aṅga*—O my boy; *lokaḥ*—this world; *tadā hi*—at once;

caura—thieves; *pracuraḥ*—too much; *vinaṅkṣyati*—vanquishes; *arakṣyamāṇaḥ*—being protected; *avivarūtha-vat*—like lambs; *kṣaṇāt*—at once.

TRANSLATION

My dear boy, the Lord, who carries the wheel of a chariot, is represented by the monarchical regime, and when this regime is abolished the whole world becomes filled with thieves, who then at once vanquish the unprotected subjects like scattered lambs.

PURPORT

According to *Śrīmad-Bhāgavatam* the monarchical regime represents the Supreme Lord, the Personality of Godhead. The king is said to be the representative of the Absolute Personality of Godhead because he is trained to acquire the qualities of God to protect the living beings. The Battle of Kurukṣetra was planned by the Lord to establish the real representative of the Lord, Mahārāja Yudhiṣṭhira. An ideal king thoroughly trained by culture and devotional service with the martial spirit makes a perfect king. Such a personal monarchy is far better than the so-called democracy of no training and responsibility. The thieves and rogues of modern democracy seek election by misrepresentation of votes, and the successful rogues and thieves devour the mass of population. One trained monarch is far better than hundreds of useless ministerial rogues, and it is hinted herein that by abolition of a monarchical regime like that of Mahārāja Parīkṣit, the mass of people become open to many attacks of the age of Kali. They are never happy in an overly advertised form of democracy. The result of such a kingless administration is described in the following verses.

TEXT 44

तदद्य नः पापमुपैत्यनन्वयं
यन्नष्टनाथस्य वसोर्विलुम्पकात् ।
परस्परं घ्नन्ति शपन्ति वृञ्जते
पशून् स्त्रियोऽर्थान् पुरुदस्यवो जनाः ॥४४॥

tad adya naḥ pāpam upaity ananvayaṁ
yan naṣṭa-nāthasya vasor vilumpakāt
parasparaṁ ghnanti śapanti vṛñjate
paśūn striyo 'rthān puru-dasyavo janāḥ

tat—for this reason; *adya*—from this day; *naḥ*—upon us; *pāpam*—reaction of sin; *upaiti*—will overtake; *ananvayam*—disruption; *yat*—because; *naṣṭa*—abolished; *nāthasya*—of the monarch; *vasoḥ*—of wealth; *vilumpakāt*—being plundered; *parasparam*—between one another; *ghnanti*—will kill; *śapanti*—will do harm; *vṛñjate*—will steal; *paśūn*—animals; *striyaḥ*—women; *arthān*—riches; *puru*—greatly; *dasyavaḥ*—thieves; *janāḥ*—the mass of people.

TRANSLATION

Due to the termination of the monarchical regimes and the plundering of the people's wealth by rogues and thieves, there will be great social disruptions. People will be killed and injured, and animals and women will be stolen. And for all these sins we shall be responsible.

PURPORT

The word *naḥ* (we) is very significant in this verse. The sage rightly takes the responsibility of the *brāhmaṇas* as a community for killing monarchical government and thus giving an opportunity to the so-called democrats, who are generally plunderers of the wealth of the state subjects. The so-called democrats capture the administrative machine without assuming responsibility for the prosperous condition of the citizens. Everyone captures the post for personal gratification, and thus instead of one king, a number of irresponsible kings grow up to tax the citizens. It is foretold herein that in the absence of good monarchical government, everyone will be the cause of disturbance for others by plundering riches, animals, women, etc.

TEXT 45

तदार्यधर्मः प्रविलीयते नृणां
वर्णाश्रमाचारयुतस्त्रयीमयः ।

तदार्य धर्मः प्रविलीयते नृणां
वर्णाश्रमाचारयुतस्त्रयीमयः ।
ततोऽर्थकामाभिनिवेशितात्मनां
शुनां कपीनामिव वर्णसंकरः ॥४५॥

tadārya dharmaḥ pravilīyate nṛṇāṁ
varṇāśramācāra-yutas trayīmayaḥ
tato 'rtha-kāmābhiniveśitātmanāṁ
śunāṁ kapīnām iva varṇa-saṅkaraḥ

tadā—at that time; *ārya*—progressive civilization; *dharmaḥ*—engagement; *pravilīyate*—is systematically vanquished; *nṛṇām*—of humankind; *varṇa*—caste; *āśrama*—orders of society; *ācāra-yutaḥ*—composed in a good manner; *trayī-mayaḥ*—in terms of the Vedic injunction; *tataḥ*—thereafter; *artha*—economic development; *kāma-abhiniveśita*—fully absorbed in sense gratification; *ātmanām*—of men; *śunām*—like dogs; *kapīnām*—like monkeys; *iva*—thus; *varṇa-saṅkaraḥ*—unwanted population.

TRANSLATION

At that time the people in general will fall systematically from the path of a progressive civilization in respect to the qualitative engagements of the castes and the orders of society and the Vedic injunctions. Thus they will be more attracted to economic development for sense gratification, and as a result there will be an unwanted population on the level of dogs and monkeys.

PURPORT

It is foretold herein that in the absence of a monarchical regime, the general mass of people will be an unwanted population like dogs and monkeys. As the monkeys are too sexually inclined and dogs are shameless in sexual intercourse, the general mass of population born of illegitimate connection will systematically go astray from the Vedic way of good manners and qualitative engagements in the castes and orders of life.

The Vedic way of life is the progressive march of the civilization of the Āryans. The Āryans are progressive in Vedic civilization. The Vedic civilization's destination is to go back to Godhead, back home, where there is no birth, no death, no old age and no disease. The *Vedas* direct everyone not to remain in the darkness of the material world but to go towards the light of the spiritual kingdom far beyond the material sky. The qualitative caste system and the orders of life are scientifically planned by the Lord and His representatives, the great *ṛṣis.* The perfect way of life gives all sorts of instruction in things both material and spiritual. The Vedic way of life does not allow any man to be like the monkeys and dogs. A degraded civilization of sense gratification and economic development is the by-product of a godless or kingless government of the people, by the people, and for the people. The people should not, therefore, begrudge the poor administrations they themselves elect.

TEXT 46

धर्मपालो नरपतिः स तु सम्राड् बृहच्छ्रवाः ।
साक्षान्महाभागवतो राजर्षिर्हयमेधयाट् ।
क्षुत्तृट्श्रमयुतो दीनो नैवास्मच्छापमर्हति ॥४६॥

dharma-pālo nara-patiḥ
sa tu samrāḍ bṛhac-chravāḥ
sākṣān mahā-bhāgavato
rājarṣir haya-medhayāṭ
kṣut-tṛṭ-śrama-yuto dīno
naivāsmac chāpam arhati

dharma-pālaḥ—the protector of religion; *nara-patiḥ*—the King; *saḥ*—he; *tu*—but; *samrāṭ*—Emperor; *bṛhat*—highly; *śravāḥ*—celebrated; *sākṣāt*—directly; *mahā-bhāgavataḥ*—the first-class devotee of the Lord; *rāja-ṛṣiḥ*—saint amongst the royal order; *haya-medhayāṭ*—great performer of horse sacrifices; *kṣut*—hunger; *tṛṭ*—thirst; *śrama-yutaḥ*—tired and fatigued; *dīnaḥ*—stricken; *na*—never; *eva*—thus; *asmat*—by us; *śāpam*—curse; *arhati*—deserves.

TRANSLATION

The Emperor Parīkṣit is a pious king. He is highly celebrated and is a first-class devotee of the Personality of Godhead. He is a saint amongst royalty, and he has performed many horse sacrifices.

When such a king is tired and fatigued, being stricken with hunger and thirst, he does not at all deserve to be cursed.

PURPORT

After explaining the general codes relating to the royal position and asserting that the king can do no wrong and therefore is never to be condemned, the sage Śamīka wanted to say something about Emperor Parīkṣit specifically. The specific qualification of Mahārāja Parīkṣit is summarized herein. The King, even calculated as a king only, was most celebrated as a ruler who administered the religious principles of the royal order. In the *śāstras* the duties of all castes and orders of society are prescribed. All the qualities of a *kṣatriya* mentioned in the *Bhagavad-gītā* (18.43) were present in the person of the Emperor. He was also a great devotee of the Lord and a self-realized soul. Cursing such a king, when he was tired and fatigued with hunger and thirst, was not at all proper. Śamīka Ṛṣi thus admitted from all sides that Mahārāja Parīkṣit was cursed most unjustly. Although all the *brāhmaṇas* were aloof from the incident, still for the childish action of a *brāhmaṇa* boy the whole world situation was changed. Thus Ṛṣi Śamīka, a *brāhmaṇa*, took responsibility for all deterioration of the good orders of the world.

TEXT 47

अपापेषु स्वभृत्येषु बालेनापक्वबुद्धिना ।
पापं कृतं तद्भगवान् सर्वात्मा क्षन्तुमर्हति ॥४७॥

apāpeṣu sva-bhṛtyeṣu
bālenāpakva-buddhinā
pāpaṁ kṛtaṁ tad bhagavān
sarvātmā kṣantum arhati

apāpeṣu—unto one who is completely free from all sins; *sva-bhṛtyeṣu*—unto one who is subordinate and deserves to be protected; *bālena*—by a child; *apakva*—who is immature; *buddhinā*—by intelligence; *pāpam*—sinful act; *kṛtam*—has been done; *tat bhagavān*—therefore the Personality of Godhead; *sarva-ātmā*—who is all-pervading; *kṣantum*—just to pardon; *arhati*—deserve.

TRANSLATION

Then the ṛṣi prayed to the all-pervading Personality of Godhead to pardon his immature boy, who had no intelligence and who committed the great sin of cursing a person who was completely free from all sins, who was subordinate and who deserved to be protected.

PURPORT

Everyone is responsible for his own action, either pious or sinful. Ṛṣi Śamīka could foresee that his son had committed a great sin by cursing Mahārāja Parīkṣit, who deserved to be protected by the *brāhmaṇas*, for he was a pious ruler and completely free from all sins because of his being a first-class devotee of the Lord. When an offense is done unto the devotee of the Lord, it is very difficult to overcome the reaction. The *brāhmaṇas*, being at the head of the social orders, are meant to give protection to their subordinates and not to curse them. There are occasions when a *brāhmaṇa* may furiously curse a subordinate *kṣatriya* or *vaiśya*, etc., but in the case of Mahārāja Parīkṣit there were no grounds, as already explained. The foolish boy had done it out of sheer vanity in being a *brāhmaṇa's* son, and thus he became liable to be punished by the law of God. The Lord never forgives a person who condemns His pure devotee. Therefore, by cursing a king the foolish Śṛṅgi had committed not only a sin but also the greatest offense. Therefore the *ṛṣi* could foresee that only the Supreme Personality of Godhead could save his boy from his sinful act. He therefore directly prayed for pardon from the Supreme Lord, who alone can undo a thing which is impossible to change. The appeal was made in the name of a foolish boy who had developed no intelligence at all.

A question may be raised herein that since it was the desire of the Lord that Parīkṣit Mahārāja be put into that awkward position so that he might be delivered from material existence, then why was a *brāhmaṇa's* son made responsible for this offensive act? The answer is that the offensive act was performed by a child only so that he could be excused very easily, and thus the prayer of the father was accepted. But if the question is raised why the *brāhmaṇa* community as a whole was made responsible for allowing Kali into the world affairs, the answer is given in the *Varāha Purāṇa* that the demons who acted inimically toward the Personality of Godhead but were not killed by the Lord were allowed to take birth in the families of *brāhmaṇas* to take advantage of the age of Kali. The all-merciful Lord gave them a chance to have their births in the families of pious *brāhmaṇas* so that they could progress toward salvation. But the demons, instead of utilizing the good opportunity, misused the brahminical culture due to being puffed up by vanity in becoming *brāhmaṇas*. The typical example is the son of Śamīka Ṛṣi, and all the foolish sons of *brāhmaṇas* are warned hereby not to become as foolish as Śṛṅgi and be always on guard against the demoniac qualities which they had in their previous births. The foolish boy was, of course, excused by the Lord, but others, who may not have a father like Śamīka Ṛṣi, will be put into great difficulty if they misuse the advantages obtained by birth in a *brāhmaṇa* family.

TEXT 48

तिरस्कृता विप्रलब्धाः शप्ताः क्षिप्ता हता अपि ।
नास्य तत् प्रतिकुर्वन्ति तद्भक्ताः प्रभवोऽपि हि ॥४८॥

tiraskṛtā vipralabdhāḥ
śaptāḥ kṣiptā hatā api
nāsya tat pratikurvanti
tad-bhaktāḥ prabhavo 'pi hi

tiraḥ-kṛtāḥ—being defamed; *vipralabdhāḥ*—being cheated; *śaptāḥ*—being cursed; *kṣiptāḥ*—disturbed by negligence; *hatāḥ*—or even being killed; *api*—also; *na*—never; *asya*—for all these acts; *tat*—them; *pratikurvanti*—counteract; *tat*—the Lord's; *bhaktāḥ*—devotees; *prabhavaḥ*—powerful; *api*—although; *hi*—certainly.

TRANSLATION

The devotees of the Lord are so forbearing that even though they are defamed, cheated, cursed, disturbed, neglected or even killed, they are never inclined to avenge themselves.

PURPORT

Ṛṣi Śamīka also knew that the Lord does not forgive a person who has committed an offense at the feet of a devotee. The Lord can only give direction to take shelter of the devotee. He thought within himself that if Mahārāja Parīkṣit would countercurse the boy, he might be saved. But he knew also that a pure devotee is callous about worldly advantages or reverses. As such, the devotees are never inclined to counteract personal defamation, curses, negligence, etc. As far as such things are concerned, in personal affairs the devotees do not care for them. But in the case of their being performed against the Lord and His devotees, then the devotees take very strong action. It was a personal affair, and therefore Śamīka Ṛṣi knew that the King would not take counteraction. Thus there was no alternative than to place an appeal to the Lord for the immature boy.

It is not that only the *brāhmaṇas* are powerful enough to award curses or blessings upon the subordinates; the devotee of the Lord, even though he may not be a *brāhmaṇa*, is more powerful than a *brāhmaṇa*. But a powerful devotee never misuses the power for personal benefit. Whatever power the devotee may have is always utilized in service towards the Lord and His devotees only.

TEXT 49

इति पुत्रकृताघेन सोऽनुतप्तो महामुनिः ।
स्वयं विप्रकृतो राज्ञा नैवाघं तदचिन्तयत् ॥४९॥

iti putra-kṛtāghena
so 'nutapto mahā-muniḥ
svayaṁ viprakṛto rājñā
naivāghaṁ tad acintayat

iti—thus; *putra*—son; *kṛta*—done by; *aghena*—by the sin; *saḥ*—he (the *muni*); *anutaptaḥ*—regretting; *mahā-muniḥ*—the sage; *svayam*—personally; *viprakṛtaḥ*—being so insulted; *rājñā*—by the King; *na*—not; *eva*—certainly; *agham*—the sin; *tat*—that; *acintayat*—thought of it.

TRANSLATION

The sage thus regretted the sin committed by his own son. He did not take the insult paid by the King very seriously.

PURPORT

The whole incident is now cleared up. Mahārāja Parīkṣit's garlanding the sage with a dead snake was not at all a very serious offense, but Śṛṅgi's cursing the King was a serious offense. The serious offense was committed by a foolish child only; therefore he deserved to be pardoned by the Supreme Lord, although it was not possible to get free from the sinful reaction. Mahārāja Parīkṣit also did not mind the curse offered to him by a foolish *brāhmaṇa.* On the contrary, he took full advantage of the awkward situation, and by the great will of the Lord, Mahārāja Parīkṣit achieved the highest perfection of life through the grace of Śrīla Śukadeva Gosvāmī. Actually it was the desire of the Lord, and Mahārāja Parīkṣit, Ṛṣi Śamīka and his son Śṛṅgi were all instrumental in fulfilling the desire of the Lord. So none of them were put into difficulty because everything was done in relation with the Supreme Person.

TEXT 50

प्रायशः साधवो लोके परैर्द्वन्द्वेषु योजिताः ।
न व्यथन्ति न हृष्यन्ति यत आत्माऽगुणाश्रयः ॥५०॥

prāyaśaḥ sādhavo loke
parair dvandveṣu yojitāḥ
na vyathanti na hṛṣyanti
yata ātmā 'guṇāśrayaḥ

prāyaśaḥ—generally; *sādhavaḥ*—saints; *loke*—in this world; *paraiḥ*—by others; *dvandveṣu*—in duality; *yojitāḥ*—being engaged; *na*—never; *vyathanti*—distressed; *na*—nor; *hṛṣyanti*—takes pleasure; *yataḥ*—because; *ātmā*—self; *aguṇa-āśrayaḥ*—transcendental.

TRANSLATION

Generally the transcendentalists, even though engaged by others in the dualities of the material world, are not distressed.

Nor do they take pleasure [in worldly things], for they are transcendentally engaged.

PURPORT

The transcendentalists are the empiric philosophers, the mystics and the devotees of the Lord. Empiric philosophers aim at the perfection of merging into the being of the Absolute, mystics aim at perceiving the all-pervading Supersoul, and the devotees of the Lord are engaged in the transcendental loving service of the Personality of Godhead. Since Brahman, Paramātmā, and Bhagavān are different phases of the same Transcendence, all these transcendentalists are beyond the three modes of material nature. Material distresses and happinesses are products of the three modes, and therefore the causes of such material distress and happiness have nothing to do with the transcendentalists. The King was a devotee, and the *ṛṣi* was a mystic. Therefore both of them were unattached to the accidental incident created by the supreme will. The playful child was an instrument in fulfilling the Lord's will.

Thus end the Bhaktivedanta purports of the First Canto, Eighteenth Chapter, of the Śrīmad-Bhāgavatam, *entitled "Mahārāja Parīkṣit Cursed by a Brāhmaṇa Boy."*

CHAPTER NINETEEN

The Appearance of Śukadeva Gosvāmī

TEXT 1

सूत उवाच
महीपतिस्त्वथ तत्कर्म गर्ह्यं
विचिन्तयन्नात्मकृतं सुदुर्मनाः ।
अहो मया नीचमनार्यवत्कृतं
निरागसि ब्रह्मणि गूढतेजसि ॥ १ ॥

sūta uvāca
mahī-patis tv atha tat-karma garhyaṁ
vicintayann ātma-kṛtaṁ sudurmanāḥ
aho mayā nīcam anārya-vat kṛtaṁ
nirāgasi brahmaṇi gūḍha-tejasi

sūtaḥ uvāca—Sūta Gosvāmī said; *mahī-patiḥ*—the King; *tu*—but; *atha*—thus (while coming back home); *tat*—that; *karma*—act; *garhyam*—abominable; *vicintayan*—thus thinking; *ātma-kṛtam*—done by himself; *su-durmanāḥ*—very much depressed; *aho*—alas; *mayā*—by me; *nīcam*—heinous; *anārya*—uncivilized; *vat*—like; *kṛtam*—done; *nirāgasi*—unto one who is faultless; *brahmaṇi*—unto a *brāhmaṇa;* *gūḍha*—grave; *tejasi*—unto the powerful.

TRANSLATION

Śrī Sūta Gosvāmī said: While returning home, the King [Mahārāja Parīkṣit] felt that the act he had committed against the faultless and powerful brāhmaṇa was heinous and uncivilized. Consequently he was distressed.

PURPORT

The pious King regretted his accidental improper treatment of the powerful *brāhmaṇa*, who was faultless. Such repentance is natural for a good man like the King, and such repentance delivers a devotee from all kinds of sins accidentally committed. The devotees are naturally faultless. Accidental sins committed by a devotee are sincerely regretted, and by the grace of the Lord all sins unwillingly committed by a devotee are burnt in the fire of repentance.

TEXT 2

ध्रुवं ततो मे कृतदेवहेलनाद्
दुरत्ययं व्यसनं नातिदीर्घात् ।
तदस्तु कामं ह्यघनिष्कृताय मे
यथा न कुर्यां पुनरेवमद्धा ॥ २ ॥

dhruvaṁ tato me kṛta-deva-helanād
duratyayaṁ vyasanaṁ nāti-dīrghāt
tad astu kāmaṁ hy agha-niṣkṛtāya me
yathā na kuryāṁ punar evam addhā

dhruvam—sure and certain; *tataḥ*—therefore; *me*—my; *kṛta-deva-helanāt*—because of disobeying the orders of the Lord; *duratyayam*—very difficult; *vyasanam*—calamity; *na*—not; *ati*—greatly; *dīrghāt*—far off; *tat*—that; *astu*—let it be; *kāmam*—desire without reservations; *hi*—certainly; *agha*—sins; *niṣkṛtāya*—for getting free; *me*—my; *yathā*—so that; *na*—never; *kuryām*—shall I do it; *punaḥ*—again; *evam*—as I have done; *addhā*—directly.

TRANSLATION

[King Parīkṣit thought] Due to my neglecting the injunctions of the Supreme Lord I must certainly expect some difficulty to overcome me in the near future. I now desire without reservation that the calamity come now, for in this way I may be freed of the sinful action and not commit such an offense again.

PURPORT

The Supreme Lord enjoins that *brāhmaṇas* and cows must be given all protection. The Lord is Himself very much inclined to do good to *brāhmaṇas* and cows (*go-brāhmaṇa-hitāya ca*). Mahārāja Parīkṣit knew all this, and thus he concluded that his insulting a powerful *brāhmaṇa* was certainly to be punished by the laws of the Lord, and he was expecting something very difficult in the very near future. He therefore desired the imminent calamity to fall on him and not on his family members. A man's personal misconduct affects all his family members. Therefore Mahārāja Parīkṣit desired the calamity to fall on him alone. By suffering personally he would be restrained from future sins, and at the same time the sin which he had committed would be counteracted so that his descendants would not suffer. That is the way a responsible devotee thinks. The family members of a devotee also share the effects of a devotee's service unto the Lord. Mahārāja Prahlāda saved his demon father by his personal devotional service. A devotee son in the family is the greatest boon or blessing of the Lord.

TEXT 3

अद्यैव राज्यं बलमृद्धकोशं
प्रकोपितब्रह्मकुलानलो मे ।
दहत्वभद्रस्य पुनर्न मेऽभूत्
पापीयसी धीर्द्विजदेवगोभ्यः ॥ ३ ॥

adyaiva rājyaṁ balam ṛddha-kośaṁ
prakopita-brahma-kulānalo me
dahatv abhadrasya punar na me 'bhūt
pāpīyasī dhīr dvija-deva-gobhyaḥ

adya—this day; *eva*—on the very; *rājyam*—kingdom; *balam ṛddha*—strength and riches; *kośam*—treasury; *prakopita*—ignited by; *brahma-kula*—by the *brāhmaṇa* community; *analaḥ*—fire; *me dahatu*—let it burn me; *abhadrasya*—inauspiciousness; *punaḥ*—again; *na*—not; *me*—unto me; *abhūt*—may occur; *pāpīyasī*—sinful; *dhīḥ*—

intelligence; *dvija—brāhmaṇas; deva*—the Supreme Lord; *gobhyaḥ*—and the cows.

TRANSLATION

I am uncivilized and sinful due to my neglect of brahminical culture, God consciousness and cow protection. Therefore I wish that my kingdom, strength and riches burn up immediately by the fire of the brāhmaṇa's wrath so that in the future I may not be guided by such inauspicious attitudes.

PURPORT

Progressive human civilization is based on brahminical culture, God consciousness and protection of cows. All economic development of the state by trade, commerce, agriculture and industries must be fully utilized in relation to the above principles, otherwise all so-called economic development becomes a source of degradation. Cow protection means feeding the brahminical culture, which leads towards God consciousness, and thus perfection of human civilization is achieved. The age of Kali aims at killing the higher principles of life, and although Mahārāja Parīkṣit strongly resisted the domination of the personality of Kali within the world, the influence of the age of Kali came at an opportune moment, and even a strong king like Mahārāja Parīkṣit was induced to disregard the brahminical culture due to a slight provocation of hunger and thirst. Mahārāja Parīkṣit lamented the accidental incident, and he desired that all his kingdom, strength and accumulation of wealth would be burned up for not being engaged in brahminical culture, etc.

Where wealth and strength are not engaged in the advancement of brahminical culture, God consciousness and cow protection, the state and home are surely doomed by Providence. If we want peace and prosperity in the world, we should take lessons from this verse; every state and every home must endeavor to advance the cause of brahminical culture for self-purification, God consciousness for self-realization and cow protection for getting sufficient milk and the best food to continue a perfect civilization.

TEXT 4

स चिन्तयन्नित्थमथाशृणोद् यथा
मुनेः सुतोक्तो निर्ऋतिस्तक्षकाख्यः ।

स साधु मेने नचिरेण तक्षका-
नलं प्रसक्तस्य विरक्तिकारणम् ॥ ४ ॥

sa cintayann ittham athāśṛṇod yathā
muneḥ sutokto nirṛtis takṣakākhyaḥ
sa sādhu mene na cireṇa takṣakā-
nalaṁ prasaktasya virakti-kāraṇam

saḥ—he, the King; *cintayan*—thinking; *ittham*—like this; *atha*—now; *aśṛṇot*—heard; *yathā*—as; *muneḥ*—of the sage; *suta-uktaḥ*—uttered by the son; *nirṛtiḥ*—death; *takṣaka-ākhyaḥ*—in relation with the snake-bird; *saḥ*—he (the King); *sādhu*—well and good; *mene*—accepted; *na*—not; *cireṇa*—very long time; *takṣaka*—snake-bird; *analam*—fire; *prasaktasya*—for one who is too attached; *virakti*—indifference; *kāraṇam*—cause.

TRANSLATION

While the King was thus repenting, he received news of his imminent death, which would be due to the bite of a snake-bird, occasioned by the curse spoken by the sage's son. The King accepted this as good news, for it would be the cause of his indifference toward worldly things.

PURPORT

Real happiness is achieved by spiritual existence or by cessation of the repetition of birth and death. One can stop the repetition of birth and death only by going back to Godhead. In the material world, even by attaining the topmost planet (Brahmaloka), one cannot get rid of the conditions of repeated birth and death, but we do not accept the path of attaining perfection. The path of perfection frees one from all material attachments, and thus one becomes fit to enter into the spiritual kingdom. Therefore, those who are materially poverty-stricken are better candidates than those who are materially prosperous. Mahārāja Parīkṣit was a great devotee of the Lord and a bona fide candidate for entering into the kingdom of God, but even though he was so, his material assets as the Emperor of the world were setbacks to perfect attainment of his rightful status as one of the associates of the Lord in the spiritual sky.

As a devotee of the Lord, he could understand that the cursing of the *brāhmaṇa* boy, although unwise, was a blessing upon him, being the cause of detachment from worldly affairs, both political and social. Śamīka Muni also, after regretting the incident, conveyed the news to the King as a matter of duty so that the King would be able to prepare himself to go back to Godhead. Śamīka Muni sent news to the King that foolish Śṛṅgi, his son, although a powerful *brāhmaṇa* boy, unfortunately had misused his spiritual power by cursing the King unwarrantedly. The incident of the King's garlanding the *muni* was not sufficient cause for being cursed to death, but since there was no way to retract the curse, the King was informed to prepare for death within a week. Both Śamīka Muni and the King were self-realized souls. Śamīka Muni was a mystic, and Mahārāja Parīkṣit was a devotee. Therefore there was no difference between them in self-realization. Neither of them was afraid of meeting death. Mahārāja Parīkṣit could have gone to the *muni* to beg his pardon, but the news of imminent death was conveyed to the King with so much regret by the *muni* that the King did not want to shame the *muni* further by his presence there. He decided to prepare himself for his imminent death and find out the way to go back to Godhead.

The life of a human being is a chance to prepare oneself to go back to Godhead, or to get rid of the material existence, the repetition of birth and death. Thus in the system of *varṇāśrama-dharma* every man and woman is trained for this purpose. In other words, the system of *varṇāśrama-dharma* is known also as *sanātana-dharma*, or the eternal occupation. The system of *varṇāśrama-dharma* prepares a man for going back to Godhead, and thus a householder is ordered to go to the forest as *vānaprastha* to acquire complete knowledge and then to take *sannyāsa* prior to his inevitable death. Parīkṣit Mahārāja was fortunate to get a seven-day notice to meet his inevitable death. But for the common man there is no definite notice, although death is inevitable for all. Foolish men forget this sure fact of death and neglect the duty of preparing themselves for going back to Godhead. They spoil their lives in animal propensities to eat, drink, be merry and enjoy. Such an irresponsible life is adopted by the people in the age of Kali because of a sinful desire to condemn brahminical culture, God consciousness and cow protection, for which the state is responsible. The state must employ revenue to advance these three items and thus educate the populace to prepare for death. The state which does so is the real welfare state. The state of India should better follow the examples of Mahārāja Parīkṣit, the ideal executive head, than to imitate other materialistic states which have no idea of the kingdom of Godhead, the ultimate goal of human life. Deterioration of the ideals of Indian civilization has brought about the deterioration of civic life, not only in India but also abroad.

TEXT 5

अथो विहायेममम्युं च लोकं
विमर्शितौ हेयतया पुरस्तात् ।
कृष्णाङ्घ्रिसेवामधिमन्यमान
उपाविशत् प्रायममर्त्यनद्याम् ॥ ५ ॥

atho vihāyemam amuṁ ca lokaṁ
vimarśitau heyatayā purastāt
kṛṣṇāṅghri-sevām adhimanyamāna
upāviśat prāyam amartya-nadyām

atho—thus; *vihāya*—giving up; *imam*—this; *amum*—and the next; *ca*—also; *lokam*—planets; *vimarśitau*—all of them being judged; *heyatayā*—because of inferiority; *purastāt*—hereinbefore; *kṛṣṇa-aṅghri*—the lotus feet of the Lord, Śrī Kṛṣṇa; *sevām*—transcendental loving service; *adhimanyamānaḥ*—one who thinks of the greatest of all achievements; *upāviśat*—sat down firmly; *prāyam*—for fasting; *amartya-nadyām*—on the bank of the transcendental river (the Ganges or the Yamunā).

TRANSLATION

Mahārāja Parīkṣit sat down firmly on the banks of the Ganges to concentrate his mind in Kṛṣṇa consciousness, rejecting all other practices of self-realization, because transcendental loving service to Kṛṣṇa is the greatest achievement, superseding all other methods.

PURPORT

For a devotee like Mahārāja Parīkṣit, none of the material planets, even the topmost Brahmaloka, is as desirable as Goloka Vṛndāvana, the abode of Lord Śrī Kṛṣṇa, the primeval Lord and original Personality of Godhead. This earth is one of the innumerable material planets within the universe, and there are innumerable universes also within the compass of the *mahat-tattva.* The devotees are told by the Lord and His representatives, the spiritual masters or *ācāryas,* that not one of the planets within all the innumerable universes is suitable for the residential purposes of a devotee. The devotee always desires to go back home, back to Godhead, just to become one of the associates of the Lord in the capacity of servitor, friend, parent or conjugal lover of the Lord, either in one of the innumerable Vaikuṇṭha planets or in Goloka Vṛndāvana, the planet of Lord Śrī Kṛṣṇa. All these planets are eternally situated in the spiritual sky, the Paravyoma, which is on the other side of the Causal Ocean within the *mahat-tattva.* Mahārāja Parīkṣit was already aware of all this information due to his accumulated piety and birth in a high family of devotees, Vaiṣṇavas, and thus he was not at all interested in the material planets. Modern scientists are very eager to reach the moon by material arrangements, but they cannot conceive of the highest planet of this universe. But a devotee like Mahārāja Parīkṣit does not care a fig for the moon or, for that matter, any of the material planets. So when he was assured of his death on a fixed date, he became more determined in the transcendental loving service of Lord Kṛṣṇa by complete fasting on the bank of the transcendental River Yamunā, which flows down by the capital of Hastināpura (in the Delhi state). Both the Ganges and the Yamunā are *amartyā* (transcendental) rivers, and Yamunā is still more sanctified for the following reasons.

TEXT 6

या वै लसच्छ्रीतुलसीविमिश्र-
कृष्णाङ्घ्रिरेण्वभ्यधिकाम्बुनेत्री ।
पुनाति लोकानुभयत्र सेशान्
कस्तां न सेवेत मरिष्यमाणः ॥ ६ ॥

yā vai lasac-chrī-tulasī-vimiśra-
kṛṣṇāṅghri-reṇv-abhyadhikāmbu-netrī
punāti lokān ubhayatra seśān
kas tāṁ na seveta mariṣyamāṇaḥ

yā—the river which; *vai*—always; *lasat*—floating with; *śrī-tulasī*—*tulasī* leaves; *vimiśra*—mixed; *kṛṣṇa-aṅghri*—the lotus feet of the Lord, Śrī Kṛṣṇa; *reṇu*—dust; *abhyadhika*—auspicious; *ambu*—water; *netrī*—that which is carrying; *punāti*—sanctifies; *lokān*—planets; *ubhayatra*—both the upper and lower or inside and outside; *sa-īśān*—along with Lord Śiva; *kaḥ*—who else; *tām*—that river; *na*—does not; *seveta*—worship; *mariṣyamāṇaḥ*—one who is to die at any moment.

TRANSLATION

The river [Ganges, by which the King sat to fast] carries the most auspicious water, which is mixed with the dust of the lotus feet of the Lord and tulasī leaves. Therefore that water sanctifies the three worlds inside and outside and even sanctifies Lord Śiva and other demigods. Consequently everyone who is destined to die must take shelter of this river.

PURPORT

Mahārāja Parīkṣit, just after receiving the news of his death within seven days, at once retired from family life and shifted himself to the sacred bank of the Yamunā River. Generally it is said that the King took shelter on the bank of the Ganges, but according to Śrīla Jīva Gosvāmī, the King took shelter on the bank of the Yamunā. Śrīla Jīva Gosvāmī's statement appears to be more accurate because of the geographical situation. Mahārāja Parīkṣit resided in his capital Hastināpura, situated near present Delhi, and the River Yamunā flows down past the city. Naturally the King would take shelter of the River Yamunā because she was flowing past his palace door. And as far as sanctity is concerned, the River Yamunā is more directly connected with Lord Kṛṣṇa than the Ganges. The Lord sanctified the River Yamunā from the beginning of His transcendental pastimes in the world. While His father Vasudeva was crossing the Yamunā with the baby Lord Kṛṣṇa for a safe place at Gokulą on the other bank of the river from Mathurā, the Lord fell down in the river, and by the dust of His lotus feet the river at once became sanctified. It is especially mentioned herein that Mahārāja Parīkṣit took shelter of that particular river which is beautifully flowing, carrying the dust of the lotus feet of Lord Kṛṣṇa, mixed with *tulasī* leaves. Lord

Kṛṣṇa's lotus feet are always besmeared with the *tulasī* leaves, and thus as soon as His lotus feet contact the water of the Ganges and the Yamunā, the rivers become at once sanctified. The Lord, however, contacted the River Yamunā more than the Ganges. According to the *Varāha Purāṇa*, as quoted by Śrīla Jīva Gosvāmī, there is no difference between the water of the Ganges and the Yamunā, *but when the water of the Ganges is sanctified one hundred times, it is called the Yamunā.* Similarly, it is said in the scriptures that one thousand names of Viṣṇu are equal to one name of Rāma, and three names of Lord Rāma are equal to one name of Kṛṣṇa.

TEXT 7

इति व्यवच्छिद्य स पाण्डवेयः
प्रायोपवेशं प्रति विष्णुपद्याम् ।
दधौ मुकुन्दाङ्घ्रिमनन्यभावो
मुनिव्रतो मुक्तसमस्तसङ्गः ॥ ७ ॥

iti vyavacchidya sa pāṇḍaveyaḥ
prāyopaveśaṁ prati viṣṇu-padyām
dadhau mukundāṅghrim ananya-bhāvo
muni-vrato mukta-samasta-saṅgaḥ

iti—thus; *vyavacchidya*—having decided; *saḥ*—the King; *pāṇḍaveyaḥ*—worthy descendant of the Pāṇḍavas; *prāya-upaveśam*—for fasting until death; *prati*—toward; *viṣṇu-padyām*—on the bank of the Ganges (emanating from the lotus feet of Lord Viṣṇu); *dadhau*—gave himself up; *mukunda-aṅghrim*—unto the lotus feet of Lord Kṛṣṇa; *ananya*—without deviation; *bhāvaḥ*—spirit; *muni-vrataḥ*—with the vows of a sage; *mukta*—liberated from; *samasta*—all kinds of; *saṅgaḥ*—association.

TRANSLATION

Thus the King, the worthy descendant of the Pāṇḍavas, decided once and for all and sat on the Ganges' bank to fast until death and give himself up to the lotus feet of Lord Kṛṣṇa, who alone is able

to award liberation. So, freeing himself from all kinds of associations and attachments, he accepted the vows of a sage.

PURPORT

The water of the Ganges sanctifies all the three worlds, including the gods and the demigods, because it emanates from the lotus feet of the Personality of Godhead Viṣṇu. Lord Kṛṣṇa is the fountainhead of the principle of *viṣṇu-tattva,* and therefore shelter of His lotus feet can deliver one from all sins, including an offense committed by a king unto a *brāhmaṇa.* Mahārāja Parīkṣit, therefore, decided to meditate upon the lotus feet of Lord Śrī Kṛṣṇa, who is Mukunda, or the giver of liberations of all description. The banks of the Ganges or the Yamunā give one a chance to remember the Lord continuously. Mahārāja Parīkṣit freed himself from all sorts of material association and meditated upon the lotus feet of Lord Kṛṣṇa, and that is the way of liberation. To be free from all material association means to cease completely from committing any further sins. To meditate upon the lotus feet of the Lord means to become free from the effects of all previous sins. The conditions of the material world are so made that one has to commit sins willingly or unwillingly, and the best example is Mahārāja Parīkṣit himself, who was a recognized sinless, pious king. But he also became a victim of an offense, even though he was ever unwilling to commit such a mistake. He was cursed also, but because he was a great devotee of the Lord, even such reverses of life became favorable. The principle is that one should not willingly commit any sin in his life and should constantly remember the lotus feet of the Lord without deviation. Only in such a mood will the Lord help the devotee make regular progress toward the path of liberation and thus attain the lotus feet of the Lord. Even if there are accidental sins committed by the devotee, the Lord saves the surrendered soul from all sins, as confirmed in all scriptures.

sva-pāda-mūlaṁ bhajataḥ priyasya
tyaktāny abhāvasya hariḥ pareśaḥ
vikarma yac cotpatitaṁ kathañcid
dhunoti sarvaṁ hṛdi sanniviṣṭaḥ
(*Bhāg.* 11.5.42)

TEXT 8

तत्रोपजग्मुर्भुवनं पुनाना
महानुभावा मुनयः सशिष्याः ।
प्रायेण तीर्थाभिगमापदेशैः
स्वयं हि तीर्थानि पुनन्ति सन्तः ॥ ८ ॥

tatropajagmur bhuvanaṁ punānā
mahānubhāvā munayaḥ sa-śiṣyāḥ
prāyeṇa tīrthābhigamāpadeśaiḥ
svayaṁ hi tīrthāni punanti santaḥ

tatra—there; *upajagmuḥ*—arrived; *bhuvanam*—the universe; *punānāḥ*—those who can sanctify; *mahā-anubhāvāḥ*—great minds; *munayaḥ*—thinkers; *sa-śiṣyāḥ*—along with their disciples; *prāyeṇa*—almost; *tīrtha*—place of pilgrimage; *abhigama*—journey; *apadeśaiḥ*—on the plea of; *svayam*—personally; *hi*—certainly; *tīrthāni*—all the places of pilgrimage; *punanti*—sanctify; *santaḥ*—sages.

TRANSLATION

At that time all the great minds and thinkers, accompanied by their disciples, and sages who could verily sanctify a place of pilgrimage just by their presence, arrived there on the plea of making a pilgrim's journey.

PURPORT

When Mahārāja Parīkṣit sat down on the bank of the Ganges, the news spread in all directions of the universe, and the great-minded sages, who could follow the importance of the occasion, all arrived there on the plea of pilgrimage. Actually they came to meet Mahārāja Parīkṣit and not to take a bath of pilgrimage because all of them were competent enough to sanctify the places of pilgrimage. Common men go to pilgrimage sites to get themselves purified of all sins. Thus the places of pilgrimage become overburdened with the sins of others. But when such sages visit overburdened places of pilgrimage, they sanctify the places by their presence. Therefore the sages who came to meet Mahārāja Parīkṣit were not very much interested in getting themselves purified like common men, but on the plea of taking a bath in that place they came to meet Mahārāja Parīkṣit because they could foresee that *Śrīmad-Bhāgavatam* would be spoken by Śukadeva Gosvāmī. All of them wanted to take advantage of the great occasion.

TEXTS 9–10

अत्रिर्वसिष्ठश्च्यवनः शरद्वा-
नरिष्टनेमिर्भृगुरङ्गिराश्च ।
पराशरो गाधिसुतोऽथ राम
उतथ्य इन्द्रप्रमदेध्मवाहौ ॥ ९ ॥
मेधातिथिर्देवल आर्ष्टिषेणो
भारद्वाजो गौतमः पिप्पलादः ।
मैत्रेय और्वः कवषः कुम्भयोनि-
र्द्वैपायनो भगवान्नारदश्च ॥१०॥

atrir vasiṣṭhaś cyavanaḥ śaradvān
ariṣṭanemir bhṛgur aṅgirāś ca
parāśaro gādhi-suto 'tha rāma
utathya indrapramadedhmavāhau

medhātithir devala ārṣṭiṣeṇo
bhāradvājo gautamaḥ pippalādaḥ
maitreya aurvaḥ kavaṣaḥ kumbhayonir
dvaipāyano bhagavān nāradaś ca

atri to *nārada*—all names of the different saintly personalities who arrived there from different parts of the universe.

TRANSLATION

From different parts of the universe there arrived great sages like Atri, Cyavana, Śaradvān, Ariṣṭanemi, Bhṛgu, Vasiṣṭha, Parāśara, Viśvāmitra, Aṅgirā, Paraśurāma, Utathya, Indrapramada,

Idhmavāhu, Medhātithi, Devala, Ārṣṭiṣeṇa, Bhāradvāja, Gautama, Pippalāda, Maitreya, Aurva, Kavaṣa, Kumbhayoni, Dvaipāyana and the great personality Nārada.

PURPORT

Cyavana: A great sage and one of the sons of Bhṛgu Muni. He was born prematurely when his pregnant mother was kidnapped. Cyavana is one of the six sons of his father.

Bhṛgu: When Brahmājī was performing a great sacrifice on behalf of Varuṇa, Maharṣi Bhṛgu was born from the sacrificial fire. He was a great sage, and his very dear wife was Pulomā. He could travel in space like Durvāsā, Nārada and others, and he used to visit all the planets of the universe. Before the Battle of Kurukṣetra, he tried to stop the battle. Sometimes he instructed Bhāradvāja Muni about astronomical evolution, and he is the author of the great *Bhṛgu-saṁhitā,* the great astrological calculation. He explained how air, fire, water and earth are generated from ether. He explained how the air in the stomach works and regulates the intestines. As a great philosopher, he logically established the eternity of the living entity (*Mahābhārata*). He was also a great anthropologist, and the theory of evolution was long ago explained by him. He was a scientific propounder of the four divisions and orders of human society known as the *varṇāśrama* institution. He converted the *kṣatriya* king Vītahavya into a *brāhmaṇa.*

Vasiṣṭa: See *Śrīmad-Bhāgavatam* 1.9.6.

Parāśara: He is the grandson of Vasiṣṭha Muni and father of Vyāsadeva. He is the son of Maharṣi Śakti, and his mother's name was Adṛśyatī. He was in the womb of his mother when she was only twelve years old. And from within the womb of his mother he learned the *Vedas.* His father was killed by a demon, Kalmāṣapāda, and to avenge this he wanted to annihilate the whole world. He was restrained, however, by his grandfather Vasiṣṭha. He then performed a Rākṣasa-killing *yajña,* but Maharṣi Pulastya restrained him. He begot Vyāsadeva, being attracted by Satyavatī, who was to become the wife of Mahārāja Santanu. By the blessings of Parāśara, Satyavatī became fragrant for miles. He was present also during the time of Bhīṣma's death. He was spiritual master of Mahārāja Janaka and a great devotee of Lord Śiva. He is the author of many Vedic scriptures and sociological directions.

Gādhi-suta, or *Viśvāmitra:* A great sage of austerity and mystic power. He is famous as Gādhi-suta because his father was Gādhi, a powerful king of the province of Kanyakubja (part of Uttara Pradesh). Although he was a *kṣatriya* by birth, he became a *brāhmaṇa* in the very same body by the power of his spiritual achievements. He picked a quarrel with Vasiṣṭha Muni when he was a *kṣatriya* king and performed a great sacrifice in cooperation with Magaṅga Muni and thus was able to vanquish the sons of Vasiṣṭha. He became a great *yogī,* and yet he failed to check his senses and thus was obliged to become the father of Śakuntalā, the beauty queen of world history. Once, when he was a *kṣatriya* king, he visited the hermitage of Vasiṣṭha Muni, and he was given a royal reception. Viśvāmitra wanted from Vasiṣṭha a cow named Nandinī, and the Muni refused to deliver it. Viśvāmitra stole the cow, and thus there was a quarrel between the sage and the King. Viśvāmitra was defeated by the spiritual strength of Vasiṣṭha, and thus the King decided to become a *brāhmaṇa.* Before becoming a *brāhmaṇa* he underwent severe austerity on the bank of the Kauśika. He was also one who tried to stop the Kurukṣetra war.

Aṅgirā: He is one of the six mental sons of Brahmā and the father of Bṛhaspati, the great learned priest of the demigods in the heavenly planets. He was born of the semen of Brahmājī given to a cinder of fire. Utathya and Saṁvarta are his sons. It is said that he is still performing austerity and chanting the holy name of the Lord at a place known as Alokānanda on the banks of the Ganges.

Paraśurāma: See *Śrīmad-Bhāgavatam* 1.9.6.

Utathya: One of the three sons of Maharṣi Aṅgirā. He was the spiritual master of Mahārāja Mandhātā. He married Bhadrā, the daughter of Soma (Moon). Varuṇa kidnapped his wife Bhadrā, and to retaliate the offense of the god of water, he drank all the water of the world.

Medhātithi: An old sage of yore. An assembly member of the heavenly King Indradeva. His son was Kaṇva Muni, who brought up Śakuntalā in the forest. He was promoted to the heavenly planet by strictly following the principles of retired life (*vānaprastha*).

Devala: A great authority like Nārada Muni and Vyāsadeva. His good name is on the list of authorities mentioned in the *Bhagavad-gītā* when Arjuna acknowledged Lord Kṛṣṇa as the Supreme Personality of Godhead. He met Mahārāja Yudhiṣṭhira after the Battle of Kurukṣetra, and he was the elder brother of Dhaumya, the priest of the Pāṇḍava family. Like the *kṣatriyas,* he also allowed his daughter to select her own husband in a *svayaṁvara* meeting, and at that ceremony all the bachelor sons of the *ṛṣis* were invited. According to some, he is not Asita Devala.

Bhāradvāja: See *Śrīmad-Bhāgavatam* 1.9.6.

Gautama: One of the seven great sages of the universe. Śaradvān Gautama was one of his sons. Persons in the Gautama-gotra (dynasty) today are either his family descendants or in his disciplic succession. The *brāhmaṇas* who profess Gautama-gotra are generally family descendants, and the *kṣatriyas* and *vaiśyas* who profess Gautama-gotra are all in the line of his disciplic succession. He was the husband of the famous Ahalyā who turned into stone when Indradeva, the King of the heaven, molested her. Ahalyā was delivered by Lord Rāmacandra. Gautama was the grandfather of Kṛpācārya, one of the heroes of the Battle of Kurukṣetra.

Maitreya: A great *ṛṣi* of yore. He was spiritual master of Vidura and a great religious authority. He advised Dhṛtarāṣṭra to keep good relations with the Pāṇḍavas. Duryodhana disagreed and thus was cursed by him. He met Vyāsadeva and had religious discourses with him.

TEXT 11

अन्ये च देवर्षिब्रह्मर्षिवर्या
राजर्षिवर्या अरुणादयश्च ।
नानार्षेयप्रवरान् समेता-
नभ्यर्च्य राजा शिरसा ववन्दे ॥११॥

anye ca devarṣi-brahmarṣi-varyā
rājarṣi-varyā aruṇādayaś ca
nānārṣeya-pravarān sametān
abhyarcya rājā śirasā vavande

anye—many others; *ca*—also; *devarṣi*—saintly demigods; *brahmarṣi*—saintly *brāhmaṇas; varyāḥ*—topmost; *rājarṣi-varyāḥ*—topmost saintly kings; *aruṇa-ādayaḥ*—a special rank of *rājarṣis; ca*—and; *nānā*—many others; *ārṣeya-pravarān*—chief amongst the dynasties of the sages; *sametān*—assembled together; *abhyarcya*—by worshiping; *rājā*—the Emperor; *śirasā*—bowed his head to the ground; *vavande*—welcomed.

TRANSLATION

There were also many other saintly demigods, kings and special royal orders called aruṇādayas [a special rank of rājarṣis] from different dynasties of sages. When they all assembled together to meet the Emperor [Parīkṣit], he received them properly and bowed his head to the ground.

PURPORT

The system of bowing the head to the ground to show respect to superiors is an excellent etiquette which obliges the honored guest deep into the heart. Even the first-grade offender is excused simply by this process, and Mahārāja Parīkṣit, although honored by all the *ṛṣis* and kings, welcomed all the big men in that humble etiquette in order to be excused from any offenses. Generally at the last stage of one's life this humble method is adopted by every sensible man in order to be excused before departure. In this way Mahārāja Parīkṣit implored everyone's good will for going back home, back to Godhead.

TEXT 12

सुखोपविष्टेष्वथ तेषु भूयः
कृतप्रणामः स्वचिकीर्षितं यत् ।
विज्ञापयामास विविक्तचेता
उपस्थितोऽग्रेऽभिगृहीतपाणिः ॥१२॥

sukhopaviṣṭeṣv atha teṣu bhūyaḥ
kṛta-praṇāmaḥ sva-cikīrṣitaṁ yat
vijñāpayām āsa vivikta-cetā
upasthito 'gre 'bhigṛhīta-pāṇiḥ

sukha—happily; *upaviṣṭeṣu*—all sitting down; *atha*—thereupon; *teṣu*—unto them (the visitors); *bhūyaḥ*—again; *kṛta-praṇāmaḥ*—having offered obeisances; *sva*—his own; *cikīrṣitam*—decision of fasting;

yat—who; *vijñāpayām āsa*—submitted; *vivikta-cetāḥ*—one whose mind is detached from worldly affairs; *upasthitaḥ*—being present; *agre*—before them; *abhigṛhīta-pāṇiḥ*—humbly with folded hands.

TRANSLATION

After all the ṛṣis and others had seated themselves comfortably, the King, humbly standing before them with folded hands, told them of his decision to fast until death.

PURPORT

Although the King had already decided to fast until death on the bank of the Ganges, he humbly expressed his decision to elicit the opinions of the great authorities present there. Any decision, however important, should be confirmed by some authority. That makes the matter perfect. This means that the monarchs who ruled the earth in those days were not irresponsible dictators. They scrupulously followed the authoritative decisions of the saints and sages in terms of Vedic injunction. Mahārāja Parīkṣit, as a perfect king, followed the principles by consulting the authorities, even up to the last days of his life.

TEXT 13

राजोवाच

अहो वयं धन्यतमा नृपाणां
महत्तमानुग्रहणीयशीलाः ।
राज्ञां कुलं ब्राह्मणपादशौचाद्
दूराद् विसृष्टं बत गर्ह्यकर्म ॥१३॥

rājovāca
aho vayaṁ dhanyatamā nṛpāṇāṁ
mahattamānugrahaṇīya-śīlāḥ
rājñāṁ kulaṁ brāhmaṇa-pāda-śaucād
dūrād visṛṣṭaṁ bata garhya-karma

rājā uvāca—the fortune King said; *aho*—ah; *vayam*—we; *dhanya-tamāḥ*—most thankful; *nṛpāṇām*—of all the kings; *mahat-*

tama—of the great souls; *anugrahaṇīya-śīlāḥ*—trained to get favors; *rājñām*—of the royal; *kulam*—orders; *brāhmaṇa-pāda*—feet of the *brāhmaṇas; śaucāt*—refuse after cleaning; *dūrāt*—at a distance; *visṛṣṭam*—always left out; *bata*—on account of; *garhya*—condemnable; *karma*—activities.

TRANSLATION

The fortunate King said: Indeed, we are the most grateful of all the kings who are trained to get favors from the great souls. Generally you [sages] consider royalty as refuse to be rejected and left in a distant place.

PURPORT

According to religious principles, stool, urine, wash water, etc., must be left at a long distance. Attached bath rooms, urinals, etc., may be very convenient amenities of modern civilization, but they are ordered to be situated at a distance from residential quarters. That very example is cited herein in relation to the kingly order for those who are progressively marching back to Godhead. Lord Śrī Caitanya Mahāprabhu said that to be in intimate touch with dollars-and-cents men, or the kingly order, is worse than suicide for one who desires to go back to Godhead. In other words, the transcendentalists do not generally associate with men who are too enamored by the external beauty of God's creation. By advanced knowledge in spiritual realization, the transcendentalist knows that this beautiful material world is nothing but a shadowy reflection of the reality, the kingdom of God. They are not, therefore, very much captivated by royal opulence or anything like that. But in the case of Mahārāja Parīkṣit, the situation was different. Apparently the King was condemned to death by an inexperienced *brāhmaṇa* boy, but factually he was called by the Lord to return to Him. Other transcendentalists, the great sages and mystics who assembled together because of Mahārāja Parīkṣit's fasting unto death, were quite anxious to see him, for he was going back to Godhead. Mahārāja Parīkṣit also could understand that the great sages who assembled there were all kind to his forefathers, the Pāṇḍavas, because of their devotional service to the Lord. He therefore felt grateful to the sages for being present there at the last stage of his life, and he felt that it was all due to the greatness of his late forefathers or grandfathers. He felt proud, therefore, that he happened to be the descendant of such great devotees. Such pride for the devotees of the Lord is certainly not equal to the puffed-up sense of vanity for material prosperity. The first is reality, whereas the other is false and vain.

TEXT 14

तस्यैव मेऽघस्य परावरेशो
व्यासक्तचित्तस्य गृहेष्वभीक्ष्णम् ।
निर्वेदमूलो द्विजशापरूपो
यत्र प्रसक्तो भयमाशु धत्ते ॥१४॥

tasyaiva me 'ghasya parāvareśo
vyāsakta-cittasya gṛheṣv abhīkṣṇam
nirveda-mūlo dvija-śāpa-rūpo
yatra prasakto bhayam āśu dhatte

tasya—his; *eva*—certainly; *me*—mine; *aghasya*—of the sinful; *parā*—transcendental; *avara*—mundane; *īśaḥ*—controller, the Supreme Lord; *vyāsakta*—overly attached; *cittasya*—of the mind; *gṛheṣu*—to family affairs; *abhīkṣṇam*—always; *nirveda-mūlaḥ*—the source of detachment; *dvija-śāpa*—cursing by the *brāhmaṇa; rūpaḥ*—form of; *yatra*—whereupon; *prasaktaḥ*—one who is affected; *bhayam*—fearfulness; *āśu*—very soon; *dhatte*—take place.

TRANSLATION

The Supreme Personality of Godhead, the controller of both the transcendental and mundane worlds, has graciously overtaken me in the form of a brāhmaṇa's curse. Due to my being too much attached to family life, the Lord, in order to save me, has appeared before me in such a way that only out of fear I will detach myself from the world.

PURPORT

Mahārāja Parīkṣit, although born in a family of great devotees, the Pāṇḍavas, and although securely trained in transcendental attachment for the association of the Lord, still found the allurement of mundane family life so strong that he had to be detached by a plan of the Lord. Such direct action is taken by the Lord in the case of a special devotee. Mahārāja Parīkṣit could understand this by the presence of the topmost transcendentalists in the universe. The Lord resides with His devotees, and therefore the presence of the great saints indicated the presence of the Lord. The King therefore welcomed the presence of the great *ṛṣis* as a mark of favor of the Supreme Lord.

TEXT 15

तं मोपयातं प्रतियन्तु विप्रा
गङ्गा च देवी धृतचित्तमीशे ।
द्विजोपसृष्टः कुहकस्तक्षको वा
दशत्वलं गायत विष्णुगाथाः ॥ १५ ॥

taṁ mopayātaṁ pratiyantu viprā
gaṅgā ca devī dhṛta-cittam īśe
dvijopasṛṣṭaḥ kuhakas takṣako vā
daśatv alaṁ gāyata viṣṇu-gāthāḥ

tam—for that reason; *mā*—me; *upayātam*—taken shelter of; *pratiyantu*—just accept me; *viprāḥ*—O *brāhmaṇas; gaṅgā*—mother Ganges; *ca*—also; *devī*—direct representative of the Lord; *dhṛta*—taken into; *cittam*—heart; *īśe*—unto the Lord; *dvija-upasṛṣṭaḥ*—created by the *brāhmaṇa; kuhakaḥ*—something magical; *takṣakaḥ*—the snake-bird; *vā*—either; *daśatu*—let it bite; *alam*—without further delay; *gāyata*—please go on singing; *viṣṇu-gāthāḥ*—narration of the deeds of Viṣṇu.

TRANSLATION

O brāhmaṇas, just accept me as a completely surrendered soul, and let mother Ganges, the representative of the Lord, also accept me in that way, for I have already taken the lotus feet of the Lord into my heart. Let the snake-bird—or whatever magical thing the brāhmaṇa created—bite me at once. I only desire that you all continue singing the deeds of Lord Viṣṇu.

PURPORT

As soon as one is given up completely unto the lotus feet of the Supreme Lord, he is not at all afraid of death. The atmosphere created by the presence of great devotees of the Lord on the bank of the Ganges and Mahārāja Parīkṣit's complete acceptance of the Lord's lotus feet were sufficient guarantee to the King for going back to Godhead. He thus became absolutely free from all fear of death.

TEXT 16

पुनश्च भूयाद्भगवत्यनन्ते
रतिः प्रसङ्गश्च तदाश्रयेषु ।
महत्सु यां यामुपयामि सृष्टिं
मैत्र्यस्तु सर्वत्र नमो द्विजेभ्यः ॥१६॥

punaś ca bhūyād bhagavaty anante
ratiḥ prasaṅgaś ca tad-āśrayeṣu
mahatsu yāṁ yām upayāmi sṛṣṭiṁ
maitry astu sarvatra namo dvijebhyaḥ

punaḥ—again; *ca*—and; *bhūyāt*—let it be; *bhagavati*—unto Lord Śrī Kṛṣṇa; *anante*—who has unlimited potency; *ratiḥ*—attracting; *prasaṅgaḥ*—association; *ca*—also; *tat*—His; *āśrayeṣu*—with those who are His devotees; *mahatsu*—within the material creation; *yām yām*—wherever; *upayāmi*—I may take; *sṛṣṭim*—my birth; *maitrī*—friendly relation; *astu*—let it be; *sarvatra*—everywhere; *namaḥ*—my obeisances; *dvijebhyaḥ*—unto the *brāhmaṇas.*

TRANSLATION

Again, offering obeisances unto all you brāhmaṇas, I pray that if I should again take my birth in the material world I will have complete attachment to the unlimited Lord Kṛṣṇa, association with His devotees and friendly relations with all living beings.

PURPORT

That a devotee of the Lord is the only perfect living being is explained herein by Mahārāja Parīkṣit. A devotee of the Lord is no one's enemy, although there may be many enemies of a devotee. A devotee of the Lord does not like to associate with nondevotees, although he has no enmity with them. He desires association with the devotees of the Lord. This is perfectly natural because birds of the same feather mix together. And the most important function of a devotee is to have complete attachment for Lord Śrī Kṛṣṇa, the father of all living beings. As a good son of the father behaves in a friendly way with all his other brothers, so also the devotee of the Lord, being a good son of the supreme father, Lord Kṛṣṇa, sees all other living beings in relation with the supreme father. He tries to bring back the upstart sons of the father to a saner stage and to get them to accept the supreme fatherhood of God. Mahārāja Parīkṣit was certainly going back to Godhead, but even if he were not to go back, he prayed for a pattern of life which is the most perfect way in the material world. A pure devotee does not desire the company of a personality as great as Brahmā, but he prefers the association of a petty living being, provided he is a devotee of the Lord.

TEXT 17

इति स्म राजाध्यवसाययुक्तः
प्राचीनमूलेषु कुशेषु धीरः ।
उदङ्मुखो दक्षिणकूल आस्ते
समुद्रपत्न्याः स्वसुतन्यस्तभारः ॥१७॥

iti sma rājādhyavasāya-yuktaḥ
prācīna-mūleṣu kuśeṣu dhīraḥ
udaṅ-mukho dakṣiṇa-kūla āste
samudra-patnyāḥ sva-suta-nyasta-bhāraḥ

iti—thus; *sma*—as in the past; *rājā*—the King; *adhyavasāya*—perseverance; *yuktaḥ*—being engaged; *prācīna*—eastern; *mūleṣu*—with the root; *kuśeṣu*—on a seat made of *kuśa* straw; *dhīraḥ*—self-controlled; *udaṅ-mukhaḥ*—facing the northern side; *dakṣiṇa*—on the southern; *kūle*—bank; *āste*—situated; *samudra*—the sea; *patnyāḥ*—wife of (the Ganges); *sva*—own; *suta*—son; *nyasta*—given over; *bhāraḥ*—the charge of administration.

TRANSLATION

In perfect self-control, Mahārāja Parīkṣit sat down on a seat of straw, with straw-roots facing the east, placed on the southern bank of the Ganges, and he himself faced the north. Just previously he had given charge of his kingdom over to his son.

PURPORT

The River Ganges is celebrated as the wife of the sea. The seat of *kuśa* straw is considered to be sanctified if the straw is taken out of the earth complete with root, and if the root is pointed toward the east it is considered to be auspicious. Facing the north is still more favorable for attaining spiritual success. Mahārāja Parīkṣit handed over the charge of administration to his son before leaving home. He was thus fully equipped for all favorable conditions.

TEXT 18

एवं च तस्मिन्नरदेवदेवे
प्रायोपविष्टे दिवि देवसङ्घाः ।
प्रशस्य भूमौ व्यकिरन् प्रसूनै-
र्मुदा मुहुर्दुन्दुभयश्च नेदुः ॥१८॥

evaṁ ca tasmin nara-deva-deve
prāyopaviṣṭe divi deva-saṅghāḥ
praśasya bhūmau vyakiran prasūnair
mudā muhur dundubhayaś ca neduḥ

evam—thus; *ca*—and; *tasmin*—in that; *nara-deva-deve*—upon the King's; *prāya-upaviṣṭe*—being engaged in fasting to death; *divi*—in the sky; *deva*—demigods; *saṅghāḥ*—all of them; *praśasya*—having praised the action; *bhūmau*—on the earth; *vyakiran*—scattered; *prasūnaiḥ*—with flowers; *mudā*—in pleasure; *muhuḥ*—continually; *dundubhayaḥ*—celestial drums; *ca*—also; *neduḥ*—beaten.

TRANSLATION

Thus the King, Mahārāja Parīkṣit, sat to fast until death. All the demigods of the higher planets praised the King's actions and in

pleasure continually scattered flowers over the earth and beat celestial drums.

PURPORT

Even up to the time of Mahārāja Parīkṣit there were interplanetary communications, and the news of Mahārāja Parīkṣit's fasting unto death to attain salvation reached the higher planets in the sky where the intelligent demigods live. The demigods are more luxurious than human beings, but all of them are obedient to the orders of the Supreme Lord. There is no one in the heavenly planets who is an atheist or nonbeliever. Thus any devotee of the Lord on the surface of the earth is always praised by them, and in the case of Mahārāja Parīkṣit they were greatly delighted and thus gave tokens of honor by scattering flowers over the earth and by beating celestial drums. A demigod takes pleasure in seeing someone go back to Godhead. He is always pleased with a devotee of the Lord, so much so that by his adhidaivic powers he may help the devotees in all respects. And by their actions, the Lord is pleased with them. There is an invisible chain of complete cooperation between the Lord, the demigods and the devotee of the Lord on earth.

TEXT 19

महर्षयो वै समुपागता ये
प्रशस्य साध्वित्यनुमोदमानाः ।
ऊचुः प्रजानुग्रहशीलसारा
यदुत्तमश्लोकगुणाभिरूपम् ॥१९॥

maharṣayo vai samupāgatā ye
praśasya sādhv ity anumodamānāḥ
ūcuḥ prajānugraha-śīla-sārā
yad uttama-śloka-guṇābhirūpam

maharṣayaḥ—the great sages; *vai*—as a matter of course; *samupāgatāḥ*—assembled there; *ye*—those who; *praśasya*—by praising; *sādhu*—quite all right; *iti*—thus; *anumodamānāḥ*—all approving; *ūcuḥ*—said; *prajā-anugraha*—doing good to the living being; *śīla-sārāḥ*—qualitatively powerful; *yat*—because; *uttama-śloka*—one who is praised by selected poems; *guṇa-abhirūpam*—as beautiful as godly qualities.

TRANSLATION

All the great sages who were assembled there also praised the decision of Mahārāja Parīkṣit and they expressed their approval by saying, "Very good." Naturally the sages are inclined to do good to common men, for they have all the qualitative powers of the Supreme Lord. Therefore they were very much pleased to see Mahārāja Parīkṣit, a devotee of the Lord, and they spoke as follows.

PURPORT

The natural beauty of a living being is enhanced by rising up to the platform of devotional service. Mahārāja Parīkṣit was absorbed in attachment for Lord Kṛṣṇa. Seeing this, the great sages assembled were very pleased, and they expressed their approval by saying, "Very good." Such sages are naturally inclined to do good to the common man, and when they see a personality like Mahārāja Parīkṣit advance in devotional service, their pleasure knows no bounds, and they offer all blessings in their power. The devotional service of the Lord is so auspicious that all demigods and sages, up to the Lord Himself, become pleased with the devotee, and therefore the devotee finds everything auspicious. All inauspicious matters are removed from the path of a progressive devotee. Meeting all the great sages at the time of death was certainly auspicious for Mahārāja Parīkṣit, and thus he was blessed by the so-called curse of a *brāhmaṇa's* boy.

TEXT 20

न वा इदं राजर्षिवर्य चित्रं
भवत्सु कृष्णं समनुव्रतेषु ।
येऽध्यासनं राजकिरीटजुष्टं
सद्यो जहुर्भगवत्पार्श्वकामाः ॥२०॥

na vā idaṁ rājarṣi-varya citraṁ
bhavatsu kṛṣṇaṁ samanuvrateṣu
ye 'dhyāsanaṁ rāja-kirīṭa-juṣṭaṁ
sadyo jahur bhagavat-pārśva-kāmāḥ

na—neither; *vā*—like this; *idam*—this; *rājarṣi*—saintly king; *varya*—the chief; *citram*—astonishing; *bhavatsu*—unto all of you; *kṛṣṇam*—Lord Kṛṣṇa; *samanuvrateṣu*—unto those who are strictly in the line of; *ye*—who; *adhyāsanam*—seated on the throne; *rāja-kirīṭa*—helmets of kings; *juṣṭam*—decorated; *sadyaḥ*—immediately; *jahuḥ*—gave up; *bhagavat*—the Personality of Godhead; *pārśva-kāmāḥ*—desiring to achieve association.

TRANSLATION

[The sages said] O chief of all the saintly kings of the Pāṇḍu dynasty who are strictly in the line of Lord Śrī Kṛṣṇa! It is not at all astonishing that you give up your throne, which is decorated with the helmets of many kings, to achieve eternal association with the Personality of Godhead.

PURPORT

Foolish politicians who hold political administrative posts think that the temporary posts they occupy are the highest material gain of life, and therefore they stick to those posts even up to the last moment of life, without knowing that achievement of liberation as one of the associates of the Lord in His eternal abode is the highest gain of life. The human life is meant for achieving this end. The Lord has assured us in the *Bhagavad-gītā* many times that going back to Godhead, His eternal abode, is the highest achievement. Prahlāda Mahārāja, while praying to Lord Nṛsiṁha, said, "O my Lord, I am very much afraid of the materialistic way of life, and I am not the least afraid of Your present ghastly ferocious feature as Nṛsiṁhadeva. This materialistic way of life is something like a grinding stone, and we are being crushed by it. We have fallen into this horrible whirlpool of the tossing waves of life, and thus, my Lord, I pray at Your lotus feet to call me back to Your eternal abode as one of Your servitors. This is the summit liberation of this materialistic way of life. I have very bitter experience of the materialistic way of life. In whichever species of life I have taken birth, compelled by the force of my own activities, I have very painfully experienced two things, namely separation from my beloved and meeting with what is not wanted. And to counteract them, the remedies which I undertook were more dangerous than the disease itself. So I drift from one point to another birth after birth, and I pray to You therefore to give me a shelter at Your lotus feet."

The Pāṇḍava kings, who are more than many saints of the world, knew the bitter results of the materialistic way of life. They were ever captivated by the glare of the imperial throne they occupied, and they sought always the opportunity of being called by the Lord to associate with Him eternally. Mahārāja Parīkṣit was the worthy grandson of Mahārāja Yudhiṣṭhira. Mahārāja Yudhiṣṭhira gave up the imperial throne to his grandson, and similarly Mahārāja Parīkṣit, the grandson of Mahārāja Yudhiṣṭhira, gave up the imperial throne to his son Janamejaya. That is the way of all the kings in the dynasty because they are all strictly in the line of Lord Kṛṣṇa. Thus the devotees of the Lord are never enchanted by the glare of materialistic life, and they live impartially, unattached to the objects of the false, illusory materialistic way of life.

TEXT 21

सर्वे वयं तावदिहास्महेऽथ
कलेवरं यावदसौ विहाय ।
लोकं परं विरजस्कं विशोकं
यास्यत्ययं भागवतप्रधानः ॥ २१ ॥

sarve vayaṁ tāvad ihāsmahe 'tha
kalevaraṁ yāvad asau vihāya
lokaṁ paraṁ virajaskaṁ viśokaṁ
yāsyaty ayaṁ bhāgavata-pradhānaḥ

sarve—all; *vayam*—of us; *tāvat*—as long as; *iha*—at this place; *āsmahe*—shall stay; *atha*—hereafter; *kalevaram*—the body; *yāvat*—so long; *asau*—the King; *vihāya*—giving up; *lokam*—the planet; *param*—the supreme; *virajaskam*—completely free from mundane contamination; *viśokam*—completely freed from all kinds of lamentation; *yāsyati*—returns; *ayam*—this; *bhāgavata*—devotee; *pradhānaḥ*—the foremost.

TRANSLATION

We shall all wait here until the foremost devotee of the Lord, Mahārāja Parīkṣit, returns to the supreme planet, which is com-

pletely free from all mundane contamination and all kinds of lamentation.

PURPORT

Beyond the limitation of the material creation, which is compared to the cloud in the sky, there is the *paravyoma*, or the spiritual sky, full of planets called Vaikuṇṭhas. Such Vaikuṇṭha planets are also differently known as the Puruṣottamaloka, Acyutaloka, Trivikramaloka, Hṛṣīkeśaloka, Keśavaloka, Aniruddhaloka, Mādhavaloka, Pradyumnaloka, Saṅkarṣaṇaloka, Śrīdharaloka, Vāsudevaloka, Ayodhyāloka, Dvārakāloka and many other millions of spiritual *lokas* wherein the Personality of Godhead predominates; all the living entities there are liberated souls with spiritual bodies as good as that of the Lord. There is no material contamination; everything there is spiritual, and therefore there is nothing objectively lamentable. They are full of transcendental bliss, and are without birth, death, old age and disease. And amongst all the above-mentioned Vaikuṇṭhalokas, there is one supreme *loka* called Goloka Vṛndāvana, which is the abode of the Lord Śrī Kṛṣṇa and His specific associates. Mahārāja Parīkṣit was destined to achieve this particular *loka*, and the great *ṛṣis* assembled there could foresee this. All of them consulted among themselves about the great departure of the great King, and they wanted to see him up to the last moment because they would no more be able to see such a great devotee of the Lord. When a great devotee of the Lord passes away, there is nothing to be lamented because the devotee is destined to enter into the kingdom of God. But the sorry plight is that such great devotees leave our sight, and therefore there is every reason to be sorry. As the Lord is rarely to be seen by our present eyes, so also are the great devotees. The great *ṛṣis*, therefore, correctly decided to remain on the spot till the last moment.

TEXT 22

आश्रुत्य तदृषिगणवचः परीक्षित्
समं मधुच्युद् गुरु चाव्यलीकम् ।
आभाषतैनानभिनन्द्य युक्तान्
शुश्रूषमाणश्चरितानि विष्णोः ॥२२॥

āśrutya tad ṛṣi-gaṇa-vacaḥ parīkṣit
samaṁ madhu-cyud guru cāvyalīkam
ābhāṣatainān abhinandya yuktān
śuśrūṣamāṇaś caritāni viṣṇoḥ

āśrutya—just after hearing; *tat*—that; *ṛṣi-gaṇa*—the sages assembled; *vacaḥ*—speaking; *parīkṣit*—Mahārāja Parīkṣit; *samam*—impartial; *madhu-cyut*—sweet to hear; *guru*—grave; *ca*—also; *avyalīkam*—perfectly true; *ābhāṣata*—said; *enān*—all of them; *abhinandya*—congratulated; *yuktān*—appropriately presented; *śuśrūṣamāṇaḥ*—being desirous to hear; *caritāni*—activities of; *viṣṇoḥ*—the Personality of Godhead.

TRANSLATION

All that was spoken by the great sages was very sweet to hear, full of meaning and appropriately presented as perfectly true. So after hearing them, Mahārāja Parīkṣit, desiring to hear of the activities of Lord Śrī Kṛṣṇa, the Personality of Godhead, congratulated the great sages.

TEXT 23

समागताः सर्वत एव सर्वे
वेदा यथा मूर्तिधरास्त्रिपृष्ठे ।
नेहाथनामुत्र च कश्चनार्थ
ऋते परानुग्रहमात्मशीलम् ॥२३॥

samāgatāḥ sarvata eva sarve
vedā yathā mūrti-dharās tri-pṛṣṭhe
nehātha nāmutra ca kaścanārtha
ṛte parānugraham ātma-śīlam

samāgatāḥ—assembled; *sarvataḥ*—from all directions; *eva*—certainly; *sarve*—all of you; *vedāḥ*—supreme knowledge; *yathā*—as; *mūrti-dharāḥ*—personified; *tri-pṛṣṭhe*—on the planet of Brahmā (which is situated above the three planetary systems, namely the upper, intermediate and lower worlds); *na*—not; *iha*—in this world; *atha*—

thereafter; *na*—nor; *amutra*—in the other world; *ca*—also; *kaścana*—any other; *arthaḥ*—interest; *ṛte*—save and except; *para*—others; *anugraham*—doing good to; *ātma-śīlam*—own nature.

TRANSLATION

The King said: O great sages, you have all very kindly assembled here, having come from all parts of the universe. You are all as good as supreme knowledge personified, who resides in the planet above the three worlds [Satyaloka]. Consequently you are naturally inclined to do good to others, and but for this you have no interest, either in this life or in the next.

PURPORT

Six kinds of opulences, namely wealth, strength, fame, beauty, knowledge and renunciation, are all originally the different attributes pertaining to the Absolute Personality of Godhead. The living beings, who are part and parcel entities of the Supreme Being, have all these attributes partially, up to the full strength of seventy-eight percent. In the material world these attributes (up to seventy-eight percent of the Lord's attributes) are covered by the material energy, as the sun is covered by a cloud. The covered strength of the sun is very dim, compared to the original glare, and similarly the original color of the living beings with such attributes becomes almost extinct. There are three planetary systems, namely the lower worlds, the intermediate worlds and the upper worlds. The human beings on earth are situated at the beginning of the intermediate worlds, but living beings like Brahmā and his contemporaries live in the upper worlds, of which the topmost is Satyaloka. In Satyaloka the inhabitants are fully cognizant of Vedic wisdom, and thus the mystic cloud of material energy is cleared. Therefore they are known as the *Vedas* personified. Such persons, being fully aware of knowledge both mundane and transcendental, have no interest in either the mundane or transcendental worlds. They are practically desireless devotees. In the mundane world they have nothing to achieve, and in the transcendental world they are full in themselves. Then why do they come to the mundane world? They descend on different planets as messiahs by the order of the Lord to deliver the fallen souls. On the earth they come down and do good to the people of the world in different circumstances under different climatic influences. They have nothing to do in this world save and except reclaim the fallen souls rotting in material existence, deluded by material energy.

TEXT 24

ततश्च वः पृच्छ्यमिमं विपृच्छे
विश्रभ्य विप्रा इतिकृत्यतायाम् ।
सर्वात्मना म्रियमाणैश्च कृत्यं
शुद्धं च तत्रामृशताभियुक्ताः ॥२४॥

tataś ca vaḥ pṛcchyam imaṁ vipṛcche
viśrabhya viprā iti kṛtyatāyām
sarvātmanā mriyamāṇaiś ca kṛtyaṁ
śuddhaṁ ca tatrāmṛśatābhiyuktāḥ

tataḥ—as such; *ca*—and; *vaḥ*—unto you; *pṛcchyam*—that which is to be asked; *imam*—this; *vipṛcche*—beg to ask you; *viśrabhya*—trustworthy; *viprāḥ*—*brāhmaṇas; iti*—thus; *kṛtyatāyām*—out of all different duties; *sarva-ātmanā*—by everyone; *mriyamāṇaiḥ*—especially those who are just about to die; *ca*—and; *kṛtyam*—dutiful; *śuddham*—perfectly correct; *ca*—and; *tatra*—therein; *āmṛśata*—by complete deliberation; *abhiyuktāḥ*—just befitting.

TRANSLATION

O trustworthy brāhmaṇas, I now ask you about my immediate duty. Please, after proper deliberation, tell me of the unalloyed duty of everyone in all circumstances, and specifically of those who are just about to die.

PURPORT

In this verse the King has placed two questions before the learned sages. The first question is what is the duty of everyone in all circumstances, and the second question is what is the specific duty of one who is to die very shortly. Out of the two, the question relating to the dying man is most important because everyone is a dying man, either very shortly or after one hundred years. The duration of life is immaterial, but the duty of a dying man is very important. Mahārāja Parīkṣit placed these two questions before Śukadeva Gosvāmī also on his arrival, and practically the whole of the *Śrīmad-Bhāgavatam*, beginning from the Second Canto up to the last Twelfth Canto, deals with these two questions. The conclusion arrived at thereof is that devotional service of the Lord Śrī Kṛṣṇa, as it is confirmed by the Lord Himself in the last phases of the *Bhagavad-gītā*, is the last word in relation to everyone's permanent duty in life. Mahārāja Parīkṣit was already aware of this fact, but he wanted the great sages assembled there to unanimously give their verdict on his conviction so that he might be able to go on with his confirmed duty without controversy. He has especially mentioned the word *śuddha*, or perfectly correct. For transcendental realization or self-realization, many processes are recommended by various classes of philosophers. Some of them are first-class methods, and some of them are second- or third-class methods. The first-class method demands that one give up all other methods and surrender unto the lotus feet of the Lord and thus be saved from all sins and their reactions.

TEXT 25

तत्राभवद्भगवान् व्यासपुत्रो
यदृच्छया गामटमानोऽनपेक्षः ।
अलक्ष्यलिङ्गो निजलाभतुष्टो
वृतश्च बालैरवधूतवेषः ॥२५॥

tatrābhavad bhagavān vyāsa-putro
yadṛcchayā gām aṭamāno 'napekṣaḥ
alakṣya-liṅgo nija-lābha-tuṣṭo
vṛtaś ca bālair avadhūta-veṣaḥ

tatra—there; *abhavat*—appeared; *bhagavān*—powerful; *vyāsa-putraḥ*—son of Vyāsadeva; *yadṛcchayā*—as one desires; *gām*—the earth; *aṭamānaḥ*—while traveling; *anapekṣaḥ*—disinterested; *alakṣya*—unmanifested; *liṅgaḥ*—symptoms; *nija-lābha*—self-realized;

tuṣṭaḥ—satisfied; *vṛtaḥ*—surrounded; *ca*—and; *bālaiḥ*—by children; *avadhūta*—neglected by others; *veṣaḥ*—dressed.

TRANSLATION

At that moment there appeared the powerful son of Vyāsadeva, who traveled over the earth disinterested and satisfied with himself. He did not manifest any symptoms of belonging to any social order or status of life. He was surrounded with women and children, and he dressed as if others had neglected him.

PURPORT

The word *bhagavān* is sometimes used in relation with some of the great devotees of the Lord, like Śukadeva Gosvāmī. Such liberated souls are disinterested in the affairs of this material world because they are self-satisfied by the great achievements of devotional service. As explained before, Śukadeva Gosvāmī never accepted any formal spiritual master, nor did he undergo any formal reformatory performances. His father, Vyāsadeva, was his natural spiritual master because Śukadeva Gosvāmī heard *Śrīmad-Bhāgavatam* from him. After this, he became completely self-satisfied. Thus he was not dependent on any formal process. The formal processes are necessary for those who are expected to reach the stage of complete liberation, but Śrī Śukadeva Gosvāmī was already in that status by the grace of his father. As a young boy he was expected to be properly dressed, but he went about naked and was uninterested in social customs. He was neglected by the general populace, and inquisitive boys and women surrounded him as if he were a madman. He thus appears on the scene while traveling on the earth of his own accord. It appears that upon the inquiry of Mahārāja Parīkṣit, the great sages were not unanimous in their decision as to what was to be done. For spiritual salvation there were many prescriptions according to the different modes of different persons. But the ultimate aim of life is to attain the highest perfectional stage of devotional service to the Lord. As doctors differ, so also sages differ in their different prescriptions. While such things were going on, the great and powerful son of Vyāsadeva appeared on the scene.

TEXT 26

तं द्वयष्टवर्षं सुकुमारपाद-
करोरुबाह्वंसकपोलगात्रम् ।
चार्वायताक्षोन्नसतुल्यकर्ण-
सुभ्र्वाननं कम्बुसुजातकण्ठम् ॥२६॥

taṁ dvyaṣṭa-varṣaṁ su-kumāra-pāda-
karoru-bāhv-aṁsa-kapola-gātram
cārv-āyatākṣonnasa-tulya-karṇa-
subhrv-ānanaṁ kambu-sujāta-kaṇṭham

tam—him; *dvi-aṣṭa*—sixteen; *varṣam*—years; *su-kumāra*—delicate; *pāda*—legs; *kara*—hands; *ūru*—thighs; *bāhu*—arms; *aṁsa*—shoulders; *kapola*—forehead; *gātram*—body; *cāru*—beautiful; *āyata*—broad; *akṣa*—eyes; *unnasa*—high nose; *tulya*—similar; *karṇa*—ears; *subhru*—nice brows; *ānanam*—face; *kambu*—conchshell; *sujāta*—nicely built; *kaṇṭham*—neck.

TRANSLATION

This son of Vyāsadeva was only sixteen years old. His legs, hands, thighs, arms, shoulders, forehead and the other parts of his body were all delicately formed. His eyes were beautifully wide, and his nose and ears were highly raised. He had a very attractive face, and his neck was well formed and beautiful like a conchshell.

PURPORT

A respectable personality is described beginning with the legs, and this honored system is observed here with Śukadeva Gosvāmī. He was only sixteen years of age. A person is honored for his achievements and not for advanced age. A person can be older by experience and not by age. Śrī Śukadeva Gosvāmī, who is described herein as the son of Vyāsadeva, was by his knowledge more experienced than all the sages present there, although he was only sixteen years old.

TEXT 27

निगूढजत्रुं पृथुतुङ्गवक्षस-
मावर्तनाभिं वलिवल्गूदरं च ।
दिगम्बरं वक्त्रविकीर्णकेशं
प्रलम्बबाहुं स्वमरोत्तमाभम् ॥२७॥

nigūḍha-jatruṁ pṛthu-tuṅga-vakṣasam
āvarta-nābhiṁ vali-valgūdaraṁ ca
dig-ambaraṁ vaktra-vikīrṇa-keśaṁ
pralamba-bāhuṁ svamarottamābham

nigūḍha—covered; *jatrum*—collarbone; *pṛthu*—broad; *tuṅga*—swollen; *vakṣasam*—chest; *āvarta*—whirled; *nābhim*—navel; *vali-valgu*—striped; *udaram*—abdomen; *ca*—also; *dik-ambaram*—dressed by all directions (naked); *vaktra*—curled; *vikīrṇa*—scattered; *keśam*—hair; *pralamba*—elongated; *bāhum*—hands; *su-amara-uttama*—the best among the gods (Kṛṣṇa); *ābham*—hue.

TRANSLATION

His collarbone was fleshy, his chest broad and thick, his navel deep and his abdomen beautifully striped. His arms were long, and curly hair was strewn over his beautiful face. He was naked, and the hue of his body reflected that of Lord Kṛṣṇa.

PURPORT

His bodily features indicate him to be different from common men. All the signs described in connection with the bodily features of Śukadeva Gosvāmī are uncommon symptoms, typical of great personalities, according to physiognomical calculations. His bodily hue resembled that of Lord Kṛṣṇa, who is the Supreme among the gods, demigods, and all living beings.

TEXT 28

श्यामं सदापीव्यवयोऽङ्गलक्ष्म्या
स्त्रीणां मनोज्ञं रुचिरस्मितेन ।

प्रत्युत्थितास्ते मुनयः स्वासनेभ्य-
स्तल्लक्षणज्ञा अपि गूढवर्चसम् ॥२८॥

śyāmaṁ sadāpīvya-vayo-'ṅga-lakṣmyā
strīṇāṁ mano-jñaṁ rucira-smitena
pratyutthitās te munayaḥ svāsanebhyas
tal-lakṣaṇa-jñā api gūḍha-varcasam

śyāmam—blackish; *sadā*—always; *apīvya*—excessively; *vayaḥ*—age; *aṅga*—symptoms; *lakṣmyā*—by the opulence of; *strīṇām*—of the fair sex; *manaḥ-jñam*—attractive; *rucira*—beautiful; *smitena*—smiling; *pratyutthitāḥ*—stood up; *te*—all of them; *munayaḥ*—the great sages; *sva*—own; *āsanebhyaḥ*—from the seats; *tat*—those; *lakṣaṇa-jñāḥ*—expert in the art of physiognomy; *api*—even; *gūḍha-varcasam*—covered glories.

TRANSLATION

He was blackish and very beautiful due to his youth. Because of the glamor of his body and his attractive smiles, he was pleasing to women. Though he tried to cover his natural glories, the great sages present there were all expert in the art of physiognomy, and so they honored him by rising from their seats.

TEXT 29

स विष्णुरातोऽतिथय आगताय
तस्मै सपर्यां शिरसाजहार ।
ततो निवृत्ता ह्यबुधाः स्त्रियोऽर्भका
महासने सोपविवेश पूजितः ॥२९॥

sa viṣṇu-rāto 'tithaya āgatāya
tasmai saparyāṁ śirasājahāra
tato nivṛttā hy abudhāḥ striyo 'rbhakā
mahāsane sopaviveśa pūjitaḥ

saḥ—he; *viṣṇu-rātaḥ*—Mahārāja Parīkṣit (who is always protected by Lord Viṣṇu); *atithaye*—to become a guest; *āgatāya*—one who arrived there; *tasmai*—unto him; *saparyām*—with the whole body; *śirasā*—with bowed head; *ājahāra*—offered obeisances; *tataḥ*—thereafter; *nivṛttāḥ*—ceased; *hi*—certainly; *abudhāḥ*—less intelligent; *striyaḥ*—women; *arbhakāḥ*—boys; *mahā-āsane*—exalted seat; *sa*—he; *upaviveśa*—sat down; *pūjitaḥ*—being respected.

TRANSLATION

Mahārāja Parīkṣit, who is also known as Viṣṇurāta [one who is always protected by Viṣṇu], bowed his head to receive the chief guest, Śukadeva Gosvāmī. At that time all the ignorant women and boys ceased following Śrīla Śukadeva. Receiving respect from all, Śukadeva Gosvāmī took his exalted seat.

PURPORT

On Śukadeva Gosvāmī's arrival at the meeting, everyone, except Śrīla Vyāsadeva, Nārada and a few others, stood up, and Mahārāja Parīkṣit, who was glad to receive a great devotee of the Lord, bowed down before him with all the limbs of his body. Śukadeva Gosvāmī also exchanged the greetings and reception by embrace, shaking of hands, nodding and bowing down, especially before his father and Nārada Muni. Thus he was offered the presidential seat at the meeting. When he was so received by the king and sages, the street boys and less intelligent women who followed him were struck with wonder and fear. So they retired from their frivolous activities, and everything was full of gravity and calm.

TEXT 30

स संवृतस्तत्र महान् महीयसां
ब्रह्मर्षिराजर्षिदेवर्षिसङ्घैः ।
व्यरोचतालं भगवान् यथेन्दु-
र्ग्रहर्क्षतारानिकरैः परीतः ॥३०॥

sa saṁvṛtas tatra mahān mahīyasāṁ
brahmarṣi-rājarṣi-devarṣi-saṅghaiḥ
vyarocatālaṁ bhagavān yathendur
graharkṣa-tārā-nikaraiḥ parītaḥ

saḥ—Śrī Śukadeva Gosvāmī; *saṁvṛtaḥ*—surrounded by; *tatra*—there; *mahān*—great; *mahīyasām*—of the greatest; *brahmarṣi*—saint among the *brāhmaṇas; rājarṣi*—saint among the kings; *devarṣi*—saint among the demigods; *saṅghaiḥ*—by the assembly of; *vyarocata*—well deserved; *alam*—able; *bhagavān*—powerful; *yathā*—as; *induḥ*—the moon; *graha*—planets; *ṛkṣa*—heavenly bodies; *tārā*—stars; *nikaraiḥ*—by the assembly of; *parītaḥ*—surrounded by.

TRANSLATION

Śukadeva Gosvāmī was then surrounded by saintly sages and demigods just as the moon is surrounded by stars, planets and other heavenly bodies. His presence was gorgeous, and he was respected by all.

PURPORT

In the great assembly of saintly personalities, there was Vyāsadeva the *brahmarṣi*, Nārada the *devarṣi*, Paraśurāma the great ruler of the *kṣatriya* kings, etc. Some of them were powerful incarnations of the Lord. Śukadeva Gosvāmī was not known as *brahmarṣi*, *rājarṣi* or *devarṣi*, nor was he an incarnation like Nārada, Vyāsa or Paraśurāma. And yet he excelled them in respects paid. This means that the devotee of the Lord is more honored in the world than the Lord Himself. One should therefore never minimize the importance of a devotee like Śukadeva Gosvāmī.

TEXT 31

प्रशान्तमासीनमकुण्ठमेधसं
मुनिं नृपो भागवतोऽभ्युपेत्य ।
प्रणम्य मूर्धावहितः कृताञ्जलि-
र्नत्वा गिरा सूनृतयान्वपृच्छत् ॥३१॥

praśāntam āsīnam akuṇṭha-medhasaṁ
muniṁ nṛpo bhāgavato 'bhyupetya
praṇamya mūrdhnāvahitaḥ kṛtāñjalir
natvā girā sūnṛtayānvapṛcchat

praśāntam—perfectly pacified; *āsīnam*—sitting; *akuṇṭha*—without hesitation; *medhasam*—one who has sufficient intelligence; *munim*—

unto the great sage; *nṛpaḥ*—the King (Mahārāja Parīkṣit); *bhāgavataḥ*—the great devotee; *abhyupetya*—approaching him; *praṇamya*—bowing down; *mūrdhnā*—his head; *avahitaḥ*—properly; *kṛta-añjaliḥ*—with folded hands; *natvā*—politely, *girā*—by words; *sūnṛtayā*—in sweet voices; *anvapṛcchat*—inquired.

TRANSLATION

The sage Śrī Śukadeva Gosvāmī sat perfectly pacified, intelligent and ready to answer any question without hesitation. The great devotee, Mahārāja Parīkṣit, approached him, offered his respects by bowing before him, and politely inquired with sweet words and folded hands.

PURPORT

The gesture now adopted by Mahārāja Parīkṣit of questioning a master is quite befitting in terms of scriptural injunctions. The scriptural injunction is that one should humbly approach a spiritual master to understand the transcendental science. Mahārāja Parīkṣit was now prepared for meeting his death, and within the very short time of seven days he was to know the process of entering the kingdom of God. In such important cases, one is required to approach a spiritual master. There is no necessity of approaching a spiritual master unless one is in need of solving the problems of life. One who does not know how to put questions before the spiritual master has no business seeing him. And the qualification of the spiritual master is perfectly manifested in the person of Śukadeva Gosvāmī. Both the spiritual master and the disciple, namely Śrī Śukadeva Gosvāmī and Mahārāja Parīkṣit, attained perfection through the medium of *Śrīmad-Bhāgavatam.* Śukadeva Gosvāmī learned *Śrīmad-Bhāgavatam* from his father, Vyāsadeva, but he had no chance to recite it. Before Mahārāja Parīkṣit he recited *Śrīmad-Bhāgavatam* and answered the questions of Mahārāja Parīkṣit unhesitatingly, and thus both the master and the disciple got salvation.

TEXT 32

परीक्षिदुवाच

अहो अद्य वयं ब्रह्मन् सत्सेव्याः क्षत्रबन्धवः ।
कृपयातिथिरूपेण भवद्भिस्तीर्थकाः कृताः ॥३२॥

parīkṣid uvāca
aho adya vayaṁ brahman
sat-sevyāḥ kṣatra-bandhavaḥ
kṛpayātithi-rūpeṇa
bhavadbhis tīrthakāḥ kṛtāḥ

parīkṣit uvāca—the fortunate Mahārāja Parīkṣit said; *aho*—ah; *adya*—today; *vayam*—we; *brahman*—O *brāhmaṇa; sat-sevyāḥ*—eligible to serve the devotee; *kṣatra*—the ruling class; *bandhavaḥ*—friends; *kṛpayā*—by your mercy; *atithi-rūpeṇa*—in the manner of a guest; *bhavadbhiḥ*—by your good self; *tīrthakāḥ*—qualified for being places of pilgrimage; *kṛtāḥ*—done by you.

TRANSLATION

The fortunate King Parīkṣit said: O brāhmaṇa, by your mercy only, you have sanctified us, making us like unto places of pilgrimage, all by your presence here as my guest. By your mercy, we, who are but unworthy royalty, become eligible to serve the devotee.

PURPORT

Saintly devotees like Śukadeva Gosvāmī generally do not approach worldly enjoyers, especially those in royal orders. Mahārāja Pratāparudra was a follower of Lord Caitanya, but when he wanted to see the Lord, the Lord refused to see him because he was a king. For a devotee who desires to go back to Godhead, two things are strictly prohibited: worldly enjoyers and women. Therefore, devotees of the standard of Śukadeva Gosvāmī are never interested in seeing kings. Mahārāja Parīkṣit was, of course, a different case. He was a great devotee, although a king, and therefore Śukadeva Gosvāmī came to see him in his last stage of life. Mahārāja Parīkṣit, out of his devotional humility, felt himself an unworthy descendant of his great *kṣatriya* forefathers, although he was as great as his predecessors. The unworthy sons of the royal orders are called *kṣatra-bandhavas*, as the unworthy sons of the *brāhmaṇas* are called *dvija-bandhus* or *brahma-bandhus*. Mahārāja Parīkṣit was greatly encouraged by the presence of Śukadeva Gosvāmī. He felt himself sanctified by the presence of the great saint whose presence turns any place into a place of pilgrimage.

TEXT 33

येषां संस्मरणात्पुंसां सद्यः शुद्ध्यन्ति वै गृहाः ।
किं पुनर्दर्शनस्पर्शपादशौचासनादिभिः ॥३३॥

yeṣāṁ saṁsmaraṇāt puṁsāṁ
sadyaḥ śuddhyanti vai gṛhāḥ
kiṁ punar darśana-sparśa-
pāda-śaucāsanādibhiḥ

yeṣām—of whom; *saṁsmaraṇāt*—by remembrance; *puṁsām*—of a person; *sadyaḥ*—instantly; *śuddhyanti*—cleanses; *vai*—certainly; *gṛhāḥ*—all houses; *kim*—what; *punaḥ*—then; *darśana*—meeting; *sparśa*—touching; *pāda*—the feet; *śauca*—washing; *āsana-ādibhiḥ*—by offering a seat, etc.

TRANSLATION

Simply by our remembering you, our houses become instantly sanctified. And what to speak of seeing you, touching you, washing your holy feet and offering you a seat in our home?

PURPORT

The importance of holy places of pilgrimage is due to the presence of great sages and saints. It is said that sinful persons go to the holy places and leave their sins there to accumulate. But the presence of the great saints disinfects the accumulated sins, and thus the holy places continue to remain sanctified by the grace of the devotees and saints present there. If such saints appear in the homes of worldly people, certainly the accumulated sins of such worldly enjoyers become neutralized. Therefore, the holy saints actually have no self-interest with the householders. The only aim of such saints is to sanctify the houses of the householders, and the householders therefore should feel grateful when such saints and sages appear at their doors. A householder who dishonors such holy orders is a great offender. It is enjoined, therefore, that a householder who does not bow down before a saint at once must undergo fasting for the day in order to neutralize the great offense.

TEXT 34

सांनिध्यात्ते महायोगिन्पातकानि महान्त्यपि ।
सद्यो नश्यन्ति वै पुंसां विष्णोरिव सुरेतराः ॥३४॥

sānnidhyāt te mahā-yogin
pātakāni mahānty api
sadyo naśyanti vai puṁsāṁ
viṣṇor iva suretarāḥ

sānnidhyāt—on account of the presence; *te*—your; *mahā-yogin*—O great mystic; *pātakāni*—sins; *mahānti*—invulnerable; *api*—in spite of; *sadyaḥ*—immediately; *naśyanti*—vanquished; *vai*—certainly; *puṁsām*—of a person; *viṣṇoḥ*—like the presence of the Personality of Godhead; *iva*—like; *sura-itarāḥ*—other than the demigods.

TRANSLATION

Just as the atheist cannot remain in the presence of the Personality of Godhead, so also the invulnerable sins of a man are immediately vanquished in your presence, O saint! O great mystic!

PURPORT

There are two classes of human beings, namely the atheist and the devotee of the Lord. The devotee of the Lord, because of manifesting godly qualities, is called a demigod, whereas the atheist is called a demon. The demon cannot stand the presence of Viṣṇu, the Personality of Godhead. The demons are always busy in trying to vanquish the Personality of Godhead, but factually as soon as the Personality of Godhead appears, by either His transcendental name, form, attributes, pastimes, paraphernalia or variegatedness, the demon is at once vanquished. It is said that a ghost cannot remain as soon as the holy name of the Lord is chanted. The great saints and devotees of the Lord are in the list of His paraphernalia, and thus as soon as a saintly devotee is present, the ghostly sins are at once vanquished. That is the verdict of all Vedic literatures. One is recommended, therefore, to associate only with saintly devotees so that worldly demons and ghosts cannot exert their sinister influence.

TEXT 35

अपि मे भगवान् प्रीतः कृष्णः पाण्डुसुतप्रियः ।
पैतृष्वसेयप्रीत्यर्थं तद्गोत्रस्यात्तबान्धवः ॥३५॥

api me bhagavān prītaḥ
kṛṣṇaḥ pāṇḍu-suta-priyaḥ
paitṛ-ṣvaseya-prīty-arthaṁ
tad-gotrasyātta-bāndhavaḥ

api—definitely; *me*—unto me; *bhagavān*—the Personality of Godhead; *prītaḥ*—pleased; *kṛṣṇaḥ*—the Lord; *pāṇḍu-suta*—the sons of King Pāṇḍu; *priyaḥ*—dear; *paitṛ*—in relation with the father; *svaseya*—the sons of the sister; *prīti*—satisfaction; *artham*—in the matter of; *tat*—their; *gotrasya*—of the descendant; *ātta*—accepted; *bāndhavaḥ*—as a friend.

TRANSLATION

Lord Kṛṣṇa, the Personality of Godhead, who is very dear to the sons of King Pāṇḍu, has accepted me as one of those relatives just to please His great cousins and brothers.

PURPORT

A pure and exclusive devotee of the Lord serves his family interest more dexterously than others, who are attached to illusory family affairs. Generally people are attached to family matters, and the whole economic impetus of human society is moving under the influence of family affection. Such deluded persons have no information that one can render better service to the family by becoming a devotee of the Lord. The Lord gives special protection to the family members and descendants of a devotee, even though such members are themselves nondevotees! Mahārāja Prahlāda was a great devotee of the Lord, but his father, Hiraṇyakaśipu, was a great atheist and declared enemy of the Lord. But despite all this, Hiraṇyakaśipu was awarded salvation due to his being the father of Mahārāja Prahlāda. The Lord is so kind that he gives all protection to the family members of His devotee, and thus the devotee has no need to bother about his family members, even if one leaves such family members aside to discharge devotional service. Mahārāja Yudhiṣṭhira and his brothers were the sons of Kuntī, the paternal aunt of Lord Kṛṣṇa, and Mahārāja Parīkṣit admits the patronage of Lord Kṛṣṇa because of his being the only grandson of the great Pāṇḍavas.

TEXT 36

अन्यथा तेऽव्यक्तगतेर्दर्शनं नः कथं नृणाम् ।
नितरां म्रियमाणानां संसिद्धस्य वनीयसः ॥३६॥

anyathā te 'vyakta-gater
darśanaṁ naḥ kathaṁ nṛṇām
nitarāṁ mriyamāṇānāṁ
saṁsiddhasya vanīyasaḥ

anyathā—otherwise; *te*—your; *avyakta-gateḥ*—of one whose movements are invisible; *darśanam*—meeting; *naḥ*—for us; *katham*—how; *nṛṇām*—of the people; *nitarām*—specifically; *mriyamāṇānām*—of those who are about to die; *saṁsiddhasya*—of one who is all-perfect; *vanīyasaḥ*—voluntary appearance.

TRANSLATION

Otherwise [without being inspired by Lord Kṛṣṇa] how is it that you have voluntarily appeared here, though you are moving incognito to the common man and are not visible to us who are on the verge of death?

PURPORT

The great sage Śukadeva Gosvāmī was certainly inspired by Lord Kṛṣṇa to appear voluntarily before Mahārāja Parīkṣit, the great devotee of the Lord, just to give him the teachings of *Śrīmad-Bhāgavatam.* One can achieve the nucleus of the devotional service of the Lord by the mercy of the spiritual master and the Personality of Godhead. The spiritual master is the manifested representative of the Lord to help one achieve ultimate success. One who is not authorized by the Lord cannot become a spiritual master. Śrīla Śukadeva Gosvāmī is an authorized spiritual master, and thus he was inspired by the Lord to appear before Mahārāja Parīkṣit and instruct him in the teachings of *Śrīmad-*

Bhāgavatam. One can achieve the ultimate success of going back to Godhead if he is favored by the Lord's sending His true representative. As soon as a true representative of the Lord is met by a devotee of the Lord, the devotee is assured a guarantee for going back to Godhead just after leaving the present body. This, however, depends on the sincerity of the devotee himself. The Lord is seated in the heart of all living beings, and thus he knows very well the movements of all individual persons. As soon as the Lord finds that a particular soul is very eager to go back to Godhead, the Lord at once sends His bona fide representative. The sincere devotee is thus assured by the Lord of going back to Godhead. The conclusion is that to get the assistance and help of a bona fide spiritual master means *to receive the direct help of the Lord Himself.*

TEXT 37

अतः पृच्छामि संसिद्धिं योगिनां परमं गुरुम् ।
पुरुषस्येह यत्कार्यं म्रियमाणस्य सर्वथा ॥३७॥

ataḥ pṛcchāmi saṁsiddhiṁ
yogināṁ paramaṁ gurum
puruṣasyeha yat kāryaṁ
mriyamāṇasya sarvathā

ataḥ—therefore; *pṛcchāmi*—beg to inquire; *saṁsiddhim*—the way of perfection; *yoginām*—of the saints; *paramam*—the supreme; *gurum*—the spiritual master; *puruṣasya*—of a person; *iha*—in this life; *yat*—whatever; *kāryam*—duty; *mriyamāṇasya*—of one who is going to die; *sarvathā*—in every way.

TRANSLATION

You are the spiritual master of great saints and devotees. I am therefore begging you to show the way of perfection for all persons, and especially for one who is about to die.

PURPORT

Unless one is perfectly anxious to inquire about the way of perfection, there is no necessity of approaching a spiritual master. A spiritual master is not a kind of decoration for a householder. Generally a fashionable materialist engages a so-called spiritual master without any profit. The pseudo-spiritual master flatters the so-called disciple, and thereby both the master and his ward go to hell without a doubt. Mahārāja Parīkṣit is the right type of disciple because he puts forward questions vital to the interest of all men, particularly for the dying men. The question put forward by Mahārāja Parīkṣit is the basic principle of the complete thesis of *Śrīmad-Bhāgavatam.* Now let us see how intelligently the great master replies.

TEXT 38

यच्छ्रोतव्यमथो जप्यं यत्कर्तव्यं नृभिः प्रभो ।
स्मर्तव्यं भजनीयं वा ब्रूहि यद्वा विपर्ययम् ॥३८॥

yac chrotavyam atho japyaṁ
yat kartavyaṁ nṛbhiḥ prabho
smartavyaṁ bhajanīyaṁ vā
brūhi yadvā viparyayam

yat—whatever; *śrotavyam*—worth hearing; *atho*—thereof; *japyam*—chanted; *yat*—what also; *kartavyam*—executed; *nṛbhiḥ*—by the people in general; *prabho*—O master; *smartavyam*—that which is remembered; *bhajanīyam*—worshipable; *vā*—either; *brūhi*—please explain; *yadvā*—what it may be; *viparyayam*—against the principle.

TRANSLATION

Please let me know what a man should hear, chant, remember and worship, and also what he should not do. Please explain all this to me.

TEXT 39

नूनं भगवतो ब्रह्मन् गृहेषु गृहमेधिनाम् ।
न लक्ष्यते ह्यवस्थानमपि गोदोहनं क्वचित् ॥३९॥

nūnaṁ bhagavato brahman
gṛheṣu gṛha-medhinām

na lakṣyate hy avasthānam
api go-dohanaṁ kvacit

nūnan—because; *bhagavataḥ*—of you, who are powerful; *brahman*—O *brāhmaṇa; gṛheṣu*—in the houses; *gṛha-medhinām*—of the householders; *na*—not; *lakṣyate*—are seen; *hi*—exactly; *avasthānam*—staying in; *api*—even; *go-dohanam*—milking the cow; *kvacit*—rarely.

TRANSLATION

O powerful brāhmaṇa, it is said that you hardly stay in the houses of men long enough to milk a cow.

PURPORT

Saints and sages in the renounced order of life go to the houses of the householders at the time they milk the cows, early in the morning, and ask some quantity of milk for subsistence. A pound of milk fresh from the milk bag of a cow is sufficient to feed an adult with all vitamin values, and therefore saints and sages live only on milk. Even the poorest of the householders keep at least ten cows, each delivering twelve to twenty quarts of milk, and therefore no one hesitates to spare a few pounds of milk for the mendicants. It is the duty of householders to maintain the saints and sages, like the children. So a saint like Śukadeva Gosvāmī would hardly stay at the house of a householder for more than five minutes in the morning. In other words, such saints are very rarely seen in the houses of householders, and Mahārāja Parīkṣit therefore prayed to him to instruct him as soon as possible. The householders also should be intelligent enough to get some transcendental information from visiting sages. The householder should not foolishly ask a saint to deliver what is available in the market. That should be the reciprocal relation between the saints and the householders.

TEXT 40

सूत उवाच
एवमाभाषितः पृष्टः स राज्ञा श्लक्ष्णया गिरा ।
प्रत्यभाषत धर्मज्ञो भगवान् बादरायणिः ॥४०॥

sūta uvāca
evam ābhāṣitaḥ pṛṣṭaḥ
sa rājñā ślakṣṇayā girā
pratyabhāṣata dharma-jño
bhagavān bādarāyaṇiḥ

sūtaḥ uvāca—Śrī Sūta Gosvāmī said; *evam*—thus; *ābhāṣitaḥ*—being spoken; *pṛṣṭaḥ*—and asked for; *saḥ*—he; *rājñā*—by the King; *ślakṣṇayā*—by sweet; *girā*—language; *pratyabhāṣata*—began to reply; *dharma-jñaḥ*—one who knows the principles of religion; *bhagavān*—the powerful personality; *bādarāyaṇiḥ*—son of Vyāsadeva.

TRANSLATION

Śrī Sūta Gosvāmī said: The King thus spoke and questioned the sage, using sweet language. Then the great and powerful personality, the son of Vyāsadeva, who knew the principles of religion, began his reply.

Thus end the Bhaktivedanta purports of the First Canto, Nineteenth Chapter, of the Śrīmad-Bhāgavatam, *entitled "The Appearance of Śukadeva Gosvāmī."*

END OF THE FIRST CANTO

Appendixes

The Author

His Divine Grace A. C. Bhaktivedanta Swami Prabhupāda appeared in this world in 1896 in Calcutta, India. He first met his spiritual master, Śrīla Bhaktisiddhānta Sarasvatī Gosvāmī, in Calcutta in 1922. Bhaktisiddhānta Sarasvatī, a prominent devotional scholar and the founder of sixty-four Gauḍīya Maṭhas (Vedic institutes), liked this educated young man and convinced him to dedicate his life to teaching Vedic knowledge. Śrīla Prabhupāda became his student, and eleven years later (1933) at Allahabad he became his formally initiated disciple.

At their first meeting, in 1922, Śrīla Bhaktisiddhānta Sarasvatī Ṭhākura requested Śrīla Prabhupāda to broadcast Vedic knowledge through the English language. In the years that followed, Śrīla Prabhupāda wrote a commentary on the *Bhagavad-gītā*, assisted the Gauḍīya Maṭha in its work and, in 1944, without assistance, started an English fortnightly magazine, edited it, typed the manuscripts and checked the galley proofs. He even distributed the individual copies freely and struggled to maintain the publication. Once begun, the magazine never stopped; it is now being continued by his disciples in the West.

Recognizing Śrīla Prabhupāda's philosophical learning and devotion, the Gauḍīya Vaiṣṇava Society honored him in 1947 with the title "Bhaktivedanta." In 1950, at the age of fifty-four, Śrīla Prabhupāda retired from married life, and four years later he adopted the *vānaprastha* (retired) order to devote more time to his studies and writing. Śrīla Prabhupāda traveled to the holy city of Vṛndāvana, where he lived in very humble circumstances in the historic medieval temple of Rādhā-Dāmodara. There he engaged for several years in deep study and writing. He accepted the renounced order of life (*sannyāsa*) in 1959. At Rādhā-Dāmodara, Śrīla Prabhupāda began work on his life's masterpiece: a multivolume translation and commentary on the eighteen thousand verse *Śrīmad-Bhāgavatam* (*Bhāgavata Purāṇa*). He also wrote *Easy Journey to Other Planets.*

After publishing three volumes of *Bhāgavatam*, Śrīla Prabhupāda came to the United States, in 1965, to fulfill the mission of his spiritual master. Since that time, His Divine Grace has written over forty volumes of authoritative translations, commentaries and summary studies of the philosophical and religious classics of India.

In 1965, when he first arrived by freighter in New York City, Śrīla Prabhupāda was practically penniless. It was after almost a year of great difficulty that he established the International Society for Krishna Consciousness in July of 1966. Under his careful guidance, the Society has grown within a decade to a worldwide confederation of almost one hundred *āśramas*, schools, temples, institutes and farm communities.

In 1968, Śrīla Prabhupāda created New Vṛndāvana, an experimental Vedic community in the hills of West Virginia. Inspired by the success of New Vṛndāvana, now a thriving farm community of more than one thousand acres, his students have since founded several similar communities in the United States and abroad.

In 1972, His Divine Grace introduced the Vedic system of primary and secondary education in the West by founding the Gurukula school in Dallas, Texas. The school began with 3 children in 1972, and by the beginning of 1975 the enrollment had grown to 150.

Śrīla Prabhupāda has also inspired the construction of a large international center at Śrīdhāma Māyāpur in West Bengal, India, which is also the site for a planned Institute of Vedic Studies. A similar project is the magnificent Kṛṣṇa-Balarāma Temple and International Guest House in Vṛndāvana, India. These are centers where Westerners can live to gain firsthand experience of Vedic culture.

Śrīla Prabhupāda's most significant contribution, however, is his books. Highly respected by the academic community for their authoritativeness, depth and clarity, they are used as standard textbooks in numerous college courses. His writings have been translated into eleven languages. The Bhaktivedanta Book Trust, established in 1972 exclusively to publish the works of His Divine Grace, has thus become the world's largest publisher of books in the field of Indian religion and philosophy. Its latest project is the publishing of Śrīla Prabhupāda's most recent work: a seventeen-volume translation and commentary—completed by Śrīla Prabhupāda in only eighteen months—on the Bengali religious classic *Śrī Caitanya-caritāmṛta.*

In the past ten years, in spite of his advanced age, Śrīla Prabhupāda has circled the globe twelve times on lecture tours that have taken him to six continents. In spite of such a vigorous schedule, Śrīla Prabhupāda continues to write prolifically. His writings constitute a veritable library of Vedic philosophy, religion, literature and culture.

References

The purports of *Śrīmad-Bhāgavatam* are all confirmed by standard Vedic authorities. The following authentic scriptures are specifically cited in this volume:

Bhagavad-gītā, 3, 27, 38, 49, 50, 56, 57, 58, 61, 62, 79, 86, 89, 104, 108, 112, 122, 123, 135, 139, 152, 156, 157, 160–161, 164, 169, 181, 182, 183, 185, 186, 214, 225, 228, 237–238, 253, 254, 258, 259, 266, 279, 294, 302, 310, 315, 323, 331, 345, 365, 377

Brahma Purāṇa, 149

Brahma-saṁhitā, 258

Brahma-vaivarta Purāṇa, 304

Bṛhad-vaiṣṇava Tantra, 168

Hari-bhakti-vilāsa, 184

Īśopaniṣad, 248

Mahābhārata, 13, 204, 205, 364

Manu-smṛti, 215

Nīti-śāstra, 18

Padma Purāṇa, 256–257, 307

Śrīmad-Bhāgavatam, 49, 140, 193, 218, 227, 275, 283, 298, 299, 309, 310, 314, 341, 361, 383, 397

Glossary

A

Ācārya—a spiritual master who teaches by example.

Adhidaivic powers—the administrative functions delegated by the Lord to the demigods, such as control over the rain, wind, the sun, etc.

Akṣauhiṇī—a military division consisting of 21,870 chariots, 21,870 elephants, 206,950 infantrymen and 65,600 cavalrymen.

Ārati—a ceremony for greeting the Lord with offerings of food, lamps, fans, flowers and incense.

Arcanā—the devotional process of Deity worship.

Artha—economic development.

Āśrama—the four spiritual orders of life: celibate student, householder, retired life and renounced life.

Asuras—atheistic demons.

Avatāra—a descent of the Supreme Lord.

B

Bhagavad-gītā—the basic directions for spiritual life spoken by the Lord Himself.

Bhāgavata-dharma—the science of devotional service.

Bhāgavata-saptāha—a seven-day series of lectures on *Śrīmad-Bhāgavatam* given by professional reciters to a paying audience.

Bhakta—a devotee.

Bhakti—devotional service to Lord Śrī Kṛṣṇa.

Bhakti-yoga—linking with the Supreme Lord by devotional service.

Brahmacarya—celibate student life; the first order of Vedic spiritual life.

Brahman—the Absolute Truth; especially the impersonal aspect of the Absolute.

Brāhmaṇa—one wise in the *Vedas* who can guide society; the first Vedic social order.

Brahmarṣi—a title meaning "sage among the *brāhmaṇas.*"

Brahmāstra—a nuclear weapon produced by chanting *mantras.*
Brahma-tejas—the potency of a *brāhmaṇa.*

D

Devarṣi—a title meaning "sage among the demigods."
Dharma—eternal occupational duty; religious principles.

E

Ekādaśī—a special fast day for increased remembrance of Kṛṣṇa, which comes on the eleventh day of both the waxing and waning moon.

G

Goloka (Kṛṣṇaloka)—the highest spiritual planet, containing Kṛṣṇa's personal abodes, Dvārakā, Mathurā and Vṛndāvana.
Gopīs—Kṛṣṇa's cowherd girl friends, His most confidential servitors.
Gṛhastha—regulated householder life; the second order of Vedic spiritual life.
Guru—a spiritual master.

H

Hare Kṛṣṇa mantra—*See: Mahā-mantra*

J

Jīva-tattva—the living entities, atomic parts of the Lord.

K

Kaivalya—the impersonal liberation of merging into the spiritual effulgence emanating from the Lord.
Kali-yuga (Age of Kali)—the present age, characterized by quarrel. It is last in the cycle of four and began five thousand years ago.
Kāma—lust.
Karatālas—hand cymbals used in *kīrtana.*
Karma—fruitive action, for which there is always reaction, good or bad.
Karmī—a person satisfied with working hard for flickering sense gratification.

Kīrtana—chanting the glories of the Supreme Lord.
Kṛṣṇaloka—*See:* Goloka
Kṣatriyas—a warrior or administrator; the second Vedic social order.

L

Lokas—planets.

M

Mahājana—the Lord's authorized devotee, who by his teachings and behavior establishes the path of religion.
Mahā-mantra—the great chanting for deliverance:
Hare Kṛṣṇa, Hare Kṛṣṇa, Kṛṣṇa Kṛṣṇa, Hare Hare
Hare Rāma, Hare Rāma, Rāma Rāma, Hare Hare.
Mahā-ratha—a powerful warrior who can singlehandedly fight against ten thousand others.
Mahat-tattva—the total material energy, from which the material world is manifested.
Mantra—a sound vibration that can deliver the mind from illusion.
Mathurā—Lord Kṛṣṇa's abode, surrounding Vṛndāvana, where He took birth and later returned to after performing His Vṛndāvana pastimes.
Māyā—illusion; forgetfulness of one's relationship with Kṛṣṇa.
Māyāvādīs—impersonal philosophers who say that the Lord cannot have a transcendental body.
Mokṣa—liberation.
Mṛdaṅga—a clay drum used for congregational chanting.
Muni—a sage.

P

Paramparā—the chain of spiritual masters in disciplic succession.
Prasāda—food spiritualized by being offered to the Lord.

R

Rājarṣi—a great saintly king.
Rājasūya sacrifice—the great ceremony performed by King Yudhiṣṭhira and attended by Lord Kṛṣṇa.

Rāsa-līlā—the pure exchange of spiritual love between Kṛṣṇa and His most advanced, confidential servitors, the cowherd damsels of Vrajabhūmi.

Ṛṣi—a sage.

S

Sac-cid-ānanda-vigraha—the Lord's transcendental form, which is eternal, full of knowledge and bliss.

Sādhu—a saintly person.

Sampradāya—a disciplic succession of spiritual masters.

Saṅkīrtana—public chanting of the names of God, the approved *yoga* process for this age.

Sannyāsa—renounced life; the fourth order of Vedic spiritual life.

Śāstras—revealed scriptures.

Soma-rasa—a heavenly elixir available on the moon.

Śravaṇaṁ kīrtanaṁ viṣṇoḥ—the devotional processes of hearing and chanting about Lord Viṣṇu.

Śrutis—the original Vedic literatures: the four *Vedas* and the *Upaniṣads.*

Śūdra—a laborer; the fourth of the Vedic social orders.

Śūdrāṇī—wife of a *śūdra.*

Svāmī—one who controls his mind and senses; title of one in the renounced order of life.

Svayaṁvara—the ceremony in which a princess is allowed to choose her husband.

T

Tapasya—austerity; accepting some voluntary inconvenience for a higher purpose.

Tilaka—auspicious clay marks that sanctify a devotee's body as a temple of the Lord.

V

Vaikuṇṭha—the spiritual world.

Vaiṣṇava—a devotee of Lord Viṣṇu, Kṛṣṇa.

Vaiśyas—farmers and merchants; the third Vedic social order.

Vānaprastha—one who has retired from family life; the third order of Vedic spiritual life.

Varṇa—the four occupational divisions of society: the intellectual class, the administrative class, the mercantile class, and the laborer class.

Varṇāśrama—the Vedic system of four social and four spiritual orders.

Vedānta—Vyāsadeva's philosophical treatise presenting the conclusion of all the *Vedas.*

Vedas—the original revealed scriptures, first spoken by the Lord Himself.

Virāṭ-rūpa—the conception likening the physical form of the universe to the Lord's bodily form.

Viṣṇu, Lord—Kṛṣṇa's first expansion for the creation and maintenance of the material universes.

Viṣṇu-tattva—the original Personality of Godhead's primary expansions, each of whom is equally God.

Vṛndāvana—Kṛṣṇa's personal abode, where He fully manifests His quality of sweetness.

Vyāsadeva—Kṛṣṇa's incarnation, at the end of Dvāpara-yuga, for compiling the *Vedas.*

Y

Yajña—sacrifice; work done for the satisfaction of Lord Viṣṇu.

Yoga-nidrā—the mystic slumber of Lord Viṣṇu.

Yogī—a transcendentalist who, in one way or another, is striving for union with the Supreme.

Yugas—ages in the life of a universe, occurring in a repeated cycle of four.

Sanskrit Pronunciation Guide

Vowels

अ a आ ā इ i ई ī उ u ऊ ū ऋ ṛ ॠ ṝ
ऌ ḷ ए e ऐ ai ओ o औ au
ं ṁ *(anusvāra)* ः ḥ *(visarga)*

Consonants

Gutturals:	क ka	ख kha	ग ga	घ gha	ङ ṅa
Palatals:	च ca	छ cha	ज ja	झ jha	ञ ña
Cerebrals:	ट ṭa	ठ ṭha	ड ḍa	ढ ḍha	ण ṇa
Dentals:	त ta	थ tha	द da	ध dha	न na
Labials:	प pa	फ pha	ब ba	भ bha	म ma
Semivowels:	य ya	र ra	ल la	व va	
Sibilants:	श śa	ष ṣa	स sa		
Aspirate:	ह ha	ऽ ' *(avagraha)* – the apostrophe			

The vowels above should be pronounced as follows:

a – like the *a* in org*a*n or the *u* in b*u*t.
ā – like the *a* in f*a*r but held twice as long as short *a*.
i – like the *i* in p*i*n.
ī – like the *i* in p*i*que but held twice as long as short *i*.
u – like the *u* in p*u*sh.
ū – like the *u* in r*u*le but held twice as long as short *u*.

ṛ – like the *ri* in *ri*m.
ṝ – like *ree* in *ree*d.
ḷ – like *l* followed by *ṛ* (*lṛ*).
e – like the *e* in th*ey*.
ai – like the *ai* in *ai*sle.
o – like the *o* in g*o*.
au – like the *ow* in h*ow*.
ṁ (*anusvāra*) – a resonant nasal like the *n* in the French word *bon*.
ḥ (*visarga*) – a final *h*-sound: *aḥ* is pronounced like *aha; iḥ* like *ihi*.

The consonants are pronounced as follows:

k – as in *k*ite
kh – as in Ec*kh*art
g – as in *g*ive
gh – as in di*g-h*ard
ṅ – as in si*ng*
c – as in *ch*air
ch – as in staun*ch-h*eart
j – as in *j*oy
jh – as in he*dgeh*og
ñ – as in ca*ny*on
ṭ – as in *t*ub
ṭh – as in ligh*t-h*eart
ḍ – as in *d*ove
ḍha- as in re*d-h*ot
ṇ – as r*na* (prepare to say the *r* and say *na*).

Cerebrals are pronounced with tongue to roof of mouth, but the following dentals are pronounced with tongue against teeth:

t – as in *t*ub but with tongue against teeth.
th – as in ligh*t-h*eart but with tongue against teeth.
d – as in *d*ove but with tongue against teeth.
dh – as in re*d-h*ot but with tongue against teeth.
n – as in *n*ut but with tongue between teeth.

p – as in *p*ine
ph – as in u*ph*ill (not *f*)
b – as in *b*ird
bh – as in ru*b-h*ard
m – as in *m*other
y – as in *y*es
r – as in *r*un
l – as in *l*ight
v – as in *v*ine
ś (palatal) – as in the *s* in the German word *sprechen*
ṣ (cerebral) – as the *sh* in *sh*ine
s – as in *s*un
h – as in *h*ome

There is no strong accentuation of syllables in Sanskrit, only a flowing of short and long (twice as long as the short) syllables.

Index of Sanskrit Verses

This index constitutes a complete listing of the first and third lines of each of the Sanskrit poetry verses of this volume of *Śrīmad-Bhāgavatam*, arranged in English alphabetical order. The first column gives the Sanskrit transliteration, and the second and third columns, respectively, list the chapter-verse reference and page number for each verse.

A

R

S

T

U

V

General Index

Numerals in boldface type indicate references to translations of the verses of *Śrīmad-Bhāgavatam.*

A

Abhimanyu
  Kurus killed, 144
  son of, **289, 296**
Absolute Truth
  "cheating" in service of, 49
  Kṛṣṇa as, 124, 229, 260
  as skylike, 40
  See also: Reality; Supreme Lord
Ācārya. See: Authority; Spiritual master, *all entries*
Activities
  fruitive. *See:* Fruitive activities; *Karma*
  in goodness, 61
  for heavenly elevation, 135
  in ignorance, 61
  irreligious, regulated in *Vedas*, 280–281
  of Kṛṣṇa. *See:* Pastimes of Kṛṣṇa
  Lord's pleasure judges, 152–153
  material vs. spiritual, 74, 157
  Paramātmā judges, 57
  in passion, 61
  pious vs. impious, 183
  pure devotee's vs. Lord's, 300
  purification of, 177
Activities, material
  birth and death caused by, 377, 378
  failure of, 3
  trance stops, 324
  See also: Fruitive activities; *Karma*
Addresses, welcome
  Vedic vs. modern, 208
  See also: Reception
Adhama in marriage, 115
Adharma. See: Irreligion
Adhiratha, 141
Aditi
  Satyabhāmā blessed by, 109
  sons of, 22
Administrators. *See:* Kings; *Kṣatriyas;* Leaders, government
Adṛṣṭa-pūrvān subhagān sa dadarśa dhanañjayaḥ
  verse quoted, 205
Adṛśyatī, 364
Age of Kali. *See:* Kali-yuga
Agni-hotra by Dhṛtarāṣṭra, **69**
Agriculture. *See:* Cow protection; *Vaiśyas*
Ahalyā, 366
Ahaṅkāra. See: Ego, false
Air in stomach, 364
Ājamīḍha, **39**
Ajāmila, degradation of, 218
Akbar, 53
Akrūra, **100**
Akṣauhiṇī military division
  of Bhūriśravā, 142
  defined, 232
Alexander the Great under Lord's will, 53
Alokānanda, 365
Amaras defined, 252
Amartya defined, 358
Ambarīṣa, King, vs. Durvāsā Muni, 132
Ambikā, 2
"Americans" as designation, 55
Ananta, Lord
  Balarāma as, 108
  Kṛṣṇa's qualities inestimable by, 225
Andhaka, **98**
Aṅga, 141
Anger as ominous sign, **84**
Aṅgirā, historical accounts on, 365

Authority (Authorities) *(continued)*
kings followed, 368
Kṛṣṇa consciousness via, 313
Parīkṣit consulted, 368
spiritual master as, 395
See also: Disciplic succession; *Mahājanas*
Avaiṣṇavas. See: Atheists; Nondevotees
Avatāras. See: Incarnations of the Supreme Lord
Avidyā. See: Ignorance

B

"Back to Godhead" via spiritual master, 396
Bāhlika, **140**
Balarāma (Baladeva), Lord
as Ananta, 108
Arjuna angered, 8
as Kṛṣṇa's brother, 288
as Kṛṣṇa's expansion, 101
mercy of, 101
as Nityānanda, 101
protects devotees, **101**
sister of, 8
as spiritual master, 101
Being, living. *See:* Living entity; Soul, conditioned
Bengal, Karṇa ruled, 141
Bhadrā, 365
Bhadrāśva, **204**, 205
Bhagavad-gītā
See also: Bhagavad-gītā cited; *Bhagavad-gītā*, quotations from
Arjuna as medium for, 322
Bhāgavatam supplements, 156
as God's law, 249, 250
ignorance dispelled by, 162
illusion dispelled by, 162
Kurukṣetra war witnessed, 155
liberation via, 156
as Lord's sound incarnation, 155, 329
message of, 56
as panacea, 157
philosophical basis of, 156
purification via, 159
Bhagavad-gītā
topics in, five listed, 156
as transcendental, 197
as *Vedas'* essence, 155
Bhagavad-gītā, cited
on authorities, 365
on Brahman's basis, 258
on Brahmā's day, 253
on devotee's qualifications, 38
on duty, 383
on fasting, 266
on food offered to Kṛṣṇa, 62
on fools misunderstanding Kṛṣṇa, 86
on hearing Kṛṣṇa's pastimes, 301
on heavenly life as temporary, 135
on impersonalists, 310
on Kṛṣṇa as Absolute Truth, 124
on Kṛṣṇa as Supreme Brahman, 181
on Kṛṣṇa as *Vedas'* goal, 3
on *kṣatriyas*, 345
on life's goal, 182, 377
on living being's immortality, 112
on Lord and devotee's incarnations, 104, 122–123, 186
on Lord as time, 27
on Lord in heart, 139
on Lord protecting pure devotees, 57
on Lord's activities, 164, 302
on Lord's lotus feet for devotees, 183
on Lord's mission, 79
on Lord's plenary expansions, 87
on mind, 258
on nature under Kṛṣṇa, 152, 228
on occupational duty, 254
on Paramātmā, 57, 259
on perception development, 323
on preachers, 50
on real renunciation, 294
on sacrifice, 214
on social orders, 331
on spiritual world, 108
on surrender, 279, 315
on transcending modes of nature, 61, 89, 185
on *vaiśyas*, 237–238

Body, material *(continued)*
as prison, 32
social order compared to, 331
soul causes, 323
stages of, 31
as suffering, 24, 32
as temporary, 59, 61, 157
time controls, **60**
yoga manipulates, 323
Body of the Supreme Lord
at disappearance, 169, **170**
as transcendental, 87, 168
See also: Form of the Supreme Lord
Brahmā, Lord
birth of, 316
as creator, 214
day of, calculated, 253
as father, 365
Kṛṣṇa above, 53, 306, 317
as *mahājana,* 21
as mortal, 27
residence of, 28, 381
Brahma-bandhus defined, 391
Brahmacarya (student life), training for, 330
Brahmajyoti
defined, 309
impersonalist aspires to, 309
as Lord's effulgence, 227
Śiśupāla dazzled by, 169
See also: Brahman effulgence
Brahmaloka
day on, calculated, 253
death on, 27–28, 355
happiness in, 24
Brahman (impersonal Absolute), 320–321
empiricists aspire to, 350
Lord as basis of, 124, 258
See also: Brahmajyoti; Brahman effulgence
Brahman (spirit)
beyond modes of nature, 185
self as, **178**
See also: Soul
Brahman, Supreme
Bhagavad-gītā cited on, 181
Lord as, **72**
self "identified" with, 178
Brahman, Supreme
See also: Supreme Lord
Brāhmaṇa(s) (intellectuals)
Arjuna disguised as, 125
Bhīma disguised as, 129
bogus vs. bona fide, 106, 229
boy, cursed Parīkṣit, 346, 356
charity to, 43, 141
as demons in Kali-yuga, 347
devotees above, 106
Durvāsā as, 131
of Durvāsā "fed up," 133
duty of, 82, **284**–285, 289
faith of, first-class, 214
food for, 117
function of, 114
impunity for, 327
in Kali-yuga degraded, 217, 236, 303, 330, 332–334, 336, 347
king protects, 114
Kṛṣṇa disguised as, 129
Kuntī served, 132
Lord protects, **105,** 353
Mahābhārata for fallen descendants of, 155
in marriage, 115
Parīkṣit advised by, **189,** 190
protection by, 346
qualifications for, 331, 332
qualities of, 106, 229
social value of, 106, 114, 331, 346
training of, 184
as truthful, 285
as twice-born, 242
worship toward, **43**
Yadus cursed by, **151**
See also: Varṇāśrama-dharma
"*Brāhmaṇas*" as designation, 55
Brahman effulgence
impersonalists worship, 145
planets within, 108
See also: Brahmajyoti; Brahman (impersonal Absolute)
Brahmā Purāṇa cited on Aṣṭāvakra's benediction curse, 149
Brahmarṣi, Vyāsadeva as, 389

D

E

Garbhodakaśāyī Viṣṇu
Brahmā begot by, 316
Lord as, 108
Garuḍa as bird king, **309**
Gauḍīya Vaiṣṇava sect, Narottama dāsa Ṭhākura in, 35
Gautama
historical accounts on, 366
as philosopher, 256, 258
Ghaṭotkaca
Karṇa killed, 142
parents of, 7
Ghosts
God's name dispels, 393
Śiva worshiped by, 129
Goal of life. *See:* Life, goal of
Go-brāhmaṇa-hitāya ca
quoted, 353
God. *See:* Kṛṣṇa, Lord; Supreme Lord
God consciousness
as essential, 354
formula for, in society, 281–282
Kali-yuga, counteracted by, 170–171
See also: Kṛṣṇa consciousness
Goddess of fortune
as Kṛṣṇa's expansion, 317
Lord served by, **230–231, 316**
Godhead. *See: "Back to Godhead"*; Kṛṣṇa, Lord; Spiritual world; Supreme Lord
God realization
by devotional service, 37
life meant for, 249
stages of, 157
See also: Devotional service to the Supreme Lord; Kṛṣṇa consciousness
"Gods." *See:* Demigods
Gokula, location of, 359
Gold
as false exchange standard, 283
as Kali's residence, **282**–283
spiritual use of, 286
Goloka Vṛndāvana
eligibility for, 178, 184
as Kṛṣṇa's abode, 197, 293–294, 379
Pāṇḍavas attained, **184**
Goloka Vṛndāvana
as Parīkṣit's destination, 379
See also: Spiritual world; Vṛndāvana
Goodness, mode of (*sattva-guṇa*)
as bondage, 70
demigods in, 136
as enlightening, 61
ignorance vs., 280
qualities of, 106
Gopīs
Lord took, back to Godhead, 149
See also: Cowherd damsels
Gotra defined, 191
Government
corruption in, 341–344
duty of, 244–245, 247, 296
godlessness in, 55
irreligion forbidden in, **272,** 288
in Kali-yuga degraded, 238, 242, 274
leaders in. *See:* Kings; *Kṣatriyas;* Leaders, government
monarchical, 341, 342, 344
as protector, 203, 244–245, 247
spiritual responsibility of, 356
Vedic vs. modern, 190
See also: Politicians; Society, human, orders of
Greeting. *See:* Addresses, welcome; Reception
Gṛhasthas. See: Householders
Guṇas. See: Modes of material nature
Guru
defined, 312
See also: Spiritual master, *all entries*

H

Haṁsas defined, 319
Happiness
in Brahmaloka, 24
conditioned souls seek, 3
by God's laws, 250
by religious principles, 222
for society, 173, 176
spiritual life as, 355

J

L

M

Modes of material nature *(continued)*
body under, 135
Brahman beyond, 185
conditioned souls under, **60,** 74
freedom from, 55, 71, 74, 89, 162, 184
senses under, 74
as suffering, 90
time above, 61
transcendentalists beyond, 350
Yudhiṣṭhira transcended, **178**
See also: Nature, material; *names of specific modes (goodness, passion, ignorance)*
"Mohammedans" as designation, 55, 273
Mokṣa
life beyond, 182–183
See also: Liberation
Monarch. *See:* King
Monarchy
democracy vs., 341, 342
See also: Government; Kings
Money, paper vs. gold, 283
Money by magic wand, material life compared to, **150**
Monists. *See:* Māyāvādīs
Monkeys, modern society as, **343**
Moon
as heavenly planet, 135, 305
Soma as, 365
Śukadeva compared to, **389**
Moon-god. *See:* Candra; Soma
Mothers, seven listed, 115
Mūḍhas defined, 87
Mysticism. *See:* Kṛṣṇa consciousness; Meditation; *Yogīs*
Mystic power
of Dhṛtarāṣṭra, **75**
of Durvāsā, 131
of Kṛṣṇa, 133, 316
Vasiṣṭha's vs. Viśvāmitra's, 365
of *yogī,* 75
Mystics
devotees vs., 356
goal of, 350
See also: Devotees of the Supreme Lord; Sages; Transcendentalists; *Yogīs*

N

Nagarāṁś ca vanāṁś caiva nadīś ca vimalodakāḥ
verse quoted, 205
Naimiṣāraṇya sacrifice
deathlessness at, 199
in post-Parīkṣit era, 288, 289
as uncertain, **303**
Yamarāja invited to, **198–200**
Naimiṣāraṇya sages
quoted on Sūta's narration, **302–306, 308, 309, 311**
Yadu dynasty demise disturbed, 167
Nakula, 6
Nāmācārya defined, 313
Names of God
demons vanquished by, 393
as God Himself, 315
Rāma vs. Kṛṣṇa, 360
Rāma vs. Viṣṇu, 360
See also: Chanting the Lord's holy names; Supreme Lord, *appropriate entries*
Nanda Mahārāja, 104, 226
Nandinī cow, 365
Napoleon under Lord's will, 53
Naptā, 142
Nārada Muni
as *devarṣi,* 389
Kṛṣṇa's supremacy accepted by, 181
Kuvera's sons condemned by, 167
as *mahājana,* 21
musical instrument of, 50, **78**
at Parīkṣit-Śukadeva meeting, 389
past life of, 78
as philosopher, 52
as pure devotee, 50, 52
as soothsayer, 68, 70, **75–76**
as spaceman, 19, 78
Vyāsadeva instructed by, 16
Nārada Muni, quotations from
on body, **60**
on lamentation as ignorance, **58–59**
on Lord as controller, **53, 55, 57**
on Lord as time, **65**

S

Sense gratification *(continued)*
life wasted on, 201
materialists pursue, 34
society degraded by, **343**, 344
speculative philosophy as, 319
warning against, 319
See also: Activities, material; Body, material; Desire, material; Enjoyment, material; Fruitive activities; Happiness, material; Life, material; Sex life
Senses
conditioned souls controlled by, 74
devotional service fulfills, 71
five listed, 71
Lord beyond, 155
in Lord's service, 323
mind controls, 177
modes of nature control, **74**
purified vs. conditioned, 106
yoga controls, 69–**71**, 324
Yudhiṣṭhira purified, **176**
See also: Body, material
Serpent. *See:* Snake
Servants of God. *See:* Devotees of the Supreme Lord
Service to God. *See:* Devotional service to the Supreme Lord
Sex life
among castes, 115
illicit, in Kali-yuga, 202
illicit, in kingless society, 343
rāsa-līlā hearing cures, 329
See also: Desire, material
Shower of flowers for Parīkṣit by demigods, **374–375**
Sind Pakistan, former name of, 143
Sindhudeśa, 143
Sin
atonement for, 353
devotees free of, 38, 346
freedom by ceasing, 361
in Kali-yuga minimized, 298
Lord saves devotee from, 352, 361
Lord's lotus feet absolve, 361, 383
Sin
in material world unavoidable, 361
mental vs. actual, 298
pilgrimage places remove, 362, 392
punishment for, 21
pure devotional service absolves, 257
sacrifice counteracts, 215–216
surrender absolves, 279, 315
Śiśupāla
as "Kṛṣṇa conscious," 17
Lord vanquished, 67, 169
Sītādevī as Rāma's wife, 41, 226
Śiva, Lord
Arjuna pleased, **134**
demons worship, 129
Durvāsā as incarnation of, 132
Gāndhārī worshiped, 5
Ganges sanctifies, 359
ghosts worship, 129
Jarāsandha worshiped, 129
Jayadratha blessed by, 144
as Kālabhairava, 129
Kṛṣṇa above, 53, 306, 317
as Mahābhairava, 129
as *mahājana*, 21
Rāvaṇa worshiped, 129, 134
wife of, **134**
worship toward, for husband, 5
Sky, Absolute Truth compared to, 40
Snake
Kali-yuga *brāhmaṇas* compared to, 336
Śamīka Ṛṣi garlanded with, **328**
time compared to, **60**
Society, human
animal slaughter disrupts, 63
basic principles of, 354
Bhāgavatam's role in, 281, 288
brāhmaṇas in, 106, 114, 331, 346
brahminical culture in, 211
bull's importance in, 211
cow protection vital for, 106, 240, 246
cow's importance in, 194, 195, 211
demons disturb, 127
devotional service needed in, 299
evil in, 265

T

Y